CLEARER THAN TRUTH

A VOLUME IN THE SERIES

Culture and Politics in the Cold War and Beyond

Edited by

EDWIN A. MARTINI
and
SCOTT LADERMAN

CLEARER THAN TRUTH

The Polygraph
and the
American
Cold War

JOHN PHILIPP BAESLER

University of Massachusetts Press
Amherst and Boston

ISBN 978-1-62534-325-3 (paper); 313-0 (hardcover)

Designed by Sally Nichols
Set in Minion Pro
Printed and bound by Maple Press, Inc.

Cover design by Thomas Eykemans
Cover photo by Ed Westcott, *Lie Detector Test,* c. 1945. Courtesy of the
U.S. Department of Energy.

Library of Congress Cataloging-in-Publication Data

Names: Baesler, John Philipp, author.
Title: Clearer than truth : the polygraph and the American Cold War / John
    Philipp Baesler.
Description: Amherst : University of Massachusetts Press, 2018. | Includes
    bibliographical references and index. |
Identifiers: LCCN 2017050240 (print) | LCCN 2018012586 (ebook) | ISBN
    9781613765647 (e-book) | ISBN 9781613765654 (e-book) | ISBN 9781625343130
    (hardcover) | ISBN 9781625343253 (pbk.)
Subjects: LCSH: Lie detectors and detection—United States—History—20th
    century. | Lie detectors and detection—Moral and ethical aspects—United
    States. | Internal security—United States—History—20th century. |
    Allegiance—United States—History—20th century. | United
    States—Politics and government—1945–1989. | Cold War—Political
    aspects—United States.
Classification: LCC JK468.L5 (ebook) | LCC JK468.L5 B34 2018 (print) | DDC
    327.1273—dc23
LC record available at https://lccn.loc.gov/2017050240

British Library Cataloguing-in-Publication Data
A catalog record for this book is available from the British Library.

Some of this book's main arguments come from two of the author's earlier publications:
"Die Macht des Lügendetektors im amerikanischen Sicherheitssystem" [The power of
the lie detector in the American security system], in *Das Erbe des Kalten Krieges* [The
legacy of the Cold War], ed. Bernd Greiner (Hamburg: Hamburger Edition, 2013), 128–
47; and "From Detection to Surveillance: U.S. Lie Detector Regimes from the Cold War
to the War on Terror," *Behemoth: A Journal on Civilization* 8, no. 1 (April 2015): 46–66.
Thanks to the editors for permission to reproduce this material.

For Jenny and Lotte

CONTENTS

PREFACE

I have never taken a polygraph test, and despite my awareness of the strictly limited significance of its results, the
thought of maybe doing so in the future—if only for fun and games—
makes me a bit jittery. Such is the aura of intimidation attached to the
machine and the rickety curves it produces when hooked up to a body.
It is this aura that turned me toward exploring the various ways in
which the history of a technology that promises relentless pursuit of
truth intersects with American Cold War history and the development
of the U.S. national security state.

This book investigates how polygraph interrogations first found their
way into use by agencies of the American federal government in the
context of the emergency of war, and how they subsequently became an
established sword and shield of "national security" as part of the American Cold War. In a struggle that U.S. officials defined as a life-or-death
contest between American fair play and communist duplicity, I argue
that the polygraph offered rigorous objectivity, sustaining American
core values while facilitating the unremitting pursuit of enemies. Yet
polygraph interrogations—scientifically questionable and inherently
confrontational—elicited protestations from citizens who felt their conscience and honor violated. In the wake of the profound crisis of legitimacy that American national security agencies, particularly the Central
Intelligence Agency, experienced after the late 1960s, the tide of public
opinion turned decisively against the polygraph. And yet, entrenched
in the permanent bureaucracies that the Cold War had created, the

polygraph survived various attacks by Congress and civil liberties advocates, ready to reemerge with renewed support after the attacks of September 11, 2001. I maintain that the story of the polygraph's Cold War
career illustrates the multifaceted, contingent political and social negotiations that went into the creation of the American Cold War. I also
argue that the persistence of the polygraph is a powerful statement about
how bureaucratic practices that began as emergency measures came to
be permanent, as if carved into the marble of the monuments along the
national mall in Washington. Because "national security" has become
so embedded in daily political discourse, I suspect that most Americans
do not stop to think very often about how they came about framing the
purpose of their government and the civic values it represents that way.
All the more crucial, I believe, to retrace our steps.

As somebody who came to the United States to attend graduate
school, I became aware of the ideological ambiguity of American civic
nationalism long before I took my first course in American history.
Being a country of immigrants, open to anybody who is willing to live
by its ideals and offering a level playing field to all, is a source of collective pride for most Americans. And yet, underneath the affirmation
of this high ideal, one can easily pick up a murmured lament that the
social order that maintains American values is fragile. Consequently,
Americans from the beginning have sought to exclude those they
deemed unworthy of the privilege of entering the country or participating in its civic life. As a German born long after 1945, the moment
when I checked the "no" box next to the question on the immigration
questionnaire that inquired whether I had ever been a member of the
Nazi Party, formed the first small echo of that long history in my mind.
Ever since, the elaboration of "national security" in American history
has been a preoccupation of mine; studying the history of the polygraph allowed me to focus my attention on a specific aspect of that
history, bringing together in the process perspectives from diplomatic,
political, and intellectual history, as well as the history of science and
technology. At the same time, I always kept the big question—namely,
what the history of polygraph says about America and Americans in
general—in mind. While the secret nature of some of that history kept
a number of lines of inquiry closed and at times only permitted titil-
lating glimpses into events, it is my sincere hope that this book offers

a fresh perspective on the dialectical relationship between measures to keep the nation secure and the perpetual feeling of insecurity that drives the implementation of those measures.

On the journey from developing my first academic interest in the history of U.S. foreign relations to finishing this manuscript, I have incurred many debts that I am happy to acknowledge. I begin with Clemens Zimmermann and Detlef Junker, who kindled my curiosity for American history many years ago at Ruprecht-Karls-Universität Heidelberg. At Indiana University, I am grateful to Nick Cullather for the invaluable advice and guidance he gave me during my graduate studies and beyond. John Bodnar, Jim Capshew, and Dror Wahrman asked pertinent questions that sharpened my focus as I began to turn my dissertation into a book manuscript. My thanks also go to Ken Alder, Gordon Barland, Susan Carruthers, Barbara Cornblath, Martin Endreß, Bernd Greiner, David Johnson, Melissa Littlefield, Chad Parker, John Prados, Regina Ammicht Quinn, Benjamin Rampp, Chris Stone, and Klaas Voß, who all offered generous feedback and suggestions, whether in writing or in conversation. I am particularly obliged to my wife, Jennifer Stinson, and my awesome father-in-law, Robert Stinson, both of whom are fine historians in their own rights, and to Allison Peters, Ann Garcia, and Sabine Bickford; their careful reading improved the manuscript immeasurably. Finally, I am grateful to Matt Becker, Rachael DeShano, Eric Schramm, and everybody at the University of Massachusetts Press for guiding the manuscript through the publication process.

Historians without sources are like fish out of water. I am therefore grateful to all the librarians and archivists at the following institutions who made it possible to research this book: the Herman B. Wells Library at Indiana University, the Zahnow Library at Saginaw Valley State University, the National Archives in College Park and Washington, DC, the Library of Congress, the Wisconsin Historical Society, the archives of the National Academy of Sciences in Washington, DC, the Bancroft Library at the University of California, Berkeley, the Special Collections and University Archives at the University of Oregon, the Columbia University Rare Books and Manuscripts Library (many thanks to Ellie Engel for providing research assistance), the Boston Public Library, and the Rare Books and Manuscripts Collection at the

University of California, Irvine (I am most thankful to Alix Norton for her assistance). I also thank George Maschke for making documents available on his website, antipolygraph.org. In addition, I am most grateful to the Indiana University Department of History, the Organization of American Historians, Indiana University East, the McNutt family, the Ruth B. Lilly Foundation, the Doris Quinn Foundation, and Saginaw Valley State University for providing me the necessary financial assistance to finish this project.

Lastly, I want to thank my family. My mother, Astrid Baesler, and my late father, Wolfgang Baesler, enabled me to pursue my passion. I hope this book makes them proud. I thank my brother, Axel, for many hours of stimulating discussion. Most of all, I thank my wife, Jennifer, for her unyielding encouragement, care, and love, our cat companion, Signe, for providing unreserved emotional support, and our daughter, Charlotte, who brightened my days (and slept through some nights) during the final stages of the process. I dedicate this book to them.

CLEARER THAN TRUTH

Introduction

The aspiring Central Intelligence Agency intern was ambitious and bright. His college fraternity had elected him their president and he was eyeing law schools. He had passed initial screenings, been flown to CIA headquarters, and had handled himself gloriously during a weekend of interviews and tests. But all was about to unravel when he faced the last hurdle in front of him—the polygraph exam. The young man struggled with the question "Have you ever used drugs?" He wondered if inhaling the dope of friends who had smoked in his presence counted. Why did the CIA still concern itself with such trifles? Then came the question that truly threw him off: "Have you ever had sex with a man?" In the early 1990s, the Agency still considered homosexual employees to be security risks, so saying "yes" would have immediately ended his chances, stellar qualifications notwithstanding. The problem was that the young man kept a dark secret, which until this point he had not shared with anybody: a male cousin had sexually abused him when he was seven years old. Both had been boys, and since no penetration had taken place, could one even use the phrase "sex with a man"? How to answer? "The anxiety rose in me," he would later write, "like dust from a thing long neglected and abruptly disturbed." When the young man answered in the negative, "the needle scratched wildly on the paper—lie." And then the dams broke: "As soon as the test was over, I turned to the [interrogator] and the things that I had never let spill from my lips came pouring out. All of it." After his confession, he pleaded for a retest. This time he answered "yes," but again the needle moved in a sharp curve that indicated he was lying. Years later the same man, Charles Blow, now a columnist for the *New York Times*, concluded, "It took a machine designed to catch liars to help me see that I didn't yet know my own truth."[1]

Stories like this proliferate in the history of the polygraph. Although the experiences Americans have when they confront the machine vary, certain themes ring out with clarity: the sudden confrontation with one's conscience; the anxiety and confusion aroused by the demand to boil down questions with complex individual connotations to a simple "yes" or "no"; the dread when confronted with the lie detector's judgment; the need to unload one's mind right away. Experiences such as the one described by Blow speak to a remarkable power of the polygraph and cry out for explanation.

They also pose questions: can simple physiological responses such as the ones measured by the polygraph—changes in blood pressure, pulse, breathing depth, and skin conductivity—reliably indicate that a person is lying? How significant can the findings of the polygraph be? How should these findings be used? Such questions—ranging from the philosophical to the technical—gain in significance and number when we put them in the context of the history of the American Cold War, when polygraph tests proliferated in the United States. What considerations made American leaders argue for the polygraph test? What ideological, bureaucratic, and political purposes did administrators and policymakers pursue when they insisted on polygraph exams, even on applicants for lowly internships? Did the test improve American national security? How would one even go about measuring if it did?

The issue of resistance to the polygraph is equally significant. Why did so many Americans insist that demanding polygraph tests of citizens was an abomination that approximated the totalitarian methods of the Soviet Union? Someone fully aware of the controversies that surrounded the polygraph was George Shultz, secretary of state during the Reagan administration, who once angrily noted that he would resign immediately if he were ever asked to take a polygraph exam. "I am deeply concerned about the attitudes and atmosphere in [Washington, DC] at present regarding these so-called lie detectors," Shultz fumed. "I don't even like to use the phrase 'polygraph' because it implies precision where precision does not exist. We all know what they pretend to be—lie detectors. But the truth is . . . that those machines cannot detect lies in a scientifically reliable manner." Even so, he conceded, "Lie-detector tests have a limited place in our security program, to a different extent in different agencies. But they must not become an excuse or a substitute for a real security program."[2] Despite his objections, Shultz could not quite bring himself to condemn polygraph tests *tout court*. The conflicted mind of the secretary of state indicates yet another reason to explore the ambiguous significance of the polygraph in the history of American national security policy.

What follows is a comprehensive history of the polygraph as a symbol and tool of American Cold War policy. One of my central claims is that because many Americans perceived the Cold War as a project to protect not only their physical safety but also their spiritual purity, justifications for the use of the polygraph must be understood as Cold War narratives—tales about the American fight against a relentless, amoral, and therefore deceitful, totalitarian enemy: communism. This book shows that the discourse of the polygraph joined a variety of stories to forge a new American national identity: the hard-nosed, masculine aura of the instrument embodied a persona for Cold War America based in skepticism and cold, hard data, but also committed to fairness and honesty. Yet according to its critics, using such an instrument of intimidation threatened to erode the binary of "free world" versus "slave world." To some, the methods that polygraph champions called for undermined the very values of justice, equality, and the presumption of innocence they claimed to protect. Polygraph debates thus revealed deep-seated fears many Americans had about the self-defeating character of Cold War policy: that by fighting communism, America was losing its democratic ethos. The polygraph, in short, became a site of controversy over the very nature of American Cold War policies.

The story of how a technology with questionable scientific credentials came to be used by official governmental agencies on a mass scale also informs and deepens our understanding of the routine implementation of Cold War policies. Security agencies conducted hundreds of thousands of polygraph tests in the decades after World War II. Administrators did not value these tests because of their scientific precision, but because of their utility in daily practice: they allowed for the timely processing of large numbers of security checks, and they could be administered in such a way that they produced actionable results as to the security reliability of individuals. In short, the polygraph was an instrument that made the American Cold War state possible. Yet one of the drawbacks of the polygraph was that it cast a shadow of doubt over the loyalty of individuals who asserted their patriotism and innocence. The often-traumatic experience provoked fierce protests from Americans across ideologies lines. I conclude that the polygraph was a quick-fix technology promising a definite scientific test of elusive values such as loyalty, and thus that it embodied fundamental conflicts in the interplay of American Cold War ideology and practice.

One of the conflicting demands the Cold War made on Americans was calling on them to value their freedom while remaining in a state of permanent alert.[3] The polygraph, so its advocates claimed, was one method to square this circle. To them, it represented a promise of objectivity, neutrality, and fairness along with effective deterrence of spies and traitors. This promise explains, at least in part, the attraction that the polygraph held for CIA security officers who needed to both appeal to talented applicants and deter potential security risks. Indeed, a certain utopian urgency was part of America's hardboiled Cold War. "By the dim, reflected light of the Soviet moons, the United States resolved to change," wrote historian Walter McDougall, describing the impetus behind America's leap into space after the Sputnik shock of 1957, when the successful Soviet launch of the first satellite into space plunged many Americans into an existential crisis. By the same token, some idealistic strategists and scientists desperately searched for a way to avoid the catastrophe of nuclear war by making politicians trustworthy again with the help of the polygraph. Seen this way, the story of the polygraph shares a striking family resemblance with other hallmarks of Cold War scientism—the belief that rigorous application of scientific methods could improve education, policymaking, and ultimately America's democratic ethos. Only if we analyze the history of the polygraph as a narrative driven by American Cold War ambitions, similar to the story of Neil Armstrong's heroic conquest of the moon,

can we understand how and why technological truth detection entered
the arsenal of the U.S. national security state.[4]

This book delineates a similarly complex history of the political and
legal compromises that American polygraph policies forged. For every
thousand tests conducted, the polygraph could potentially produce a
staggering 150 false positives. With such an error rate, the lie detector
accused the guiltless by the thousands and often caused shell-shocked
individuals to confess to crimes they did not commit. Casting suspicion on innocent people was not simply a glitch in the system; it was
inherent to the very methodology of polygraph exams. This book takes
a fresh look at the atmosphere of suspicion and paranoia often associated with Cold War culture. It shows that in the case of the polygraph, the practice of "security first" was bound to create suspicion
and destroy lives. Further, the use of the lie detector to screen government employees, identify spies, or extract intelligence from potential
defectors became the subject of repeated congressional investigations.
Government agencies, scientists, labor unions, and individual citizens
contributed to the debate, which culminated in legislation that prohibited the use of the polygraph by private businesses in 1988. Yet the
law exempted polygraph use for purposes of national security. This
part of the story reveals a previously unacknowledged entrenchment
of "national security" practices in the face of increasingly organized
citizen opposition. Far from diminishing its relevance amid such opposition, the lie detector's bureaucratic success created a legal precedent
to shelter a controversial technology from future challenges.

Thus, the history of the polygraph and the history of the American Cold War are mutually illuminating and intertwined. My approach
bears out and specifies Daniel Yergin's claim that the doctrine of
national security "was born of technical and political transformations
and out of men's experience and understanding of them. A political
and bureaucratic struggle over the postwar military establishment
gave the doctrine additional force."[5] From 1945 on, a dangerous world
with dangerous new enemies and weapons seemed to call for global,
proactive ways to protect the nation, but the implementation of a new
strategy became the subject of a political-bureaucratic struggle among
federal agencies. The polygraph existed before the national security
state; indeed, its ready availability was one of its virtues to anxious

policymakers who aimed to create that state. But only after 1945 did the polygraph and the U.S. national security state enter into a permanent, mutually beneficial relationship. The polygraph is therefore a particularly significant artifact of American Cold War history.

While this book mostly focuses on specific events in the post–World War II period, it aims at illuminating broader themes and the ways in which a number of historical trends culminated in U.S. policies after 1945. These themes are—in brief outline—as follows.

Sincerity and Power in the American Imagination

The social history of the polygraph reaches back into early modernity and the creation of western commercial society. It shines light on America's struggle to define sincerity as the country developed an exuberant, reckless, and risky form of capitalism in the nineteenth century. As inherited differences of social status eroded, writers, philosophers, and scientists in the Anglo-American world began to devise methods of detecting the inauthentic. As Lionel Trilling argued, it was the phenomenon of social mobility that introduced the figure of the villain or trickster in modern English literature and made sincerity—matching inner self and social norms—a middle-class ideal. During the eighteenth century, the English literary world was obsessed with fraud and hoaxes and discussed means to uncover them. A little later, within the crowded urban landscapes of nineteenth-century America, advice literature addressing anxieties about hypocrisy and the threat it posed to Victorian notions of middle-class virtue abounded.[6] At the same time, the burgeoning American market economy also suggested advertisement and self-promotion—mastery of the art of appearance—as a useful tool for economic and social advancement. While confidence men appear in the popular imagination of many cultures, historian Walter McDougall declared "hustling" to be the archetypical American activity and Herman Melville's *The Confidence-Man* (1857) to be the quintessential American novel. Put differently, legitimate and illegitimate market activity became hard to distinguish in modern America, which opened the door for lie detector advocates to offer yet another marketable service.[7]

The historiography of American capitalism raises important questions regarding the relationship among democracy, market society, and sincerity, because only in a society that valued individual achievement and maintained a distinction between the private and the public sphere could the choice between truth and lies become a source of individual empowerment. In Victorian England, writers like Thomas Hardy or Oscar Wilde (who famously declared lying a form of art) often wrote about characters with an authentic existence on the margins of middle-class respectability. These characters forged such an existence by pursuing the opposites of sincerity—secrecy, masquerade, reserve, and invention.[8] In the more prosaic history of American capitalism and the importance it placed on salesmanship, individuals often struggled to maintain a strict distinction between advertisement and deception. Honesty and sincerity therefore held a precarious place in the American national imagination and in economic practice.

Accusations of hypocrisy have long existed toward world powers whose methods and morals appear to exist in conflict. The founding fathers had struggled to defend themselves against charges of two-facedness coming easily against a nation supposedly based on liberty but tolerant of the institution of slavery.[9] In the realm of foreign policy, statesmen and academics in Germany, England, and America fired off mutual charges of hypocrisy when their countries began to compete for global power in the 1890s. The liberal British empire of the Victorian age, so the Germans argued, had acquired its dominance by force, yet its defenders claimed that British supremacy was benevolent since it facilitated global trade. While British writers countered that German *Realpolitik* was little more than an elaborate justification for naked Machiavellianism, German historian Friedrich Meinecke famously argued that it was the British who practiced "the most effective kind of Machiavellianism, which could be brought by the national Will of power-policy to become unconscious of itself, and to appear (not only to others, but also itself) as being pure humanity, candor and religion."[10] Such accusations were easily transferred to America, the new preponderant global power after the Second World War. Charges of hypocrisy stung many American diplomats, as when it came to explaining Jim Crow practices in the nation's capital to foreign diplomats.[11]

By that time, however, the communist tactics of propaganda and infiltration served as a suitable foil to contrast American sincerity with communist deceit. "The Communist Party, USA, has been and is engaged in an all-out war against American freedom," FBI director J. Edgar Hoover declared in his (ghostwritten) 1958 bestseller *Masters of Deceit.* "Its tactics of confusion, retreat, advance, infiltration, and hypocrisy are in full play." Hoover warned of communist "terrorism, espionage, sabotage, lying, cheating." The defense of American national character would acquire new urgency when U.S. foreign policy attempted to advertise America's core values and, in the process, define American national identity.[12]

According to polygraph examiner Gordon Barland, by the early 1990s, polygraphs as a routine investigation tool in law enforcement had spread to fifteen countries other than the United States, and overall fifty-five countries retained some public or private polygraph resources.[13] Still, no country came even close in its reliance on the machine. Given the exceptionally wide use of the technology in the United States, it is not surprising that historians have raised the question of whether lie detection reveals something transcendent about the American national character. For example, in his authoritative group biography of the main characters who drove the development of the machine—William Marston, an academic psychologist who ended up as a comic book writer; John Larson, a psychologist-police officer who at the end of his life came to call the machine "Frankenstein's Monster"; and Leonarde Keeler, the son of a famous poet who made the polygraph his claim to fame—Ken Alder emphatically calls finding out liars "an American obsession."[14] In contrast, since a variety of groups in American society participated on different sides in the debates over the polygraph and national security, this book highlights the conflicting demands Americans made of each other as they negotiated the need for both security and personal freedom. The result was a negotiated compromise that failed to satisfy either proponents or critics of the polygraph.

In contrast to Alder's broad identification of lie detection with the American character, this study highlights the intense conflicts that the purposes of polygraph tests sparked among citizens and its role in national security policymaking. I want to explain not only why the lie detector became so popular in the United States, but also why it was attacked so enthusiastically at different times. Despite occasional spectacular appearances in celebrity cases, the polygraph has not become the standard expert witness before American courts. Nor did American psychology utilize it on a broad basis during the rise of the "therapeutic ideal" in postwar America, when top psychologists played a major role in government-sponsored efforts to emotionally manage the population.[15] After three major investigations, Congress passed the 1988 Employee Polygraph Protection Act, which prohibited private companies from polygraphing applicants and from random testing of current employees. Exempted were companies concerned with national security, as well as national security agencies of the government. Since the polygraph borrowed legitimacy from the discourse of national security, we need to understand the history of this symbiotic relationship from the viewpoint of its supporters and its critics.

Surveillance Technologies and Global Power

As a variety of scholars in the fields of science and technology studies, sociology, literary studies, and the history and philosophy of science have established, the polygraph originated in nineteenth-century psychology, physiology, and criminology. The Victorian Age saw the rise of technologies to map individual appearance and open it to analysis. Accompanying the development of photography, for example, was a hope that the formal portrait would offer, as historian Alan Trachtenberg described it, "surety that persons were knowable in their visage, the image offering a surrogate for face-to-face sociality in an increasingly distended social order." Artists such as the daguerreotypist Montgomery Simons, who in 1853 created a series of thirty portraits to build an exhaustive display of human emotions, believed that "a pictured face manifested inner-ness." While the abolitionist Frederick Douglass firmly believed in photography as a means to reveal the human dignity of freedmen after the American Civil War, the white American middle and upper class employed photography to highlight racial and social distinctions. The "mug shot" also defined rather than liberated the individual. Making an early appearance in the history of photography (French authorities began to photograph prisoners in 1841), it

became an instrument of surveillance and governance, allowing criminologists to search out types of criminals. Even as Kodak's affordable
photo technology and the introduction of the U.S. Postal Service's one-
penny stamp for postcards allowed millions of Americans to experiment with photographic self-expression at the end of the nineteenth
century, the appearance of gruesome lynch photography reminds us
that technology could be used to brutally constrict the ability of individuals to define themselves.[16]

The search for traces of in-born criminality made Victorian criminologists in Europe develop further technological devices to use the
body itself, rather than testimony, as a witness. The medical technology
that led to the development of the polygraph measured physiological
changes in the human body invisible to the eye. Beginning in the 1860s,
European physiologists such as Étienne-Jules Marey in France, Vittorio
Benussi and Angelo Mosso in Italy, and Frederick Peterson in England
developed devices to measure and record blood pressure, pulse rates,
and respiration. In the first decade of the twentieth century, Swiss psychologist Carl Jung employed the new galvanometer. It featured an
electrode to detect galvanic skin resistance (sweat) by measuring an
electric current running through a finger. Jung employed the device
in combination with word association tests (first developed by Francis
Galton in England). During these tests, the subject would be asked to
freely associate based upon words read by the examiner. Jung's goal in
matching the chart of the galvanometer with the speed and content of
the stated word associations was to identify emotional pathology—the
sick mind. Hence, he mainly tested subjects with a variety of diseases
such as epilepsy. This concern with the abnormal mind as a human
type was prevalent in much of the early use of lie detection technology
such as the galvanometer. Nonetheless, it set the stage for the polygraph
to become a means to measure "normal" people and to monitor their
behavior, as Geoffrey Bunn has convincingly shown.[17]

Given that terms such as "criminality" escaped a strictly medical
definition, discourse surrounding the detection of certain types of individuals was to a prominent degree socially constructed. This holds true
especially for concerns about the female offender, whom criminologists
such as Cesare Lombroso or physicians such as Havelock Ellis viewed
as uniquely influenced by their physique. To them as to others in the

Victorian era, "the female body was associated with nature, passivity, emotionality, and irrationality." According to Geoffrey Bunn, it was Lombroso's research to detect female emotions that "led to a search for ordinarily invisible signs of crime within the body." Only when these physiological assumptions about criminality came under sustained critique by psychologists and social reformers such as Frances Kellor in the 1890s was the search for "criminal types" slowly abandoned. Still, prominent polygraph advocate William Moulton Marston titillated audiences in 1928 with a test of the supposedly varying emotionality of blonde, brunette, and red-headed women. Keeping the gendered agenda of the instruments that led to the development of the polygraph in mind, we need to realize that exerting social power remained a concern when polygraph tests were unleashed on homosexuals, communists, and other marginal groups of people in the twentieth century.[18]

It was often fear of social disintegration that drove these technological developments and endowed them with cultural significance. We can, for example, see the birth of Victorian detective fiction like Sir Arthur Conan Doyle's Sherlock Holmes stories as an example of cultural fantasies about the power of truth to reaffirm social order. Indeed, Ron Thomas notes that the lie detector might be called "the fulfillment of a dream inspired by nineteenth-century detective fiction."[19] Expanding on the theme of the interrelatedness of science, literature, and technology, Melissa Littlefield argues that crime and science fiction literature throughout the twentieth century advertised the possibilities of lie detection beyond what science could offer. Such literature particularly elided the challenges of interpreting the charts produced by physiological data.[20] According to Robert Michael Brain, the interaction between artistic imagination and the oddly symmetric charts of the new laboratory instruments even facilitated the rise of modernism in the fine arts. An intuitive viewing of the inscription of physiological data on paper would, so the hope of avant-garde intellectuals and artists, inspire a new formalist aesthetic. This aesthetic would utilize technological instruments and media such as film as extensions of the human sense organs and forge a new understanding of human nature based on the clues provided by those instruments.[21] The penetrating analysis of the human body by recording physiological data thus could be based on pessimism about the effect of modern mass society *and* inspire utopian visions of what it meant to be human. My study is based on an appreciation of the dynamic interaction between the research that led to the lie detector and the different cultural contexts in which the graphs that the polygraph produced could exert their influence. But in contrast to existing studies, this book focuses on American foreign policy as the site of discourses of the polygraph.

While many scientists of the early twentieth century explored new ways to police populations by mapping and defining the inner life of individuals, a peculiar parallel activity took place: Western policymakers and their advisors mapped out global geography in search for danger spots to be policed more efficiently as well. With Presidents William McKinley and Theodore Roosevelt, U.S. foreign policy attempted to reimagine the global landscape and developed new doctrines of state authority and national security fit for the industrial age and America's global economic ambitions. For example, the 1907 Roosevelt Corollary to the Monroe Doctrine, in which President Roosevelt unilaterally claimed American police authority in the Caribbean, complemented the American building of the Panama Canal, one of the technological wonders of the modern world. Indeed, the first decades of the twentieth century saw the radical shrinking of western conceptions of time and space, due to modern technologies such as the telegraph, telephone, steamboat, and railroad. These changes inspired the English geographer Halford Mackinder to develop the concept of "geopolitics." This concept stressed the impact of geography on the global balance of power, but it also highlighted how modern technologies began to strike at that balance. Mackinder argued that the advent of modern communication and transportation technology shrank the globe to a "closed system" of interdependent power relations.[22]

President Woodrow Wilson was a crucial transitional figure in American geo-strategic thinking. As the British-German war on the Atlantic raged after 1914, Wilson was haunted by the specter of an interdependent world—full of opportunity but also danger—in which modern technology threatened to globalize all conflicts so that no country, even the United States, could stand apart anymore. This view of the globe as a shrunken space laid the intellectual foundation for the domino theory. Popularized by President Dwight D. Eisenhower during the early 1950s, the domino metaphor of conflict suggested that any local conflict could spiral out of control. As a consequence, the domino theory highlighted the need for proactive U.S. policies to prevent a potentially catastrophic chain reaction. Modern technology therefore had distinctly dystopian implications for many policymakers: it established a sense of the impossibility of an unthreatened homeland.[23] The interplay between a sense of global threat and a belief in a unique American ability to benevolently police the globe was one major factor that set the stage for the American Cold War.

The Polygraph and the Concept of Cold War

This book aims to provide a narrative of the American Cold War. Historians have, with some notable exceptions, avoided methodological questions about how to conceptualize the compelling yet elusive concept of "the Cold War." In a recent survey of the historical literature, Anders Stephanson observes that historians too often use the term as an "empty marker of time" with no analytical payoff. Applied as "shorthand for an amorphous epoch of enormous span," the term confuses rather than clarifies which events of the period between 1945 and 1991 should be termed "Cold War" and what criteria should be used to make that call. For Stephanson, the Cold War was less an objective playing out of events than a narrative of America existing in mortal danger, justifying an offensive national posture and denying legitimacy to Soviet geopolitical interests.[24]

The ways in which the Cold War was a break with, or a continuation of, older American policy principles remains, in the final analysis, a matter of interpretation. One analytical challenge is that while the Cold War put many American long-term goals—such as a global system of free trade—temporarily on hold, in the minds of U.S. policymakers, it *ultimately* was meant to serve those ends.[25] In addition, the process of *how* the United States came to assume expansive military, political, and economic obligations was historically contingent. It depended on the sense of global responsibilities that came with America's unique position of power at the end of a period that had seen two world wars within a generation.[26] In short, the American Cold War arose from circumstance but also according to numerous, and at times contradictory, predispositions in American political culture and economy. Because

use of the polygraph was in many cases driven by a sense of mortal threat to American values, this book is then a Cold War history and, as in other Cold War histories, circumstances, contingencies, and coincidences matter.

While the concept and narrative of the Cold War came to be used and redefined by non-American actors as well, my book follows Stephanson's lead in analyzing the Cold War as a narrative that was embedded in American debates. I also agree with Stephanson and other historians that, since most American policymakers grudgingly came to accept the Soviet Union as a fellow great power by the early 1960s, the Cold War as a narrative rapidly lost plausibility among American publics and policymakers.[27] As a consequence, this book also investigates the practices that cemented elements of the Cold War after "containment" had lost its hegemonic status as the "privileged American narrative during the Cold War."[28] The polygraph thrived at the beginning of the American conflict with the Soviet Union and came under attack in the early 1960s. The fact that it became a target of persistent criticism, yet still existed in a more limited sphere of "national security" practice, suggests that its history should be understood as part of Cold War history, and that narratives of the powerful lie detector were containment narratives.

I would like to further emphasize that the history of the polygraph as a tool and symbol of the Cold War is consonant with existing approaches to American Cold War history. Historian Melvyn Leffler characterizes U.S. global strategy during and after World War II as, first, the encouragement of the economic and political consolidation of Western Europe; second, the pursuit of a nuclear arms race; and, third, vigorous opposition to allegedly communist nationalism in the Third World. When we abstract from this analysis, we can see that the strategy of containment was based on the perceived need to impose order on a world seen as chaotic—a world in which even the threat of an opponent capable of harnessing human and material resources demanded preparedness to actively intervene anywhere in the world and overwhelm any potential enemy. Based on these assumptions, the U.S. strategist Paul Nitze stated in 1950, "To seek less than preponderant power would be to opt for defeat."[29]

The American Cold War worldview can be seen as an inherently technological view: an outlook on the world that demanded constant surveillance, assessment, and intervention through technology. A technological outlook is foundational for ruling foreign populations in modern times. Rule by technology, according to Gyan Prakash, is "an enframing that acts upon and organizes the world so as to make it available as a resource."[30] American methods of rule by technology did not grow evenly. This outlook originated with slavery, as when Southern states introduced numbered passes to identify slaves working outside their home plantation.[31] However, the U.S. federal government at first did not match the ability of late nineteenth-century industrial enterprises to systematically collect, store, and assess information to identify citizens. Only after the "colonial laboratory" of the Philippines post-1898—with the creation of a comprehensive surveillance system that utilized (among other things) index cards based on intelligence from photography, fingerprints, and a network of local informants run by the Military Information Division and its affiliated indigenous organizations—did government officers such as Ralph Van Deman proceed to unleash these surveillance techniques on American society at home during World War I. The technological outlook therefore began to erode distinctions between the domestic and foreign realms even before the onset of the struggle with the Soviet Union.[32] Although the technological power of the U.S. government grew unevenly, variations of a technological outlook were nevertheless pervasive in the imagination of a settler society bent on conquering a continent with the help of modern technologies such as the railroads.[33]

However, the worldview of technology competes with rival imperatives, meaning that different groups can make ownership claims to governmental power. For example, after declaring independence in 1947, Indian Hindu nationalists declared the technologically mobilized colonial state their own, claiming correspondence between its newly configured natural and human resources—the "legible" outer sphere—and its ancient, spiritual, inner sphere. Thus, for Prime Minister Jawaharlal Nehru, India viewed through the frame of imperial technology could be transformed into an entity ruled by domestic elites for the benefit of postcolonial Indians, rather than by Westerners for their own benefit.[34]

The at-times paradoxical relationship between national identity and technology can also be seen in political discussions over the American national security state after 1945. During World War II, the federal government radically expanded its ability to govern the daily lives of citizens and formed new corporatist partnerships with private industries in the name of protecting individual liberty. "By cloaking new obligations to the state in this fusion of liberalism (with its valorization of freedom and equality) and nationalism (with its demand for unity, order, and loyalty), the federal government could expand its power radically without triggering opposition."[35] The controversies over the creation of the national security state—its ever-increasing defense budget, the terrifying development of nuclear technology, and the establishment of opaque bureaucracies such as the National Security Council and the Central Intelligence Agency—were also laden with rhetoric of national identity: the Truman administration justified these measures as a means to protect American values. Only by appropriating the traditional American discourse of freedom and imbuing it with new technological meaning could the Truman administration and its successors justify the new power of the state. Thus, U.S. national security policy attempted to avoid the specter of a "garrison state"—sociologist Harold Lasswell's vision of totalitarianism, in which an all-powerful civilian-military elite would dominate society.[36] American militarization would instead mean mobilization of American human and material resources through corporatist public-private networks, consisting of government agencies and the private defense industry.[37]

This expansion of the American state during and after World War II led to a paradox: security policy became intensely inward-looking, even as its sphere of action grew global. The wider the reach of U.S. power, the more intensely Americans discussed their national purpose. As a result, public discussions of foreign policy were often driven by partisan politics and vice-versa.[38] America's "global nationalism" assumed the necessity for a global grand strategy to protect what was uniquely *American*.[39] We can observe the impact of globalized domestic politics in the intense, but often unacknowledged, militarization of popular culture and domestic policy debates (from the "War on Poverty" to the "War on Drugs"), which—interrupted by the Vietnam War—underwent a resurgence under President Ronald Reagan in the 1980s. Military power often became imbued with the mythical ability to solve political problems, and "national security" often served as a placeholder for a variety of domestic debates.[40] Historians have studied congressional attempts to rein in the empowered executive branch at different times after 1945, but the repeated and often heated controversies about federal polygraph policies have been ignored so far.[41]

This book shows that discussions about the value or danger of the polygraph were a prominent part of the many debates to define the elusive term "national security" that became a powerful doctrine justifying American state-building during and after the Second World War. As one foreign relations textbook defines it: "U.S. national security is the ability of national institutions to prevent adversaries from using force to harm Americans or their national interests and the confidence of Americans in this capability."[42] National security therefore has physical and psychological connotations. Through the history of the polygraph, this study analyzes the meaning of "national security" as Americans negotiated it (often heatedly) with each other. An analytical focus on national security, Melvyn Leffler succinctly states, "demands that as much attention be focused on how the American government determines its core values as on how it perceives external dangers."[43] Leffler recently summarized his findings thus: "What I had learned was that national security itself was an amorphous notion shaped by external realities, domestic circumstances, and personal perceptions. It meant different things to different people at different times. It was a dynamic concept, always changing, always contentious."[44] This history of the polygraph may serve as a case study of Leffler's insight. How did polygraph debates express different ideas about American core values? How does the history of the polygraph as a tool of national security transform our understanding of the technological project to create security and protect democracy?

The Polygraph and the Political Power of Measurements

The polygraph lastly illustrates the theme of *measurement* and the danger inherent in basing national policy on measurable data alone. National security policy had to iron out contradictions and changes and often pursued ad-hoc policies rather than following well-established doctrines. As the political scientist David Campbell reminds us, "The constant (re)writing of national purpose and the objectives of national security policy . . . so that which is contingent and subject to flux is rendered more permanent" is the task of the national security state.[45] The polygraph was one technology that promised to *measure* security and establish an objective, scientific (and therefore fair and democratic) standard for achievable policies. But the question is: What exactly *did* the polygraph measure? How does a machine measure imponderables such as loyalty to democratic values?

Measurements such as numbers of Soviet troops, missiles, bombers, and so on were highly coveted during the Cold War, partly because they allowed the calculation of risk. In his classic study *Strategies of Containment*, historian John Lewis Gaddis points out the strategic shift from George Kennan's conception of limited strong point defense to the comprehensive global policies outlined in security document NSC-68 that took place in the early 1950s. By 1950, after the outbreak of the Korean War, American policy was becoming increasingly based on worst-case scenarios of Soviet threat.[46] This shift was due to an increased valuation of risk minimization: U.S. policy came to focus on Soviet military capabilities at least in part because capabilities could be *measured* more easily than intentions. Without sources of human intelligence inside the Kremlin (at least until the early 1960s), American policymakers often had to guess the intentions of the secretive Kremlin leadership. However, after the development of the U-2 spy plane in 1954, it became easier to measure what the other side was capable of. In fact, both superpowers in the end tended to interpret the adversary's immense military capabilities as a measure of the other side's aggressive intentions.[47] This book suggests the history of the polygraph is part of the history of risk management in U.S. national security policies.

In addition to risk management, this study also attends to technology as a means for establishing governmental control. As Paul Edwards reveals in his book *The Closed World*, the strategy of nuclear deterrence led to the development of digital technologies for global surveillance, for example the Distant Early Warning Line, an interconnected system of radar stations in the Arctic region of the Atlantic coast, which NATO installed in 1957. But deterrence also created closed-world discourse. This discourse included "the language, technologies, and practices that together supported the visions of centrally controlled, automated global power." Under this analytical heading, we can detect a unifying theme in U.S. national security policy: it calculated the predictability of human behavior in game theory, was often driven by worst-case scenarios of global war, and produced cognitive science that modeled human thinking after computer technology.[48] The history of the polygraph is part of the history of the American project to create predictability by reducing human conscience to measurable data. In this sense as well, the history of the polygraph is part of Cold War history.

Another finding of this book that contributes to our larger understanding of U.S. national security policy is how a practice that at first was only an improvised, on-the-spot solution became enshrined in practice and eventually turned into established policy. The history of the polygraph therefore suggests the path-dependent character of U.S. Cold War policies.[49] Bureaucratic convenience simply trumped science when it came to federal polygraph practices. In this context, my study discusses the way the executive branch of government—especially the CIA—used the polygraph to fight off congressional oversight. By emphasizing its critical contribution to national security, the CIA managed to carve out a sphere of control for itself by claiming the self-regulating, scientific nature of the polygraph as a neutral procedure. This discussion builds on the finding of historian Theodore Porter, who argues that quantitative methods allow American bureaucracies freedom from meddlesome outsiders (especially Congress) by depersonalizing knowledge and power. Using abstract knowledge gained from numbers is a strategy of modern government in the western world that especially resonates with traditional American distrust of elites and central authority. According to Porter, "Objectivity lends authority to officials who have very little on their own."[50] In a broader sense, the polygraph is therefore part of larger cultural forces that created what media theorist Neil Postman called "Technopoly." To Postman, Technopoly "consists in the deification of technology, which means that the culture seeks its authorization in technology, finds its satisfaction in technology, and takes its orders from technology." As part of this culture of technology, "Machines eliminate complexity, doubt, and ambiguity" and determine which questions people ask themselves and therefore direct their thinking.[51] My study tells the story of one technology that contributed to the larger technological cultures of the twenty-first century, in which issues of national security and personal freedom are still at the forefront of public debates.

My investigation proceeds as follows. Chapter 1 outlines the scientific challenges of establishing sufficiently precise polygraph tests. My hope is that clarifying the underlying methodological issues of the polygraph beforehand facilitates an easier flow of the historical narrative. In chapter 2 I discuss the American researchers who pioneered lie detection technology: Hugo Münsterberg, William M. Marston, John Larson, and Leonarde Keeler. This chapter discusses the context and first use of truth technology in the spectacular 1907 court trial of International Workers of the World leaders, who stood accused of assassinating Idaho governor Frank Steunenberg—a case followed closely by the national press. The chapter discusses the first systematic testing of lie detection technology during World War I. I also analyze how emerging "modern" threats—transnational terrorism, socialist ideology, and border-crossing crime—became the prime target of the lie detector. While one group of lie detector advocates favored a therapeutic use of the technology, its preponderant use (highlighted by sensational press coverage) became the deterrence of threats and the detection of criminals.

In chapter 3 I lay out the introduction of the lie detector in the national security state that American civilians and the military created during World War II. This chapter illustrates the extent of its use—first in prisoner-of-war camps, then in the screening of federal employees for loyalty and security in the initial stages of the Cold War. I explore the role of nuclear weapons development, which laid the basis for a new, invasive protocol of security, and the demands for submission to this protocol from federal employees. This chapter therefore demonstrates the concurrent rise of the U.S. national security state out of the emergency situation of World War II and the deployment of the polygraph by the federal government as an emergency measure, which achieved permanence due to the development of nuclear weapons.

Chapter 4 tracks polygraph controversies in the public sphere during the early Cold War years, with particular emphasis on new fears of totalitarian government methods. The investigations of anticommunist members of Congress (such as Joseph McCarthy and Richard Nixon) hold a prominent place, but the investigative journalism of Dwight Macdonald and other journalists and academics—as well as responses from American citizens—are the focus of this chapter. The analysis highlights the ambiguous position of the polygraph as both a harbinger and a perceived protector from undue governmental power. The main finding of this chapter is that the polygraph added to, rather than subdued, the social anxieties caused by the domestic Cold War in 1950s America.

Chapter 5 builds a larger interpretive and factual frame for the role of national security discourse in relation to the polygraph. It develops the early history of U.S. Cold War policies and the creation of the CIA, which came to embody the new powers of the national security state. The CIA was a secret executive agency that was charged with implementing the strategy of containment while being largely shielded from congressional oversight. In this chapter I illustrate the striking family resemblance of U.S. Cold War strategy, ideology, and narratives with polygraph discourse.

In chapter 6 I track the way the polygraph became integrated into the CIA's bureaucratic procedures. I conclude that despite attempts to make the polygraph a routine part of security procedures, the technology became embroiled in internal turf wars between professional interrogators, field agents, and security personnel. Bureaucratic needs therefore shaped the use of the technology. Further, this chapter illustrates that the sheer quantity of information produced by the lie detector obscured questions of how to properly assess the "security reliability" of individuals. Agencies such as the CIA could never resolve such questions. While the polygraph became a symbol of the relentless power exuded by federal security agencies, it revealed the inherent weaknesses of bureaucratized security procedures. Just like the polygraph, the CIA relied on reputation to establish credentials as a protector of national security.

In chapter 7 I discuss in detail the debates from the 1950s and 1960s to integrate the polygraph into U.S. nuclear deterrence strategy in order to overcome the stalemate in arms control. Largely confined to social scientists and policy analysts, this debate apparently never reached policymakers themselves. It nevertheless highlights the hopes and limitations of the polygraph's ability to establish cooperation between the two main nuclear powers—the United States and the Soviet Union—by functioning as a substitute for genuine trust building measures. The main argument of this chapter is that attempts to incorporate the polygraph into nuclear arms control give a strong indication of the limits of technological and game-theoretical solutions to the political conflicts underlying the arms race.

In chapter 8 I follow congressional investigations of the lie detector in the 1960s, 1970s, and 1980s. I focus in particular on John Moss and Bella Abzug in the House of Representatives and Sam Ervin in the Senate. This discussion shows that opposition to the polygraph reflected the growing importance of the individual "right to privacy" during and after the 1960s. Dozens of labor union publications and increased coverage by trade journals and within the scientific community drove this opposition. However, this chapter also argues that concern over the propriety and scientific credentials of polygraph technology transcended domestic political battle lines while simultaneously confirming the Cold War consensus that extensive measures against foreign threats were necessary. Lack of agreement on the scientific credentials of the polygraph thus led to a need to borrow ideological credentials from the national security state. This explains the persistence of polygraph tests in the federal government. "National security," this study concludes, now had the power to trump science and civil rights.

I conclude with an epilogue that highlights the continued relevance of the issues discussed in the preceding chapters. Especially after the attacks of September 11, 2001, "national security" became an even more powerful discourse, undermining political opposition to preemptive military action abroad and invasion of privacy both in the United States and abroad. In this context, "new and improved" ways to detect deception continue to enjoy currency as well. However, I also argue that the paradigm of truth technology seems to have shifted from detection of specific deceptive statements to all-encompassing surveillance of populations with the help of Big Data. Security discourses and practices continue to evolve, but it is my hope that this study of the polygraph and the American Cold War will help to forge a historically grounded discussion of the uses and limits of truth technology.

CHAPTER 1

How the Polygraph Does and Does Not Work

During a standard polygraph test, two soft rubber belts are strapped around a subject's stomach and chest, measuring the subject's breathing. Two wires are fastened on the ends of two of the subject's fingers, measuring skin conductance of electricity. Then a blood pressure cuff is placed around the subject's upper arm, measuring pulse and variations in blood pressure. In short, the polygraph determines a selection of responses from the autonomic nervous system. In the traditional, analog polygraph test, all measurements are hooked to a modestly sized box, which sits on a table between examiner and subject. During a typical exam, between nine and fifteen questions are asked in intervals of about fifteen seconds, with all physiological responses recorded on a continuous roll of paper. Digital technology has come to replace the box and the role of paper, so that, since the 1980s, most polygraph tests use computers to score the physiological responses. The test is usually repeated two or three times. It is preceded by a pretest interview, during which the examiner discusses the procedure and the questions with the subject. It concludes with a post-test interview, which offers the subject the chance to clear up any issues on their chart. It is therefore useful to distinguish between the polygraph *test* and the polygraph *examination,* a procedure that includes interviews before and after the test.[1]

Nonpractitioners, especially in academic psychology, have been mostly skeptical of the lie detector test's validity—that is, its ability to measure what it claims to measure: a specific, universal, and reproducible physiological lie response that can be untangled from individual, evolutionary, and cultural context. According to communications scholar Mark Knapp, the ability to effectively deceive others is a valuable trade when seen from an evolutionary perspective. Since natural selection rewards successful lies, humans have learned to lie effectively. Further, there is no firm boundary between truthful and deceitful communication. Equivocation, irony, white lies, and other subtle forms of deceit map a wide range of verbal and nonverbal human interaction. These forms of deceit involve complex cognitive states, such as self-deception, that make a physiological demarcation between truth and falsehood difficult.[2] Research in controlled laboratory situations suggests that some behavioral clues—such as higher vocal pitch, nervousness, or blinking—are correlated with deception; yet research subjects' rate of success in detecting deceit is little better than a coin toss.[3] Overall, humans have an ambiguous attitude toward deception. While societies value truthfulness and rely on trust in everyday social interactions, lying within limits has been found to be frequent. Rather than calculating costs and benefits of lying versus truthfulness, argues psychologist Dan Ariely, humans frequently engage in deception yet still want to view themselves as decent people. Fear of punishment or expectation of rewards, therefore, does not correspond with lower or higher likelihood of deception.[4] As a result, the basic methodological assumption of the polygraph—namely, that lying requires extraordinary mental exertion—is questionable. This raises the issue of what exactly the lie detector examination does.

In the controlled setting of a lie detector examination, truthfulness can be framed as compliance with the interrogator's questioning. By comparing responses to relevant and irrelevant questions and—more importantly—juxtaposing mental stress arising from intrusive control questions with anxiety that accompanies responses to the target questions (what the interrogator is really interested in), the lie detector examination attempts to isolate the deceptive consciousness from mere nervousness. This is why during the pretest interview, subjects are asked about any reasons why specific questions might cause them stress even when they answer truthfully. In the post-test interview, the subjects might be prompted to explain spikes in their curve in response to target questions; the lie detector test is then repeated.

The problem with this approach is that the subjects might not be aware of why they respond to certain questions more strongly than to others. For example, due to unresolved psychic conflicts, subjects might respond strongly to the question, "Have you ever stolen more than ten dollars?" because they have recently inherited a large sum of money of which they don't consider themselves worthy. Further, while it is possible to concoct scenarios in a laboratory setting in which the truthfulness of statements can be precisely defined, the psychic stress that questions cause in a subject cannot be reproduced that easily. That is because the consequences of a "failed" polygraph exam are naturally much more severe in real life than in a scientific study. As a result, the responsiveness of subjects in laboratory tests may not resemble responsiveness in real-life situations. Similarly, disagreements between interrogator and subject about how to interpret a response often cannot be resolved by external verification of the facts at hand. In such situations, the interrogator must press for a confession, since the correctness of the chart interpretation might otherwise never be confirmed. This state of affairs results in a dearth of field studies that measure the so-called external validity of the polygraph exam.

These and other methodological issues of polygraph exams were thoroughly assessed in a nineteen-month investigation for the National Research Council (NRC) by a group of researchers under Stephen Fienberg, a professor of statistics at Carnegie Mellon University. The study was commissioned by the U.S. Department of Energy and released in 2002, yet it highlighted issues that critics of the polygraph had raised long before.[5] On a basic level, the NRC study found that polygraph research was of low quality: fewer than one in three polygraph studies fulfilled minimal scientific standards. Most studies concerned themselves with application of existing procedures rather than underlying theory or even improved technique. Accordingly, there was "inertia among practitioners about using familiar equipment and techniques that rely on 1920-era science."[6] After analysis of acceptable research, the study concluded nevertheless that in specific event investigations, when relevant factual details are known and the significance of questions can be better assessed, lie detector tests performed "at rates well above chance, though well below perfection." However, the scientists also warned that "polygraph accuracy may be degraded by countermeasures" and judged that "its accuracy in distinguishing actual or potential security violators from innocent test takers is insufficient to justify reliance on its use in employee security screening in federal agencies."[7]

As for "construct validity," defined as a convincing theory as to why the test measures what it claims to measure, the NRC found that polygraph research offers as potential answers fear, arousal, or excitement, the conflict between two incompatible reactions, a conditioned response to lying, or the anticipation of punishment in case of being found out. In other words, there were many theories about the polygraph test's construct validity. All theories leave open possibilities for error, since, for example, fear of punishment might be present even in truthful examinees, who might anticipate the repercussions of a wrong call. Due to these problems, David Lykken developed an alternative approach based on the "orientating theory" of lie detection. Lykken stated that hearing a question with stress-triggering information is enough to cause a physiological response because it focuses the subject's attention. For example, a burglar who used a red Toyota as a getaway car would respond more strongly to any question involving a "red car" than questions that do not contain the trigger information. On the basis of this theory, Lykken developed the concealed knowledge test, a line of questioning that compares responses to a variety of questions with or without information relevant to the investigation at hand.[8] But the assumption underlying Lykken's orienting theory runs counter to the common practices used by most polygraph practitioners, such as the practice of discussing the questions before the test in order to avoid startling the subject. Consequently, after decades of practice there was no agreed-upon theory of what the polygraph test legitimately measured.

Further, the NRC study insisted that physiological data recorded by the polygraph are not universal and can vary among individuals:

The physiological responses measured by the polygraph do not all reflect a single underlying process such as arousal. Similarly, arousing stimuli do not produce consistent responses across these physiological indicators [blood pressure, skin conductivity, heart rate] or across individuals. This knowledge implies that there is considerable lack of correspondence between the physiological data the polygraph provides and the underlying constructs that polygraph examiners believe them to measure.[9]

As a result, the questions chosen by the examiner can influence the test results, as can the responses from different examinees to the same questions as well as a number of other variables that polygraph research has failed to calculate. Therefore, "the basic science relevant to the polygraph suggests that it can at best be an imperfect instrument, but it leaves unclear the degree of imperfection."[10]

Another crucial issue the NRC study examined was polygraph use for security screening purposes—that is, the use of lie detector tests to identify the suitability of applicants or employees for work in federal security agencies. The study identified two major problems. First, U.S. security agencies did not agree on what findings they considered severe enough to warrant denial of employment for applicants or termination of employment for employees. As a result, the predictive value of the test remained unclear. While federal statistics on the utility of the polygraph often counted the detection of small infractions of security protocol or lies about insignificant matters as true positives (that is, the correct identification of a deceptive statement), the purported goal of the screenings was to identify serious threats to U.S. national security. As the NRC researchers put it, "Assessing the polygraph's accuracy for screening cannot be done without agreement on the criterion—what it is supposed to be accurate about. The committee has seen no indication of a clear and stable agreement on what the criterion is, either in general or within any particular organization that uses polygraph screening."[11] Homosexuality is a good example of this problem. For the longest time—indeed, until the 1990s—the Central Intelligence Agency considered homosexuality as a disqualifier for employment for reasons relating to both morale within the agency and the perceived susceptibility of a homosexual to blackmail. Yet as cultural acceptance of homosexuality increased, this criterion lost its value, and the CIA eventually adjusted its policy. What other criteria that intelligence agencies have been using to define suitability for employment might be subject to change in the future?

In addition, since applicants who flunked polygraph tests due to failure to disclose minor infractions were denied employment, it was also impossible to compare their job performance and loyalty with those who passed the test. This lack of comparison data goes a long way toward explaining the continued controversies over not just the validity, but also the utility of the polygraph test. There is simply no consensus as to how reliable a predictor of future loyalty a failed polygraph test is. "Perhaps most critical," emphasized the NRC analysts,

> it is necessary to make inferences about future behavior on the basis of
> polygraph evidence of past behavior, such as illegal drug use, to future
> behavior of a different kind, such as revealing classified information.
> We have not found either any explicit statement of a plausible theory
> of this sort in the polygraph literature or any appropriate evidence of
> construct validity.[12]

Worse still, the NRC found a second, even more critical shortcoming of polygraph tests as a means of screening applicants or employees in federal security agencies. In order to correctly identify spies who attempt to infiltrate an intelligence agency, the test *has* to result in accusations of spying against many innocent people. This is because polygraph examiners, in order to calibrate the test to be sufficiently sensitive to identify deceptive individuals in large pools of people, have to make the test sufficiently unspecific. This lack of specificity will result in many false positives (individuals who show signs of anxiety for reasons unrelated to lying but are nevertheless identified as deceptive). The study gave the following example of the tradeoff between sensitivity and specificity of the test in employment screening. If we assume ten spies in a population of ten thousand applicants for a job, and the test is set sensitive enough to identify eight of the ten spies, it will result in 1,598 wrongly accused applicants.[13] Yet federal examiners did not have a clear understanding of this fact, namely that there were different appropriate measures of accuracy—the "decision threshold"—for different purposes.[14] Instead, it appeared that examiners often relied on informal criteria to judge a person as either nervous or deceptive. This finding offers a mathematical explanation for the accusations hurled against lie detector tests in screening procedures. It further justifies the claim of many polygraph practitioners that the quality of the test ultimately depends on the experience of the examiner.

Many polygraph examiners maintain that they are interrogators who use the machine as a tool of the trade. They argue that a successful polygraph examination is an art more than a science and that the test will lead, ideally, to a confession. Especially in specific interrogations, examiners insist, an unexplained "deception indicated" can be given with a strong sense of confidence, while during screenings the polygraph test often leads to admissions of crimes or other lapses of ethics that otherwise would have remained unnoticed. The amount of credence polygraph examiners give to the scientific value of the test varies, but they usually agree that the validity of the test depends on the quality of the examiner. CIA polygraph examiner John Sullivan's attitude may serve as a typical defense of the polygraph that does not rely on science. Sullivan admits to the scientific limitations of the polygraph but argues that "in the real world, there is no better screening device than a polygraph instrument in the hands of a good examiner—'good examiner' being the operative word."[15] Similarly, former Army Intelligence polygraph examiner Gordon Barland argues that phrasing precise control questions is crucial. He maintains that experienced examiners do not judge responses in screenings the way they would in specific investigations. Rather, they will incorporate other indicators such as behavior into their judgment and will retest the subject, with differently worded questions if necessary, resulting in a lower amount of false positives in real life than studies show. Barland also insists that the deterrent effect of the test should not be underestimated.[16]

There is evidence that experienced examiners can conduct effective polygraph interrogations and that the prospect of a polygraph exam has deterred potential or actual spies from entering national security agencies. On the other hand, the appeal of the polygraph comes to a large degree from its family resemblance with science and its aura of objective, precise technology. Early developers and practitioners of the polygraph test counted on this aura, and most polygraph examiners still employ it today. It is a result of these various perceptions of the polygraph exam—part science, part art—that its role and effectiveness in U.S. security policies remains so controversial. Another consequence of this state of affairs is that the polygraph exam is often experienced by subjects as an expression of overbearing, powerful authority, while polygraph examiners consider themselves marginal, misunderstood, and unjustly under attack. These varying perspectives on the polygraph present another reason to consider the lie detector a fascinating lens through which to study U.S. national security policies.

I use the terms "lie detector" and "polygraph" interchangeably, unless a passage is meant to emphasize the significance of one term or the other in a specific context. In general, the most meaningful difference between the two designations is that the term "lie detector" was coined by popular culture (apparently it was first employed in 1909 in the novel *The Yellow Circle* by Charles Walk)[17] and thus emphasizes the role reputation has played in the rise of the technology. "Lie detector" also tends to emphasize the instrument itself rather than the skills of an examiner using it. The term encourages a tendency to endow the instrument with agency of its own. "Polygraph," on the other hand, was the name chosen by the man who patented the technology, Leonarde Keeler. Among the other names Keeler considered were "Emotograph" and "Respondograph." "Polygraph" is a generic term for any device performing "many writings" simultaneously and therefore tends to highlight the discretionary power of the operator. As a seemingly technical term, "polygraph" can also be interpreted as suggesting scientific correctness, professionalism, and technical prowess.

CHAPTER 2

Truth to Remake Society

At first he denied everything. But after three days of solitary confinement, followed by interrogation by the most experienced officer in the nation's most notorious detective agency, the suspect finally confessed the truth: he was part of an international conspiracy to terrorize the United States that had already killed seventeen people. After an extraordinary rendition had brought his alleged coconspirators into state custody, a protracted court battle ensued under the watchful eye of the national and international press. Months of investigation did not produce any corroborating evidence for the charge of conspiracy. The fate of the accused hung on the sincerity of one man, who in the meantime had undergone a religious conversion. Was he telling the truth?

Such were the dramatic circumstances under which modern lie detection was introduced to the American public in 1907. The witness for the prosecution was "Harry Orchard," one of the many pseudonyms Albert E. Horsley had used throughout his vagrant life. The alleged coconspirators were William "Big Bill" D. Haywood, secretary and treasurer of the Western Federation of Miners (WFM); Charles H. Moyer, the union's president; and G. A. Pettibone, a former member of its Executive Committee. They had been arrested secretly in Denver, Colorado, at WFM headquarters and brought to Boise, Idaho, by special train. Orchard was held for the bombing death of former Idaho governor Frank Steunenberg on December 30, 1905. As governor, Steunenberg had broken up a WFM strike by invoking martial law, an act the WFM considered a betrayal. After days of interrogation by James McParland of the Pinkerton Detective Agency, Orchard wrote a sixty-page confession claiming to have conspired with Haywood, Moyer, and Pettibone, but Steunenberg's murder had only been the latest plot. A bare-knuckle legal fight ensued between James H. Hawley and Idaho senator-elect William Borah for the prosecution and Edmund F. Richardson and Clarence Darrow for the defense, which included bribing witnesses and engaging in mutual espionage.[1]

The ambitious promoters of lie detection sought recognition outside the scientific community through sensational press coverage, such as the trial of the leaders of the WFM. If the lie detector thrived on a sense of crisis, so did state building generally in twentieth-century America, where the federal government would deliver justifications for centralized authority that the country's federal structure and culture of local autonomy had long denied it. At the same time, the early history of lie detection and the polygraph also highlights the unease that many retained about the test. The authority of the machine competed with the experts in science, law, and government.

In the early twentieth century, psychologists in the United States fought to enhance the status of their discipline by demonstrating its usefulness to solve social problems. German scholar Hugo Münsterberg proved a driving force in this development. Born of Jewish parentage in 1863, Münsterberg converted to Protestantism as a young man and eventually left Germany for the United States. His career illustrates the rich exchange of scientific and social reformist ideas across the Atlantic at the turn of the twentieth century.[2] In the United States, Münsterberg's humanistic interests came through, leading him into the Boise courthouse in 1907 equipped with laboratory instruments. Münsterberg was a man of broad knowledge and even broader ambitions. He received his Ph.D. in psychology from Leipzig University under the influential Wilhelm Wundt and an M.D. from Heidelberg. He was familiar with the philosophy of German Idealism and Darwin's theory of evolution. Influenced by his mentor Wundt, Münsterberg developed a theory of mind that rested on the idea that subjective states of minds, such as thoughts and emotions, could be identified by measuring correspondent activity in the brain and vice-versa. He then tried to apply his findings to ethical and social problems.

Münsterberg was a man of his time. Psychologist William James lured him to Harvard University and gave him lavish opportunity to expand on his laboratory psychology. In Germany, Münsterberg had built an extensive laboratory of equipment for measuring minute physiological data, such as chronoscopes to calculate reaction time, a sphygmamograph to measure pulse rates, and instruments to determine a subject's perception of colors or the direction of sounds. At Harvard, Münsterberg eventually built forty rooms worth of experimental equipment. His colleagues honored him with the presidency of the American Psychological Association in 1898 and the American Philosophical Association in 1908. Münsterberg's action theory of consciousness—which assumed a feedback loop between human physiology and the environment as the origin of consciousness—broadly fit the functionalist and behaviorist direction American psychology was taking at the time.[3]

But Münsterberg's drive to prove the social significance of his research on the one hand, while insisting on the exclusive authority of the scientist on the other, created, as one of his biographers put it, "conflicting interests and incongruent ambitions." His unrelenting self-promotion would eventually set Münsterberg on a confrontation course with his equally aspiring colleagues. When the Great War erupted in 1914, his political activities and cooperation with the German embassy made him suspect to the Anglophile northeastern elite. By the time of his death in December 1916, Münsterberg had lost much of his clout in the profession, although his vision of applied psychology was firmly in line with the goals of many in his discipline.[4]

The social and political crises of the time provided ambitious psychologists such as Münsterberg with abundant opportunities. By the time Harry Orchard's trial began in the spring of 1907, the United States had experienced decades of political violence. Anxious middle-class observers worried about new immigrants, violent foreign ideologies such as anarchism, and the rapid speed of industrialization. Events such as the Chicago Haymarket bombing of 1886, the Pullman Strike of 1894, and the assassinations of Presidents James Garfield and William McKinley in 1881 and 1901 dominated the headlines of the mass circulation newspapers. The globalization of the labor market fueled American economic power, yet the individual immigrant—sometimes described as overly passive, sometimes as overly aggressive, almost always as dangerous for democracy—came to stand for every unwanted development in American life. Many shared author Henry James's dread of "the terrible little Ellis Island."[5]

One of the most frightening specters haunting early twentieth-century America was that of the mad assassin who, armed with modern weapons such as dynamite (invented by Alfred Nobel in 1863), spread his "propaganda by deed" with the help of wireless communication and mass print media. The case of President McKinley's assassin, Leon Czolgosz, a U.S.-born unemployed steel worker from Ohio with no connections to political groups, raised two equally uncomfortable questions: Was American society so out of control that it could drive a man insane, or were American political institutions so corrupt that a sane man could be justified in killing the president? Under President Theodore Roosevelt's leadership, the federal government in 1903 banned anarchists from legal immigration *and* initiated federal oversight of large corporate institutions. Just as the "alienists," the mental pathologists who examined Czolgosz, sharply disagreed as to whether heredity or environment were to blame for his deed, American Progressive reformers also diverged on the remedy for the ills of industrial society.[6]

The question of Harry Orchard's truthfulness was so explosive that even the grandiloquent Münsterberg could hardly have exaggerated it. "The crime ranks with the assassination of Lincoln, Garfield, and McKinley," declared the *New York Times*, taking a stance favorable to the prosecution.[7] Correctly observing that the legitimacy of U.S. unionism itself was on trial, Münsterberg also recognized the transnational political aspects of the court battle when he observed, "The whole country wanted clearness as to whether Western socialism was really working with the means of an anarchism that overshadows the nihilism of Russia." Prosecutor William Borah answered that question in his closing argument: "I saw Idaho dishonored and disgraced. . . . I saw murder—no, not murder, a thousand times worse than murder; I saw anarchy wave its first bloody triumph in Idaho." Nothing less than American democracy appeared to be at stake at a time when mostly imagined but occasionally real anarchist conspiracies filled the pages of sensationalist newspapers and potboiler novels on both sides of the Atlantic.[8]

The mystery of Harry Orchard was irresistible. One aspect of his testimony that baffled contemporary observers was the incongruity of his stoic demeanor and the explosive content of his testimony. He told a "horrible, revolting, sickening story" of murder upon murder, yet "there was nothing theatrical about the appearance on the stand of this witness. . . . Orchard spoke in a soft, purring voice, marked by a slight Canadian accent, and except for the first few minutes that he was on the stand he went through his awful story as undisturbed as if he were giving the account of a May Day festival."[9]

Was this credible testimony? Maybe one could go by the witness's appearance. When he was arrested, Orchard sported a disheveled look that many respectable Americans associated with tramps and criminals. But after his arrest he was clean-shaven and came to court in a three-piece suit. This killer, as *McClure's* put it, looked "like nothing so much as your milkman." In fact, his "nervous eyes, the compressed lips" and "hardened face muscles" had been replaced by "good-natured diffidence, breaking easily into an ingenuous smile."[10] *Times* correspondent Oscar King Davis concluded that Orchard's incredible story had to be true precisely because it was so incredible: "Lies are not made as complicated and involved as that story. Fiction so full of incident, so mixed of purpose and cross-purpose, so permeated with the play of human passion, does not spring offhand from the most marvelous fertile invention."[11]

Therefore, Davis was less concerned with the particulars of Orchard's life story. Rather, it seemed to come down to whether one believed in, as the defense called it, the witness's "narrative" of transformation from sinner to sincere Christian. That Orchard had committed murder was not the question. But was he still *a murderer*? Was the story sincere or was it all just an elaborate ruse to escape the gallows? Again the *New York Times* correspondent had made up his mind:

It is indeed a modern miracle, this change in Orchard. It has taken the
most abandoned, depraved, inhuman wretch, whom no abyss or infamy
seemed deep enough to check, and transformed him into a man serene
and sure, imperturbable under any assault, who has balanced his books
and squared his account with life, and whose only purpose now is to
make such reparation as he can by telling the whole infamous truth about
himself and his work, wherever it may lead, whatever it may cost.[12]

For Davis, Orchard had presented a convincing case of a successful
American makeover: the achievement of redemption by creating a new
identity. Orchard expressed this creed in an interview with the *Denver
Post*: "I think that in no other country in the world can a man get such
an opportunity to succeed as he can here. I think that nowhere else
can he get such cordial friendship and so much sympathy if he fails
and tries honestly to rise again."[13] With the help of ghostwriter George
Kibbe Turner, Orchard also prepared a manuscript of his "autobiography" for *McClure's*, which was published in the summer and fall of 1907.
This story was largely a bland, factual telling of Orchard's upbringing in
Ontario, his failed business attempts, and his decline into a life of crime.
The story, however, climaxed with Orchard's subsequent conversion in
prison. He affirmed, "I was tired of such a life and wanted to reform and
ask God's forgiveness."[14]

Whether intended or not, Orchard's makeover from violent, atheist
labor radical to respectable middle class Christian fit a larger agenda of
Protestant religion at the turn of the century—expressed, for example,
in the Reverend Charles Sheldon's 1896 bestseller *In His Steps*. Sheldon
and his followers believed that faith could domesticate the lower classes
and in the process reinvigorate the Protestant middle class. For those
who believed in the power of personal redemption to heal society,
Orchard's story was therefore especially appealing.[15]

But was Orchard's transformation narrative too good to be true?
Toward the end of the trial, the German psychologist entered the scene
to solve the riddle with the help of laboratory psychology. Münsterberg
at the time saw himself on a crusade against torture. He professed to
reject brutal methods of interrogation not only "from sentimental horror and from aesthetic disgust" but even more so from "the instinctive
conviction that the method is ineffective in bringing out the real truth."[16]

The science of psychology had to step up and show its usefulness: "Whoever claims that he can whistle must finally prove it by whistling."[17] Juxtaposing his own neutral, scientific approach with the charged political atmosphere of the trial, Münsterberg later narrated his journey toward correct diagnosis. In this later telling, he was at first skeptical and applied his own knowledge of eugenic discourse on criminality to size up Orchard: "I saw him from the side and his profile, especially the jaw, appeared to me most brutal and most vulgar. I saw also the deformation of the ear, the irregularity in the movement of the eyes and the abnormal lower lip. That this was the profile of a murderer seemed to me not improbable, but that this man had become a sincere religious convert and an honest witness seemed to me . . . quite incredible." Invoking the demonic view of criminals so typical of eugenicists, Münsterberg voiced his agreement with Clarence Darrow that "Orchard was a monstrous liar."[18]

Münsterberg therefore set up his readers for a surprise when he concluded, after administering a battery of tests, that Orchard spoke the truth. The psychologist used the reaction-time test, measuring with a chronoscope the fractions of a second it took Orchard to freely associate to a careful mix of innocuous words such as "river," "ox," or "yoke" and loaded words such as the names of Orchard's alleged victims, based on the idea that a guilty mind would hesitate in its response to loaded words in order to avoid giving itself away with an overly quick and revealing response. The chronoscope revealed no such hesitation in Orchard's responses. "Confession," for example, prompted "truth" in no more time than innocent words (eight-tenths of a second).[19] Therefore, a piece of modern technology, administered by an expert, finally revealed the truth. Or did it?

Münsterberg confessed that trickery had played a prominent role in the test. "If he [Orchard] thought that he, the experienced poker player, could easily hide his innermost mind and could deceive me with cant and lies, I turned the tables on him quickly. . . . I used some . . . illusions, and soon he was entirely under the spell of the belief that I had some special scientific powers."[20] Münsterberg did not describe what kind of tricks he used. However, he was more explicit about his strategy to distract Orchard from the real purpose of the tests. He told his subject that by using word associations he "shall learn all from the ideas which he [Orchard] would bring up."[21] By suggesting that the test was about answers rather than reaction time, Münsterberg hoped the witness would give himself away by involuntary emanations from his mind. Such suggestive "working" of test subjects was a first that Hugo Münsterberg introduced as a permanent feature of lie detection.

For Münsterberg, his tests also had been a success because of the speed and efficiency with which he had managed to "pierce into the mind" of the accused. This was another major aspect of lie detector discourse this trial showcased: "As far as the objective facts are concerned my few hours of experimenting were more convincing than anything which in all those weeks of the trial became demonstrated."[22] But what "objective facts" could Münsterberg really ascertain? If anything, Orchard's reaction to the psychologist's questions might have proved that Orchard believed his own story. Maybe he was a sincere liar.

Münsterberg's arguments for his tests were repeated many times in the coming decades. Still, lie detection would also become embedded into narratives. The single utterance would become reintegrated into lie detector stories that explained a case and could translate the data of the test back into the language of contemporary society. Münsterberg did so at the end of his narration of Orchard's case: "I pressed his [Orchard's] hand as that of an honest reliable gentleman, and, with full feeling of the responsibility, I felt ready to affirm that every word in Orchard's confession is true."[23] In other words, Orchard had not just uttered statements he himself believed to be true, but he was an "honest, reliable gentleman," the kind of sincere person ready to be readmitted into society.

Alas, the moment of triumph did not last. On the train back east a tired Münsterberg revealed his findings to a reporter, who promptly filed a story for the *Boston Herald*. The leaking of the diagnosis to the press before a verdict had been reached backfired disastrously. Haywood's defense attorneys and many newspapers, including the *New York Times*, attacked Münsterberg's statements as unwise. Editorials in labor publications called him "an intellectual prostitute" and "a shameful charlatan" since he had come on behalf of a magazine looking for publicity. This name-calling was painful. Münsterberg and S. S. McClure agreed not to print the article on his experiments he had prepared. *Whilshire's Magazine's* added another caveat: "The learned professor seemingly neglected to take into consideration the fact that another expert psychologist, Professor McParland [the Pinkerton Agency's star detective], had been previously working on the subject for sixteen months."[24] Could not a comprehensive rehearsal of a story beat lie tests? "Countermeasures" was another issue that lie detection technology would have to face time and again.

Münsterberg's humiliation showed how easily these tests, when conducted in a political atmosphere, could spark a firestorm. Publicity was a double-edged sword, since fame and infamy lay close together in the court of public opinion.[25] Lie detection's claim to be the proper replacement for torture or the "third degree" also raised doubts from the start. One *New York Times* editorial warned that despite Münsterberg's claim to the contrary, his apparatuses "are not quite devoid of cruelty, and would be likely, it seems to us, to throw a timid innocent person into fits."[26] Münsterberg's writings do not suggest that he consciously used his tests to intimidate his subjects. Later practitioners of lie detection did.

Scientific lie detection did not solve the case, nor would it solve any of the big court cases in twentieth-century U.S. history. The jury found the defendant William Haywood not guilty due to lack of corroborating evidence. To add insult to injury, the trial turned Haywood into a celebrity of international socialism. He went on a celebrated tour to Europe in 1910 on behalf of the Socialist Party of America (SPA) and would soon after head the International Workers of the World (IWW), a genuinely American labor union that nevertheless would be crushed by the federal government as a threat to national security in 1917. Only under the threat of life in prison did Haywood jump bail and flee to the Soviet Union, where he died as a lonely exile in 1928.[27] Even J. Anthony Lukas's exhaustive study of the case failed to come to a firm conclusion as to the defendants' guilt, and the case will likely never be settled. Harry Orchard died in prison in 1952, never having changed his story.

Yet lie detection resonated in American society because it offered a way to reconcile political traditions of personal autonomy with the organizational challenges of modern industrial society. William James poignantly expressed how deeply his later professional conflicts with Münsterberg were connected to their respective general visions of society: "I want a world of anarchy, Münsterberg one of bureaucracy, and each appeals to 'nature' to back him up."[28] But it is too simple to employ James as the representative American libertarian counterpart to Münsterberg's Teutonic program of authoritarianism. Achieving social control through efficient application of ordering principles rapidly became a mainstream ambition of American psychology. Columbia University's James McKeen Cattell expressed the hyperbolic attitude among many American psychologists when he declared in 1904, "I see no reason why the application of systematic knowledge to the control of human nature may not in the course of the present century accomplish results commensurate with the nineteenth-century applications of physical science to the material world."[29] Similarly, psychologist Herbert Nichols—a student of H. Stuart Hall and instructor at Harvard under Münsterberg—wrote in 1893, "The twentieth century will be to mental science what the sixteenth century was to physical science, and the central field of its development is likely to be America."[30] The difference between Münsterberg and many of his American colleagues was thus more one of tone than substance.

Placing Münsterberg in proper context shows that his pioneering work in lie detection was part of an ambitious Progressive agenda of social engineering among many American psychologists who aspired to use the polygraph for broad social disciplinary purposes. The history of lie detection in the twentieth century would be a negotiation of the precise place of the technology within the administration of justice, the surveillance regime of workers in large corporate entities, and, eventually, federal agencies. Both American capitalism and the federal government would therefore shape Münsterberg's project to their needs, while American political traditions of libertarianism would limit its reach.

Broad application of lie detection technology became possible when Münsterberg took a decisive step away from the preoccupation with in-born degradation. A focus on heredity had defined late nineteenth-century physiology and eugenics and featured most prominently in the work of Cesare Lombroso.[31] Lombroso's 1876 book *Criminal Man* had offered a meticulous study of cranial physiognomy and posed a causal connection between anatomy and deviant behavior. The Italian criminologist suggested guidelines to identify criminal types of persons through external measurement. Other researchers followed this lead and concluded that "the brains of criminals exhibit a deviation from the normal type, and criminals are to be viewed as an anthropological variety of their species," as Austrian physician Moritz Benedikt asserted in 1881. Lombroso's encyclopedic maps of degeneration corresponded with his political program of containing social disorder by excluding the allegedly inferior.[32]

While this kind of science was the stuff for lurid fiction (Bram Stoker's description of Count Dracula, for example, drew from Lombroso), it soon lost traction. Lombroso committed the cardinal mistake of confusing correlation with causation when he inferred the roots of criminality from the physiology of criminals. Further, the development of statistics soon replaced his strict science of causation with probabilistic thinking about crime, where "causal understanding moved in the direction of increasing specificity, multiplicity, complexity, probability, and uncertainty."[33] Such thinking rejected Lombroso's bold claims for the predictive power of anatomy. But some of his research methods were repurposed. In particular, Lombroso had employed a special glove he used to register blood pressure changes that he hoped would give away clues about the physiological make-up of criminals. Such methods could be employed for different ends, not to catch the born criminal but the occasional liar.[34]

As we saw, Hugo Münsterberg juxtaposed his own approach with eugenic ideas of telltale physiology. In contrast to Lombroso's politics of separating inferior human material from society, Münsterberg employed his laboratory instruments in the cause of Progressive social reform, especially during the last decade of his life. In his 1908 essay "The Prevention of Crime," the scholar distanced himself from theories of "born criminals" and specifically attacked the work of Lombroso. While criminals had "insufficient capacity and resistance of the central nervous system," Münsterberg asserted, "no man is born a criminal; but society gives him, without his will, the ruinous injection." Deducing from his action theory of consciousness, Münsterberg called for an ambitious program to study the effect of a variety of stimuli—from tobacco and tea to light conditions, bad air, exhaustive sports, and many more—"that enter the daily life of the masses." His broad goal was to map nothing less than the effects of modern life on the individual: "What the commercialism of our time or the vices of the street, the recklessness of the masses and the vulgarity of the newspapers, the frivolity of the stage and the excitement of the gambling-hells, may mean for the weak individual cannot better be understood than through the microscopical [sic] model of it in the experimental test which allows subtle variations." Ultimately, Münsterberg wanted to build a social reform program based on the results of laboratory findings that would inoculate the individual against such stimuli: "The public welfare must give through work, through politics, through education, through art, through religion, to everybody a kind of life interest and life-content in which envy is meaningless."[35]

Psychological experiments could also lead the way to reforms in government institutions and criminal justice. After administrating a number of tests on perception and memory in his Harvard laboratory, Münsterberg claimed to have established the unreliable nature of witness testimony. Having found that "associations, judgments, suggestions, penetrate into every one of our observations," he warned against "the blind confidence in the observations of the average normal man."[36] Münsterberg also called for vocational guidance through aptitude tests to find the right person for the right job in industrial society. He campaigned for adjustment of work conditions to identify "the most rational scheme" for the "arrangement of tool and apparatus by systematic experiments in the psychological laboratory," and equally systematic study toward "eliminating all superfluous movements and . . . training in those movement combinations which were recognized as the most serviceable ones." Münsterberg believed that industrial work could be fulfilling and would not depend on a system of monetary inducements such as the one proposed by Frederick Winslow Taylor.[37] At the same time, contemporary researchers such as Münsterberg's compatriot, the sociologist Max Weber, noted that psycho-physiological accounts of daily activities shortchanged the sociocultural context of human behavior. For example, how could graphic measurements distinguish between mental fatigue derived from overwork, or from boredom? What about workers' habits after hours that influenced their performance on the factory floor? This criticism of laboratory psychology was not exclusive to Weber. Many have taken issue with its seeming reduction of complex human motivation to simplistic measurements.[38]

Either way, Münsterberg's interest in lie detection was part of his reform program to adjust the individual and American mass society to each other and to avoid heavy-handed social legislation. For example, Münsterberg argued against prohibition of alcohol. Voluntary temperance was crucial because the very variety of pleasures that American consumer society offered led to lack of attention and introspection, which in turn resulted in restlessness and nervousness. In a particularly telling passage of his essay collection *American Problems*, Münsterberg pondered the American character:

> The foreigner who studies the American character will always be deeply impressed by the wonderful striving for self-assertion, self-perfection, and self-realization, which gives meaning and significance to this greatest democracy of the world. But there is one trait which he instinctively perceives, in spite of all his enthusiasm in the strength and glory of the New World. He cannot help feeling the lack of accuracy and thoroughness, the superficiality, the go-as-you-please character of the work; and this ultimately means the lack of voluntary attention. . . . Every feature of our social life shows an unwillingness to concentrate attention. Only that which can be followed without effort is welcome.[39]

Such judgment might still ring true in the age of iPods, instant messaging, and social networking websites.[40] Indeed, decrying the lack of mental discipline as the result of the rigors *and* comfort created by modern urban life was widespread among middle-class thinkers of various professions and interests. Münsterberg was therefore part of a larger chorus warning of cultural decline due to lack of consistent effort, often identified with feminization of society.[41] As a consequence, Münsterberg emphasized the confession as a means of self-discipline:

> No longer do we write letters full of feeling which our grandparents wrote: we of to-day dictate notes. We do not keep emotional diaries: instead, we subscribe to the clipping bureau. . . . The businesslike soberness of our modern times has taken away this chance for confession; and many a nervous system might be wrecked, where a confessional might have saved it.[42]

Münsterberg concluded this line of thought with advice to resocialize criminals by applying his brand of psychology to the confession. In 1908, after his controversial intervention in the Boise trial, Münsterberg would write with now uncharacteristically restrained optimism:

> The man who confesses puts himself again on an equal ground with the honest majority; he belongs again to those who want a healthy justice;

he gives up his identity with the criminal and eliminates the crime like a foreign body from his life. . . . The psychologist—I say it with hesitation, as my observations on that point may not yet be complete enough, and the subject is an entirely new one—may even be able to find out by his experiments whether a true confession is authentic or not.

Under Münsterberg, modern lie detection developed into one aspect of "a systematic education in self-control," a program of social engineering in which the administration of a confession ritual could be part of a general effort to adjust mental sensibility to the environment and to restore the subject's identity.[43] Not addressed was the question of power. Would the expert guide the subject toward restored mental health? Or was more forceful intervention necessary? What if there was disagreement between expert and technology on the one hand and the subject on the other hand? Münsterberg's writings remained silent on these questions.[44]

Münsterberg was among the first to experience how quickly the neutral expert could be drawn into political controversy, and he encountered the first suspicions that his modern methods might not be all that different from the old-fashioned "third degree." By turning away from the search for types of criminals and focusing attention on the individual and "the lie" as a distinct entity, he opened the question as to whether "the psychologist may in the future use his mental microscope to make sure whether there are lies in the mind of the subject."[45] Just as during the Great War, in which James Montgomery Flagg's Uncle Sam would directly point at the individual citizen and proclaim that he wanted "you," the lie detector promised (or threatened?) that it would soon be able to do the same. However, it is also crucial to emphasize that Münsterberg's program saw psychology as an aide to affirm truthfulness rather than detect lies. The reformed liar was supposed to be reintegrated into society rather than banished on the basis of suspicions. This positive program would fall by the wayside when the polygraph began to be used for national security purposes.

Münsterberg's student William Moulton Marston achieved a breakthrough in lie detection on the basis of experiments he conducted in his mentor's Harvard laboratory. Marston's work established the supremacy of the blood pressure measurement as the most reliable instrument of lie detection and introduced the graph as the visible manifestation of the deceptive mind. The graphical depiction of a subject's blood pressure curve would translate any testimony into a different kind of story—one that was readable by the deception expert—and establish the authority of deception tests. After all, how could laypersons argue with a graph taken from their own body?[46] Blood pressure was a peculiar measurement. Undetectable to the individual, it took modern medical technology rather than an experienced medical practitioner to measure it. Soon after French physiologist Étienne-Jules Marey introduced his sphygmograph—an instrument that created a graphic record of the human heartbeat—in 1859, the leading British medical journal *Lancet* celebrated, "The finger is substituted by an instrument of precision, which replaces impressions by recorded facts self-analyzed." Like the thermometer, the sphygmograph did not simply amplify human perception but reconstructed it via graphic representation.[47] Around the time of Marston's experiments, the significance of blood pressure entered the public mind. Calls to keep high blood pressure "under control" became a constant reminder about the hidden dangers in the lives of stressed consumers.[48] Unlike breathing, blood pressure was completely outside the realm of conscious control. Blood pressure was the ideal measurement to detect deception: it was elusive to the subject yet precisely measurable.

In 1915 at Münsterberg's laboratory, Marston employed fellow students to convince a jury of their peers of the truthfulness of their testimony in an elaborately concocted scenario. He then applied his sphygmomanometer. While the jury was correct in barely half the cases, intermittent blood pressure measurements found the liar 96 percent of the time. Marston was ecstatic: "In a word, a uniform and significant systolic pressure curve was established by the results, as symptomatic of the deceptive consciousness. . . . The behavior of the b.p [blood pressure] . . . constitutes a practically infallible test of the *consciousness of an attitude of deception.*"[49] Marston claimed that by recording a rise in blood pressure in response to specific questions, he could successfully exclude other factors causing an emotional response and isolate the attitude accompanying a conscious lie. But this approach also meant that Marston's experiments equated truthfulness and compliance in following his directions, all under highly controlled circumstances with the ability of the researcher to compare a subject's truthful testimony with the curve created by the "deceptive consciousness."[50] Marston further asserted that he had found (through follow-up interviews with his subjects) that fear was the main emotion accompanying a conscious lie and that the blood pressure curve was the result of the mental activity necessary to suppress this fear: "A significant lying curve is a function of the struggle between the involuntary impulse to express fear in response to awareness of danger [of being caught in a lie], and the voluntary focusing of attention to exclude the fear from consciousness." Yet paradoxically, the large majority of his subjects testified they had enjoyed lying more than telling the truth.[51] Lie detection developed with this fundamental question unresolved: What exactly causes a significant psycho-physiological response when a subject lies? The polygraph would do without a coherent theory of lying.

America's entry into the Great War gave Marston a chance to prove the usefulness of his research in the real world. He was only one of many American scientists eager to establish their worth in a national emergency. Leading American scientists in 1916 founded the National Research Council (NRC). As would be the case in World War II (albeit on a much larger scale), scientists in the NRC developed a number of projects that they deemed promising in the pursuit of victory. What scientists sought above all was actual testing and application by the government itself, particularly the military. The NRC allowed for the first testing of lie detection for the purpose of national security. Confessing "my very selfish motive in desiring such work," Marston wrote in April 1918, "should my tests prove successful, military organization experience . . . would be invaluable for fitting me for systematic extension of deception work."[52] The federal government at the time was in the process of becoming a large bureaucracy in need of modern administration. The number of U.S. federal employees in 1900 had been 230,000 and would climb to 645,000 in 1920.[53]

Marston received patronage from psychologist Robert Yerkes, another former student of Hugo Münsterberg. Yerkes led the war effort to use mental aptitude tests on draftees, expanding on another area of applied psychology that Münsterberg had pioneered.[54] Marston initially offered his services to Yerkes in this context, "possibly fitting myself to put into operation the tests you [Yerkes] intend ultimately to use in all the camps [for military training]? . . . Could any use be made of my b.p. [blood pressure] deception test in connection with the draft? . . . Why couldn't valuable data, at least, be obtained by giving some of the draftees the b.p. deception test at the Laboratory or even at the place of medical examination?"[55] By the end of the war, having tested 1.7 million army recruits, American psychologists under Yerkes had legitimized mental testing to establish individual differences within the range of "normal" mental ability. But the border between "normal" and "feebleminded" was still contested. American psychologist Henry Herbert Goddard had concluded that it was hopeless to base the diagnosis on observable behavior. Observation created only subjective, imprecise, and not mutually exclusive categories. Alfred Binet's test to measure child development on the other hand promised precise categories according to how a patient's answers to increasingly difficult questions corresponded with the statistical mean.[56]

Exploring the usefulness of his test for governmental purposes by applying Binet's test to the contentious issue of mass immigration, Goddard found in two studies at Ellis Island in 1910 and 1912 that 40 percent of immigrants scored within the range of "feebleminded," below what Goddard considered normal mental aptitude. Such results found eager echo among proponents of immigration restrictions. And yet, Goddard also came to see Binet's supposedly objective, universally valid questions as alien to the background of many immigrants. Goddard therefore repeatedly recalibrated his test and moreover came to realize through follow-up investigations that a low score did not correspond with low social adaptability. Most low-scoring immigrants seemed to get by in America just fine. Thus the social usefulness of aptitude testing was still unclear.[57]

Mass application of aptitude tests during World War I, however, erased such concerns and turned psychologists into boosters. The group under Yerkes developed Army Alpha, a pencil-and-paper multiple-choice test that could be administered to thousands of recruits within one hour and was easily scored. By December 1917 Army Alpha was given on a mass scale at training camps across the country. Testers found a 25 percent illiteracy rate and a generally low average mental age among recruits. Southern African Americans scored lowest, officers highest.

Such results comfortably fit existing views among the military brass, even though it is less clear if they had an immediate influence on the recruitment effort. Still, the exercise changed the nature of intelligence testing in the United States, from a concern for feebleminded individual children to a mass exercise that established where "normal" Americans fit within educational and vocational hierarchies.[58] Historians have come to judge Yerkes' tests as methodologically flawed and practically useless for testing individuals from a variety of different backgrounds. A careful critic of rigid testing scales before the war, Yerkes apparently changed his attitude in government employment. Likely knowing better, he came to endorse screening tests that confirmed prejudices of mental inferiority, in particular of African American recruits.[59] Historian James Reed suggests that Yerkes and his colleagues embraced the results of hastily designed tests due to a "deeply felt need to prove that psychologists had technologies analogous to those of physical scientists, and thus deserved higher status and support."[60]

Lie detection under Münsterberg and Marston and aptitude testing embarked on similar journeys: toward confrontations between individual citizens and large corporate entities, such as the military, employers, or universities. At the same time, controversies over the validity of the fundamental assumptions underlying all mental testing (rather than simply the reliability or accuracy of the methods used) remained.[61] Lastly, just as the "pathological liar" disappeared from the sight of lie detection research during Marston's first experiments, aptitude testing also shifted toward mass application among the general population.

For all mental testing, national emergency was significant because it helped overcome skepticism. One of Marston's sponsors assured the assistant attorney general: "I have looked into the matter enough to feel sure that this is not a joke or a freak [sic] which some people would consider it at first thought. It is really a serious matter."[62] Marston further realized that to show their usefulness, deception tests needed to identify authentic emotions. His first goal in his work for the NRC was therefore to show that "the behavior of b.p. [blood pressure] is substantially the same under actual conditions as it has proved to be under experimental laboratory conditions."[63] Having reviewed Marston's initial Harvard experiment, psychologist Edward Thorndike was "still a little shaky about his [Marston's] results," but thought they deserved "a real try and with real cases."[64] Thus the mutual benefits for lie detection and national security were established. Both worked from and with authentic fear, such as fear of foreign danger or fear of being caught in unlawful activity.

Marston's thirty additional experiments with Harvard students for the NRC resulted in promising rates of detection. He reported to Yerkes a correct detection rate of 93 percent using his own blood pressure test, claiming that breathing and word association had proven less reliable.[65] This success encouraged Marston and the NRC to seek government sponsorship for additional tests.[66] Here Marston tried to directly profit from the war culture of forced voluntarism. Introducing Marston to Assistant Attorney General Warren, Richard Hale, secretary to the Massachusetts Bar Association, opined that the "ideal material would be the slackers [draft dodgers] who come into the United States Attorney's Office in Boston prepared to tell a glib story. These people would waive all constitutional rights and all that sort of difficulty or nothing would be done. In their anxiety to be believed they would cheerfully submit themselves to Mr. Marston's experiments."[67] This example illustrates how, to the individual American, forced voluntarism became a demand of good citizenship and loyalty. The lie detector test therefore became a site of confrontation between the demands of the national security state and notions of personal autonomy.

Lack of time probably prevented the exemption board of the Boston District Attorney's office to set up an arrangement with Marston for testing suspected draft dodgers before the December 14 meeting of the Psychology Committee of the NRC. Instead, he worked on twenty or so cases from the probate office of the Boston Municipal Court, mostly cases of larcenists and drug users applying for probation. Marston considered these subjects not ideally suited for his new focus on "normal" emotional activity. He privately complained of the "low grade mentality and psychopathic tendencies" of individuals usually dealt with in the probate office, yet was enthusiastic when he could report a perfect record in all cases where his test findings could be confirmed by other information.[68]

On December 14, 1917, the Psychology Committee authorized follow-up work under a subcommittee headed by Robert Yerkes. Marston was optimistic that his tests would produce "the same or better results in real life than they produce in the Laboratory"—in other words, that the test could detect authentic emotion. Beyond that, his goal was to prove usefulness for specific governmental purposes: "It is *not* a question of convincing the intelligent people [of the army intelligence division] that we can do the trick but of actually getting an official chance *to do work for them.*" By more laboratory tests "we'll not gain a thing." Instead, Marston wanted to show to the government that "these tests can be used in certain definite ways." That meant showing government agencies that deception tests served their needs. Yerkes recommended Marston to Secretary of War Newton Baker. The Army Intelligence Division, headed by another former Münsterberg student, Major Nicholas Biddle, expressed interest in Marston's work as well. However, due to lack of actual cases at the New York office of the Bureau of Investigation in early 1918, Marston, having overcome a case of the mumps, ended up conducting more experiments with concocted scenarios, this time for army intelligence at Camp Greenleaf in Georgia, the same camp where his colleagues were developing Army Alpha.[69]

The aspiring Marston made the best out of the situation. His experiments could still show value to "military situations arising in connection with courts martial . . . or in connection with investigations of alleged enemy agents by the Military Intelligence Department, where Psychological Examiners might be required to test the truth of the story of the person under suspicion." Further, they could "determine the extent to which these deception tests could be confided to non-expert operatives."[70] To this end, thirty-five volunteer recruits were given an opportunity to steal a number of items from a room and were granted ten minutes to decide whether to lie or tell the truth about what they had done. Marston as well as seven pairs of army intelligence agents then cross-examined and gave the blood pressure test to the volunteers. While the intelligence agents, having apparently received minimal training by Marston, made twenty-six correct calls (74.3 percent), Marston claimed thirty-three correct calls and therefore a success rate of 94.2 percent. This result led Marston initially to assert "considerable practicable value, even when applied by non-experts" to the test. Yet this result defied the scientific principle of reliability: that other researchers could replicate a result. Reliability remained another vexing issue for lie detection.[71]

Marston's work during the war is significant for the history of lie detection because it sheds first light on a number of methodological problems of the test. For one, the Camp Greenleaf experiment led Marston to assert that, in order to correctly interpret the blood pressure curve, the administrator needed to be "personally cognizant of all the conditions in the light of which the curve must be interpreted."[72] In other words, administration of the test and interpretation of the curve should remain with one expert. This was due to the fact that in two instances, Marston and his intelligence operators had made correct judgments of deception despite incorrect blood pressure recordings because they had been present at the examination and had noted problems with the recording of the blood pressure curve. Therefore, the *judgment and skill* of the examiner, rather than the recorded physiological responses of the subject, became crucial for the interpretation of test results. This would elevate the role of the expert who administrated the test. In the future, deception tests would increasingly be under the control of one operator responsible for all aspects of the examination.

Second, Marston's enthusiasm caused others to doubt the validity of the test. After reviewing Marston's fervent reports about his experiments at Harvard, John Shepard, a University of Michigan psychologist and chair of the Committee on Tests for Deception, deemed the results "certainly very suggestive." But as to the interpretation of the blood pressure curve, he counseled caution: Recent research had shown that "organic changes are an index of activity, of 'something doing,' but not of any particular kind of activity. . . . The same result would be caused by so many different circumstances, anything demanding equal activity (intellectual or emotional) that it would be practically impossible to decide any individual case."[73] What was the difference between emotional disturbances due to the nervousness that might accompany lying, fear of the consequence of telling a lie, or any other kind of disturbance? The same concern had already caused Marston to abandon the psycho-galvanometer test of sweat, yet he held firm on his blood pressure test. If there was no deceptive sweat, there could still be deceptive fear.[74]

Shepard advised the addition of "strongly licentious or horrible or other emotional material" to raise the emotional level of the "true" answers in hypothetical test scenarios and compare them with

emotional activity accompanying a lie.[75] The methodological question this point raised continued to be a fundamental one and directly
attacked the value of Marston's claim to have isolated fear as the primary
emotion in lying: Could the test really distinguish fear of being caught
lying from any other fear? What about fear of the test itself? Shepard's
call for provocative scenarios further explains the scandalous reputation of lie detection and its association with "improper" investigations.
What better way to induce emotional activity in subjects than to evoke
shame and stress-inducing topics, especially sexual material? Eventually, this insight would lead to the development of a "control question"
test that compared responses to irrelevant, relevant, and irrelevant yet
anxiety-inducing questions.

Lastly, Marston's reporting to Robert Yerkes on another case illustrated the thin line between the scientific measurement of objective
data and the assertion of socially conditioned prejudice. Investigating
the theft of drawing instruments and a codebook at the surgeon general's office in Washington, DC, in January 1918, Marston tested seventy
African American employees and found "a very marked discrepancy
between the behavior of negro and white b.p."[76] Marston concluded
that "the factor of voluntary control, which, with white men, seems to
make a deception rise regular and almost an absolute one, apparently
is almost altogether lacking in negroes, so that, tho [sic] the change is
really even more sharp and extreme, it is vastly more difficult to estimate norm plus excitement."[77] In other words, as Marston later put
it, because of the "extreme emotionality of negroes," changes in their
blood pressure curve were harder to interpret as evidence of deception.
As John Shepard had pointed out, the ambiguity of graphic traces of
emotional activity was a fundamental methodological problem, since
one had to infer a specific cause (such as fear of being caught lying)
from physiological responses that could be caused by a variety of mental states. Asserting inherent racial differences only entrenched this logical fallacy into polygraph methodology.[78]

Marston's work therefore straddled a fine line between "promising"
and "too good to be true." Harvard psychology professor Herbert
Langfeld deemed his former student Marston "entirely trustworthy,"
"resourceful," and "very intelligent." Yet Langfeld also had "a mere
suspicion" that Marston "may be slightly overzealous in grasping

opportunities, which causes him to take the corners a little too sharply."[79] In view of such statements, historian Ken Alder sees the lie detector as a reflection of the desires of its creators. I would add that fellow psychologists had already criticized Marston's mentor Hugo Münsterberg for neglecting to present his laboratory data clearly. One critic charged that Münsterberg seemed to hold the view that "facts are relative and negligible—the theory's the thing."[80] Psychoanalyst C. G. Jung had attacked Münsterberg for not giving him sufficient credit for the development of the word association test either.[81]

Marston envisioned a variety of tests, administering blood pressure, word association, and breathing tests *subsequently* rather than in one *simultaneous* polygraph recording. He used the limited tests he did manage to conduct during the war mainly to improve his hardware and to assert the primacy of his blood pressure test against word association and breathing tests. In short, he did not develop a *poly*graph test that unified different measurements in one procedure.[82]

Still, Marston was on his way to creating a *practical* test. He highlighted "the simplicity of the apparatus and method of [the blood pressure] test" as "its first recommendation for practical use."[83] He further recognized the appeal of graphic representation. After his first Harvard test in the spring of 1917, Marston described what he thought was the curve of a liar: "b.p. increases during deception assumed . . . when graphically represented, a regular curve, with the height approximately at that point in the subject's story which marked the crisis, or climax, of the whole 'job' of that particular deception."[84] In other words, Marston's noncontinuous blood pressure graph still followed the overall arch of the subject's testimony. He still wanted to assess the validity of the story. But he already recognized what would eventually become the smoking gun of lie detector tests: the swift spike of the graph accompanying a particular utterance in response to an unexpected question. "When the subject thinks the 'job' is all done, however, a sudden significant question may cause a short, sharp rise in the b.p."[85] Later, the polygraph test would only look for that short moment of tension, even though Marston had recognized that even during a truthful story a sharp rise of blood pressure could occur if the subject was surprised or upset by a question.

Practical tests also remained inherently questionable to critics committed to strict laboratory test design. In order to meet the demands of practical value, tests needed to show that they could work with authentic emotions and that testing could be simple enough to be conducted by administrators with minimal training. Therefore, the need for practical success shaped the way deception tests would be developed and administered. The NRC, which left most of its research incomplete due to the short duration of American participation in the war, also reflected the impetus to apply rather than thoroughly test lie detection. The subsequent application of lie tests to real-life situations therefore did not take place under the auspices of the federal government, but on a local level—in the nation's urban police departments.

John Larson was a psychologist interested in forensic research who decided to work in the most progressive police department in the nation under chief August Vollmer in Berkeley, California. Larson read Marston's account of his wartime experiments and decided to continue the work under Vollmer. He was joined in 1922 by Leonarde Keeler, the son of Vollmer's friend, California poet laureate Charles Keeler. The two developed—at first together, then in competition with each other—a lie detector test with a standardized polygraph that combined blood pressure and pulse readings, breathing depth, and (on some models) skin resistance. In the 1930s, Larson would retreat into clinical research and become a determined critic of Keeler, who carried lie detection into mass application at numerous police departments around the country and at private, corporate businesses from his home base in Chicago. From this position of strength, the polygraph would reenter federal service in World War II and eventually the Cold War.[86]

August Vollmer looms large in the history of American police administration. As chief of police in Berkeley from 1909 to 1932, he developed an idealistic program for crime prevention through community policing, cutting edge technology, and effective administration. His system of keeping records on the basis of "modus operandi" was a pioneering work of criminal profiling. His introduction of Robert Yerkes' Army Alpha test for police recruits, creation of a crime laboratory with fingerprint and handwriting analysis units, as well as systematic academic training in the sciences, law, and sociology at the college level earned him the title of "father of modern police administration."

Vollmer envisioned modern police work as administering scientific knowledge within the limits of local civic culture: "The character of the community is but a reflection of the character of its residents, and no matter how many laws are on the books, enforcement can go no farther than the citizens will permit."[87] He communicated his ideas through books, as president of the International Association of Chiefs of Police (IACP), and other prominent national work.[88]

His spiritual kinship to Münsterberg illuminates Vollmer's interest in lie detection. Both supported efforts to scientifically study the effect of modern society on individual behavior and adjust the administration of justice accordingly. Like Münsterberg, Vollmer emphasized prevention of crime: "If he [the policeman] would serve his community by reducing crime he must go up the stream a little further and dam it up at its source."[89] Though not free of personal prejudices, Vollmer envisioned the role of police as objective, neutral investigators of the causes of crime in the name of prevention, what he called "our principal function." In a speech as president of the IACP in 1922, Vollmer stressed, "The public can furnish a thousand different reasons for the crooked act, but the wise policeman remains silent, ventures no opinion, knowing that every factor must be investigated before an intelligent explanation can be given for the individual's failure to conform to the rules made to govern our conduct."[90]

Like the German psychologist, Vollmer also worried about modern life facilitating crime. Two decades earlier, Hugo Münsterberg had recognized that "the more complex the machinery of our social life, the easier it seems to cover the traces of crime and to hide the outrage by lies and deception."[91] Vollmer also stressed the transitory nature and accelerated speed of modern life as challenges for police administration:

The lawbreaker even more than the honest citizen appreciates the twentieth-century speed of communication and transportation which has made it possible to express distance in terms of seconds, minutes, or, at most, hours instead of weeks and months. Equipped with the 'latest' inventions, he respects no boundary lines, conducts his operations where most convenient, and speedily flees from the jurisdiction of the local authority.[92]

Yet American police departments in the 1920s and 1930s were plagued by the persistence of urban machine control over police administration, low salaries due to postwar inflation, ferocious white backlash to the Great Migration of African Americans to the North, and violent labor struggles in the Great Depression. The thankless task of enforcing prohibition further created an underlying atmosphere of crisis among officers.[93] In retirement Vollmer vented his frustration: "Police . . . are the helpless tools—and victims—alternately of politician and reformer, and the indifferent, uncomprehending taxpayer foots an enormous and perfectly needless bill."[94]

For Vollmer, "the overwhelmingly indifferent, negative attitude of the public" was "the greatest handicap of all" to effective police work.[95] Therefore, while the professionalization push of the post–World War I era eventually succeeded in wrestling control over policing away from political machines, police departments, especially in cities, soon felt under siege again. Police professionalization was a genuine grassroots movement coming from local police chiefs. Yet, many officers felt misunderstood by the public and the outside experts who assessed their work. In the absence of national structures for local government, American police reformers relied on stop-gap measures created in response to the social crises of the day. In addition, they also competed with federal police authority. J. Edgar Hoover's Federal Bureau of Investigation (renamed in 1935) was built *in parallel* with new local and state police units. The polygraph came into being in this highly competitive environment. In hindsight, we can see that its development as a tool for police reform foreshadowed its use as a tool for national security policy during the Cold War. In both situations, a perceived crisis aided the acceptance of the technology.[96]

The polygraph developed into a crime fighter at a time when the local knowledge of the cop on the beat had to compete with the scientific ideals of police administration to "get results" under the watchful eye of the national press. Polygraph tests were one of the many compromises between the ideal of voluntarism and community autonomy on the one hand and forceful policing authority on the other. American police administrators did not quite know how to reconcile the two. Toward the end of his active career Vollmer struck a pessimistic tone and advocated a voluntary universal fingerprint registration of all citizens. "Communists, anarchists may be followed from place to place and their activities noted," while "injured and unconscious persons may be identified," he asserted. However, a 1935 fingerprint registration drive, with President Roosevelt and other prominent citizens such as John D. Rockefeller and Walt Disney submitting their prints to the FBI's Civil Identification Division, petered out quickly amid protests from the American Civil Liberties Union. This episode illustrated the ill fit between the traditional American culture of voluntarism and the new calls for surveillance and control.[97]

John Larson and Leonarde Keeler transformed Marston's deception test into a police procedure that would invest authority with alleged scientific objectivity, while maintaining at least a patina of voluntarism. Radically simplifying Marston's approach, Larson developed the simple yes-or-no routine of interrogation, mixing innocuous with relevant questions for comparison. He also created a method to measure an amalgam of pulse and systolic blood pressure continuously on a roll of paper that could be examined during and after the test. Keeler would register a patent for a portable machine and called it "polygraph" in 1931. In Berkeley between 1921 and 1923, Larson and Keeler tested 861 people in 313 cases involving everything from petty theft to sexual deviance to violent crimes. They found that the longer the interrogation, the more crimes people confessed to. Establishing the proper limits of the test soon competed with exploring its seemingly endless possibilities.[98]

The first spectacular newspaper stories about the lie detector raised doubts in the conscientious Larson that eventually led him to repudiate the polygraph as his "Frankenstein's Monster." With the encouragement of Vollmer, Larson pursued the "open science model" of research by testing the technology at the Chicago Institute for Juvenile Research and similar clinical institutions. Larson became an accredited authority on deception by publishing his findings in scientific journals and through his authorship of the first authoritative textbook on the test.[99] In contrast, the likable and flexible Leonarde Keeler used the polygraph as his ticket to fame. Keeler pursued the "proprietary know-how" model of science by patenting his polygraph and publicizing and advertising the social utility of his intellectual property.[100]

Keeler refined the polygraph in Los Angeles (where he followed August Vollmer in 1923) and in Chicago, two metropolises that contrasted starkly with the picturesque Berkeley. August Vollmer's one-year stint as LA's chief of police from 1923 to 1924 was a disaster, mainly due to massive resistance to his attempts to discipline the force and opposing political interference from above. Lie detection, on the other hand, caught on due to the fact that the "Keeler Polygraph" incorporated the proprietary know-how model of lie detection into preexisting urban police culture: The very vagueness of the name combined the authority of a machine with the discretion of its operator and made it usable in a variety of contexts.[101]

The separation of clinical use and police work was gradual. Larson and Keeler worked at various times at the Chicago Institute for Juvenile Research and were reunited with August Vollmer when he took a position at the University of Chicago in 1929. Larson developed a noncoercive clinical approach that made the polygraph examiner team up with a psychologist, a physician, and a lawyer.[102] Successful testing at the Illinois State Penitentiary in Joliet led Keeler to Northwestern University's Scientific Criminal Detection Laboratory, where he first tested Chicago cops in support of Vollmer's effort to eradicate corrupt police officers. Resistance faded when Keeler took another decisive step in his work for the Chicago police in the 1930s, calibrating the use of the test in order to extract confessions and thereby "getting results," meaning getting confessions. Keeler made sure that most police officers mastered the six-week training courses at his crime lab in Chicago. Even August Vollmer would come to call the polygraph "a modified, simplified and humane third degree," rather than a substitute for police violence. In 1939 when Keeler surveyed police departments using his interrogation technique with the polygraph nationally, he found that 60 percent of suspects labeled "deceptive" by an initial test would go on to confess to *something*—a heaven sent to overworked police officers.[103]

Thus, polygraphs multiplied. Under the discretion of autonomous local police departments, tests went on for hours and pried confessions from exhausted suspects who were confronted with charts they did not understand and accusations that the machine proved they were lying. In the absence of national guidelines for policing, polygraphing became local practice enhanced by the authority of technology and a family resemblance to science. While the test was voluntary, suspects faced the accusation that any resistance to it was an indirect admission of guilt. When other pupils of Vollmer such as C. D. Lee began to sell their own versions of the Keeler Polygraph, more and cheaper lie detectors became available by the mid-1930s.[104]

The last point emphasizes the role of the corporate capitalism of the United States in the rise of the polygraph. In 1939, Keeler founded Keeler Inc. and entered the personnel management business, offering a two-week orientation course and a full six-week course. He had envisioned expanding into corporate business for a while. In a letter from 1929 Keeler unveiled to Vollmer his blueprint for using the polygraph in the corporate world:

> I find large department stores lose large sums of money each year through the crooked twists of employees. . . . Now, suppose we are placing a competent operator with blood pressure machine in the store and examine all of the employees (possibly each person could be tested only once in every four or six months, with the test kept in daily use), what would the effect be? I believe we would quickly weed out the "lifters" and gangs that I know to be working in the store, eliminate these, and put "the fear of the Lord" in the others. Due to our actual weeding out process and the psychological effect on all employees probably the enormous losses would be reduced [by] some seventy-five per cent or more.[105]

Again, the success of the lie detector depended on reputation for social usefulness, which in the corporate world meant effective cost cutting. This goal included the actual reduction of theft by employees, but also control over morale among the largely nonunionized bank clerks and department store salespeople.[106]

At this point Keeler's career converged again with that of William Moulton Marston, who combined John Larson's scientific ambition with Keeler's salesmanship. At first Marston continued to publish scholarly articles on the nature of emotions and wrote academic books, most notably *The Emotions of Normal People* in 1928, which attempted to incorporate the lie detector into a rather idiosyncratic theory of primary emotions. Having already worked in Hollywood briefly in the 1920s, by the early 1930s Marston completely changed his strategy and interests. Marston made himself the primary salesman of the polygraph by launching a career as a psychological consultant, with advice columns in several mass publications such as *Century* magazine. He advertised products such as razor blades with the lie detector. Marston's crowning achievement in promoting the utopian powers of lie detection, however, took place in 1941, when he introduced the truth lasso–swinging comic book character Wonder Woman.[107]

Both Keeler and Marston saw themselves as benevolent authorities, good cops who employed a machine as their bad cop counterpart. According to his sister Eloise, "Nard" Keeler liked to help people prove their innocence: "Nard's empathy and concern for people, combined with his knowledge of psychology, often made him seem more like a family counselor than a police interrogator."[108] To promote her brother's effort, Eloise even wrote a short play during the 1930s, in which a group of people in an Agatha Christie–style scenario correctly identifies a murderer with the help of an "inventor" and his polygraph. They also inadvertently catch a stealing butler, who is promptly forgiven, having cleansed his conscience with the help of the polygraph.[109]

William Moulton Marston also believed that the urge to deceive needed to be broken—gently, to be sure—in order to achieve "crime elimination." He called the lie detector "psychological medicine, if you like, which will cure crime itself when properly administered." Periodic testing would establish genuine trust among people, Marston believed: "But after all have been tested a new spirit of mutual trust and confidence always prevails. . . . It is inevitable that sooner or later the Lie Detector will bring about this condition of mutual trust in all large business and financial organizations."[110] He envisioned a society that enforced truth and encouraged trust without contradiction. Marston therefore remained a student of his mentor Hugo Münsterberg to the end.

Marston also contributed to a court case that restricted the legal status of lie detection until the end of the twentieth century. In August 1921, James A. Frye, an African American, confessed to the murder of a prominent black Washington, DC, doctor, but later retracted the confession. Frye's defense counsel contacted Marston, then working at George Washington University, who gave Frye a lie detector test and found him to be truthful in denying the murder. When the defense attempted to introduce this evidence into court, Chief Justice of the District Court Walter McCoy denied the move out of hand and did not even allow evidence to establish that Marston was an expert on lie detection. The sixty-two-year-old McCoy demanded "common knowledge" of the merits of a scientific technique to even hear it, and since he had never heard of the lie detector, he "was not willing to take chances." However, the judge was open to reading Marston's publications and hinted that he "may decide differently next year, but not now."[111] A jury found James Frye guilty of second-degree murder, and Marston would claim that his test had saved the defendant's life, since the jury had at least heard of the fact that Frye had passed Marston's test.

Frye's defense appealed before the U.S. Court of Appeals for the District of Columbia. The court rejected lie detector evidence once again and in the process handed down a decision that would become known as the "Frye test." It would guide U.S. judicial practice in admitting scientific evidence into the 1990s:

> Just when a scientific principle or discovery crosses the line between the experimental and demonstrable stages is difficult to define. Somewhere in the twilight zone the evidential force of the principle must be recognized, and while courts will go a long way in admitting expert testimony deduced from a well-recognized scientific principle or discovery, the thing from which the deduction is made must be sufficiently established to have gained general acceptance in the particular field in which it belongs.[112]

This decision—only two pages long, citing no precedent—proved crucial because it demanded sufficient evidence that the principle of a scientific procedure, in other words the underlying assumption of what it supposedly did, had to be generally accepted. In this case, it was necessary to show the validity of the claim that variations in blood pressure indicated a deceptive mind. This was a much more fundamental requirement than simply demanding that the technology in question accurately measured a physiological response. Second, "general acceptance in the particular field in which it belongs" meant that the scientific community of psychologists had to accept the validity of lie detection before the courts would. Judges would merely follow the scientific community.

In 1923, one may assume, psychologists had not accepted the lie detector yet due to its novelty. However, this mistrust never changed substantially. Subsequent estrangement between psychologists and legal scholars, on the one hand, and the community of lie detector enthusiasts in law enforcement and the national security establishment, on the other hand, was rather influenced by competing professional prerogatives, as Ken Alder and Tal Golan have argued.[113] Professor of law Charles McCormick in 1926 asked eighty-eight psychologists for their opinion as to whether the research conducted until then by Marston, Larson, and others was sufficiently solid to recommend the lie detector to courts and juries. Of thirty-eight respondents, eighteen agreed (with varying qualifications), thirteen disagreed, and seven voiced opinions too ambiguous to allow for qualification one way or another. More significantly, almost all psychologists emphasized that only a qualified expert should conduct and interpret such tests, that at best deception tests could only aid an investigation but never be a hundred percent accurate, and that more research was necessary. McCormick thus summed up his findings: "[There is] a preponderance of belief in the significance to some degree of the tests, but a fairly evenly divided opinion on the question of whether they are suitable for consideration by courts. The scientific view being still one of suspended judgment, the courts must obviously wait for further verification and wider acceptance of the validity of these tests before relying upon their results as evidence."[114] Such consensus never materialized.

The consequences of the Frye ruling were manifold. Nobody could be convicted or acquitted in a U.S. court on the sole basis of a polygraph test, and ever since, no court could force a witness or a defendant to take a polygraph test. However, upon mutual agreement between defense and prosecution, the test could be introduced as evidence, and once a subject had agreed to it, anything they said during the test was admissible in court. After Leonarde Keeler in 1935 managed to get a Wisconsin jury to hear his testimony in a pharmacy holdup case, "prior stipulation" became the only basis for polygraph admissibility in U.S. criminal courts.[115] This meant that polygraph advocates had reason to aspire to scientific acceptance, but the unregulated field of plea-bargaining remained wide open to them.

This state of affairs denied the technology the kind of judicial credentials Hugo Münsterberg had envisioned. The "black box" of the polygraph did not replace the "black box" of the closed jury deliberation.[116] Things began to change somewhat in the 1990s. In the 1993 case

Daubert v. Merrell, the U.S. Supreme Court established more detailed guidelines as to what criteria made scientific evidence worthy of consideration in court. Such guidelines included publications in peer-reviewed journals, a program of scientific testing, and a known error rate. Then, in 1998, a majority of U.S. Supreme Court judges announced that courts should not be concerned that juries would be overwhelmed by the "aura of infallibility" of the lie detector test. The case *Scheffer v. United States* involved a military officer whose request to submit the result of a polygraph test exonerating him of guilt for a failed drug test was denied. A majority also ruled that juries should hear all available evidence, especially when a procedure such as polygraph testing was so wide-spread and accepted in other areas. Still, the court rejected Scheffer's request and thus perpetuated the polygraph's contested existence.[117]

Federal authorities remained equally skeptical, sensational press coverage notwithstanding. In the early 1920s, American mass culture developed a fascination with magic yet scientific crime-fighting technologies such as "Lie Detectors" or "truth serum." Popular crime fiction such as "The Achievements of Luther Trant" by Chicago newspapermen Edwin Balmer and William MacHarg speculated already in 1907—the year of the Steunenberg trial—about the possibilities of locating deception in the mind of the criminal.[118] Local and national press accounts of spectacular cases in which a "lie detector" confronted criminals began to abound. "The newspapers baptized the lie detector; they named the device, launched its career, gave it its purpose," historian Ken Alder concludes.[119] Further, in a time when inventors such as the Wright brothers or Henry Ford enjoyed the standing of modern explorers in American culture, the status of "invention" endowed the lie detector with a mythical authority.[120] At this time, Texas obstetrician Robert House also argued for the possibility of locating traces of truthful memory in the body through the application of sodium pentothal. After newspapers coined the phrase "truth serum," this technology made a similar career as an allegedly objective yet scientifically questionable technology, joining the polygraph in the arsenal of Keeler's Chicago Crime Laboratory in the 1930s.[121]

Given these findings, it is tempting to describe the polygraph mainly as a public discourse inhabiting the popular imagination. However, the institutional credentials of the state—police agencies as well as the federal national security state—sustained lie detection research during and after World War I and assured massively extended use of the test during the Cold War *against* an increasingly skeptical press, as subsequent chapters show.

As Hugo Münsterberg had learned on his journey west, not all publicity was good publicity. The public relations disaster of the Red Scare of 1919–1920 was another case in point. J. Edgar Hoover had been a key organizer of the Red Scare, but because he distanced himself from the disgraced William J. Burns, who had enmeshed the Bureau of Investigation in the Teapot Dome scandal by ordering harassment of critics of Secretary of the Interior Albert Fall, Hoover managed to keep his image clean (even Roger Baldwin's newly founded American Civil Liberties Union [ACLU] supported his appointment). While Hoover took an active—at times obsessive—interest in the public image of his FBI, the power his agency acquired in the 1930s came from cooperation with the New Deal, not publicity in and of itself. The expanded definitions of federal crimes that Attorney General Homer Cummings signed into law in 1934 and that led to creation of the *Federal* Bureau of Investigation were part of an expansion of federal power across the board. Advocates justified such expansion as a response to the crisis of the Great Depression. While the "crime waves" of the 1920s and 1930s turned out to be exaggerated, we must note that the growth of the federal government and of federal police power proceeded rapidly and in response to perceived crises of public order.[122] The polygraph would similarly assume the role of instant crisis manager in the Cold War.

Yet the whiff of scandal never left the polygraph, which made Hoover keep a distance from it. While not eschewing publicity by any means, Hoover emphasized the FBI's competence. At a time when the "third degree" and a reputation for corruption made police officers sometimes indistinguishable from the gangsters themselves, "respect for respectability" was supposed to set the FBI apart from urban police departments as well as Hollywood gangster movies of the 1930s. After the public relations disasters of "slacker raids" and the "Red Scare" between 1918 and 1920, "fighting crime" was an activity that would again require the partnership of federal bureaucracy and citizen volunteers. As Hoover put it in a 1931 article, "Our problem today is whether the forces of government or outlawry must dominate. You must be either with or against government. There is no middle ground. We must have the support of the public. Citizens of this country must become enemies of crime." In order to win the public trust, New Dealers embraced a conservative image of the FBI as one of the "symbols of national regeneration and a powerful state that was well organized, honest, and resolved to serve the people."[123]

We can therefore conclude that by the mid-1930s, J. Edgar Hoover embraced popular culture as a source of institutional power and let it be known that reporters who produced anything less than the most fawning coverage of the FBI would meet his undying wrath.[124] But he did so to impress upon the public his ideal of the well-dressed, educated, restrained, brave, God-fearing, and family-loving—in short, "professional"—white male police officer.[125] Even though there is evidence that Hoover inquired about the lie detector in 1935, it did not become the kind of standard equipment with which his FBI would be associated under his tenure.[126]

Hoover's opinion of Marston further illustrates how carefully the FBI guarded its conservative credentials against the frivolous publicity Marston sought in the 1930s and 1940s. Marston's 1938 book *The Lie Detector Test* was judged by the FBI's Technical Laboratory to be written "in an extremely egotistical vein," since Marston proclaimed his ability to make subjects "always in the future tell the truth" once they had been caught by the lie detector. When the famously petulant Hoover received notice that Marston had signed a contract to advertise Gillette razors with a lie detector test that would supposedly gauge the customers' lack of satisfaction with other blades, he splashed a handwritten note on the margin: "I always thought this fellow Marston was a phony and this proves it."[127]

The FBI kept a safe distance from Marston's efforts to popularize his tests. Without the authority of August Vollmer, lie detection might have remained a curiosity. Without the emergencies of two world wars, the American state might have declined its services. The fact that Hoover's FBI remained skeptical of the test shows that there was no inherent bureaucratic push for the technology. However, the advent of World War II and the Cold War would change the institutional dynamics among federal agencies and open the door for the lie detector.

CHAPTER 3

World War II, National Security, and the Search for Loyal Citizens

The armistice of November 11, 1918, was a disappointment for William Moulton Marston; the end of fighting cut short his experiments for the National Research Council (NRC). While J. Edgar Hoover kept an eye on Marston and stayed in touch with August Vollmer's and Leonarde Keeler's work in Chicago, the Navy's Bureau of Medicine and Surgery rejected a request to introduce the lie detector as a tool to screen recruits in 1923.[1] The polygraph's rise to prominence in the federal national security bureaucracy, therefore, was anything but a foregone conclusion. Only when World War II rekindled the interest of scientists and military leaders in lie detection did the polygraph become a permanent weapon in the arsenal of democracy.

The interrogation of German Prisoners of War constituted the first use of the polygraph to measure political loyalty, a practice that was continued at the nuclear facility in Oak Ridge, Tennessee, in 1946. On

66

the one hand, we can see that polygraph tests during and after World War II reflected the prominence that loyalty to democratic institutions took in U.S. political discourse. On the other hand, debates about the polygraph were often placeholders in domestic disputes about larger political issues. Fears concerning communist infiltration or a lapse into totalitarianism often played out in debates about the lie detector. Far from alleviating political clashes, the technology accentuated them.

By 1941, the technique, equipment, and experience that Leonarde Keeler had assembled were readily available to the federal government, and like others in the psychological profession, lie detector advocates stood ready to oblige their government.[2] In October 1941, two months before Pearl Harbor, University of Chicago psychologist Dael Wolfle presented a confidential fourteen-page report to an Emergency Committee of psychologists. The report was based on Wolfle's survey of current literature and his exchanges with polygraph practitioners such as Keeler, Marston, and others.[3]

Caught in the spirit of mobilization that pervaded the psychological profession, Wolfle did not dwell on problems.[4] The author concluded that blood pressure and pulse, with breathing as a control measure and galvanic skin response as an additional option, were considered reliable measures to detect deception. The report did list other methods, such as tracking a subject's eye movements and drugs, but dismissed them as experimental or unreliable. Similarly, it noted that of the six commercially available polygraph models, the ones designed by Keeler and C. D. Lee, another protégé of August Vollmer, were the most common. Wolfle also described how during the pre-interrogation interview the subject was allowed to divulge his/her story and that it was "not unusual for a suspect to confess his guilt during the course of the questioning." He was even aware of Keeler's favorite extracurricular method, a card guessing game at the beginning of an interrogation. Keeler would ask a subject to choose one of about ten cards and then instruct them to answer "no" each time the interrogator tried to guess the correct card. Wolfle dutifully noted, "As a matter of fact the deck is sometimes stacked," but neglected to ponder the ethical problems of Keeler's sleight of hand.[5] The report further emphasized that only experienced examiners could interpret polygraph data competently and that not more than a dozen people in the United States fulfilled the necessary requirements at the moment.

Wolfle further highlighted the lie detector's potential utility. He dwelled on the success rates of experienced polygraph examiners in real-world investigations and estimated that 80 percent accuracy was possible with highly experienced personnel. Wolfle did not explain how he arrived at that number, but it was within the range of what Keeler usually claimed. As for the polygraph's potential usefulness in a coming war, the report suggested that the technique could be used to examine witnesses and suspected foreign agents or sympathizers, to prescreen workers in defense industries for potential saboteurs, and to retest workers in responsible positions for deterrence. On this last point, Wolfle emphasized that "testing in this way would deter many individuals from active sabotage by greatly increasing the fear of detection. The exaggerated popular belief in the infallibility of the lie detector works here to its advantage." The report concluded that "the methods for the detection of deception have been adequately worked out," that sufficient equipment existed, and that a small core of highly competent examiners stood ready.[6]

Wolfle's report was written entirely from the perspective of the polygraph community around Keeler. It uncritically reiterated high success rates and endorsed possible applications of the lie detector without discussing methodological, legal, or ethical problems. In particular, the report did not raise the issue that interrogations of limited pools of subjects in specific cases entailed a methodology entirely different from screening large numbers of people. Further, the report simply assumed a deterrent function in periodic screening due to the polygraph's reputation as an infallible machine, again without providing supporting evidence or voicing ethical concerns about deceiving subjects.

As it happened, support from the academic community was not required, since Leonarde Keeler had ties to the military. While Keeler's heart disease and alcoholism prevented him from joining the service in 1942, his polygraph did in 1944: first to solve murder cases under Army jurisdiction, then to test the loyalty of German POWs.[7] In contrast to World War I, resistance to conscription into the war against fascism was minimal among Americans, and the problem of enemy aliens was solved heavy-handedly through so-called internment camps.[8] However, the approximately 378,000 Germans kept in camps on U.S. soil from 1943 to 1946 created a unique opportunity to test the political usefulness of the polygraph.

The murder of a German POW by fellow inmates in March 1944 at the Papago Park camp in Phoenix, Arizona, initiated Keeler's involvement. Colonel Ralph Pierce of the Army Security Intelligence School in Chicago asked him for assistance. Keeler narrowed a list of 125 suspects down to twenty who showed suspicious spikes on their polygraph chart when asked about specific circumstances in connection with the murder. Of those twenty, seven confessed after the Army used different interrogation methods, such as sleep deprivation and forcing the accused to breathe through a gasmask with an onion in it. They were hanged at Fort Leavenworth on August 24, 1945, in the last mass execution in American history.[9]

In August 1944, Pierce received permission to purchase a Keeler Polygraph for the school.[10] He and Keeler cooperated again in early 1945 in the case of Byron Russell, a civilian employee of the Postal Exchange at Fort Huachuca in Bisbey, Arizona, who had been robbed and stabbed to death in April 1944. Private Robert Cunningham, a soldier found near the crime scene, accused two other privates of the murder, but the FBI dropped the case due to insufficient evidence. In January 1945, Keeler interrogated the suspects for three days on his polygraph with the assistance of Pierce and another military officer. On the third day, Cunningham confessed to the murder and passed a subsequent polygraph test. Pierce, who had already trained with Keeler, endorsed the polygraph wholeheartedly after this real-world success.[11]

The next big coup for Pierce and Keeler were the polygraph interviews of German POWs whom the Army planned to use as a civilian police force in the American occupation of Germany. The enemy's mind had been a target of psychological warfare throughout the war. Many American psychologists subscribed to some version of Erik Erikson's diagnosis: "It is as if the German nation as a whole could be likened to a not uncommon type of adolescent who turns delinquent."[12] In the spring of 1945, the Army created a police school in Fort Wetherill, Rhode Island, to train several thousand POWs for police work. From August 10 to August 18, 1945, Keeler, Pierce, and a team of assistants interrogated 270 German POWs "regarding their attitudes and intentions regarding sympathy with the Nazi Party at the time it was in power, at the present time; and their willingness to cooperate fully with the American Occupational Forces." In addition to questions about membership in Nazi organizations as well as past and current sympathies, the first round of questions included inquiries such as "Do you advocate Communism in Germany?" and "Do you intend to cooperate fully with American forces?" and "Do you believe in religious freedom?"[13] A second list, apparently prepared for those with unsatisfactory results in the first round, included questions about criminal activity, masturbation, homosexuality, and rape, as well as this: "Do you think Hitler is a great man?"[14] The Army stated matter-of-factly: "Prisoners of war who do not pass the polygraph test will be rejected for the project."[15] The personal questions, as Keeler knew by now, were sure to create embarrassment in anybody and could provide another control measure against physiological reactions to the political questions.

Thirty-six percent of subjects were rejected, not only because of Nazi background or sympathies, but also due to health problems, emotional instability, unwillingness to cooperate, and criminal records.[16] Keeler's short case summaries do not reveal how all these factors were weighted, or whether the interrogation team applied any consistent criteria for their judgments other than that they rejected subjects who admitted to—or whose test results indicated—current Nazi sympathies. Among those without such emotional indications, however, some were rejected while others were not. One subject, for example, indicated "no disturbance" whatsoever in his polygraph, including questions about Nazi sympathies. But since he had been a member of the Nazi party since 1934 and a block leader, he was rejected. In contrast, another subject who admitted some Nazi sympathies passed. He received the following diagnosis:

> This subject professes no political party affiliations. He was a leader in the Catholic Youth movement. . . . He stated that he believes the Nazi principles were correct in most respects, but their religious doctrine made it impossible for him to join. He was in doubt about the value of the Nazi party, because they claimed to represent the Fatherland but were against his religion. He gave no reactions to pertinent questions, and is recommended.[17]

Since U.S. occupational regulations prohibited association among German veterans, the graduates of Fort Wetherill did not constitute special units. There is no record to judge whether passing Keeler's test improved the performance of these police units, but the indiscriminate weighing of ideological attitudes was the sign of a poorly designed test. Not that these questions were irrelevant, but it appears that Keeler's test made no effort to establish the significance of the answers in any systematic way. Put differently, the report featured 270 individual judgments, many of which may have been correct on a common-sense level. The documentation, however, does not suggest a methodologically constructed test.

How exactly *should* Americans have approached the reeducation of Germans? Nazi sympathies among POWs prevailed even after months of imprisonment. As a result, many American political and military leaders considered reeducation a waste of time. Some academics such as sociologist Talcott Parsons warned that disillusioned Germans might even turn toward communism instead of democracy, while others suggested following the communist example and using the officers among the POWs as shock troops to form a Germany in the victor's image. Press reports of well-fed Nazis frolicking in camps in the heart of America increased the political pressure to do *something* constructive. The Army's Special Project Division (SPD), put in charge of POW reeducation in 1944, appealed to what they perceived as the German appreciation of high culture with a humanistic program. But after months spent taking academic courses in German and U.S. history in SPD training camps at Fort Getty and Fort Wetherill, 70 percent of the graduates of the special education program still did not believe the reports of death camps, and half of them insisted that the Jews were still Germany's main problem. Although the majority claimed they would not fight the war again and did not consider Germans a superior race, was the program not a success? As historian Ron Robin concludes, "The endorsement of reeducation was not derived from any meaningful assessment of the task at hand; it was a political decision based on domestic consideration."[18]

Keeler's tests also illustrated how quickly loyalty investigations could create bad blood. During the summer of 1945, Fort Wetherell experienced a crisis among its staff when Major General Lerch of the Army's Office of the Provost Marshal General (PMG), which was in charge of the SPD, purged a number of faculty members due to alleged communist sympathies. Lerch's dislike of intellectuals was probably aggravated by pressure from a congressional military affairs committee. Red baiting quickly became a way to advance a career in government, and Lerch soon moved into U.S. military command in Korea.[19] In his report, Colonel Pierce noted that camp commanders at Fort Wetherill had "some misgivings about the use of the polygraph as a means of screening, fearing that it would interfere with their school's work, adversely affect the morale among prisoners, etc." He noted that none of the Germans objected to the test. However, the fact that some flunked the questions regarding whether they intended to cooperate with the U.S. occupation and whether they were faking their attitude of cooperation diminished the significance of this observation. More importantly, Pierce was convinced that the polygraph "increased the morale of those with a sincere desire to cooperate and make the project a success. The prisoners with sincere anti-Nazi attitudes seemed anxious to weed out the Nazis among their group and to appreciate the efforts of the American authorities to do this."[20] Some POWs rejected from the police program learned their lesson so well that in October 1945 in a letter to the PMG, they accused several of their camp instructors of communist sympathies, claiming they had been removed from the program because of their forceful anticommunism.[21] At that point, civilian academic instructors, military officers, the camp chaplain, and the POWs had all become suspicious of one another.

Pierce and Keeler did not ask whether encouraging denunciation should be part of teaching democracy. In any case, another study of German POW camps in the United States stresses the sociological significance of these camps as places *sui generis*. Removed from the discipline of both their own military and their culture at home, life for soldiers in these camps developed unpredictable dynamics as both captors and captives adjusted to the new circumstances. Behavior such as submissiveness to their captors reflected less a deeply ingrained authoritarian personality than an adjustment to the situation at hand. What lessons the exceptional situation in a POW camp could teach for reconstruction and political reeducation at home should have been derived from careful study, not from a quick polygraph exam.[22]

Democratic values also interact with partisan political beliefs. Leonarde Keeler supported the Republican Party, but little else is known about his political views. In a private letter to his aunt before the 1940 election, Keeler diagnosed "a world-wide trend toward totalitarian forms of government," saw FDR as part of this trend, and believed that the president's supporters were "either consciously or subconsciously in favor of the totalitarian form of government or some sort of a national socialistic government." If the United States were to join the war in Europe, Keeler stated, American democracy was done for.[23] The New Deal and FDR's schemes to wrestle power away from the Supreme Court were often criticized as signs of "totalitarian" or "fascist" tendencies by conservative opponents who used these terms to create a contradistinction to whatever they viewed as the proper definition of democracy. Whatever Keeler had in mind in this letter, his words suggest that he rejected regulatory intervention in the economic life of the nation.[24] It is a twist in the lie detector's story that Keeler did not ponder the possibility that the lie detector could become a potent weapon to *increase* the power of government bureaucracies.

Did the lie detector alleviate distrust, or did its very availability justify *continued* distrust? William Marston firmly believed the former, but Keeler's pessimism about the American political system suggests that the lie detector could become a tool to stoke up fears about the integrity of America's democratic order. The relationship between democracy and testing sincerity was thus complicated and contained multiple ironies: for one, when the polygraph became entangled in the McCarthyite anticommunist crusade, many conservative libertarians with political views similar to Keeler's listed the polygraph as Exhibit A among totalitarian tendencies in the country that were *undermining* basic decency and human relations. Second, after the end of World War II, CIA leaders showed few qualms about employing former Nazi war criminals, such as the Ukrainian Mikola Lebed, whose partisans were considered "a terrorist organization" by the Justice Department, or the former head of the Eastern Division of the *Abwehr*, Hitler's military intelligence service, Reinhard Gehlen. There is no indication that Gehlen was ever given a polygraph, maybe because American officials trusted his judgment and loyalty in the anticommunist fight (to little avail, since Gehlen's organization was infested with Soviet spies).[25] Apparently, it could be in the interest of national security to cooperate with former Nazis.

To highlight one last irony: it was to a large degree the imperative of fighting Soviet totalitarianism that led U.S. occupation officials to end the program of "denazification" in West Germany in the late 1940s and to enroll the largely unreconstructed German people into the struggle. Put differently, Americans began to fight fire with fire. It is true that many German scholars and intellectuals offered their services to the American occupational forces and in the process developed influential theories of democratization that forged an intellectual "western" Cold War community.[26] However, for the majority of Germans, it was the myth of "Nazism without Nazis" and not a thorough confrontation with the past that created the consensus on which an ultimately successful postwar democracy was built. Until the generational change of the 1960s, this myth remained powerful, if never completely uncontested.[27] None of this was foreseeable in 1945, nor was it preordained. But German postwar history suggests the prediction of human behavior was beyond the capacity of the lie detector or any other test.

When World War II ended, questions of loyalty were directed not just at Germans, but at Americans as well. After the POW screening, the leaders of the Manhattan District facility in Oak Ridge invited Colonel Pierce for a demonstration. Given that Oak Ridge produced enriched Uranium 235, the fuel for nuclear weapons, it was "imperative that only personnel of unquestioned integrity and loyalty be employed" there. After a visit in December 1945, Pierce was given the job to polygraph selected personnel at Oak Ridge in February/March 1946.[28] Oak Ridge in rural Tennessee employed thousands of workers from various parts of the country with various skills and educational backgrounds. Their lives and work were ruled by strict regulations, including racial segregation. It was not until after Hiroshima that the federal government even admitted to the facility's existence.

Pierce and Keeler initially tested 690 Oak Ridge workers. Since Keeler was unwilling to move to the rural South, Russell Chatham, another one of Keeler's protégés from the Chicago Crime Laboratory, took on the job at Oak Ridge. Chatham's team of eleven examiners was a fixture there, testing approximately 50,000 engineers and other workers before, during, and after employment. They handled up to one hundred cases a day. With this workload, individual tests could only last about twenty minutes, with two sets of questions and some time in between to clear up problems. This procedure set the precedent for the polygraph as a technological tether for a whole population.[29] Among the first 690 workers tested, stealing tools and supplies was the most common infraction the test uncovered (seventy-five admitted to it). Nine employees had taken product material, another seven ratted out others who had. Those were cases of small thefts. A few admitted radioactive spills they had not reported. Others had used false names at some point in their lives. These 18.7 percent "adverse admissions" were hardly politically radioactive. The purpose of these screenings, however, was to enforce continued loyalty. Under Russell Chatham, questions included, "Do you intend to do damage to this project or the United States?" and "Are you in sympathy with Communism or the Communistic form of government?" According to John Trovillo, a psychologist and collaborator of Chatham, the trustworthiness of a person could be inferred from questioning their intent.[30]

The civilian Atomic Energy Commission (AEC), which took over Oak Ridge and all other nuclear facilities from the military on January 1, 1947, continued the polygraph program. The most likely explanation is the political pressure the AEC faced from House Un-American Activities Committee (HUAC) chairman J. Parnell Thomas, a Republican from New Jersey, whose June 1947 *Life* magazine article "Reds in Our Atom-Bomb Plants" charged that Oak Ridge and other installations were "heavily infested" with communists. Thomas had received information about left-leaning tendencies from the Oak Ridge Security files that were leaked to him, in all likelihood, by the FBI. In part to release political pressure, the AEC, headed by New Deal Liberal David Lilienthal, revoked security clearances for many Oak Ridge scientists and initiated loyalty investigations. Although clear evidence is lacking, it is reasonable to assume that the continuation of the polygraph program was part of the political back-and-forth among HUAC and other congressional forces, different factions within the AEC, and the Federation of American Scientists (FAS), the organization of former Manhattan Project workers.[31]

Responses to a 1951 survey, which, it should be emphasized, was not anonymous, suggest either that workers knew what their employer wanted to hear, or that some workers indeed appreciated the tests. One senior physicist responded, "I have a personal satisfaction in passing each test, to have a recalibration so to speak. Knowledge that I would be taking the test again would surely influence me if I had any intent of doing wrong." Many agreed that it was a good "deterrent," with one secretary pointing out that "the program of periodic testing makes us more security conscious, even on little conversations." A security officer claimed that the polygraph had reduced "chatter" (accidental disclosure of classified information) by "70 percent."[32] AEC spokesman Morse Salisbury told the Associated Press in 1951, "I think they love it there. It is a good guard on a loose tongue. When a man knows he's going up against this machine, he thinks about it when he starts talking."[33] Historian Ken Alder argues that AEC employees were glad they could point to proof of their loyalty, thus alleviating the pressure of permanent suspicion. If this is true, the polygraph highlighted the climate of fear in the early Cold War rather than reducing it.

Anthropological research allows us to see polygraph testing as an initiation ritual of the kind accompanying all socialization processes. In environments shrouded in secrecy, members of a group tend to see themselves as bound together by a shared sense of importance, which in turn is the flip side of high demands on them such as submission to security procedures and anonymity. As anthropologist Hugh Gusterson put it, "[Secrecy] segregates laboratory scientists as a privileged but somewhat isolated elite; it inculcates a sense of group loyalty; and it thrusts on laboratory scientists an amorphous surveillance, which can become internalized." Yet in practice, as Gusterson found in his study of the nuclear research laboratory at Livermore in the mid-1990s, those scientists also tended to ignore secrecy measures such as classification of documents if it hindered their daily work routine, resulting in a regime of secrecy measures that is pervasive, indeed open-ended, but also incomplete and subject to ad hoc twisting by the employees.[34] Lie detector tests at Oak Ridge might have helped scientists to internalize the importance of secrecy and their own elevated status as keepers of secrets, but we do not know if the tests affected their daily work routine.

Market forces apparently disposed of the issue of loyalty testing at Oak Ridge. Accepting work in a climate of permanent suspicion is one thing in a labor market in which supply exceeds demand. This is especially true in low-paying jobs that do not require special skills. But nuclear scientists and engineers had enormous pull in the postwar era. Universities offered rewarding research work under less stringent conditions and perhaps a less secretive environment. When 40 percent of senior physicists and chemists had abandoned work at Oak Ridge in 1947–1948, and when a major AEC contractor, Carbide and Carbon Chemicals Corporation, complained that it was losing personnel to other employers, the Oak Ridge polygraph program was in trouble.[35] After the *New York Times* disclosed polygraph use in the federal government and revealed the Oak Ridge program in a page-one story in December 1951, publicity turned negative as well.[36] The AEC abandoned the program in early 1953 to the chagrin of Russell Chatham, who darkly hinted to the press that hundreds of prospective or current AEC employees had admitted to major crimes or membership in "Un-American" organizations.[37] Apparently, lie detector screenings always revealed just enough derogatory information to justify alarmism, but maintaining qualified personnel was a higher priority for the AEC at that point.

If it accomplished anything, the Oak Ridge polygraph program signified that the AEC claimed rightful authority over nuclear secrets. The AEC, however, had to constantly reaffirm its standing, and in the process it also claimed superior authority to judge individual life stories. It did so most prominently by stripping J. Robert Oppenheimer, who had been the chief scientist at the Los Alamos laboratory during the war, of his security clearance after an extensive loyalty investigation. From 1945 on, Oppenheimer had treated a careful balance between supporting the militarization of science and at the same time advocating the "pure" scientific ideal of rational, international, open discourse. Oppenheimer became politically vulnerable when, as chairman of the AEC's General Advisory Committee, he opposed the development of the hydrogen "super" bomb in October 1949. At once, Oppenheimer's past personal connections to communist front organizations and members of the Communist Party came back to haunt him. AEC chair Lewis Strauss and Oppenheimer's scientific competitor Edward Teller jumped at the opportunity to take him down.[38] In the spring of 1954, the Personnel Loyalty Board of the AEC conducted hearings that unearthed the fact that Oppenheimer had not divulged all details of the information his friend Haakon Chevalier had provided to him concerning the transfer of scientific information to the Soviet Union in 1943. No conclusive proof was found, however, that Oppenheimer himself had been a communist in the 1930s or 1940s or that he had ever engaged in espionage.

Nor did accusations that his advice had substantially delayed the development of the hydrogen bomb produce credible evidence. Nevertheless, the AEC revoked his security clearance in June 1954.

The AEC Personnel Security Board justified the decision thus:
"There can be no tempering with national security, which in times of
peril must be absolute. . . . Any doubts whatsoever must be resolved in
the interests of the national security." However decisive such a statement appeared, it revealed unresolved problems rather than a clear
understanding of what the acceptable demands of the state toward the
individual would be. As the board admitted,

> On the one hand, we find no evidence of disloyalty. Indeed, we have
> before us much responsible and positive evidence of the loyalty and love
> of country of the individual concerned. On the other hand, we do not
> believe that it has been demonstrated that Dr. Oppenheimer has been
> blameless in the matter of conduct, character, and association. . . . Any
> person whose absolute loyalty to the United States is in question, aside
> from present or former Communist affiliations of associations, should
> be rejected for Government service.[39]

Oppenheimer's career in and out of the center of the national security state is instructive. It poses the question of "the relationship between
truth and worldly power: between the intellectual and the polis, 'pure science' and technology, charisma and bureaucracy."[40] Rather than criticizing U.S. national security policy from the outside—as Albert Einstein and
Niels Bohr did—or embracing the rewards it offered to willing participants such as Edward Teller, Oppenheimer remained committed to both
the persona of the charismatic, humanistic thinker who remained true
to the quest for ultimate truth, and advisor to power within the world of
politics. The enigma of Oppenheimer and his eventual ousting illustrates
the ultimate impossibility of that double commitment. The threat of the
atomic bomb set the persona Oppenheimer had constructed for himself
on a collision course with the priorities of the American national security
bureaucracy. Neither he nor other scientists committed to the principle of
open government movement could avoid that conflict.[41]

The Oppenheimer hearings unfolded simultaneously with Joseph
McCarthy's Army hearings, which inaugurated the senator's downfall
and the end to the worst postwar anticommunist hysteria. The AEC

stressed that "the people of our country can be reassured by this proceeding that it is possible to conduct an investigation in calmness, in fairness" and "that loyalty and security can be examined within the frameworks of the traditional and inviolable principles of American justice."[42] The Oppenheimer case highlighted, however, that in the American Cold War standards of security depended on some measure of loyalty, which opened the door to government investigations into an individual's private beliefs.

The public outcry over Oppenheimer's ousting despite the fact that he was not found to be disloyal attested to Oppenheimer's celebrity status. His case gains even greater significance when we consider general problems of loyalty investigations. Initiated by President Truman in 1947, loyalty investigations of thousands of federal employees from the outset had a political character. Fed their information by the FBI, loyalty review boards made their decisions on the basis of J. Edgar Hoover's alarmist views on the dangers of communism. Even so, until 1950 the vast majority of federal employees were reinstated after their review board had heard their case. The outbreak of the Korean War, however, inflamed partisanship anew, and under conservative pressure, the Truman administration established stricter standards, making "reasonable doubt" of a person's loyalty sufficient reason for dismissal. President Eisenhower extended this strict standard to the whole federal workforce, establishing "security" rather than "loyalty" as the goal of investigations.[43]

To what extent should investigations target not only actual deeds, but thought? How far should the requirements of security be allowed to reach into the personal history of Americans? The AEC Personnel Board saw the issues. It asserted, "The necessary but harsh requirements of security should not deny a man the right to have made a mistake, if its recurrence is so remote a possibility as to permit a comfortable prediction as to the sanity and correctness of future conduct."[44] But it emphasized its priorities emphatically:

> There remains also an aspect of the security system which perhaps has had insufficient public attention. This is the protection and support of the entire system itself. It must include an understanding and an acceptance of security measures adopted by responsible Government agencies. It must include an active cooperation with all agencies of Government properly and reasonably concerned with the security of our

country. It must involve a subordination of personal judgment in the light of standards and procedures when they have been clearly established by appropriate process. It must entail a wholehearted commitment to the preservation of the security system and the avoidance of conduct tending to confuse or obstruct.[45]

This statement reads like the Magna Carta of the national security state: The federal government asserted the right to demand compliance with its security rules, not only for the sake of protecting secrets, but to protect "the entire system itself." The individual had to "subordinate personal judgment" and comply with the rules. But the board also asserted core values of American democracy: the board explicitly refused to cut Oppenheimer slack for his elevated status and therefore asserted the egalitarian character of national security measures. Security depended on "active cooperation" and "wholehearted commitment" of citizens and promised "appropriate process" according to "clearly established" standards, therefore echoing the language of "due process" in the U.S. Constitution that protected individual rights. Means and ends of national security were declared to be in perfect harmony.

Unlike Oppenheimer, who retreated to the Institute for Advanced Study in Princeton, New Jersey, the polygraph managed to find a permanent place in the national security state as part of these "standards and procedures." His case came at the tail end of the drama of public accusations and denunciations commonly referred to as "McCarthyism," which was succeeded in time by more bureaucratized security investigations and institutionalized surveillance of citizens. While the Cold War thus became normalized, the tension between its means and ends persisted. The polygraph illustrates the dilemmas of a political-scientific system arguing for rational discourse as the means to realize core liberal values. The internal conflict of the state claiming to be committed both to modern bureaucratic rationality—the efficiency to protect itself—and liberal core values—what gave meaning to bureaucratic procedures—played out as a public drama in the case of Robert Oppenheimer.[46] Yet it also became an institutionalized endless rerun through the practice of lie detection. Like Oppenheimer the scientist, the machine "came to embody cultural tensions rooted in the development of the secular, modern conception of truth as 'a thing of this world,' . . . truth *as* power as well as cultural tensions *between* truth and power."[47]

Given the untimely end of the polygraph at Oak Ridge, its history also illustrates the limits of the powers of the national security state. Nuclear power created mistrust of the government, especially when scientists in the early 1950s began to warn of the hazards of nuclear fallout produced during tests. As with other aspects of Cold War strategy, the U.S. national security state used public relations campaigns to strengthen morale among its employees and reassure the public. The polygraph was tested as a trust-builder in this context as well, and its limits illustrate further the limits of the emergent national security state in convincing American citizens of its trustworthiness.

When the AEC resumed nuclear testing in 1951 at its new facilities in Nevada, the Army tracked the emotional responses of U.S. soldiers witnessing a nuclear blast during a maneuver code-named Desert Rock I on November 1, 1951, and again during Desert Rock IV in March 1952. On both occasions, two different research teams recorded soldiers' attitudes toward the use of nuclear weapons in battle before indoctrination, after indoctrination, and during and after the blast itself. While the Army Human Resources Research Office (HumRRO) relied on questionnaires, a team from Johns Hopkins University's Operational Research Office (ORO) used personal observation, recorded interviews and reactions, and employed polygraph tests before and after the nuclear explosions. In both cases, HumRRO painted an upbeat picture of soldiers' responses and reported that indoctrination had achieved high confidence (exceeding 70 percent) in the safety of entering a battlefield after a nuclear blast. Few soldiers complained of physical problems after the blast except for some trouble with the eyes. The ORO study, on the other hand, showed "significant physiological disturbance" among soldiers during and after the blasts, "more physiological disturbance . . . than their verbal responses indicated." During the second test, soldiers showed fewer physiological signs of anxiety and managed to dismantle their weapons during the blast without impairment. However, given that these maneuvers were carefully staged, ORO insisted that the results were of little value. Real tests needed "danger, surprise, and fatigue approximating those found in combat, or when atomic weapons are actually used in combat operations."[48] The AEC never again ordered such polygraph tests with nuclear weapons.

This short but devastating episode (given the long-term damage done to the health of these unwitting men) illustrated the dialectic of secrecy and publicity in the management of national security. If democracy depended on the free exchange of information, how could the government justify secrets guarded by a military classification system of knowledge that restricted the flow of information? In the case of nuclear power, the AEC soon concluded that popular fears of the health hazards deriving from nuclear fallout demanded good publicity to counter such fears. Proactive measures included ways to prove the usefulness of weapons testing and other nuclear activity. For example, the AEC launched Project Plowshare to great fanfare in 1958. The goal of this amply funded research project under Edward Teller was to develop ways to use nuclear explosions for engineering purposes by blasting harbors into coastlines, canals to connect rivers, or tunnels through mountains. Terms such as "safety feasibility" employed by Plowshare scientists suggested that the seemingly unpredictable hazards of nuclear fallout could be calculated. However, after ten years of frantic search for a spectacular demonstration of nuclear power's safety feasibility and much resistance from local scientists, journalists, and citizens, Project Plowshare disappeared back into the laboratory and onto graphs and maps.[49] Polygraph results remained sufficiently unpredictable to be of little use in this project. In the case of the atomic soldiers, however, they did give a correct diagnosis: nuclear weapons *were* scary.

The press often depicted nuclear power in recklessly optimistic terms, at least until the early 1960s. AEC-friendly magazines such as *Life, Business Week,* or *U.S. News and World Report* often praised the "AEC men" (maybe echoing J. Edgar Hoover's G-men from the 1930s) in stories featuring impressive pictures of the mushroom cloud and the results of nuclear blasts.[50] Nuclear blasts were spectacular and intimidating, while the scientific principles behind them were elusive to the non-initiated. Yet the question was whether these stunning displays invoked trust or fear of the government in the American public—in other words, if the project of "calibrating public perceptions of the nuclear danger" would yield the appropriate amount of politically usable fear while avoiding debilitating terror among Americans citizens. Such a project proved beyond the control of federal authorities and evinced complicated responses from American popular culture. Film, television, and other media extensively dealt with "the Bomb," but their treatment evades easy categorization as either "pro" or "anti" nuclear weapons.[51]

The polygraph worked according to the logic of intimidating but not terrifying performance that was similar to nuclear deterrence.[52] In his 1930 article, "A Method for Detecting Deception," Keeler suggested that each test should be initiated by a preamble read to the subject: that the machine "so far has proved a very reliable means of detecting the innocence or guilt of man, and I'm sure we will not fail in your case." The secret of the self-fulfilling prophecy was thus to simply announce it. Keeler also boasted, "75% of the guilty suspects confess" without the need for analyzing their physiological measures.[53] Keeler's associate Fred Inbau suggested a similar speech in his 1942 textbook *Lie Detection and Criminal Interrogation:*

> If you are telling the truth, you have nothing to worry about—the instrument will indicate you are telling the truth, and I'll report that fact to the officers who requested me to make this test. However, if you are not telling the truth, the machine will show it; and I'll tell you so, and then I'll ask you to let me hear the truth. That's fair enough, isn't it? And you don't mind taking the test, do you?[54]

The card guessing game, of course, was another part of this logic of performance, which went back to Hugo Münsterberg, as we have seen. As long as the audience was dazzled, its creators believed, the lie detector worked.

Given the spectacular way the polygraph has performed in American culture, particularly as an actor in police and courtroom dramas, this analysis has much to offer in explaining its appeal. Further, many aspects of U.S. deterrence policies were meant to assuage domestic public opinion, as were projects such as Chatham's polygraph program at Oak Ridge. Part of the appeal of the lie detector, however, was its promise of scientific precision. As we will see, a true lie detector was envisioned by some Americans to break *through* the bluffs of "massive retaliation" or "second-strike capability," not to maintain their spell. Therefore, the lie detector's promise always relied at least in part on its association with "legitimate" science and the expectation that it would eventually work the way the public imagined it: as a foolproof scientific instrument.

Throughout the Cold War, communism put on the most impressive performances of people's acceptance of the social system. Yet even the most festive May Day parades did not save economically bankrupt and politically corrupt systems, which for the most part relied on invasive internal spy apparatuses to keep track of dissent, while citizens had to continue performing socialistic utopianism on official occasions.[55] Similarly, nuclear power and the policy of nuclear deterrence never enjoyed unquestioned agreement in the United States. The horrors of World War II created "an age of doubt" and a "culture of contingency," as one historian called it. Even mainstream culture of the 1950s bubbled with discord, if often only symbolically and sporadically, culminating the in the black humor of early-1960s movies such as *The Manchurian Candidate* or *Dr. Strangelove* that mocked Cold War obsessions with communism and misplaced trust in nuclear deterrence. Not even the Cuban Missile Crisis could convince more than a few thousand Americans to build private bomb shelters.[56] By the early 1960s and the signing of the Test Ban Treaty of 1963, the superpowers began to cautiously move toward the principle of coexistence.

National security policies and the polygraph enjoyed a symbiotic relationship. Rather than positing the success of the polygraph based on its spectacular performance, however, we should see that the polygraph endured on borrowed legitimacy rather than triumphing in its own right. Like two drunken men at the end of a long night at the bar, the national security state and the polygraph leaned on each other, maintaining a precarious balance.

CHAPTER 4

The Polygraph and the Specter of Totalitarianism Within

ike a shot of potent medicine, the Second World War revived the United States but left many Americans wondering about the aftereffect. Beginning in 1940, defense spending revived the depressed economy. Mass employment, in turn, sparked hopes for a permanently elevated standard of living in a self-sustaining consumer economy guided by the light touch of tax incentives and other indirect federal intervention. The experience of comradeship in battle eased prejudices and facilitated a less ethnic and more civic sense of national identity among sixteen million men and women who had joined the armed forces. Fighting fascism also restored a sense of purpose and mission in the American political system. President Roosevelt's Four Freedoms offered a blueprint for a future in which American principles would provide liberty and prosperity for all, even hinting at the possibility that the nation might finally tackle the "American dilemma" of racism. A new sense of patriotism seemed to imbue the American people and led them to accept the expanded power of the state as necessary and beneficial.[1] To be sure, the veneer of racial progress often turned out to be rather thin upon inspection, and the valorization of the war as "good" turned out to be largely the cultural work of nostalgia.[2] Nevertheless, in 1945 many Americans concluded that the country had been granted a new lease on greatness.

Among American intellectuals, the legacy of World War II was ambiguous. Many contemporary critics, especially on the Left, negotiated an uneasy peace with American democracy as the war against fascism yielded to the war against communism.[3] Nevertheless, four dangers loomed in the shadows of postwar prosperity: American violence unwittingly imitating the violence of undemocratic regimes; freedom at home lost in a consumer society ruled by corporate opinion-makers and anonymous state bureaucracies; surrender to Stalin's brutal regime abroad due to a lack of will to resist it; and the slippery slope from well-intentioned welfare state policies toward dictatorship. These threats converged in the specter of "totalitarianism" and demanded vigilance toward American democracy and its potential to turn on itself.

Prominent theologian Reinhold Niebuhr pondered the first danger by stressing the larger implications of mass warfare in his 1944 book *Children of Light and the Children of Darkness*. Sobered by the Great Depression and global war, Niebuhr warned, "The excessively optimistic estimates of human nature and of human history with which the democratic credo has been historically associated are a source of peril to democratic society; for contemporary experience is refuting this optimism and there is danger that it will seem to refute the democratic ideals as well."[4] American democracy received a distinct justification from Niebuhr: It was not possible because of human idealism and virtue, but necessary because of human fragility and self-destructiveness. Niebuhr's sense of existential dread, shared by writers as diverse as Norman Mailer, Ralph Ellison, and Betty Friedan, encouraged determined action with a sober mind, but in doing so he robbed American values of their missionary righteousness.[5] Following Niebuhr, historian Arthur Schlesinger Jr. noted in his 1949 book, *The Vital Center,* a founding document of Cold War liberalism, that modern society had facilitated greater human freedom, but hand in hand with this freedom had come an anxiety over new responsibilities. Schlesinger saw as the consequence a loss of moral certainty and identity: "By making choices, man makes himself: creates or destroys his own moral personality."[6] Which course would America, now endowed with unprecedented power to create or destroy, choose? Only a course of "realism" that avoided extremes could steer clear of catastrophe, or so it appeared to liberal intellectuals such as Niebuhr and Schlesinger.

Recent American actions were cause for concern. When America dropped atomic bombs on Japanese civilians in August 1945, Niebuhr struggled with the terrible calculus offered by the Truman administration, namely that in the long view the bombs had saved lives, especially American lives.[7] Niebuhr was not alone in his ambivalence: contemporary editorials and other accounts sensed a "cultural crisis" over Hiroshima and Nagasaki, with deep anxiety over the forces unleashed as well as cautious hope and determination to contain them.[8] Atomic bombs added a terrible urgency to Niebuhr's concerns: How much violence could a democracy inflict on others before becoming the evil it was fighting? Even though Niebuhr exaggerated what he saw as a lack of tragic sense in American culture (Did the Puritans not have a sense of existential anxiety? Was the Blues not an acknowledgment of tragedy?), in the Atomic Age many intellectuals joined Niebuhr in demanding a farewell to illusions of American innocence and a sober, realistic attitude in conducting foreign relations.

Concerns about the second danger—American political freedom undermining itself at home—had considerable currency due to the writings of European émigrés, especially Jews who had escaped Hitler's Germany. For example, in his bestselling 1941 book *Escape from Freedom*, German émigré psychologist Erich Fromm declared freedom "a psychological problem" inherent in Western society generally, not just Germany: "Modern man is still anxious and tempted to surrender his freedom to dictatorships of all kinds, or to lose it by transforming himself into a small cog in the machine, well fed, and well clothed, yet not a free man but an automaton." In this analysis, the accomplishments of American society created only an illusion of freedom: "The right to express our thoughts . . . means something only if we are able to have thoughts of our own. . . . Modern man lives under the illusion that he knows what he wants, while he actually wants what he is *supposed* to want."[9] This condemnation of inauthentic mass man—lost in urban crowds and helpless against the onslaught of advertising and mass media—was one echo of discourse on totalitarianism in U.S. postwar discussions among writers and social scientists who were less concerned with capitalism's failures but rather its resounding success, even though most rejected Fromm's call to replace social democracy and planned economy for consumer capitalism.[10]

A third way in which the specter of totalitarianism entered the imagination of American writers and readers were visions of the formidable powers of totalitarian societies to destroy individuality. Most prominently, British author George Orwell's dystopian novel *1984*, published in the United States in 1949, impressed critics with its power to capture the "psychology of capitulation," the "methodology of terror that enables them [totalitarian regimes] to break human beings by getting inside them," as *Partisan Review* critic Phillip Rahv wrote. "The victim crawls before his torturer, he identifies himself with him and grows to love him. That is the ultimate horror."[11] Such descriptions of totalitarianism also found their way into policy documents such as NSC-68, drafted in 1950 mainly by the head of the State Department Policy Planning Staff Paul Nitze, but based on extensive interviews with a variety of policymakers: "Being a totalitarian dictatorship, the Kremlin's objectives [sic] in these policies, is the total subjective submission of the peoples now under its control. The concentration camp is the prototype of the society which these policies are designed to achieve, a society in which the personality of the individual is so broken and perverted that he participates affirmatively in his own degradation."[12] In addition, Hannah Arendt's massive study *The Origins of Totalitarianism*, published in 1950, emphasized the strong family resemblance between Hitler's Germany and Stalin's Soviet Union in their capacity to forge mass movements out of rootless modern individuals, close the ranks of their own followers through conspiracy theories and outright lies, and use everyday terror as a method of government. In this view, totalitarian regimes were relentless juggernauts driven to restless expansion by the logic of total mobilization. Arendt's vision frightened many American writers into staunch opposition to Soviet policies in each and every case, even though this was hardly what the émigré philosopher had intended, while popular press coverage and movies painted a picture of communism as a vast concentration camp that could easily be juxtaposed with the alleged personal freedom that escape to the West offered.[13] Once the Cold War took shape, to many Americans fears of communist persuasion techniques co-mingled with concerns about weak-willed Americans consumers, prone to fall prey to insidious "brainwashing" methods.[14]

Lastly, libertarian economists warned that the newly acquired powers of the New Deal welfare state could contain the seeds of dictatorship. Beginning in the mid-1930s, Austrian economists Ludwig von Mises and Friedrich Hayek added intellectual heft to the warnings of conservatives such as former president Herbert Hoover that the rise of large federal bureaucracies such as the Social Security Administration and the political influence of industrial labor unions could result in a new "collectivism" that would lead America down a slippery slope from economic planning to total dictatorship. Hayek's polemic *The Road to Serfdom*, first published in 1944 and read by millions of Americans in a *Reader's Digest* version, became a foundational text for those who saw socialism as the first step toward fascism. This view, at first expressed only by organizations such as the John Birch Society, eventually became influential in forging a fundamentalist critique of the welfare state as essentially totalitarian. Making a related argument, Ludwig von Mises emphasized in his 1944 book *Omnipotent Government* that the cause of recent world wars had been government interference in the global economy, which consequently would have to be avoided in order to prevent totalitarianism.[15]

Such fears of totalitarianism, often contradictory and ambivalent, contributed to a sense of "nightmarish pessimism" in public discussion about the totalitarian threat looming behind the sunny face of postwar prosperity. Based on these observations, I conclude that fear of totalitarianism was a cause *and* a consequence of the American Cold War confrontation with the Soviet Union, a self-fulfilling prophecy of and a response to events.[16]

In this chapter I make three claims. First, the polygraph channeled such abstract fears about creeping totalitarianism at home into a specific practice. American security agencies—with the help of the mobilized psychological profession—researched "totalitarian methods" of interrogation with grim determination. They studied techniques of disorientation, sensory deprivation, and self-inflicted pain allegedly used by Nazi German concentration camp guards and Chinese and Soviet communists to break an individual's will.[17] To most Americans, however, such activities remained obscure until the post-Watergate revelations of the mid-1970s. The polygraph, on the other hand, was in actual use at home and therefore allowed a debate over the limits of governmental interference with the individual and his/her conscience. In short, the polygraph was a prism that reflected the debate of the new powers of the state in its effort to protect "national security" against the totalitarian threat. Second, the polygraph's family resemblance to more reputable social-scientific measurements made it usable for participants on different sides of the political debate, which discouraged united fronts of support and opposition and reflected general ambivalence over the usefulness of testing and other scientific measures of subjective attitudes. Third, limiting polygraph use through regulation had the ironic effect of normalizing the test and therefore bolstering the polygraph's credentials within the discourse of "national security."

In the early 1950s, the polygraph became a matter of public debate. The first politician who took on the machine was Senator Wayne Morse of Oregon. Elected to the Senate in 1944 as a Republican, Morse left the GOP in 1952 and became a Democrat two years later. The Senate "maverick" of his time, Morse defended the internment of Japanese Americans during World War II and voted for the 1950 Internal Security Act that mandated registration of Communist organizations and allowed deportation of members, but he also opposed police wiretaps and criticized President Truman's Executive Order 9835 of 1947 that prompted loyalty investigations of over three million federal employees. As chair of the Senate Foreign Relations subcommittee on Latin America, he criticized U.S. support of military dictators. In 1964 he was one of only two senators who voted against the Gulf of Tonkin Resolution granting President Lyndon Johnson a free hand to escalate the war in Vietnam.[18]

Morse's opposition to the lie detector grew out of his commitment to individual privacy and his insistence on Congress's oversight privileges over the executive branch. The senator expressed ambiguity about national security policies in a speech he gave on the use of polygraphs in the Pentagon on the Senate floor on January 17, 1952. As a member of the Armed Services Committee, Morse requested information on polygraph procedures in the Department of Defense and professed shock at what he found out. He concluded that polygraphing applicants for federal employment was "a repugnant, abhorrent, and outrageous procedure."[19] Morse's specific objection was the disconnect between policies and core values he saw in the use of the lie detector, namely that it introduced an attitude of "the end justifies the means" that could not be squared with individual freedoms: "As a constitutionalist . . . I say today . . . that the end never justifies the means, when the means cannot be reconciled with the basic guarantees of personal liberty and freedom set forth in the Constitution." Morse continued to claim that he would not "yield to any colleague in the Senate of the United States in zeal in fighting communism" and that he had "no objection" to the polygraph, as long as it was "surrounded with the procedural safeguards available to any defendant in an American courtroom." Yet Morse concluded his criticism by framing the debate in terms of a dichotomy between freedom and totalitarianism and formulated an argument that would resonate throughout the American Cold War: "In our fight against totalitarianism we ourselves should not adopt totalitarian techniques and tactics."

What Morse really objected to, therefore, was the change of values that polygraph tests could produce, namely a "forgetting" of the "the presumption of innocence," and the idea that "doubt, and doubt alone, is all that is necessary in order to ruin the reputation and the economic future of a fellow American."[20] Presumption of innocence was a basic feature of the American legal system, and good reputation was a condition for success in a market society. The mere act of ordering an upstanding citizen to take a polygraph as a routine procedure without a specific suspicion seemed to imply an assumption of guilt with the potential to smear a good reputation. It might have been one thing to force polygraph exams on suspected criminals or mental patients, but it was quite another to have the government conduct tests on a mass basis.

Despite his robust statement, Morse's criticism contained easily missed ambiguity.[21] The senator refused to pinpoint whether the polygraph test was an inherently totalitarian technique, or whether it was only a lack of proper procedural protections that made it so. If the latter was the case, Morse may have endorsed the test with the addition of satisfactory oversight. While Morse did not spell out such issues, he squarely faced the question of how far the government could go in demanding proof of loyalty from its citizens. The context of his speech was the implementation of unprecedented means to police political expression, such as mass loyalty investigations, which President Truman initiated for every federal employee in 1947, or broad anticommunist legislation such as the Smith Act of 1940, which had made it illegal to advocate or teach the violent overthrow of the government. When the Supreme Court in 1951 upheld the conviction of twelve members of the Communist Party of the United States (CPUSA) based solely on the party's written material, it made thought crimes as punishable as actual deeds and effectively outlawed membership in the party itself. The enforcement of the Smith Act after 1948 broadened the spectrum of inadmissible speech and behavior and opened the door for the exclusion of communists from all areas of public life.[22]

Having threatened to introduce anti-polygraph legislation if the tests continued, Morse accepted assertions by Secretary of Defense Robert Lovett that testing had been halted. However, Lovett apparently only banned use in his *immediate* office of twenty employees while leaving general use in the Pentagon untouched.[23] As lie detector stories continued to trickle into the news, Morse and his staff continued to question federal agencies about polygraph practices. The senator helped uncover more polygraph stories for a major expose in the liberal highbrow magazine *The Reporter* in 1954.[24]

In that article, Dwight Macdonald investigated what the author called a "dark corner of our governmental practices."[25] Macdonald's piece, building on Anthony Leviero's reporting for the *New York Times* from a few years earlier, was the most detailed rendering of polygraph controversies yet. A former Trotskyist who had been among the first of the New York intellectuals to break with Stalinism, Macdonald had opposed U.S. intervention in World War II and struggled to find an ideological home in postwar America. The fiercely independent Macdonald became a lukewarm supporter of U.S. Cold War policies, famously proclaiming in a debate with Norman Mailer at Mt. Holyoke College in 1952, "I choose the West. . . . I prefer an imperfectly living, open society to a perfectly dead, closed society."[26] At that point Macdonald had given up on developing the coherent anarcho-pacifistic philosophy he had pursued in his journal *politics* from 1943 to 1949 and instead made himself a name as a caustic critic of American consumer culture.

Macdonald presented powerful anecdotes about the toll the practice was taking on citizens. These counter narratives to the heroic polygraph stories presented by its boosters effectively revealed the emotional responses and associations the tests evoked in its subjects. In investigating the furor surrounding the polygraph, Macdonald was shedding light on a state of political confusion created by a procedure that seemed to define loyalty as a testable mental attribute. He revealed the struggle between traditional ideas of voluntary citizenship with the new demands of the national security state. The novelty of this regime after World War II was that it targeted white-collar workers in search of government employment. This group was likely to feature many individuals fiercely proud of their educational achievements, skills, and loyalty.

Macdonald conceded the technology's "usefulness for certain police and commercial investigations," but quickly focused on the phenomenon of mass security screenings being instituted in the Department of Defense's National Security Agency (NSA), the CIA, and the Army's Operations Research Office (ORO). Mass screenings had their peculiar problems. First was the search to find simple Yes or No answers to "complex and vague questions," often targeting "inclination or intention rather than . . . fact." Second was the moral question whether "citizens accused of no crime [should] have to subject themselves to a lie test in order to convince their superiors of their honesty."[27] These were precisely the questions that the enforcement of the Smith Act and the loyalty investigations of the Truman and Eisenhower administrations had raised. Drawing from a number of "horror stories," Macdonald focused on the inappropriate behavior of examiners at the NSA.

The first set of objections Macdonald presented focused on a sense of violated privacy among job applicants, who assumed that voluntary service to their government showed good citizenship and were therefore outraged by doubt of their motives. Such emotions often accompanied a sense of class privilege, something a "gentleman" would not have to put up with. One of the peculiar cases Macdonald reported was the case of one Richard Roe, an employee of the NSA.[28] "I was willing, even eager, to take the test because I believed in its scientific reliability," Macdonald quoted Roe. "But halfway through, I felt like someone being tried in a Moscow purge." What disturbed Roe and produced that peculiar association? It was what Roe described as the "total lack of empathy" on the examiner's side when Roe attempted to fend off the question "Have you ever been sympathetic to Communism?" He explained that he had studied Marxism in college and was sympathetic to some Marxist doctrines but not others. "I got the impression that he [the examiner] considered anyone who had studied Marx to be ipso facto a security risk and also that he personally wanted me to fail."[29] Roe's (and Macdonald's) class bias showed in their telling of a Moscow-trial-in-reverse of a college graduate with even-keeled political and intellectual views by "an examiner who may or may not have gone to high school." However, Macdonald also captured how the polygraph test created a genuine sense of violation in many subjects, particularly in persons volunteering for government employment in national security agencies. Another story dealt with a young woman who expressed "humiliation of being treated as a suspected liar and a criminal." Macdonald asserted, "The folklore of NSA is full of stories about these tests."[30]

Many federal employees or candidates for federal jobs considered themselves above such testing. As one of Macdonald's sources put it: "I believe that when you go through the motions of the lie test you lose your usefulness as a public servant because you have submitted to something no gentleman can tolerate: You have let a machine verify your word of honor."[31] Yet this assumption overlooked the logic of the national security state: it was precisely an individual's willingness to submit to security investigations of their "honor" that made them reliable in the new bureaucracies of the state. Insistence on a code of gentlemanly honor echoed the findings of prominent contemporary critics such as Columbia University sociologist C. Wright Mills, one of the few intellectuals of the American Left who was free to criticize contemporary society without having to work through a past commitment to communism. In his 1956 book *The Power Elite*, Mills argued that a Lockean "classic democracy" assumed that "the individual conscience was the ultimate seat of judgment and hence the final court of appeal." Yet American society made the public of autonomous individuals into a mass of people incapable of speaking up, voicing dissent, putting views into action, or escaping the deep reach of what Mills coined the "power elite," the "effective units of power, . . . the huge corporation, the inaccessible government, the grim military establishment." Mills warily observed, "We have moved considerably along the road to the mass society. At the end of the road there is totalitarianism, as in Nazi Germany or in Communist Russia."[32] In this line of argument, polygraph screening could be read as a signpost along the way toward totalitarianism because it demanded that individuals submit their individual conscience to be verified by a standardized procedure.

Macdonald's article was a hard-hitting expose on the abuses dealt out by the polygraph, but it stopped short of condemning the technology itself and instead attacked the credentials of the examiners. When the piece discussed the abusive behavior of NSA examiners, it stressed that all were graduates of Leonarde Keeler's polygraph school, which Macdonald was quick to point out "had fallen into disrepute after the death of its founder in 1949."[33] Published in a magazine meant as a platform of critique from inside the Cold War consensus, the article refrained from outright dismissal of the validity of the polygraph if administered by an expert. For some, Macdonald's critique therefore did not go far enough. One sarcastic reader compared the author's demand for stricter licensing of polygraph examiners to calls by "legitimate" astrologers to "silence the quacks who give astrology a bad name."[34]

Still, Macdonald registered profound unease at the violation of individual conscience in the name of bureaucratic necessity. The title Macdonald had chosen for his expose, "The Lie Detector Era," indicated how much of what he found resonated with his larger concerns. Macdonald's article continued an argument he had made in his essay "The Root Is Man" eight years earlier. In that essay Macdonald had emphatically argued for a new minimalist political program, "working from the individual to society rather than the other way around." Echoing other prominent theorists of bureaucracies such as Harrold Laswell and James Burnham, Macdonald argued that "bureaucratic collectivism" had become the heir to both capitalism and socialism as the only viable form of social and political organization. Macdonald added that since history had ceased to be the carrier of progress, timeless moral values such as "truth, justice, love" needed to be reasserted.[35] If bureaucratic efficiency could replace the big ideologies of the nineteenth century, the line between American liberty and Soviet totalitarianism was becoming blurry; efficient administration would rule supreme over hollowed-out values. C. Wright Mills echoed this concern in an essay Macdonald published in the same issue of his journal *politics,* in which Mills exhorted American intellectuals to pursue a "politics of truth," a personal commitment to take responsibility to always speak truth to power. Mills warned that "when irresponsible decisions prevail and values are not proportionally distributed, you will find universal deception practiced by and for those who make the decisions and who have the most of what values there are to have."[36] In short, both authors warned of the power of large corporate structures to entice individuals to give up their personal responsibility to uphold moral values.

We get further insights on the debate about personal and public morality in citizens' responses sent to Morse upon his speech and the publication of the *Reporter* articles two years later. A number of writers identified themselves as current employees in government service or rejected applicants for government jobs. Their letters reveal strong sentiments of how the polygraph test violated their sense of patriotism. A correspondent writing from the AEC Oak Ridge facility proudly conveyed, "My ancestors were in this country before the Revolution, fought in it and in every war since and in their small way helped to build this great country. I have always been proud of my heritage and considered myself a good citizen. It came as quite a shock to me that my dignity and integrity as such was to be determined by a gadget." Another writer by the name of Rutledge closed with the postscript, "I am very proud that the signature 'Rutledge' is in the Constitution and Declaration of Independence."[37] Other writers voiced a second, related theme in objections to polygraph screening: the conformity that life and work in mass organizations seemed to engender. One such writer told of her rejection of an assignment due to her refusal to take the test and asserted that "thoughtful people were willing to put their love for their country above every trial as long as they believed that their government was backing them up. . . . I refused [the polygraph test]. But I doubt that that fact or the reasons for it are included in what must be by now a voluminous file under my name."[38] Such a comment expressed fear that individual subjectivity—notions of honor and duty informed by personal convictions—did not register with bureaucracies working according to their own rules. Another writer echoed this concern by stating that citizens were "becoming conditioned more every day to obeying bureaucratic decrees without question. This seems to me to foster communism and totalitarianism."[39]

Fortune magazine columnist William Whyte took this concern over conformity one step further and argued in his bestselling *The Organization Man* that employment in large organizations fostered the psychic need to identify with the corporation, bank, or government agency one worked for. In a not-so-faint echo of George Orwell, Whyte found that American white-collar workers indeed came to love Big Brother. He called for small acts of defiance such as cheating on the ubiquitous personality tests, whose pretentions at both validity and scientific accuracy the author dismissed with acidic disdain. Rather than predicting human behavior, Whyte found that constant tests to establish normal behavior "intensify a mutual deception we practice on one another. Who is 'normal'? All of us to some degree have a built-in urge to adjust to what we conceive as the norm, and in our reach we can come to feel that in the vast ocean of normality that surrounds us only we are different. We are the victims of one another's facades."[40] Whyte identified the psychic toll coming from the "fake it till you make it" culture that originated with Dale Carnegie's brand of self-help literature and motivational speaking.[41]

While Whyte's criticism highlighted a fear of the rule of bureaucracy—demanding conformity and inauthenticity, keeping personal records—the polygraph also touched the limit of bureaucratic procedures many employees were willing to put up with. Stories of outrage over lie detector use in businesses periodically appeared in the press. For example, according to a 1951 *Business Week* story, when president W. J. Tastet of the Washington, DC, hardware store Fries, Beall & Sharp hired a security company to test its 122 employees to explain a drop in profit margins, he claimed, "We believe our employees are honest, and we're just trying to prove it." An unnamed employee was quoted as responding, "Mr. Tastet thinks the employees all feel better now that they have purged themselves. They don't. They're scared and unhappy." *Business Week* reported that "the whole business is touchy to begin with, and on top of that it seems to give everybody associated with it the same sense of guilt and shame that a small boy feels when he's caught in the jam closet."[42] Visceral emotional disgust at the physical experience of being tested added to moral outrage over presumption of guilt and concern over conformity. One Armed Forces Security Agency employee who wrote Senator Morse reported his "extreme discomfort" with "intimate" and "insulting" questions, concluding that "I felt entirely subdued and at the mercy of the operator" and commended Morse for his fight to prevent "such a degrading experience" for federal employees.[43]

Such emotional responses highlight that even those who did not object to the logic of invasive security investigations *felt* violated by the polygraph procedure. In other words, the experience of being strapped to the polygraph had the potential to change the perception of security investigations. For example, journalists Joseph and Stewart Alsop, two unrelenting Cold War boosters and Georgetown high society players, compared the polygraph to the embrace of an octopus whose "electric tentacles" produced an "overwhelming impulse to tell all . . . in order to appease the octopus machine." They declared taking the test an "experience almost intolerably unpleasant." The Alsop brothers did not object to security measures, indeed they declared the CIA's reasoning in introducing the tests "entirely sensible." But the polygraph called up the totalitarian Other of the Cold War: "The old right to personal privacy is eroded away, and we begin palely to imitate the system we fear."[44]

Such foreboding might also have driven the Alsops to publicly defend J. Robert Oppenheimer and even Henry Wallace at the time of their respective loyalty investigations.[45] Therefore, understanding resistance to the widespread introduction of polygraph tests outside of criminal investigations demands attention to the sensibilities of the people who experienced it. The history of the polygraph reminds us that Cold War security culture needs to be understood not only in terms of content—how anticommunist themes entered public discourse—but also in terms of how this content was bound up with emotion.[46] Polygraph experiences, the confrontation with the polygraph as a material object, made abstract fear of "mass society" palpable and imbued it with emotional content.

However, others disagreed, and a number of Senator Morse's correspondents expressed support for the lie detector. One declared, "Were I, innocent, accused, my great desire would be to receive such a test. I can conceive of no objection to it except by scoundrels who fear detection." Another one thanked Morse for his effort "to abolish the lie detector for applicants for government jobs" but showed concern about cover-ups: "If there are actions to cover up communists in the State Department

I wish you would take whatever action that becomes necessary to correct this situation." Such sentiments were sometimes embedded in an argument that reversed the claims of patriotism that many former government employees had expressed. "Any true American should not be afraid to take the lie detector test and especially when holding a defense job," announced one letter, adding that Morse and convicted spy Ethel Rosenberg (wife of Julius Rosenberg) "should go to Russia. I doubt if either of you would pass a test."

This view of patriotism, now defined as the willingness to *submit* to a lie detector, was often expressed within the context of an anti–New Deal aversion to elitism: "If that Roosevelt gang Alger Hiss etc. were only given the lie detector test we would be a hell of a lot better off today."[47] Such statements suggested that the lie detector had an egalitarian appeal: it could clear the innocent because it was out of the hands of the East Coast elite associated with the New Deal and the State Department. They also highlighted the class element in polygraph discussions: depending on one's viewpoint, the polygraph could either bring down snobbish elites whose patriotism was questionable or destroy the reputation of qualified Americans who resented their patriotism being questioned.

Anticommunism played a prominent role in Americans' responses to the lie detector. "With the United States actively engaged in battle with the insidious forces of Communism, every good American is more than willing to prove that he is loyal beyond question," another letter stated. Yet showing that anticommunism in the 1950s did not equal McCarthyism, this letter continued, "In order to protect our state secrets, I urge that a careful study be given to the idea of giving lie-detector tests to *all* government servants and employees, from top to bottom. This would be an effective way to deal with crackpots such as Senator McCarran and Senator McCarthy." Similarly, another correspondent stated, "It is, in my opinion, outrageous that a man has to be investigated for government jobs at all. But after the Hiss case, one can sympathize with the suspicion that must be cast on all American citizens. . . . Not only does [the polygraph] save the taxpayer the burden of lengthy, expensive clearance . . . but it is more efficient in catching the disloyal who are growing smarter all the time and may throw investigators off the track indefinitely."[48]

Therefore, some cautious supporters of the lie detector saw it as independent of the political machinations of both New Deal elites and witch hunting demagogues, and efficient in clearing questions of loyalty. We may even hear faint echoes of Hugo Münsterberg's technocratic vision that objective technology would be able to solve political conflicts. Responses to Morse's speech generally showed that the polygraph as a screening tool could be invoked for more than one ideological purpose. Both proponents and opponents claimed refusal and submission as respective markers of patriotism; it could be interpreted both as a harbinger of and protector from totalitarianism, and it could bolster or rein in an intrusive federal bureaucracy. In short, contradictory responses to the polygraph reflected the deeply contradictory response to the threats of totalitarianism from within and without that marked the formation of the American Cold War and resulted in what historian Andrea Friedman calls the "scattershot nature of Cold War repression" that mostly closed, but on occasion also opened, doors for citizen dissent.[49] In Cold War America, William Marston's dream of exercising a therapeutic, loving authority with the polygraph gave way to a grim regime of calculated risk management.

Its boosters praised the polygraph as a prime example of progressive technology in the service of fairer and more efficient administration of justice. Critics such as Dwight Macdonald, however, insisted that "decent human relations cannot be maintained in an atmosphere in which everyone is presumed to be lying." He pointed out that European nations such as West Germany and France rejected the polygraph as "a violation of basic human rights" and closed with the warning that the procedure left no physical traces but hurt "the spirits of a good many government employees" and "the fabric of American democracy."[50] In short, Macdonald feared that intrusive government could sap the democratic ethos of the United States. This was his most basic objection to the polygraph during the "Lie Detector Era."

Macdonald did not spell out whether he favored an all-out ban on the polygraph. He trusted neither people nor institutions, was neither a populist nor a technocrat. He shared with intellectuals like Reinhold Niebuhr and Arthur Schlesinger Jr. a sense that danger was coming from either too much or too little democracy.[51] "Realism" was the new motto for many postwar intellectuals. Macdonald, in addition, agreed with another prominent cultural critic, literary scholar Lionel Trilling, that in technocratic America there was "a drift toward a denial of the emotions and the imagination" that was as deplorable as it was irresistible.[52] In the critic's eye, the polygraph might have been another instance of a culture bent on simplifying and organizing human complexity. But maybe not all scientific means of surveying and measuring the individual had to be dismissed. Was it not better to keep an eye on dangerously fragile modern man? Indeed, it should be noted that many critics of U.S. postwar society came from new academic disciplines, such as sociology and social psychology, which argued that observable data confirmed the validity of their dire warnings. Beginning with Erich Fromm's survey of Frankfurt workers' attitude toward authority in the family in 1932, which fueled the Frankfurt School's rejection of traditional Marxist trust in the working class as the carrier of progress, empirical study of popular attitudes became a major feature of postwar social science. Examples of such works are Theodor Adorno's *The Authoritarian Personality* and David Riesman's *The Lonely Crowd,* both published in 1950.[53] The irony here was that some critics used broad generalizations derived from one form of testing—the survey with questionnaires—to diagnose the ills of a society becoming atomized by, among other things, too much testing.

Lionel Trilling recognized that irony when he analyzed the relation between measuring human experience and social engineering. As he explained in an essay on the first Kinsey Report of 1948, "There is something repulsive in the idea of men being studied for their own good. . . . The act of understanding becomes an act of control." Trilling compared the social sciences to loving parents smothering their children with understanding. And yet, as science had come to dominate culture, "perhaps only science could effectively undertake the task of freeing sexuality from science itself." In other words, Trilling hoped that scientific proof of the variety of human experience could counteract tendencies to enforce uniform cultural norms through science, as he claimed the science of sexuality had done before Kinsey: "There is something right in turning the Report loose on the American public—it turns the American public loose on the Report. . . . And perhaps only science could effectively undertake the task of freeing sexuality from science itself. Nothing so much as science has reinforced the moralistic or religious prohibitions in regards to sexuality."[54]

Relating Alfred Kinsey's approach to the study of sex and the polygraph's approach to the detection of deception is instructive. In their
methodologies, the two could not have been more different. Kinsey
used sympathetic interviews with subjects who volunteered to give
intimate details about themselves and would remain anonymous in his
published study. He collected specific data from which he and his team
drew general conclusions. The polygraph exam was the exact opposite. It used a confrontational procedure, based on general assumptions about human physiology, to extract intimate specific details from
people who were reminded in subtle or not-so-subtle ways that they
better "volunteer" for the test. These data were used to judge specific
individuals as to their veracity and in cases of larger screening procedures, to predict future behavior. Kinsey's research design and many of
his conclusions were later subjected to methodological criticisms from
fellow scientists, but for the public, and Kinsey himself, his research
still posed the supremely uncomfortable question of just how much
intimate detail about the inner lives of individuals society could take,
and how quickly private inclinations could interfere with supposedly
objective research.[55]

In this fundamental sense, public responses to the *Reports* showed
a resemblance between Kinsey's softer scientific reach into the human
psyche and the polygraph's direct confrontation between authority and
the isolated individual.[56] On first look Kinsey's *Sexual Behavior in the
Human Male* bluntly juxtaposed scientifically gathered facts with social
norms. It claimed that 37 percent of American men had had at least one
homosexual encounter since puberty and that 4 percent were exclu-
sively homosexual. Such findings caused a public outcry of various
public authorities, as when *Life* magazine called the study "an assault
on the family as a basic unit of society, a negation of moral law, and a
celebration of licentiousness." Kinsey's study on American women in
1953, which found, among other things, that 25 percent of white middle-
class women under forty had committed adultery and that almost half
of American women had engaged in premarital sex, caused even more
vicious responses in its attack on prevailing ideas of the asexual woman
who was allegedly happy to please only her husband and had few if any
sexual needs of her own.[57]

But was this research strictly descriptive? Trilling didn't think so (and neither did Kinsey's conservative critics). Counting orgasms may have already suggested that more was better. By making human sexuality measurable, Trilling charged, Kinsey silently made quantity a measure of quality. In other words, objective data assumed a normative function: "It [the study] is itself by no means averse to letting the idea of the Natural develop quietly into the idea of the Normal."[58] Trilling came down in support of Kinsey's research only because he believed society would be better off confronting its prevailing norms with the norms implicit in Kinsey's numbers. In other words, the impact of Kinsey's research was not a function of simply "letting the numbers speak," and Trilling supported it due to his own conviction that there were too many sexual double standards prevailing in the United States.

We can apply the issue of quantity and quality to the lie detector: It was not necessarily liberating when employers knew what their employees had confessed to during polygraph exams and judged them on a quantifiable measurement (their physiological responses) and voluntary (but in reality forced) confessions rather than the full context of their individual experience. What if a government authority replaced the empathetic scientist? Who would be in charge of deciding which intimate details were relevant to judging a person's loyalty or security reliability and which were not? Such fundamental questions required a broad social consensus. Answers to them were not implicit in the data itself.

One group of people particularly isolated from protection by law or group solidarity were homosexual Americans, the first and most viciously attacked victims of McCarthyism. Among countless other Americans, thousands of young homosexuals had come to Washington, DC, in the 1930s and 1940s to work for the new federal agencies created by the New Deal and World War II. The constant coming-and-going of federal employees had created a tolerant atmosphere in the capital. Homosexuals were one group who *profited* from the more anonymous, uprooted urban life decried by so many social scientists. While Kinsey's research was received by many gays and lesbians as liberating and would prove so generally in the long run, at the time it arguably contributed to their persecution due to the attention the reports focused on the issue of homosexuality.[59]

Beginning in 1947, the State Department used polygraph exams together with a master list of people implicated in any investigation on homosexuality (by 1950 the list contained approximately 3,000 names) and close cooperation with the vice squad of the Washington police department. After a 1950 Senate investigation, the effort picked up faster pace. A 1952 manual for interrogators included a nine-page section on recognizing gays that suggested profiling of applicants by asking about "hobbies, associates, means of diversion, places of amusement, etc." as well as "unusual traits of speech, appearance, or personality." In case of suspicion, a polygraph would be given.[60] Under President Eisenhower, former FBI agent Scott McLeod purged homosexuals from the State Department even more aggressively. The FBI's Sex Deviate program passed information on to many other government agencies. Historian David Johnson estimates that these investigations led to about 1,000 alleged homosexuals dismissed from State Department service and 5,000 overall from government service.[61]

Attacks on homosexuality had a strong political quality, for suggesting that liberal diplomats were closet homosexuals was part and parcel of McCarthyite rhetoric. Next to the intended emasculating effect, the "advantage" of such charges was that the accuser did not have to prove disloyal behavior, such as espionage, on the side of the accused. Rather, private impropriety (that, as the argument went, could be used to blackmail a person) could earn somebody the label "security risk," which under President Eisenhower became sufficient reason for dismissal from government service. Further, the charge of homosexuality had a convenient self-fulfilling quality: the more public condemnation of "risky" behavior one could whip up, the bigger the scandal such behavior could potentially cause, which in turn made blackmail potentially more devastating.

While prominent figures in the Truman administration such as the diplomats Dean Acheson and Charles Bohlen could count on their high public profile for protection, a lesser-known figure such as Charles Thayer, Bohlen's brother-in-law and former head of Voice of America, the official U.S. propaganda radio service, was momentarily dismissed in 1951 when he confessed to one homosexual act and a subsequent polygraph test found him to be a homosexual (a second test was judged inconclusive). Thayer promptly traveled to Switzerland, where he requested a battery of other tests, including sodium pentothal and a Rorschach test, and received the happy diagnosis that he was not gay.[62] However, most suspected security risks lacked the option of finding the right test to exonerate them. Many of them resigned preemptively when suspicion fell on them. Leonarde Keeler himself had been fully aware of the way polygraph exams invited piecemeal confessions of singular acts (as had been the case with Thayer), especially when the interrogator stressed that confessions in the pretest interview could clear the way for the test itself. When the test would show more suspicious jumps corresponding with the suspect's answers, further partial admissions eventually allowed the interpretive jump to full diagnosis: admissions of singular acts could be added up to "homosexuality"—and therefore "security risk"—as the final judgment on the subject.[63]

The Lavender Scare continued into the 1960s. FBI director J. Edgar Hoover in particular remained on the lookout for any loosening of restrictions on homosexuals in federal employment. As a response, the East Coast Homophile Organizations (ECHO), an umbrella group that united four different gay rights groups in early 1963, issued a pamphlet "How to Handle a Federal Interrogation." The pamphlet included eleven points of advice, including "sign nothing, take no lie detector test, offer no names."[64] Only in 1975 did the government move away from its policy of making homosexuality a cause for dismissal, with intelligence agencies lagging further behind.[65] This state of affairs powerfully illustrated how the charged political atmosphere of the Cold War made human intentions suspect and how the polygraph was used to unearth evidence of sexual inclinations that could be used politically. In fact, sexualized politics crossed lines of class or political ideology. Joe McCarthy's working-class brand of masculinity competed with the gentile brand of the "imperial brotherhood," in historian Robert Dean's phrase, that many of his establishment opponents represented. Yet both sides employed sexual gossip and homosexual innuendo as a political weapon. For example, liberal columnist Drew Pearson hammered on the alleged intimate relationship between McCarthy's associates Roy Cohn and G. David Schine, and television anchor Edward R. Murrow deftly exploited footage of McCarthy crying after he received flowers from a male admirer. "Queering" McCarthy therefore suggested that he was a demagogue driven by feminine emotions and was not to be trusted.[66] Similarly, gossip about J. Edgar Hoover's alleged cross-dressing ways—and the way contemporary and later political opponents of Hoover came to embrace such gossip—can be seen as evidence that it is impossible to separate political from sexual discourse, as indeed Hoover himself found it impossible to separate private morality from public virtue.[67]

The polygraph's complicity in the Lavender Scare marks the beginning of the use of an allegedly objective technology as one avenue to fix sexual, and with it political, identity at a time when much hard evidence of espionage and other activities was kept secret from the public and from Congress to protect the sources and methods of secret government espionage projects.[68] The American experience in this regard was not unique, given that the Royal Canadian Mounted Police (RCMP), beginning in the late 1950s, also initiated an increasingly comprehensive program to target and remove homosexuals from public life. By 1961, the RCMP had already identified 460 homosexuals and reported that about one-third had either resigned or been removed from public life. By the late 1960s, the number of targeted individuals had risen to about 9,000. The leader of the RCMP effort, Don Wall, described the threat that homosexuals allegedly posed to Canadian national security in similar terms as his U.S. counterparts, namely as one of reliability rather than disloyalty: gays were vulnerable to blackmail, secretive, good at deceiving their surroundings and themselves, did not share the morality of the majority, and kept to themselves.[69]

Significantly, the Canadian Lavender Scare also included the search for a "fruit machine," a psycho-physiological series of tests to detect homosexual orientation in individuals. In a 1980 interview, Wall distanced himself from U.S. use of the polygraph that he had observed in Washington, DC, in the early 1960s:

Their approach . . . tended to be mechanistic. They wanted a gimmick. An easy way of determining whether a guy was a homosexual or not. And their prime tool was the polygraph machine which was used in most of these agencies as part of the selection procedure or if a doubt was raised about a guy's behavior after he had been in the service for a while he would be brought back and was subjected to what to my mind was a pretty horrendous series of tests that were stacked up next to a polygraph and asked a series of very pointed questions the purpose of

which was essentially to arise anxiety to the point where he would confess. . . . I found it to be an intrusive and essentially unfair process. In
the report that I made to the government of Canada when I got back I
strongly recommended against the use of that approach.[70]

However, the research that Carleton University psychologist Frank
Wake pursued on behalf of the Canadian government in the following
years bore more than a passing resemblance to lie detector methodologies. Similar to Hugo Münsterberg's dismissal of Lombroso's criminal
type, Wake rejected the idea of a single homosexual type and assembled
an apparatus of technologies to detect homosexual preference. These
tests included measurements of sweat and perspiration, word association tests, and most significantly a pupillary response test in which
subjects were shown images of nude men and women as well as artistic
depictions of nudity while a camera measured widening of the pupils
in response to the images. Just like the polygraph, this test aimed at
matching nervousness with a distinct involuntary physical response to
specific stimuli in order to identify homosexual inclinations. Just like
with the polygraph, the researchers eventually had to concede that no
specifically homosexual physiological response could be found. Apparently, lack of research subjects killed the project off in 1967.[71]

Blanket suspicion toward homosexuality did not divide the Cold
War camps, either. Heterosexual masculinity and homophobia were a
prominent part of political discourse in communist countries such as
East Germany, where homosexuality was a weapon in interparty rival-
ries and the state security services infiltrated sections of the Lutheran
church providing shelter for homosexuals. Just like U.S. security services, the Ministry for State Security (today known as the "Stasi") saw
gays as part of an unreliable, amoral subculture that was hard to control and vulnerable to foreign blackmail. Yet at the same time it turned
blackmailed homosexuals into informers and on occasion praised their
supposed special talents for treason on behalf of the authorities.[72]

It remains doubtful whether blackmail was ever a significant threat to
either side. As was revealed in the early 1990s, the KGB in 1957 attempted
to blackmail Joseph Alsop into cooperating with Soviet intelligence efforts
after it had obtained pictures of Alsop having sex with a man in a Moscow hotel room. Alsop refused and reported the recruitment attempt.[73]
Since the mid-1920s, such "honey traps" were part of the communist

intelligence repertoire, but they were mostly used against heterosexual individuals, primarily single women who worked in administrative positions.[74] In the words of former KGB General Oleg Kalugin, "The CIA and Western intelligence services used sexual blackmail against our people, and we employed it even more frequently against our adversaries. Catching people with their pants down was a prime way of compromising and recruiting them. As long as men would be men and women would be women, lust would play a role in the spy wars."[75]

Fear of subversion, therefore, tended to reinforce preexisting sociocultural prejudices on both sides of the Iron Curtain. It led to the cultural construction of a radically different enemy and inaugurated state oppression of populations deemed unreliable through attempts to identify and exclude them. The polygraph fit into the American version of this Cold War construction.

As things stood in the 1940s and 1950s, hard evidence of citizen loyalty or disloyalty was often missing, so insinuation and doubt reigned. In this context, critics such as Dwight Macdonald also decried the use of the polygraph as a way to taunt political opponents. Lie detectors worked perfectly as part of such stagecraft. Both Congressman Richard Nixon and Senator Joseph McCarthy, the two politicians most willing to make political careers by unearthing communist elements in the federal government, publicly challenged their respective opponents to take or refuse lie detector tests, since refusal to take the test could easily be interpreted as an indirect admission of guilt. At the height of McCarthy's power in 1953, *The Reporter* commented on "the vogue of the lie detector:" "Whenever anything we say is called a lie by somebody, we may be invited to take a lie-detector test. Our devotion to our country, to our family, or to plain decency may have to be checked by a mechanical gadget."[76] The art of the bluff was nothing new in American political discourse, but the lie detector added an aura of scientific neutrality and efficiency to it. The scientific credentials of the technology were just serious enough to be intimidating.

Nixon succeeded in damaging the credibility of former State Department employee Alger Hiss. He used the polygraph to highlight the perception of Hiss among conservatives as an insincere, rootless bureaucrat who had lacked the will to resist communism. McCarthy similarly used the polygraph as a public threat and taunt, demanding tests of witnesses in congressional hearings, of those who were subjects of loyalty investigations, and generally of any government officials in "sensitive posts" throughout the heyday of his notoriety. Macdonald quoted McCarthy as browbeating a witness with the taunt, "I think you are lying! I do not think you can fool the lie detector. You may be able to fool us. I have been told you are very, very smart. . . . I am convinced you cannot fool the lie detector."[77]

Yet McCarthy also used the polygraph to play defense. Before the Senate investigation into McCarthy's own improprieties, he suggested polygraph tests for all witnesses, including himself. In statements before the press he repeatedly stressed the scientific stature of the machine, expressing his "complete confidence in this scientific instrument when it is operated properly" and stressing that only voluntary examination was admissible, "otherwise it would be a violation of [witnesses'] Fifth Amendment rights against self-incrimination."[78] Therefore, McCarthy could point at the polygraph's veneer of scientific neutrality and highlight his concern for correct and constitutional procedure, while still profiting from its intimidating effect. After all, who could possibly object to an effective, neutral procedure? If all participants agreed on the polygraph, McCarthy intoned, "we might be able to end this thing in twenty-four hours rather than twenty-four days."[79] Thus McCarthy used the polygraph as a taunt to attack others and to protect himself.

Alger Hiss confronted such pressures in 1948 when Richard Nixon and the House Un-American Activities Committee (HUAC) goaded him to take a polygraph. A lawyer himself, Hiss after the trial professed to realize that polygraphs were "unreliable booby traps" that were dangerous "because of the impression [their] casual mention by the Committee might make on a technically uninformed public." However, in the very act of expressing his reservations toward the polygraph, Hiss had to credit its proximity to scientific procedure—in other words its public reputation—by adding, "I certainly don't want to duck anything that has scientific or sound basis."[80] Hiss was cornered, since Nixon's taunt to fly in Leonarde Keeler, "a prominent Chicago criminologist" and "the leading authority in the Nation" on polygraphs, was reported in the press. Nixon convinced HUAC chairman Parnell Thomas to allow "a scientific lie test" if Hiss volunteered.[81] Nixon banked on the adverse effect on public opinion that Hiss's refusal of the polygraph would have. To that end, the congressman made sure that his offer to Hiss was leaked to the newspapers before Hiss had a chance to weigh his options. Nixon used his power over government secrets deftly as he pitted the polygraph's scientific reputation against Hiss's reputational defense.[82]

The spectacle of Alger Hiss refusing the polygraph resembled many other courtroom scenes in which Americans accused of disloyalty asserted constitutional protection against self-incrimination ("taking the Fifth") and countless accusers interpreted such assertions as indirect admissions of guilt. Disloyalty was rarely proven in these performances. Rather, for many contemporary observers the purpose of getting witnesses to implicate others was to establish a public record of willingness to submit to security procedures—in other words to participate in a ritual that affirmed the purpose of the investigations. In the same vein, Whittaker Chambers's willingness to undergo a polygraph examination to prove his claim that Alger Hiss had been a communist spy was an example of the ritual performed by scores of other friendly witnesses who "named names" of supposed subversives in a public display of loyalty. To inform was therefore a character test in which individuals had to affirm their personal aversion against denunciation by prefacing their confessions with expressions of disgust, only to proceed to give away names anyway.[83] Similarly, Nixon juxtaposed Chambers's willingness to take the test with Hiss's refusal, as Ken Alder put it, "[as] pitting unrehearsed frankness against elitist shilly-shallying."[84]

In short, polygraph tests had to fit a narrative, yet they threatened to take away authority of individuals over their own life story. Few people in early Cold War America knew more about the power of narrative than Chambers himself. His 1952 autobiography *Witness* made Chambers a significant figure in postwar U.S. history. Apart from the hard evidence in the form of documents he produced from a pumpkin on his farm, the reasons Whittaker Chambers became a celebrated figure of the conservative movement were the pathos of his conversion story (including an attempted suicide), the gravitas his elegant writings bestowed on his anticommunism, and the apparent earnestness of his repentance. The perpetually ill-clothed and overweight Chambers even *looked* like a martyr. The polygraph was only one element in this religious conversion narrative. As he wrote in *Witness*, "There is a difference of opinion about the accuracy of the lie detector test. . . .

Nevertheless, I did not believe it possible that a test which had been in use some time, could possibly be so far out that it would fail to show a preponderance of truth, when truth was spoken, over error. Therefore, I answered yes."[85] While admitting to some mistakes in his testimony (Hiss's defense would especially target the fact that Chambers had initially erred in dating his first meeting with Hiss), Chambers throughout the trial insisted on a "preponderance of truth" in his testimony. His humble attitude toward the polygraph reflected the general image of the humble sinner that Chambers tried to project through his writings.

His supporters had better reasons to believe Whittaker Chambers than a lie detector test, but offering to take the test added credibility to Chambers's apparent willingness to submit to higher authority. In his memoirs Chambers averred, "Between man's purpose in time and God's purpose in eternity, there is an infinite difference in quality."[86] Chambers professed a faith without certainty and yet brimmed with missionary conviction. Even political opponents such as Arthur Schlesinger Jr. admired his passion and the courage of his choice against communism, even if they rejected Chambers's insistence on Christianity as the only effective counter-faith. However, liberals such as Schlesinger had difficulty agreeing on a measure to distinguish principled from fanatical anticommunism and remained divided by McCarthyism. Chambers, on the other hand, had shown courage and moreover managed to reconcile metaphysical doubt with political certainty, at least during his time at the center of public controversy. Eventually Chambers lost faith in the sincerity of McCarthy's brand of anticommunism and withdrew into private life.[87]

The public spectacle of various polygraph tests probably changed few partisan minds on either side of an emotional political confrontation. Maybe Hiss was more correct than he realized when he pointed out that the polygraph "registere[d] more emotion than anything else." An additional irony was that delivering more credible emotional testimony would in fact have *bolstered* Hiss's case, since even his supporters despaired at Hiss's apparent aloofness and came to doubt his assertion that "I am not lacking emotion in this business."[88] Since the whole affair seemed to leave Hiss a tad too unconcerned, we might wonder if a "failed" polygraph test would have helped Hiss's credibility by making a mechanical case for his professed outrage at the accusations against him. As for Whittaker Chambers, he offered to take another polygraph test on live television for the program *Newsweek Views the News* during Hiss's first perjury trial in 1949. Chambers had to be dissuaded by the FBI and prosecutor Thomas Murphy, who both feared that the publicity might taint the jury pool.[89]

In the highly politicized context of HUAC's and McCarthy's investigations, the polygraph's resemblance to scientific procedure therefore did little to alleviate political polarization among partisan lines. Just as Nixon's supporters could take Hiss's refusal to take the polygraph as a sure sign of guilt, Hiss's defenders on the political left condemned it as "trial by ordeal" that mostly worked because "many criminals have been so frightened by the prospect of having to take the test that they have confessed while sitting around waiting for it to start," as one editorial put it. One's attitude toward the polygraph could therefore mark one's political position in the early Cold War period, and apart from two retrospective fluff pieces on August Vollmer and the early days of polygraphing in Berkeley, published in *Reader's Digest* in 1947, press coverage of the polygraph was rarely as starry-eyed during the Cold War as it had been during the 1920s and 1930s.[90] In the occasional popular culture reference, such as a 1955 episode of the TV police drama *Highway Patrol,* the lie detector helped clear a wrongfully suspected citizen and cornered the real culprit who dutifully maintained that polygraph evidence was not admissible in court and could not be believed.[91] However, at a time when many demanded a "realistic" attitude toward the "ironic" if not "tragic" nature of current times, hard-boiled depictions of the polygraph did not necessarily disqualify it.

We can therefore conclude that the polygraph was one marker used to establish boundaries in the midst of political controversies in the early Cold War. In an age when many Americans feared an unknown enemy, the "scientific" polygraph promised *some* clarity. Yet contrary to that promise, it tended to amplify confrontations over totalitarianism, particularly questions of whether it could happen in the United States as well. These debates took place in many arenas. While especially early Cold War television tended to idealize law enforcement, even no-holds-barred patriotic movies of the early fifties, such as *My Son John, I Led Three Lives,* or *I Was a Communist for the FBI,* made room for some ambivalence. These movies portrayed the impending breakdown of family structures under the strain of communist duplicity and immorality, but also—often inadvertently—by invasive FBI surveillance methods and mutual suspicion among Americans. Either way, the role of economic and social conditions in shaping political views was largely absent from public discourse, despite America's rapidly growing economy and the impact it had on political and social relations. As a result, psychologized depictions of the communist menace often hinted at seduction and confused sexuality as a major source of political deviance.[92]

To return once more to the iconic figure of Alger Hiss: the aloof bureaucrat embodied vague anxiety rather than concrete fear of totalitarianism. Stephen Whitfield asserts that Hiss "wore no beard, spoke with no accent. . . . [He looked like] the man in the office across the hall on Wall Street or State Street. If this man could be a spy, anybody could."[93] Perhaps we should specify: Hiss spoke with no foreign accent, but he embodied the weak, effeminate white-collar bureaucrat who could be a communist, a homosexual, or a spy.[94] For those who voiced open or silent support for McCarthyism, the western organization man and not the eastern anarchist threatened American democracy in the early Cold War, and the polygraph was often, but not always, their weapon. On the other hand, members of the East Coast elite such as Charles Thayer, who saw themselves now under attack by descendants of Irish-Catholic or Eastern European immigrants, associated the polygraph with danger coming from people they still considered newcomers. Privately, Thayer mused that "their devilish polygraph" helped McCarthy and his fellow thugs to "abandon the old Anglo-Saxon standards of justice and ethics and replace them by a system of terror modeled on the European dictators, of the Gestapo and GPU."[95]

The spectacular comings and goings of Nixon and McCarthy gave mid-1950s scholars occasion to ponder the larger implications of growing security culture on the one hand and continuing acrimony in public debate on the other. The result was a call for moderation. However, the demise of spectacular congressional hearings in the mid-1950s did not end the systemic, behind-the-scenes anticommunism the FBI had practiced all along and would continue to practice until the post-

Watergate/post-Vietnam period. This style of anticommunism depended
on silent subversion of allegedly communist organizations, anonymous
informants, and wire-tapping. Even though his FBI had maintained close
ties to HUAC, McCarthy, and other theatrical anticommunists, J. Edgar
Hoover was protective of the institutional power of the Bureau.[96] Therefore, invasive security procedures remained uncontested if they
appeared to be "moderated" by common sense and bureaucratic control. In a similar move, the Eisenhower administration would adopt a
policy of managing the Cold War by finding the right middle ground
between complacency and panic. Avoiding extremes was the political
motto of the mid- to late 1950s.

The question was whether the polygraph would find a place in this
normalized Cold War. The Eisenhower administration was soon concerned that it could lose control over purges it had helped spark by
appointing the zealous McLeod to rid the State Department of homosexuals. As a consequence, Eisenhower and Secretary of State John Foster Dulles denied Joseph McCarthy's request to have Charles Bohlen
polygraphed when Eisenhower nominated Bohlen for the post of
ambassador to the Soviet Union in 1953. Dulles did not "want to take
the risk of using a test" that could "produce confusion" and "would
not be reliable." In other words, the polygraph might not produce the
desired clearance for Bohlen.[97]

The polygraph, a loose gun and potentially dangerous to the national
security state itself in the wrong hands, subsequently became involved
in debates over the proper administration of state secrecy. Sociologist
Edward Shils argued in 1956 that in the age of nuclear power and global
conflict, concerns about securing vital information became intertwined
with deeper cultural and indeed psychic conflicts. Shils saw American
history full of those conflicts. Nativism was nothing new in a nation
assimilating a constant influx of immigrants from various ethnic backgrounds. Fear of subversion was maybe natural in a society that professed to demand from citizens nothing more than sincere loyalty to
its political system. Public theater and populist demagoguery might be
unavoidable in a freewheeling federal democracy that pitted regional
and ideological camps against each other in a regular succession of
elections. But in the age of totalitarian enemies and nuclear secrets,
the stakes in these conflicts had been raised. The result was an intense

symbolic battle involving politicians, scientists, businessmen, and intellectuals that seriously threatened "the balance of publicity, privacy and secrecy which will maintain liberties." Shils warned that the result was increasing polarization between two camps, one demanding absolute security and unquestionable loyalty, the other casting itself as the defender of American liberty. Both extremes were dangerous: "The perfectionists of security and loyalty, like the perfectionists of justice and freedom, are a menace to freedom, to justice and security and to the order to which loyalty is demanded."[98] In the political climate of the 1950s, Shils found "an irrational adhesion of the three elements: fear of secrets, dependence on secrets, and dependence on publicity."[99] Suspecting conspiracy behind every façade chipped away at American democracy because it was intolerant of the differences people had beyond their agreement on the basic values of civil justice and liberty.

Shils's call for moderation and balance had great currency among intellectuals at the time. Historians like Richard Hofstadter agreed that the succession of international crises since World War II had opened an unlimited field for the paranoid imagination of domestic populists.[100] However, as we have seen, it was not only the populist demagogues like McCarthy who demanded the surrender of privacy, but indeed the very governmental agencies that McCarthy and the other populists attacked. Partly as a response to McCarthy's attacks, the executive shut the doors to congressional inquiries. The East Coast elites heavily represented in much of the U.S. foreign policy establishment had their own cult of secrecy and conspiracy, and after the conservative onslaught on the New Deal, the CIA became "one of [the elite's] last throws, a secret bastion of power that could be shielded from democratic scrutiny on the pretext of national security."[101] My examination of the polygraph, therefore, shows that it was a weapon that worked both ways, as a shield of the bureaucracy and a sword of the populist challengers, because even the most mundane bureaucratic procedures could be politicized.

As we have seen, the development of the polygraph as an employee-screening device predated government use. The ubiquity of the polygraph in postwar America cannot, therefore, be explained as a trickle-down effect of national security practices, as some contemporaries claimed.[102] Rather, the language of protecting commodities, such as money handled in banks, expensive items sold in jewelry stores, and so on, began to be applied to government and the commodity it now had to protect—state secrets. Businesses before and during the Cold War argued that polygraphing employees could bring down the costs of defrauding. *American Business* estimated in 1951 that defrauding by employees cost U.S. businesses around $600 million (one of many numbers used) and advised: "Business seems justified in taking every possible precaution to safeguard its funds and property. The person who wants a position of responsibility should be willing to undergo such a test in order to get it."[103] In the Cold War the polygraph augmented the case to protect precious commodities (material or symbolic), but it intensified preexisting anxieties about the probing eye of an all-knowing totalitarian government.

Polygraph debates further emphasized the need to keep an eye on the weak, effeminate American male who was susceptible to undue sexual, moral, and political influences. For example, beginning in 1953, Americans could read about low morale that supposedly had prevailed among POWs in Korean prison camps. In stark contrast to the manly resolve of past generations of American servicemen captured by the enemy, these soldiers were missing "the historical American standards of honor, character, loyalty, courage and personal integrity."[104] Even more shocking stories told of American Airmen accusing the military of waging germ warfare, and POW's refusing repatriation during prisoner exchanges in early 1954. Such outrageous behavior led to theories of "brainwashing," a term popularized by journalist Edward Hunter in a string of books, most prominently 1951's *Brainwashing in Red China*. Fears of the unlimited power of behaviorist methods of using outside stimuli to break an individual mind and change somebody's core beliefs resonated with journalists such as Vance Packard. The general public came to suspect that weak modern individuals, especially young men who were raised by overbearing mothers, apparently lacked the moral core to resist the power of reward and punishment. These debates were not created by the results of polygraph tests, but the lie detector fit the agenda of those who were concerned about "soft" American men.

Just as the hysteria generated by the public phase of McCarthyism subsided after 1954, most Americans eventually awoke from this Cold War nightmare. By the early 1960s, three major studies commissioned by the Air Force and the Army found no correlation between POWs' political beliefs and their inclinations toward collaborating with their captors. In addition, British psychologist Cyril Cunningham agreed with American physicians Lawrence Hinkle and Harold Wolff of Cornell University, who researched communist interrogation methods for the CIA, that sense deprivation and isolation were much more likely explanations for the behavior of some captured servicemen than insidious Pavlovian techniques to reprogram the brain. Similarly, upon closer inspection, communist "brainwashing" in the POW camps for United Nations soldiers turned out to be straightforward ideological indoctrination.[105] However, just as the end of public confrontations and show trials did not end political suppression of dissent, the end of the brainwashing panic did not inaugurate greater trust in the American consumer citizen among political and scientific elites. In fact, a kind of "silent" McCarthyism, characterized by institutionalized surveillance of suspect citizens, continued in the United States and among its allies across the Atlantic.[106]

"Vital Center" liberals such as Edward Shils mistakenly ascribed obsession with secrets not only to those they considered "radicals" on the Right such as Richard Nixon and Joe McCarthy, but also to men on the Left such as C. Wright Mills, whom Shils called "a sort of Joe McCarthy of Sociology."[107] Yet they were correct in highlighting how international affairs had raised the stakes for domestic political debates. Therefore, concern with keeping and uncovering secrets continued, driven by institutionalized national security policies and continuing Cold War tensions. The "Sputnik Shock" of 1957 replaced fears of immediate conventional war and the popular appeal of communism to "soft" Americans with an equally intense apprehension over Soviet technological capabilities. The complacency of the weak-willed American consumer remained a concern, but now it was in the face of Soviet industrial prowess rather than communism's subversive powers of persuasion.[108] With this "technological analog to the Red Scare," totalitarian victory remained just around the corner.[109]

Sociologist Francis Rourke concluded in 1961 that all branches of federal government—executive bureaucracy, Congress, and the courts—bore responsibility for creating a regime of official secrecy. Rourke found no fewer than 172 federal statutes permitting or encouraging the withholding of information from the public in 1960, citing as a prominent example the Atomic Energy Act of 1946. However, Rourke also noted that secrecy was only the flip side of publicity and warned, "Through the skillful use of secrecy and publicity [the government] can wield an influence over public opinion not altogether different from that enjoyed by the autocrats of modern totalitarianism." Nowhere was this ability more striking than in "defense and foreign affairs," but many government agencies, Rourke found, began to use "possession of countless records of private citizens and business firms" and the threat of publicizing evidence of illegal activity to enforce compliance in the private sector.[110]

For Rourke as for Shils, the American tradition of scrutinizing government had to be counterbalanced with the legitimate need for government secrecy. Finding the middle ground between these two poles was the task of democracy, and, as we have seen, the polygraph was equally concerned with protecting secrets (shielding information from subversive elements) and publicizing them (the public shaming of suspected subversives). Therefore, the polygraph had become part of the "dilemma" of democracy in Cold War America.

CHAPTER 5

Truth and National Security in the American Cold War

When George Kennan, the father of the Containment doctrine, resigned from the State Department in early 1953, he decried his failure to forge what he considered a rational American Cold War strategy. Instead of clear-headed pursuit of a cogent policy, Kennan only saw a farrago of lofty goals miles ahead of the means to achieve them. Kennan also noticed a new watchword: national security. He fumed: "Like any political absolute, the idea of service to the 'national security' is used as a stalking horse for 1000 ulterior purposes and often assumes forms that constitute an invitation to ridicule."[1] Ridiculous or not, in the formation of the American Cold War, "national security" became the dominant doctrine to implement Cold War policies. Administrations from President Truman on asserted wide authority to define which expressions of citizen dissent were inside and outside legitimate government control and which actions by foreign leaders constituted an attack on American national security.

The crucial innovation, as legal philosopher Giorgio Agamben argues, was not that the government asserted power to respond to emergency situations, but rather that it claimed *ahead of* any specific emergency a potentially unlimited freedom to do so.[2] In defining American Cold War strategy, I take my cue from Anders Stephanson's observation that "there is no strategy, and certainly no account of it, that is not at the same time discursive and ideological."[3] To analyze the U.S. pursuit of "national security" therefore assumes that means and ends of foreign policy were not self-evident to policymakers or to the public, but were subject to question and change. Further, the pursuit of these goals was not simply a reaction to policies of the Soviet Union. Rather, it emanated from what policymakers defined as deeply held American ideals as well as specific policy goals.[4] Attention to how abstract core values translate into specific policies assumes neither coherence nor consensus. Instead, by explicitly questioning "national security" as a discourse, we can examine the role it played in forging a consensus that often obscured how specific policies were supposed to realize American values. We should therefore be aware that "national security" was never a clear or uncontested doctrine. If U.S. government agencies time and again justified using the polygraph with the needs of "national security," incoherence in the use of the machine can explain incoherence in the term "national security," and vice-versa.

U.S. policymakers often presented the Cold War as a competition of truth against lie, open press against censorship, pragmatic problem-solving against ideological rigidity, and a national community of mutual trust against a top-down political system based on intimidation. In this chapter I further explore the discursive and institutional context of national security on the one hand and the core value of truthfulness on the other hand by discussing the role of propaganda and covert action in the creation of truth as a core value in U.S. national security policies as they developed in the early Cold War. It was this context, I argue, that gave the polygraph a discursive and institutional home and made it a productive technology to further cement the discourse and institutions of national security. In short, I argue that the polygraph became an integral part of the American Cold War.

Propaganda was a way to explain *and* to fight the Cold War. It was used to counter Soviet competition in contested areas, rally the home front in the United States and allied countries, and pave the way for more aggressive intervention if necessary. Yet the paradox of U.S. Cold War propaganda was that denial was part of its practice. After all, only totalitarian societies used propaganda, according to American Cold War discourse. Moreover, early U.S. propagandists soon realized that strident words had to be followed by strident action to remain credible, which was not always prudent in the Atomic Age. Therefore, truth in propaganda had to be contained, controlled, and managed.

Propaganda was ubiquitous at the end of World War II. Nazi Germany had fought a racial *Weltanschauungskrieg*, a war of ideologies, to the bitter end, and the Soviet Union had imposed a strict top-bottom ideological interpretation of world events that posed "monopoly capitalism" as the root of fascist expansionism (and would apply that interpretation both to Nazi and U.S. Cold War policies). Even western democracy seemed incapable of expressing its political values without obfuscation. In his 1946 essay "Politics and the English Language," George Orwell identified the connection between language and the disastrous politics of his time:

> In our time, political speech and writings are largely the defense of the indefensible. Things like the continuance of British rule in India, the Russian purges and deportations, the dropping of the atom bombs on Japan, can indeed be defended, but only by arguments which are too brutal for most people to face, and which do not square with the professed aims of political parties. Thus political language has to consist largely of euphemism, question-begging and sheer cloudy vagueness. . . . In our age there is no such thing as "keeping out of politics." All issues are political issues, and politics itself is a mass of lies, evasions, folly, hatred, and schizophrenia.[5]

Obfuscating rhetoric also served diplomatic purposes. President Roosevelt exhausted himself fashioning a personal relationship of trust with Stalin, glossing over ideological and strategic differences. He cabled Winston Churchill in 1942, "I think I can personally handle Stalin better than either your Foreign Office people or my State Department. Stalin hates the guts of all you top people. He thinks he likes me better, and I hope he will continue to do so." On occasion of the opening of the Dumbarton Oaks conference in August 1944, which established the ground rules for the postwar United Nations organization, FDR asserted, "I got to know him [Stalin], he got to know me . . . you cannot hate the man that you know well." At the Tehran conference in November 1943 and on other occasions, Roosevelt's Soviet ambassador Averell Harriman overheard him give Stalin assurances that the United States understood Russia's desire for "friendly" regimes in eastern Europe, and that Roosevelt would not "start a war" over Soviet policies in Baltic states.[6] For many U.S. policymakers, Roosevelt's strategy seemed to be built on vague promises and doubletalk, but for the president, personal trust between leaders and diplomacy conducted with a wink and smile were indispensable.[7]

The situation fundamentally changed in the summer of 1945, not only because of Roosevelt's death, but also because Germany and Japan finally collapsed and wartime rhetoric needed to be forged into institutional forms. When U.S. and Soviet priorities began to diverge and mutual distrust ensued, U.S propaganda began to define the two countries as defined by radically different core values. Under President Harry Truman and thereafter, U.S. foreign policy became less idiosyncratic than under FDR and instead was based on achieving bureaucratic consensus on how to translate Roosevelt's war for freedom into specific policies.

However, despite this shift in style, the United States did not give up on FDR's insistence that freedom was indivisible—in other words, that the United States could not be secure until freedom everywhere was secure and that therefore nothing short of "unconditional surrender" of the enemy was acceptable. The inability of American policymakers to solve specific issues of postwar reconstruction in Europe and Asia developed in an inverse relationship to the ideological rigidity that these policymakers presented to the voters at home. Faced with many challenges in the fragile postwar world, the United States thus continued to take on vague enemies such as "totalitarianism," "chaos," and "expansionism." In such a conception of total threat, there was little room for personal trust building and deal making until much later in the era of détente. For ten years after the Potsdam meeting of July–August 1945, there would be no summit between the United States and the Soviet Union.[8]

Already during the Second World War, Anglo-American intellectuals had averred that Western democracy represented truth and that truthful propaganda worked best. British and American psych-warrior-scholars such as F. C. Bartlett, Richard Crossman, and Daniel Lerner argued that forcefully distributed white propaganda in the form of leaflets and radio broadcasts against German populations and soldiers was most effective.[9] Their attitude might well have been genuine, but it also reflected the favorable strategic situation of the Allies since 1943: Allied propaganda could afford truthfulness about the military situation more than Nazi propaganda. In the Cold War, the situation was similar. Edward Barrett, a former *Newsweek* editor who acted as Assistant Secretary of State for Public Affairs from 1950 to 1953, defined the double task of fighting for and with truth in his book *Truth Is Our Weapon*. Once confronted with the exhortation not to be "too squeamish" about the truth in propaganda, Barrett recalled himself replying, "I argued that truth and truth alone should be America's weapon in official propaganda." While maintaining adherence to truth as an inner value defining American identity, Barrett nevertheless continued, "Those of us who argue for sticking to the truth are not solely motivated by ethics. We are convinced that truth offers not only the moral course but the cold, practical, effective course."[10] Such statements, forceful as they may sound, concealed considerable anxiety among American propagandists since World War I about the supposedly weak grasp American citizens had of basic political concepts and their susceptibility to totalitarian propaganda. In some ways, American Cold War information policy was justified as a prophylactic measure: propaganda against propaganda.[11]

After World War II, propaganda[12] institutions such as the Office of War Information (OWI) were dealt budget cuts, but the Truman administration in 1948 upgraded American overt and covert information activities to thwart communist electoral victories in Italy and France. Propaganda often targeted different audiences simultaneously. Beginning with the Italian election, the government rallied ethnic organizations in the United States to support U.S. policies in the old country. Given the popularity Benito Mussolini had enjoyed among some leading Italian Americans before the war, a "Letters to Italy" campaign—in which thousands of Italian Americans wrote to relatives in Italy, encouraging them to reject communism—was a chance to both influence the Italian election and to enforce domestic loyalty in the United States. A similar strategy was pursued in the "Campaign of Truth," beginning in 1950, when the ostensibly private "Common Council for American Unity" began to publish articles in over 900 foreign language publications in the United States, with instructions on how to effectively convey the blessings of liberty to recipients of letters abroad. Shortly thereafter, the United States Information Agency (USIA) also began targeting audiences in Iraq, Egypt, and other Muslim countries, mostly with written materials that emphasized the atheistic nature of Soviet communism.[13] Expanding on the distribution of written material, covert support of "citizens' committees" by the CIA quickly evolved into a vast network of voluntarism. Groups such as the "National Committee for a Free Europe," the "People to People" campaign, or the "National Student Association" all served as CIA front organizations and were consciously modeled after communist fronts—but now in the service of the U.S. core value of truth.[14]

Mao's victory in the Chinese civil war in the fall of 1949 and the stunning outbreak of the Korean War in June 1950 removed second thoughts about pro-active global propaganda among most U.S. policymakers. The United States would invest considerable efforts in the coming decades to advertise and implement freedom all over the world. Yet the failed 1956 Hungarian uprising, encouraged by the CIA-financed Radio Free Europe, posed uncomfortable questions about fiery propaganda and its relation to grand strategy: encouraging the overthrow of communist governments in the age of nuclear war was reckless. While toning down its rhetoric, the United States kept radio, TV, and print media, exchange programs, and other efforts in its repertoire, constantly honing the message and agonizing over the influence (or lack thereof) these measures had on their audiences.[15] In short, from the beginning propaganda was meant to raise morale at home, among allies, and beyond. Policymakers agreed that it was necessary, but its effects were never quite clear.

Cold War policy documents show how American propaganda discourse took shape. A State Department review of the first U.S. propaganda activities from 1950 placed propaganda in U.S. Cold War strategy: "There is wide agreement that the present situation calls for positive action to extend the use of propaganda in support of our common objectives. The threat of Soviet-Communist tyranny cannot be met by material means alone. If we are to achieve the kind of world in which freedom can endure, we must employ all the means at our disposal to strengthen the unity of purpose and the moral determination of the free nations of the world."[16]

Since George Kennan had warned that Soviet-led "propaganda machines" would be utilized "to undermine [the] general political and strategic potential of Western powers," U.S. propaganda was defended as a necessary, not freely chosen, response. The Soviet Union used "deceit, distortion, and lies . . . systematically . . . as a matter of deliberate policy." Only because "the Russians have pitched the battle on the psychological front" did America need "the wherewithal to counter them."[17] Further, Washington policymakers conceived strict loyalty to truth as a marker of Western identity. As William Benton, former Undersecretary of State for Public Affairs, asserted in a speech in 1948, "We are deeply wedded to fact and fair argument. Our social, political, and moral patterns would not permit us to use the Soviet type of propaganda." When the Smith-Mundt Act of 1948 provided congressional sanction for revived propaganda, the new assistant secretary, George Allen declared, "Let us be certain that the Voice of America represents genuine American principles—American democracy and liberty and freedom." This concern with core values led, for example, to propaganda efforts by the State Department to provide publications "which portray America's spiritual and religious values in true perspective," such as *Christian Century* and the Bible in U.S. information centers abroad.[18] American propaganda would not depend on the art of persuasion as much as "the timely and persistent *demonstration* of the superiority of the idea of freedom."[19]

To demonstrate one's own dedication to freedom, American propaganda had to "expose the falsities of Soviet pretentions."[20] George Kennan had pioneered this rhetorical trope in the "Long Telegram" he had written from his station in Moscow in February 1946 to get the attention of his superiors in the State Department. Imbued with "Oriental secretiveness and conspiracy" as well as utter devotion to Marxist-Leninist ideology, "The very disrespect of Russians for objective truth—indeed, their disbelief in its existence—leads them to view all stated facts as instruments for furtherance of one ulterior purpose or another."[21] Kennan repeated this analysis in his 1947 "Mr. X" article in *Foreign Affairs*, which introduced the U.S. Cold War worldview to the domestic elite:

Their [Soviet] particular brand of fanaticism, unmodified by any of the Anglo-Saxon traditions of compromise, was too fierce and too jealous to envisage any permanent sharing of power. From the Russian-Asiatic world out of which they had emerged they carried with them a skepticism as to the possibilities of permanent and peaceful coexistence of rival forces. . . . Here caution, circumspection, flexibility, and deception are the valuable qualities; and their value finds natural appreciation in the Russian or the Oriental mind.

Kennan interpreted totalitarianism as a disease that might befall western societies as well: "[Totalitarianism] is a condition made possible by modern police weapons, a state into which any great national entity *can* relapse, if it doesn't watch its step."[22] He employed the idea of totalitarianism as pathology on other occasions, such as in a talk at Harvard University symposium on totalitarianism in 1954. Here Kennan also called it a "straitjacket" that could be fitted onto every modern society and warned: "I was repelled from the start [in the 1920s] by certain features of Russian Communism apparent even in the shadows: notably, its reckless injustice, its shocking physical cruelty, and its congenital untruthfulness. . . . All societies have varying degrees of vulnerability to totalitarian tendencies and of resistance to them. . . . If we go too far in behaving as they [the Soviets] do, we are lost."[23]

This diagnosis of totalitarianism as an Eastern disease that could spread to the West was a change from earlier assessments. While late nineteenth and early twentieth-century U.S. scholars, journalists, and diplomats working in Russia often decried Russian naïveté and incurable backwardness, they also praised the simple-minded honesty of Russian peasants. After Lenin's ascent to power, however, many American Russia experts asserted that the thin veneer of European civilization had been removed from Russia, and that communist rule took advantage of the Asiatic tendencies among Russians to be apathetic in the face of despotic rule, sluggish, suspicious, cruel, and xenophobic. *New York Times* correspondent William Duranty, for example, synthesized these trades into "Oriental duplicity" in his widely read reporting. Kennan had clearly soaked up these influences upon his first visit to the Soviet Union in 1933, when the United States established diplomatic relations with Stalin's regime.[24]

For Kennan and other Russia specialists, duplicity was an essential marker of Soviet behavior, which they variously explained with geography or ideology. This was the Western technological view on less "civilized" people that we can recognize from earlier periods, as for example when British colonial official Sir William Herschel justified fingerprinting Indians in 1858 and the biologists Edward Henry and Sir Francis Galton, the creators of the modern fingerprint system based on classification of the hand in loops, whorls, and arches, asserted that Westerners would not have to give their prints due to their superior trustworthiness. Creating the self-reporting body—whether in form of mug shots, fingerprints (especially helpful since Westerners often confused dark-skinned subjects on photos) or other technologies such as the polygraph—therefore went hand in hand with ideological juxtapositions of civilized truthfulness with uncivilized deceit.[25]

Soviet ideology also contributed to American discourse of truth as a weapon. Applying his own logic of emergency—namely the need to prepare the road from the dictatorship of the proletariat to the Revolution—Vladimir Lenin espoused a strictly instrumentalist view of morality, asserting that it merely served social ends. Even after his break with Stalin, Leon Trotsky continued to claim that deception was a legitimate means toward a justified end—the communist revolution. In his 1938 essay "Their Morals and Ours," Trotsky argued: "A society without social contradictions will naturally be a society without lies and violence. However there is no way of building a bridge to that society save by revolutionary, that is, violent means. . . . It remains to be added that the very conception of *truth* and *lie* was born of social contradiction."[26]

Like the American national security state, the institutionalized revolution of the Soviet Union therefore declared a necessity as the norm. By doing so, communists ended up letting their goals dictate their means and invited a response in kind from the Americans.[27]

To what ends did Soviet officials lie? As Kennan realized, duplicity could be interpreted as a defensive strategy, namely to conceal how "primitive" and backward the country was. The proverbial "Potemkin Village," ordered by Boris Godunov during the disastrous interregnum of the early seventeenth century to conceal a famine, lent itself to a similar interpretation of Russian deception as a defensive means to hide the sad state of Russian society and economy that western visitors

encountered in travels through the Soviet Union in the 1930s.[28] Stalin
himself often commented on the need to overcome the Russian position of backwardness toward the West, as when he admonished industrial managers in Moscow in 1931: "We are 50 or 100 years behind the
advanced countries. We must make good this distance in 10 years.
Either we do it or they will crush us."[29] American observers could not
easily separate Soviet policies as either based on expansive Marxism-
Leninism or on defensive Oriental (at times also called "Slavic") secretiveness. Even so, Kennan's diagnosis of Soviet expansionism caught
their fancy more than his occasional insistence on their defensiveness.
"Containment" therefore did not offer an unambiguous interpretation
of Soviet duplicity. It was as much Kennan's authoritative tone and the
vividness and comprehensiveness of his depiction of Russian/Soviet
character as the accuracy of his analysis that appealed to military leaders and politicians in Washington. Kennan spoke like a doctor giving
a long awaited diagnosis, and in 1946 U.S. policymakers were eager to
hear what ailed the world situation.[30]

In the 1950s, another aspect of Kennan's diagnosis of the Soviet
threat gained currency among American intellectuals. The *Department
of State Bulletin* ran a series on Soviet methods of information control
and indoctrination toward its own people in 1951, and throughout the
Cold War American social science applied their methodologies to the
analysis of totalitarian society. Academic discourse moved away from
assumptions of a radically different national character and instead
resorted to social science methods to explain Soviet ideology and society.[31] This distinction, to be sure, still allowed American leaders to claim
that their methods were radically different from Soviet ones, but since
universal theories of human development and the availability of modern technology made all societies vulnerable to totalitarianism, America was in danger as well. In the "Long Telegram," Kennan therefore
exhorted Americans to "cling to our own methods and conceptions of
human society. After all, the greatest danger that can befall us in coping
with this problem of Soviet communism is that we shall allow ourselves
to become like those with whom we are coping." U.S. diplomats would
echo this ethos time and again: "As long as we keep constantly in mind
the goal of truth, we have few worries about the outcome of the battle
of ideas. We shall win."[32]

But there were paradoxes in truthful propaganda. Propaganda entailed an inherent impetus toward exaggeration. Could the United States fight fire with fire and not get burned? How are we to understand, for example, Secretary of State Dean Acheson's famous remark that the Truman administration had to sell the danger of communism to Congress by packaging facts in the most effective way? In his memoirs Acheson proclaimed, "The task of a public officer seeking to explain and gain support for a major policy is not that of the writer of a doctoral thesis. . . . If we made our points clearer than the truth, we did not differ from most other educators and could hardly do otherwise."[33] As political scientist John Mearsheimer points out, the role of deception in international politics remains understudied, but politicians such as Dean Acheson more often speak "clearer than truth" to domestic audiences than to foreign leaders, who already assume that their conversation partners will not be completely forthcoming.[34]

Then there was the issue of self-defeating policies. NSC-68, the grand strategy outline that President Truman requested on the eve of the Korean War and that became a powerful Cold War declaration of faith, glossed over the problem of harmonizing means and ends when it stated, "Thus we must make ourselves strong, both in the way in which we affirm our values in the conduct of our national life, and in the development of our military and economic strength." The document affirmed, "Translated into terms relevant to the lives of other peoples, our system of values can become perhaps a powerful appeal to millions."[35] But such a statement already assumed that the creation of the national security state was in harmony with American values. By 1950 Kennan's interpretation of Soviet expansionism as part and parcel of totalitarian government had become a powerful justification for policies of military preparedness and confrontation that represented a departure from the tradition of military demobilization after large conflicts. While Acheson and Truman publicly justified such policies to rally the American public, NSC-68 (mainly drafted by Kennan's successor Paul Nitze) used language just as strident. It therefore implicitly justified the use of potentially questionable means:

Unwillingly our free society finds itself mortally challenged by the Soviet system. No other value system is so wholly irreconcilable to ours,

so implacable in its purpose to destroy ours, so capable of turning to its
own uses the most dangerous and divisive trends in our own society, no
other so skillfully and powerfully evokes the elements of irrationality in
human nature everywhere, and no other has the support of a great and
growing center of military power.[36]

Cold War discourse therefore demanded potentially contradictory
national security policies. From C. Wright Mills's critique of the "Power
Elite" in 1956 to President Dwight Eisenhower's warning about the pro-
defense lobbies of the "Military-Industrial Complex" in 1961, Americans struggled to define the proper relation between means and ends
in the Cold War. The trope of the "military-industrial complex" came
to represent the many aspects of the question how military preparedness could be maintained within a society dedicated to individual freedom.[37] However, if "irrationality" in human behavior was at the heart of
American Cold War assumptions, then making the mind readable and
human behavior more predictable were of utmost importance. Propaganda and psychological research took aim at the mind; covert action
went further and also aimed at influencing the behavior of individuals
and groups. In both endeavors, the polygraph could play a role.

Some observers have noted the peculiar fact that the CIA is not only
among the most secretive of U.S government agencies, but also among
the most famous. Intelligence is one of the precious few aspects of government endowed with a mystique and a reputation. Until the 1960s,
"the Agency" (and to a lesser degree its domestic counterpart, "The
Bureau") on the one hand represented the quintessential modern
bureaucracy: secretive, impenetrable, all-knowing, and efficient. On the
other hand, the CIA also enjoyed a celebrity status, an image of being
the heroic daredevil among government agencies. We can view the
CIA as the American answer to Lenin's vanguard party, whose secrecy
and fame formed a dialectic relationship. To establish itself within the
bureaucratic turf wars of postwar Washington, the CIA took on the
"culture-defining" task of clandestine operations.[38] Director of Central
Intelligence Allen Dulles told his future successor Richard Helms, "If
there's no real money involved," neither Congress nor the military were
likely to take the CIA seriously. It therefore had to spend money on

covert action, and it did. By 1952, clandestine operations consumed 70–80 percent of the entire CIA budget.[39] The CIA was seen as the part of the government that was *doing* something during the frustratingly complex Cold War. With minimal oversight, the agency nurtured a cult of action that often led to disastrous failures or unforeseen blowback.[40]

Like the propagandists, CIA covert operators justified their existence as a response to a fight somebody else had started. Preparedness was the order of the day after Pearl Harbor, and since modern war required total mobilization of resources, the United States needed to be comprehensively informed about the state of mobilization of its adversaries. An internal Treasury Department memo from May 1946, co-authored by Richard Bissell, who would later be in charge of the CIA's U-2 spy plane program, captured the new thinking about the need for comprehensive, permanent mobilization after World War II: "Modern warfare" affected "the entire organism of the state," and the nation's "economic, social, and political life. . . . Planning and mobilizing for the common defense are inseparable . . . from planning and mobilizing for the general welfare of the nation."[41] Unity of intelligence, military command, and political decision-making would thus be democracy's first line of defense. The result of these considerations, through the National Security Act of 1947, was the creation of the Central Intelligence Agency, the office of Secretary of Defense, the Joint Chiefs of Staff, and a National Security Council. Democracies henceforth needed to be prepared to preempt totalitarian attacks. But how could these new powers be squared with a belief in limited government? This was one of the problems at the heart of the process that created the CIA and the national security state.

Few in postwar Washington doubted the need for a central place to collect and evaluate information about potential foreign threats. In particular, the Navy, represented by Admiral James Forrestal, the first secretary of defense, supported an agency that would prevent another Pearl Harbor. The specific powers of the agency that was created, however, developed concurrent with the events of the early Cold War. General William Donovan's Office of Strategic Services (OSS), founded in June 1942, had been the first U.S. agency that gathered and evaluated intelligence and exercised operational control over its use, conducting clandestine operations in enemy territory. Donovan was the type of valiant Wall Street lawyer turned super-spy who was the stuff of legends on which the CIA would later draw. However, throughout the war the OSS remained under military control, and after the war President Truman disbanded the somewhat disconcerting organization in October 1945. The creation of a permanent American intelligence establishment was not the work of one man, nor was it a preordained outcome of World War II.[42]

The founding of the CIA rather was the result of a convoluted process of intra-governmental wrangling.[43] This intense bureaucratic fight over knowledge and power among a number of intelligence-gathering departments of the federal government ended with a qualified victory for the idea of a central intelligence agency. Already in July 1946, Hoyt Vandenberg, director of the Central Intelligence Group (the CIA's predecessor, still lacking staff or budget authority), created the Office of Research and Evaluation (ORE). The expressed purpose of the ORE was to secure the right to evaluate—and disseminate to decision makers—intelligence coming from all gathering agencies, and to begin gathering intelligence on its own. This right was expressed in the National Security Act of July 26, 1947. The act charged the CIA with the production of strategic knowledge: for the purpose of "coordinating the intelligence activities of the several Government departments and agencies in the interest of national security," the CIA had to "correlate and evaluate intelligence relating to national security."[44] In the following months, the CIA acquired the authority to access the intelligence produced by other departments and "produce and disseminate national intelligence," that is, intelligence "that covers the broad aspects of national policy and national security."[45] The head of the CIA was thus to be, at least in theory, a Director of Central Intelligence (DCI) and would possess exactly the kind of authority the OSS had never achieved.

In the coming years, it was especially DCI Walter Bedell Smith, the irascible but widely respected former chief of staff of President Eisenhower, who aggressively consolidated the CIA's ability not only to analyze, but also to create strategic intelligence. During Smith's tenure from 1950 to 1953, the ORE's tasks became more precisely defined through the creation of the Office on National Estimates (ONE), the Office of Research and Reports (ORR), responsible for economic analysis of the Soviet Union, and the Office of Current Intelligence (OCI), housing specialists on individual countries and producing focused reports, in contrast to ONE's task of creating wide-ranging synthetic reports. All three offices were supervised by a Board of National Estimates (BNE), whose task it would be to provide expert evaluation of the intelligence produced by the CIA. In addition, under Smith's leadership a Directorate of Intelligence was created, which included an Office of Collection and Dissemination and an Office of Scientific Intelligence.[46] We can therefore discern two essential bureaucratic moves in the development of this basic CIA organizational structure: compartmentalization of tasks and supervision by committee.

The National Security Act also acknowledged the relation of knowledge to the exercise of power in creating such knowledge. It stated that the CIA not only created national intelligence, but it was also "responsible for protecting intelligence sources and methods from unauthorized disclosure" (section 102 (d) (3)) and to "perform such other functions and duties related to intelligence affecting the national security as the National Security Council may from time to time direct" (section 102 (d) (5)).[47] While it was the latter sentence, section (d) (5), upon which further expansion of CIA authority to conduct espionage and other operations would be based in the coming years, section (d) (3) established independent authority for the CIA to create its own methods to vet intelligence. The use of the polygraph would be based on the authority to establish methods deemed necessary for intelligence, an authority that was independent from procedures and regulations applicable to other government agencies. The right to create its own rules in protecting national security was therefore noted in the CIA's bureaucratic birth certificate and it would carry the use of the polygraph through the Cold War and beyond, by and large shielding it from congressional challenges.

The beginning of espionage, counterespionage, and covert activities—the other major tasks of the CIA—was intimately interwoven with the development of those intelligence-gathering structures, as well as with the perceived need to counter aggressive policies by Communist governments. Between 1947 and 1950—and before major reforms within ORE—CIA failure to predict major foreign events prompted calls to take active measures in order to prevent such setbacks in the future. The origins of U.S. willingness to preempt threats in cases of incomplete intelligence flowed from the rapid fire of events the United States confronted from 1948 to 1950: the communist coup in Czechoslovakia in early 1948, which coincided with highly contested elections in Italy and the Soviet blockade of West Berlin; the communist victory in the Chinese civil war during 1949 and the concurrent testing of the first Soviet nuclear bomb; and the North Korean attack on South Korea in June 1950.

CIA mythology has it that those intelligence failures were due to a reluctant DCI, Roscoe Hillenkoetter, and overly cautious politicians, exposing the need for rapid expansion of espionage and covert action capabilities. Yet as historian Rhodri Jeffries-Jones notes, for example, a CIA estimate of December 1947 missed the first Soviet explosion of a nuclear bomb by sixteen months, predicting it for early 1951 rather than August 1949. According to Jeffries-Jones, that was "an appreciable but surely not disgraceful margin of error."[48] In the realm of political/ military events, the Soviet blockade of West Berlin had not come out of the blue, either. In fact, U.S. policymakers had expected a Soviet move in Berlin as early as December 1946 and squeezed the maximum pro- paganda value out of an event that until today serves as the iconic first chapter of a Cold War narrative that placed a heroic West under siege by the insatiable and unpredictable expansionism of the Soviet Union.[49]

As for more proactive policies, in his Executive Order of October 1, 1945, President Truman had transferred the OSS's "special operations" staff to the War Department, where it was quickly wound down. The task of OSS covert operations during World War II had mainly con- sisted in assisting or establishing resistance movements in enemy terri- tory and "morale operations" directed at enemy soldiers and civilians, such as dropping leaflets exhorting enemy soldiers to surrender. While the War Department kept a skeleton crew of clandestine intelligence collection and counterintelligence units (renamed Strategic Services Unit [SSU]), direct action such as sabotage was abandoned. However, by early 1947 CIG had absorbed the War Department's SSU and incor- porated it into a new unit, the Office of Special Operations (OSO). It therefore possessed the means to collect secret information by itself.[50]

Around the same time, military leaders and the State Department began lobbying for the development of "psychological warfare" capabil- ities that could quickly be folded into military structures if war broke out. Until September 1947, such proposals stressed the need for such capabilities "in time of war or threat of war." However, by that time the State Department began to stress the need for political propaganda in Western Europe to support noncommunist forces there. "Covert action" therefore came to fulfill similar, if not identical, needs by representatives of both the U.S. diplomatic and military establishment. As a result, by December 1947 consensus had been achieved to create permanent authority for such operations and to institutionally separate "overt" propaganda authorized under NSC 4—under the auspices of the Assistant Secretary of State for Public Affairs—from "covert" activities related to secret propaganda and intelligence gathering, authorized under the guidance of NSC 4's twin brother, NSC 4-A.

The upper ranks of the new CIA began to demand this authority for themselves. CIA officials argued, "All concerned must appreciate that this Agency is and must be the sole agency to conduct organized foreign clandestine operations." More precisely, they averred, "The similarity of operational methods involved in covert psychological and intelligence activities and the need to ensure their secrecy and obviate costly duplication renders the Central Intelligence Agency the logical agency to conduct such operations."[51] In April 1948, discussions about a covert action unit ensued anew. The State Department favored a separate agency under its control, while the CIA warned against duplication of its covert action unit established under NSC 4-A. Eventually, NSC 10/2 from June 17, 1948, generated the Office of Special Projects (later Office of Policy Coordination [OPC]), a quasi-independent component of the CIA. The director of the OPC would be appointed by the secretary of state and receive instructions from State and Defense. Hence, the OPC sat as uneasily within CIA as did CIA within the overall national defense structure.

Political (if not institutional) consensus over the need for clandestine capabilities was strong. By the time NSC 10/2 was issued, the State Department already anticipated that the OPC "might at a later date be incorporated in CIA." Within five years, the OPC had swallowed all "extra-curricular activity" and had come under the sole leadership of the Director of Central Intelligence and therefore the CIA.[52] This development was a logical consequence of the secretive, intentionally vague mandate given by section 102 (d) (5) of the National Security Act, which only allowed the CIA to perform "other functions and duties" related to intelligence activities."[53]

In the wake of the Bay of Pigs disaster in 1961 and revelations of the extent of CIA covert activities during congressional hearings in the mid-1970s, many former shadow warriors suffered public bouts of bad conscience. Harry Truman himself confessed publicly in 1963, "For some time I have been disturbed by the way the CIA has been diverted from its original assignment. It has become an operational arm and at times a policy-making arm of Government. . . . I never had any thought when I set up the CIA that it would be injected into peacetime cloak and dagger operations."[54] However, the legal and strategic ambiguity of covert operations—as well as the blurring of the distinction between war and peace—had been present at the creation of the CIA and had been fully noted by its founders. In a memo from September 1947, when such operations became the subject of intense internal discussion, CIA General Counsel Lawrence Houston warned that section 102 (d) of the National Security Act "could bear almost unlimited interpretation. . . . We do not believe that there was any thought in the minds of Congress that the Central Intelligence Agency under this authority would take positive action for subversion and sabotage."[55] If such activities were undertaken, they would only remain legal if authorized by the National Security Council. NSC 4-A thus specifically charged the DCI with "ensuring that such psychological operations are consistent with U.S. foreign policy and overt foreign information activities, and that appropriate agencies of the U.S. government . . . are kept informed of such operations which will directly affect them."[56] Yet in a memo from December 2, 1947—shortly before approval of NSC 4-A—CIA Deputy Director Wright stressed, "The pattern of our foreign operations will not permit supervision of these activities by other agencies if it is to be maintained as an efficient and secure operation and the conduct of Black psychological operations must fit into the over-all operational pattern [of the CIA]."[57] In other words, internal CIA operational and bureaucratic structures were prohibitive of strict supervision. Yet the very legality of covert action in accordance with section 102 (d) (5) of the National Security Act depended on authorization by an outside authority, the National Security Council.

Therefore, U.S. policymakers were fully aware that it was practically impossible to reconcile secret operations as means of U.S. policy with the overt goals of policy as established by the president and the heads of major departments in the National Security Council. The OPC became a hot potato that could not comfortably be placed into any bureaucratic lap, not even within the CIA. Harmony between American core values and the national security policies charged with translating these values into specific goals therefore proved next to impossible and had to rest on a cultural consensus and the good intentions and patriotic spirits of the decision-making elite, not the law or institutional structures.

The virus of covert operations was spreading into the body politic in even more ways. All internal discussion papers of late 1947 and early 1948 discussed what came to be known as "plausible deniability" as a defining characteristic of covert operations. NSC 10/2 defined covert operations as "all activities (except as noted herein) which are conducted or sponsored by this government against hostile foreign states or groups or in support of friendly foreign states or groups but which are so planned and executed that any US Government responsibility for them is not evident to unauthorized persons and if uncovered the US Government can plausibly disclaim any responsibility for them."[58]

Hence, by definition the president had to be left sufficiently in the dark about what kind of covert operations his government was undertaking. It is true that presidents time and again would attempt control of unsupervised intelligence operations. But control also meant normalizing abnormal warfare. After 1953, President Eisenhower played a proactive role in using covert operations as a permanent tool of policy. As a major scholar of CIA history recently concluded, "It is apparent—and now largely accepted by historians—that Eisenhower *relied* upon covert operations instead of, and in preference to, conventional military force. He institutionalized covert operations precisely by creating mechanisms to manage them."[59] Similarly, beginning with Eisenhower's DCI Allen Dulles the CIA worked actively to woo Congress and the public with carefully selected stories that became famous for the way they left details open to interpretation and presented the CIA as a "regular" agency led by professionals.[60] Members of Congress, on the other hand, drew little political gain from overseeing the obscure machinations of a "schizophrenic" agency, designed to easily execute covert action while struggling to fulfill its original mission of gathering intelligence.[61]

In addition, I want to emphasize how quickly early crises converted skeptics to enthusiasts of covert action. Telling here is the evolving role of George Kennan, who as head of the new State Department Policy Planning Staff (from 1947 to 1950) was at the center of U.S. postwar foreign policymaking. Kennan had supported granting authority for covert operations within the National Security Council, yet had also added the caveat that "before giving our consent to any such activities we would wish to consider most carefully the need thereof."[62] Then, in a crisis moment in the Italian election campaign of early 1948, that need apparently arrived. Fearing panic among European partners, Kennan panicked. He advised that provoking a civil war and reoccupying the country would be preferable to a communist election victory, since such a victory would "send waves of panic to all surrounding areas."[63] In addition, Italy had strategic importance as a potential launching pad for air attacks on the Soviet Union. In April 1949 it became a founding member of NATO.[64] After the hoped-for victory of the CIA-supported Christian-Democratic party in the election on April 18, 1948, Kennan became markedly more enthusiastic about covert operations. He ardently campaigned to become State Department liaison to the OPC; it was upon Kennan's recommendation that Frank Wisner became its first director. After the Italian success, Kennan wanted covert operations to be intimately connected to the implementation of containment as developed in the State Department. In a memo discussing what became NSC 10/2, Kennan warned that a semi-independent covert organization within CIA would be "too remote from the conduct of foreign policy" and "the needs of this Government for the conduct of political warfare."[65]

Yet OPC soon slipped away, mainly because Frank Wisner's shop drastically expanded with the beginning of the Korean War in 1950, which caused a general shift of attention among policymakers away from Europe.[66] At that time, Kennan had already left the State Department. Yet a Policy Planning Staff memorandum of May 4, 1948, illustrates not only Kennan's thinking directly after the Italian election, but also the ease with which lines between legitimate and illegitimate political warfare could be crossed in broader, philosophical statements of the kind Kennan relished. While early drafts of NSC 10/2 still reserved the need for "covert operations in time of war or national emergency," Kennan considered such distinctions quaint. In contrast to both the British Empire's and the Kremlin's understanding of political warfare, "we [the United States] have been handicapped by a popular attachment to the concept of a basic difference between peace and war."[67]

Kennan egged on policymakers to join history as an existential, perpetual struggle devoid of the fair play ethos of a sporting event that the author identified as a hallmark of classic liberal thinking. Yet in a move that is equally remarkable, Kennan did not suggest that Americans rid themselves wholesale of their exceptionalist ethos and core values. Rather, he wanted to put that ethos to work. The United States should sponsor "selected political refugee committees" and conduct "overt operations, which, however, should receive covert guidance and possibly assistance from the Government. . . . What is proposed here is an operation in the traditional American form: organized public support of resistance to tyranny in foreign countries."[68] CIA support for "private" liberation committees—the performance of grassroots democracy under the grand maestro CIA—thus exemplifies another project in which U.S. Cold War policies attempted to square a circle: the value of free citizen associations had to be advertised by groups covertly sponsored by the government.

Kennan subsumed "all the means at a nation's command, short of war, to achieve its national objectives" under political warfare. Yet the difference between war and peace—as Kennan, the eager student of Carl von Clausewitz, recognized—was only one of degree. To leave no doubt about what the United States should be thinking about, he listed projects for consideration: not only were the Truman Doctrine and the Marshall Plan "all political warfare and should be recognized as such," but in the future, the United States should consider sponsoring "support of indigenous anti-communist elements in threatened countries of the free world"; and "only in cases of critical necessity . . . direct action to prevent vital installations, other material, or personnel from being sabotaged or liquidated or captured intact by Kremlin agents or agencies."[69] Kennan did not recommend active measures to overthrow governments such as the CIA applied in Iran in 1953 and Guatemala in 1954. However, such measures could be justified by simple synthesis of his endorsement of support for anticommunist forces in "free" countries and his recommendation to engage in "Preventative Direct Action," under which the OPC subsumed sabotage, demolition, evacuation, and stay-behind operations, in addition to "support of guerillas" in countries about to be taken over by Communist forces.[70] It was not a stretch to read Kennan's recommendations as creating a doctrine of preemption.

Kennan was often quick to decry the "vast, turgid, self-centered, and highly emotional process" of decision making in Washington during the crises of the late 1940s. Yet his own enthusiastic engagement in covert action, what he later called "the biggest mistake I have ever made," serves as a good example of the emotional component of his own thinking.[71] It also showed how a clandestine operations unit, conceived by Kennan early in 1947 as a "compact, mobile and hard-hitting task force," was from the beginning a component of the U.S. policy of containment, precisely because it could avoid "panic" and exert a "sobering and restraining influence" on opponents.[72] As the Cold War became institutionalized in the United States, so did the defensive and highly emotional mindset of policymakers such as Kennan.

In sum, by the early 1950s propaganda and covert operations had been accepted as a necessary means to U.S. Cold War policies, but neither their precise goal nor their bureaucratic administration could ever be coherently defined. Was their goal to shore up democracy in the West, to undermine communism in the East, or to overthrow communism altogether? Confusion over means and ends was a birth defect of U.S. Cold War policies.[73]

We can ascribe some of the general anxiety that characterized the early formation of the Cold War in the United States to this uncertainty over means and ends. In the dark forest of new threats—as well as new ambitions—many Washington policymakers whistled familiar tunes of American core values. The reorganization and expansion of national security policies demanded justification of new institutions and policies by claiming compatibility with those values. Fear of too powerful a national government mixed uneasily with equally intense anxiety over powerlessness in the face of new threats.

One strategy to ease these fears was the creation of institutional boundaries. The first such boundary was erected when President Truman put a stop to efforts to include the FBI—domestic law enforcement—into the new foreign intelligence establishment. To prevent an "American Gestapo," the CIA in turn was denied domestic law enforcement powers. This move eased Truman's own conscience and appeased his Republican critics.[74] Yet it also led to the institutionalization of two sets of rules, one for domestic and one for foreign policy. America would not allow its own government or foreign powers the kind of secret maneuvers *within* that it would engage in *abroad*. The CIA was therefore placed squarely in the middle of competing ethics. How could a spillover from one sphere to the other be avoided? The 1956 Bruce-Lovett report on CIA covert activities asked the relevant question: "Should not someone, some-where . . . [be] calculating the impacts on our international position, and keeping in mind the long range wisdom of activities which have entailed our virtual abandonment of the international 'golden rule' . . . ?"[75] Yet this conflict remained as a legacy of early Cold War decisions, when later presidents proved to be less reluctant than Truman to use the CIA for internal operations.

Other NSC documents of the time also emphasized the need to restrain spending. As NSC 20/4 of November 1948 stated, for example, American defense policies toward Western Europe should be geared toward avoiding "permanently impairing our economy and the funda-mental values and institutions inherent in our way of life."[76] In hindsight we can see how this concern played out. While the Truman administra-tion managed to limit defense spending between 1947 and 1950 to about a third of overall expenditures and no more than 5.5 percent of the gross domestic product (GDP), the Korean War inaugurated stiff increases in military spending over the coming decades. However, since the Ameri-can economy overall grew at such impressive rates, the share of defense spending in GDP began to steadily decrease by the late 1950s. Even at the height of the Vietnam War it did not exceed about 9 percent of U.S. GDP and hovered between 4 and 6 percent for the rest of the Cold War.[77]

Contrary to the fears of some policymakers, a large defense budget therefore did not impede the American way of life economically. How-ever, U.S. prosperity became ever more intertwined with the economic health of Western Europe and Japan, in other words, with expansive economic policies.[78] Meanwhile, ideological battles at home continued. National defense, or "warfare," became a favorite bludgeon, used by self-proclaimed fiscal conservatives to limited New Deal–style "wel-fare" spending. Less than half a decade after Dwight Eisenhower ended his presidency with his famous warning against the growing power of the "Military-Industrial Complex," Lyndon Johnson declared that the

United States could "have it all," guns and butter.[79] The relation between security and the American "way of life" thus remained contested.

Another strategy of dealing with the new means to defend core values was to sweep them under a rug of secrecy. Both the White House and DCI Hoyt Vandenberg preferred not to bring up covert action when the National Security Act was submitted to Congress in March 1947, and to omit "all but the barest mention of the CIA," since the requested authorities for the CIA were "too controversial and might hinder the passage of the merger legislation."[80] Neither was there great interest in raising these questions after passage of the legislation.

Both overt and covert propaganda operations and the secretive CIA were products of bureaucratic power struggles, ideological convictions, strategic reorientation, and perceived momentary necessity. Propaganda had to present America as a vibrant citizen democracy, yet its message had to be carefully stage-managed by government agencies. The CIA was to serve peacetime diplomatic goals but also to prepare worst-case scenario plans. It had to remain within the law, to take guidance from the National Security Council, but not let political leaders in on how exactly it was executing policies. Its ambiguous purpose became the focus of criticism from inside and outside the government, beginning with the Bruce-Lovett report, an indictment of CIA covert activities in the midst of its alleged "Golden Age" yet as sharp as any later ones coming from outside the executive. With the passing of the National Security Act, the United States took the first step toward permanent militarization of its foreign policy. Historian Michael Hogan captured this legacy well when he stated, "The National Security Act . . . laid the institutional foundations of the national security state. . . . Everyone was ready to accept the permanent blurring of the usual distinctions between war and peace, citizen and soldier, civil and military."[81] Despite White House fears of controversy, Congress proved little interested in controlling the CIA. Bureaucratic turf wars mixed with ideological differences in the Senate—just as they had in the executive—and prevented effective oversight.[82] As CIA historian Michael Warner put it, "Congress stepped back" and thus "resolved the apparent contradiction of creating 'central intelligence' that was not centrally controlled."[83]

Blurring of tasks proved to be a more lasting problem than military control of foreign policy. As sociologist Harold Lasswell began to argue in the late 1930s, it was precisely a "merging of skills" that would characterize the logic of the "Garrison State," where "experts in violence" (soldiers) would use civilian management and marketing techniques (Lasswell also had mind-altering drugs in mind) to maintain a sense of threat among the population and achieve control by mastery of modern technology.[84] Maybe no other U.S. postwar national security organization came to embody precisely this merging of skills, because the fact that the CIA was not under military control did not prevent the merging of military and civilian ethos. Therefore, Lasswell's and other popular arguments of the time that commercial and military societies were "two irreconcilable types of social organization" were soon refuted in practice. The CIA and other national security bureaucracies were run by civilians, many of them businessmen, but they advertised military prowess and the ethos of war.[85] In a world of unforeseeable threats, Wilsonian "crisis internationalism" encouraged a merger of peacetime ends with wartime means.[86]

The double vision of the Soviet Union as both foe and mirror image, totalitarian Other and fellow great power, loomed large in discussions over means and ends. The 1954 Doolittle Report on CIA activities prepared on request from President Eisenhower expressed the same paradox I already described in Kennan's "Long Telegram." To fulfill its mission, the CIA was required to develop "an aggressive covert psychological, political and paramilitary organization more effective, more unique and, if necessary, more ruthless than that employed by the enemy. No one should be permitted to stand in the way of the prompt, efficient and secure accomplishment of this mission." It was in this context that the report demanded that "greater security be developed at all levels" through "immediate completion of full field investigations and polygraph examinations of the several hundred Agency personnel who have not yet been fully processed," and a general "augmentation of the present sound policy of polygraphing all new employees and all personnel returning from overseas assignments to include periodic rechecks of all personnel, on a more comprehensive basis, whenever effective counterintelligence practices indicate."[87]

In hindsight, such strident policies seemed to hark back to the failure to establish a basic institutional framework to build trust between the superpowers. Instead, the Cold War led to policies that emanated from absence of trust. What is significant is that these characteristics reached deeply into domestic policies and politics, so that any notion of a strict separation of domestic and foreign policy was unrealistic. It is precisely this border crossing that also became a characteristic of the American "national security state." In June 1946, David Lilienthal, the head of the Atomic Energy Commission, recorded some remarks by J. Robert Oppenheimer that predicted the domestic consequences of Bernard Baruch's confrontational attitude toward sharing nuclear know-how:

> [The Baruch Plan] will go to the [Security Council] and Russia will exercise her veto and decline to go along. This will be construed by us as a demonstration of Russia's warlike intentions. And this will fit perfectly into the plans of that growing number who want to put the country on a war footing, first psychologically, then actually. The Army directing the country's research; Red-baiting; treating all labor organizations, CIO first, as Communist and therefore traitorous, etc.[88]

Oppenheimer was on to something. Nuclear confrontation pulled the United States away from cooperation with the Soviet Union internationally and added strong confrontational dynamics in domestic politics. The American national security state consisted of new institutions, such as the Department of Defense and the Central Intelligence Agency, which justified their existence solely through their function in maintaining security. But further, "national security" became a discourse that served as a justification for governmental powers in a more general way. The U.S. government became a national security state after 1945. It had a penchant for secrecy instead of transparency; a tendency toward alarmist interpretation of the moves of the Soviet Union and other opponents; a concern over "morale" rather informed public discussion at home and with allies; an official suspicion of dissent; a preference for limited conflict, often through "covert action," rather than open war *or* peace. At bottom, the U.S. postwar federal government justified many aspects of its power with the need to uphold "national security," a term that became so ubiquitous in U.S. Cold War discourse that its meaning seemed to be taken for granted rather than understood or questioned.

This characterization should not be understood as a one-size-fits-all interpretation of every aspect of U.S. Cold War foreign policy since 1945. Party politics and sincere disagreements among policymakers shattered but did not break the Cold War consensus. It is also true that brutal Soviet policies in Eastern Europe and elsewhere, the secrecy surrounding its policymaking, and atomic espionage provided ample justification for U.S. policies that favored preparedness over trust. Most importantly, it should not obscure the profound changes that American polices underwent in the postwar era (especially because of the Vietnam War), and it certainly does not mean to ignore the many dissenters who argued for alternative policies. Rather, the question is how the national security state attempted to reconcile America's traditional values of freedom and open government with what many but not all Americans accepted as new demands of the world situation. National security required a technology such as the polygraph: fair, objective, and sufficiently scientific, but also intimidating, relentless, and a deterrent.

CHAPTER 6

Immeasurable Security
The Polygraph and the CIA

rank Powers had his first polygraph experience right after signing up as a pilot for the U-2 program in January 1956. In his memoirs, Powers described being called into a room, where he was confronted with the question,

> "Any objection to taking a lie detector test?" Though I had a great many, I didn't voice them, shaking my head. If this was a condition of the job, I'd do it. But I didn't like it. . . . I had never felt so completely exposed, as if there was no privacy whatsoever. If at that moment someone had handed me a petition banning polygraphs forever from the face of the earth, I would gladly have signed it. When I was asked the last question and the straps were taken off, I vowed that never again, no matter what the circumstances, would I undergo such an insult to my integrity.[1]

Yet Powers would take another polygraph test.

In July 1954, President Eisenhower's Technological Capabilities Panel, charged with assessing the nation's ability to counter a Soviet surprise attack, approved a design for a single-engine plane based on the fuselage of a jet fighter and sailplane wings. New aerial cameras and lightweight film were added. After less than two years of building and testing, the U-2 flew at Mach 0.8 at an altitude of over 70,000 feet and a range of 2,000 miles, capable of escaping Soviet air defenses and penetrating interior Russia. Under the direction of the CIA, it made its first reconnaissance flight on July 4, 1956.[2] From 1956 to 1960, twenty-three U-2 flights by U.S. and British pilots yielded strategic intelligence on Soviet military capabilities as well as tactical intelligence on current events such as the Suez Crisis of 1956. For President Eisenhower, these missions were a calculated risk: reassurance that the Soviet Union was not ahead in the production of long-range bombers or missiles was worth the hazard of provoking an incident (Premier Nikita Khrushchev secretly complained to the United States three times about the invasion of Soviet airspace). The U-2 allowed the president to pursue a test ban treaty and resist pressures by the Air Force and Congress to increase military spending.

But on May 1, 1960, disaster struck when Francis Gary Powers's plane was shot down over Sverdlovsk (today called Yekaterinburg). As was established later, the first of fourteen V-750 surface-to-air missiles launched by Soviet air defense squadrons had hit or nearly hit the rear of Powers's plane and brought it down. American authorities issued a cover story about a weather balloon gone astray and were caught flat-footed when Khrushchev presented to a stunned world audience first the remnants of the plane and then the pilot. Powers had miraculously survived and was subsequently put on trial in Moscow and sentenced to ten years in prison for espionage. President Eisenhower's eventual admission that he had authorized the fateful flight forced Khrushchev to cancel a summit meeting in Paris, meant to initiate détente between the superpowers. Powers was subsequently exchanged for Soviet KGB colonel Vilyam Fisher (alias Rudolf Ivanovich Abel). He returned home as a hero under suspicion.[3]

After his release in February 1962, the CIA interrogated Powers about the truthfulness of his account of his time in Russia, and in particular on the circumstances of his crash. After Powers was told that the agency considered him cleared, a board of inquiry under Judge E. Barrett Prettyman was set up by new DCI John McCone to prepare a statement that could be presented to the public.[4] The unclassified account of his interrogation highlighted that medical tests, a background check, and the interrogation itself had confirmed that Powers "appeared to be truthful, frank, straightforward. . . . He volunteered with some vehemence that, although he disliked the process of the polygraph, he would like to undergo a polygraph test. That test was subsequently duly administered by an expert. . . . [Powers] displayed no indications of deviation from the truth in the course of the examination."[5] Contrast this with Powers's own version of his treatment: under pressure from Prettyman's "doubts about my responses, . . . I finally reacted angrily, bellowing: 'If you don't believe me, I'll be glad to take a lie detector test!' . . . Even before the words were out of my mouth, I regretted saying them. 'Would you be willing to take a lie detector test on everything you have testified here?' . . . I knew that I had been trapped."[6]

Until his death in a helicopter accident in 1977, Powers insisted that he had acted as a loyal American under trying circumstances. For example, he claimed that he had not given up details about his mission during interrogation. Yet doubts about his account of the Mayday events persisted. Unbeknownst to him, suspicion toward Powers was due to National Security Agency (NSA) intercepts of the responses to the U-2 flights (Soviet air defenses improved measurably during the four years of U-2 flights; they had located Powers's plane even before it entered Soviet air space). Tracked radar signals indicated that on May 1, Powers's plane had dropped below its regular altitude of 65,000 feet, which had made it vulnerable to surface-to-air missile attacks. Powers, on the other hand, vehemently denied that he had allowed the plane to decline. No definite account of the incident has been established yet.[7]

The different narratives of Powers's experience emphasize several ambiguous characteristics of polygraph use by the CIA for purposes of national security. First, the claim by polygraph proponents that the test could be a witness for the defense, exonerating a willing, loyal citizen who volunteers to take it, often turned out to be less than clearcut. Second, while it relied on the rhetoric of voluntarism, in reality the pressure to take the test often mocked the idea of a voluntary test. Last, polygraph exams often served to provide official cover rather than revealing the truth of events.

Thus, the CIA's use of the polygraph illustrated both the reach and the limits of attempts to normalize national security procedures. The Agency urged use of the polygraph due to the state of emergency imposed by the

Cold War. At the same time, policymakers and bureaucrats attempted to normalize that emergency by imposing lie detector tests on employees as a regular, standardized procedure. This chapter shows how the lie detector, as a consequence, became a Cold War technology that generally embodied the appeals and inner tensions of Cold War ideology. Contradictory polygraph policies were examples of contradictory Cold War policies; emergency and normalization both characterized the lie detection culture of the Cold War. At issue was the elusive quest to find the measure of a reliable, loyal, patriotic individual, yet insisting on the reliability of the polygraph raised the questions of how to define a reliable employee or agent and at which point polygraph exams became counterproductive because they deterred promising applicants and valuable employees. This conflict played out with particular ferocity in foreign covert operations. Here, the polygraph had to contend with the authority of field agents who saw mandatory polygraph tests of sources as an intrusion on their authority by the bureaucracy at home. Despite the usefulness of the machine in the hands of interrogators who incorporated its methodology into their professional toolkit, it remained controversial not only with the general public but also within the CIA. Haunted by these challenges, CIA polygraph policies remained contradictory, improvised, and subject to passionate debate.

Because the National Security Act gave the Director of Central Intelligence (DCI) responsibility for securing intelligence sources and methods, the CIA was authorized to create its own security procedures. In June 1947, it created the Executive for Inspection and Security (I&S), which in 1950 became the Office of Security (OS) with a Director of Security (DS) who was responsible for overall security policy in the agency, including personnel security. While the CIA's internal structures changed often during the years, security procedures remained a privilege of the OS. Within the office, an Interrogation Research Branch would be responsible for the administration of polygraph tests on behalf of the agency. Significant in this arrangement was that the OS was responsible both for "approv[ing] or disapprov[ing], from a security standpoint, the employment or utilization of individuals by the Agency" (with the exception of covert personnel abroad) and "develop[ing] and conduct[ing] counterintelligence programs for the Agency security procedures." Consequently, in the OS, two functions—regular security procedures and procedures for counterintelligence—merged into one. The mission of Interrogation Research was therefore to establish two objectives: (1) a system comprehensive enough to catch potential spies and (2) procedures that were "routine" enough to handle everyone else. But one never knew who was who.[8]

Equally important for the Office of Security's bureaucratic ethos was the relentless competition with other federal agencies and the CIA's effort to fend off congressional oversight. This competition began in earnest when the FBI lost its bid to take over foreign intelligence in 1945 because President Truman was uncomfortable with the idea of one agency in control of both domestic and foreign intelligence functions. The Bureau hence lost its intelligence authority over Latin America in early 1946. This defeat resulted in the Central Intelligence Group (CIG)—and later the CIA—needing to recruit its own personnel very quickly. J. Edgar Hoover soon retaliated against the CIA in ways big and small. One was to terminate without warning FBI security checks for CIA agents. Hoover's agency had performed the checks since April 1946, when the CIG had been created as an agency lacking authority over the hiring of its personnel. Even though the FBI resumed its service from December 1948 to December 1950, it is reasonable to assume that Hoover's impulsive action prompted the CIA to establish its own security screening procedures as quickly as possible. Only after Hoover's act of defiance did DCI Roscoe Hillenkoetter demand "a directive providing the same standing in government for the results of our investigations of CIA applicants and personnel now accorded to the FBI investigations." The FBI extended the deadline to January 1, 1948, but the CIA was now under pressure to do its own security checks.[9]

Just as the FBI withdrew from CIA security checks in late 1947, the U.S. Army recommended the polygraph to the CIA. DCI Hillenkoetter ordered in August 1948 "to conduct research and planning in the use of technical devices which could improve and expedite the conduct of personnel security investigations in time of emergency" and thus authorized I&S "to test this machine [the polygraph] on any employee of CIA or any applicants for employment who may volunteer to subject themselves to this test."[10] In March 1949, I&S noted that the AEC used the polygraph at Oak Ridge and reported polygraph testing "to date show[s] definitely that it can be of inestimable aid to security." It was reported that unnamed officials were "enthusiastic about it."[11] Most likely as a result, in May 1949 the CIA used its unvouchered funds to train two officers at the Chicago Police Department, which was in charge of the Chicago Crime Laboratory where Leonarde Keeler had refined his polygraph method in the 1930s.[12] At this time, CIA officials attempted to suppress any publicity that might accompany their use of the polygraph. In early 1950, I&S reported that "to date, the polygraph program has been very carefully handled in order to insure against (1) unfavorable publicity, (2) unfavorable reaction amongst employees, and (3) unwarranted intrusion upon the personal privacy of the individual."[13]

As DS Sheffield Edwards, who held the office until 1962, further explained to incoming DCI Allen Dulles in 1953, polygraph exams became part of clearance procedures for Special Intelligence beginning in 1948. Then they spread to "routine screening of employees prior to departure for overseas assignments as well as employees returning from extended periods of overseas duty. In the fall of 1951, a procedure was initiated whereby all applicants, as a part of their entry on duty processing, were given polygraph examinations on a voluntary basis. This program has continued without interruption." Edwards concluded, "Considering the results of the polygraph program and its benefits from a security standpoint, I am convinced that its use since 1948 has immeasurably increased the security of this Agency."[14] Dulles's response was a circumspect endorsement: "The use of the polygraph as a technical aid to interrogation and adjunct to background investigation for the purpose of security clearances of employees of the agency may be continued on a voluntary basis. However, we should not forget that the polygraph can be in error and consequently proper care should be exercised in the use of information obtained from it."[15]

Dulles's caution was not atypical. It revealed how caveats about the polygraph remained as the machine found its way into the CIA and its security culture. How did this process come about? In analyzing internal CIA documents on the polygraph, we can establish two themes: First, the polygraph became "routine," as Edwards already pointed out to Dulles. Second, participation in the polygraph program was "voluntary." The Agency liked to emphasize to others that its employees not only accepted but also embraced the polygraph. As the Acting Director of Security emphasized in 1955:

> All applicants [for CIA employment] have for some time been asked to volunteer for a polygraph interview because of the need in the unusually sensitive work of this Agency to take the most stringent security precautions in the national interest. Our applicants and employees have realized this unusual necessity, and their spirit of cooperation and willingness has been most heartening. In over 20,000 cases, only six persons have failed to volunteer for this interview.[16]

Indeed, by early 1955 the CIA reported to the National Security Council that it had eliminated backlogs in nonpolygraphed personnel, responding to a complaint Admiral Doolittle had expressed in his report of the previous year.[17] However, making a "voluntary" polygraph test a routine was recognized as a challenging task. As early as January 1950, Edwards recognized that "the [polygraph] screening of individual employees . . . should be handled as routinely as possible so as to eliminate any apprehension individual employees may feel concerning the program."[18] Throughout the history of the agency, these calls had to be repeated time and again. For example, each screening needed to be "an orderly and periodic review and updating of the clearances of all Agency employees, and it should not be viewed as coercive or threatening in any way," DCI Stansfield Turner asserted in 1978.[19]

On many occasions, CIA officers expressed pride in the professional way the agency handled this touchy subject. In 1963, the Inspector General Report on personnel security cited the polygraph as "one of our major security strengths. The degree to which it is accepted by Agency employees stems largely from the care with which the program is administered." The report highlighted "the professionals who have made a career in security," and concluded:

> Good personnel security results in part from the cooperation of all concerned. Personnel security, employee morale, and the Agency image are inseparably bound together. . . . We do not and could not aspire to total security. Our open society has an inherent resistance to police-state measures. The existence of narrow and rigid security restrictions would not only have an undesirably inhibiting effect on many employees but would make it impossible for us to hire persons having the qualities we

seek. To meet these complex problems, the Office of Security has developed a philosophy that seeks to engender a sense of security responsibility in our employees, in whom considerable trust is then placed. This principle is perhaps easier to enunciate than it is to describe, but we believe . . . that this philosophy does exist and that it is effective.[20]

In short, the CIA aimed at nurturing a security culture than was stringent but consistent with U.S. core values. The term "security responsibility" captured this ethos. To formalize polygraph interrogations, the CIA designed a polygraph agreement for applicants and employees in 1957. On the form, individuals signaled that "I . . . after having been informed of my rights under the Constitution, do, of my own free will and without any compulsion, duress, or promise of reward or immunity, agree to an interview with officials of the Central Intelligence Agency, during which I will participate in Polygraph tests." This statement was carefully worded. As the Office of Security opined at the time, "A short agreement would be less likely to raise questions in the minds of a prospective polygraph examinee."[21] Similarly, a polygraph agreement for current employees stated that "the Agency uses Polygraph testing as a routine procedure" and that "every employee of the Agency will be requested to participate in Polygraph interviews from time to time."[22] Neither agreement form changed significantly from the 1960s to the 1980s.

As the federal government developed more elaborate guidelines for security procedures, the CIA attempted to adjust and "follow Civil Service Commission (CSC) procedures as closely as possible" even though it was exempted from a number of requirements. Among them was a ban on polygraph screening the CSC had implemented in 1969. The CIA emphasized that written consent was required for a polygraph test, and that "all questions asked during a polygraph examination must have specific relevance to the individual being polygraphed and to the purpose of the particular inquiry."[23]

Criticism of the polygraph came often from bureaucratic competitors, which gave CIA executives opportunity to advertise their polygraph policy as a measure of distinction. In 1954, a task force led by General Mark Clark surveyed the CIA as part of the Hoover Commission (chaired by former President Herbert Hoover), which evaluated all federal agencies. Significantly, clandestine activities were kept off-limits, evaluated by a separate committee under Air Force general James Doolittle. Concerned about the agency's attrition rate, some on General Clark's task force questioned the polygraph program.[24] One member in particular, Colonel McGruder, "exploded over the subject of the polygraph, a favorite bad dream of his." CIA members complained about the notion, which they took McGruder to hold, that the Office of Security had to "act as Dorothy Dix for all the disgruntled workers. . . . McGruder thinks that just as the AEC (his alma mater) threw out the idea of the polygraph, so should we."[25] Insisting on the polygraph therefore began to distinguish the CIA from most other executive agencies entrusted with national security issues. By the same token, the CIA used its polygraph program to advertise its elite status to presidents under political pressure. One such presentation to Lyndon Johnson in October 1964 apparently caused the president to state that he was "appalled" that "no other Government agency has such a [polygraph] program," and that "every Government agency having access to classified information should have such a program." While the CIA pledged to prepare "a first-class briefing with the best briefers we can marshal," congressional opposition to the polygraph nevertheless began to get momentum in 1964.[26]

When challenged by Congress, the CIA again defended the polygraph aggressively. By the 1970s, the focus on anticommunism had lost most of its pull. However, the responsibility to protect intelligence "sources and methods" according to Section 102 (d) (3) of the National Security Act provided a strong argument for polygraph use. In a 1975 letter to Congresswoman Bella Abzug (then chair of the House Subcommittee on Government Information and Individual Rights), DCI George H. W. Bush warned that a complete prohibition of polygraph use in the federal government would "seriously impair" him "from complying with his statutory responsibility under the National Security Act." Bush justified the polygraph not only because it uncovered security-relevant information and had "proven reliability," but also because it was "a useful and comforting confirmation of other screening procedures."[27] Yet this policy of security overkill was based on circular logic: If the polygraph found something other screening procedures had missed, it proved an essential additional tool of security. If it found nothing, it was a welcome affirmation of the rest of the security program.

By the early 1980s, the polygraph's status as a tried-and-true method was one of the strongest arguments for maintaining it. In 1980, the DCI's Security Committee insisted: "The utility of the polygraph interview as part of security processing has been demonstrated by empirical means. . . . These practical results, plus more than thirty years' experience, make the use of the polygraph in security screening truly unique and indispensable."[28] Defenders of the polygraph did not advertise it as a lie detector, but simply as an additional means to reduce risk. According to former case officer and recruiter Tom Gilligan, the polygraph "may be an imperfect instrument in the hands of imperfect people, but it is far and away CIA's principal defense against hostile penetration, the Agency's main concern. . . . Thus, there is a great emphasis on, and need for, screening new hires thoroughly—for this purpose, the polygraph is generally the toughest screen of all." Gilligan's advice for job candidates was to "be absolutely candid and straightforward in the initial process and thereby avoid the polygraph problem altogether."[29]

At the end of the Cold War, therefore, the polygraph had become thoroughly embedded in the CIA's security procedures. That did not mean, however, that there was no internal opposition to the use of the machine.

If the polygraph is a "gadget," it has to work effortlessly. By making the "routine" polygraph exam part of the CIA's professional culture, agency officials attempted to create unquestioned authority for the polygraph, even though official CIA documents usually downplayed its role. The polygraph was, after all, merely an "aid" to investigation, not a "lie detector." As a technology that used intimidation as a central source of its methodology, however, the polygraph did not—indeed could not—function without friction, even within the CIA. For example, former chief of CIA counterintelligence James Olsen called polygraph exams "an awful but necessary ordeal. We all hate them. . . . A polygraph examination . . . is rude, intrusive, and sometimes humiliating. . . . It's a grueling process."[30] Similarly, former analyst Scott Breckinridge confessed:

> As with many laymen, I entertained reservations about "lie detectors"—
> reservations later modified because of the way CIA polygraph operators
> handled their work. Had I known in advance I may never have left [my

hometown]. . . . To say I was annoyed understates it considerably. . . .
As I later came to know the standards and practice employed by CIA's
polygraph people, my confidence in the agency's process grew, although
I knew of people who I know had no problem who did not fare well on
the polygraph.[31]

Many accounts of polygraph experiences come from the memoirs
of former case officers. Often written after a less than amicable end to
government service, they should not be taken at face value. On the
other hand, even supporters of the polygraph, such as Olsen and
Breckinridge, confirmed the problematic place of the polygraph in
CIA security procedures due to its sheer unpleasantness. The fact that
they still supported the polygraph points to a role of the machine that
goes beyond routine procedure. The mystique of the polygraph mimics
the mystique of the CIA.

A good example of a polygraph war story that maintains the mystique of the test while being embedded in a critical narrative is Philip
Agee's 1975 memoir *Inside the Company: CIA Diary.* Agee joined the
CIA in 1957 and worked as a case officer in Latin America before resign-
ing in 1968 out of protest, as he claimed, against the agency's support
for oppressive regimes. In the aftermath of his resignation, Agee's story
became a public affair when he revealed the names of hundreds of U.S.
covert agents as well as other trade secrets. Agee was forced to leave
several Western European countries due to U.S. diplomatic pressure
and took up temporary residence in communist Grenada, Nicaragua,
and Cuba. In *Inside the Company* Agee relayed the terror that the test
incited in applicants who had passed all screening procedures and
were now faced with the polygraph. "It seems that the main part of the
apparatus crosses the breasts, which makes some of the girls nervous,
and the main questioning is on homosexual experience, which makes
some of the boys nervous. There are stories of nervous breakdowns,
ambulances and even suicide."[32] Describing his own polygraph exam,
Agee ascribes special powers to it: "How stupid to think I could beat
the machine! . . . During the pre-test interview I had given my interrogator several half-truths, partly because I simply resisted his invasion of
my life, and partly because I was curious about the effectiveness of the
machine. Foolish child!"[33] Despite having heard rumors that persistent

denials would "beat the machine," Agee depicted his polygraph test as a defeat. Repeated runs of questions left the interrogator unsatisfied. An "agonizing" three-day wait made Agee ready to confess everything. To his surprise, Agee received the good news that he had passed, which left him and the reader of his memoir even more baffled as to what exactly had happened during and after the polygraph exam. In contrast to other accounts, this is not a "debunking" account of the polygraph. If nothing else, in this telling the polygraph comes across as an impressive demonstration of the hurdles applicants have to clear in order to be admitted to the exclusive club that is the CIA. After the test, Agee insisted he made "no more arrogant jokes about the polygraph."[34]

Yet the polygraph's exact powers remain unclear in this narrative; we never find out what exactly made the polygraph examiner unsatisfied, nor do we hear about the role the polygraph chart played in the final decision-making of the agency. Other polygraph stories are similarly baffling. For example, when aspiring case officer Lindsay Moran applied at the agency in the late 1990s, her polygraph interrogator told her "you're not doing well" and claimed that she was hiding a past crime. Moran reports that she did not understand what the problem was, but was nevertheless told in the end that she had passed after a reinterview. Worse still, after a year abroad and another polygraph exam ("just as harrowing"), her interrogator told her that he only accused her of lying in order to get a confession out of her.[35] Stories such as these cannot be independently verified. They nevertheless speak and contribute to the mystique of the polygraph test.

The problems caused by the impression of mystery surrounding the polygraph came through in official CIA documents as well. In October 1953, the Chief of the Interrogation Branch began giving lectures to new personnel "concerning the enigma of the polygraph" to clear up "distorted impressions about it."[36] The Interrogation Research Branch reported that after such briefings, "employees are less nervous and more receptive to the polygraph interview."[37] CIA polygraph policymakers, however, always had to reckon with resistance inside and outside the agency. Within the Security Office, it was acknowledged in a 1956 memo that normalization of the polygraph was in fact not possible: "It is [...] recognized that there are many elements within the Agency and outside the Agency opposed in varying degrees to the polygraph program and

that we must make use of it in such a manner that we will give its enemies no cause to clamor for its elimination from our security program."[38]

Among the fundamental problems was the question of whether
the "routine" polygraph was a bureaucratic fiction, given the frequent
exemptions granted to certain personnel. Again, CIA memoir literature
occasionally hints at exemptions to polygraph exams. According to his
son's account, high-ranking case officer and Vienna station chief John
H. Richardson Sr. refused the polygraph exam required of him when
the Central Intelligence Group transitioned into the Central Intelligence Agency: "If they didn't trust him after all his years of service, he
said, they could damn well fire him. Finally [counterintelligence officer]
Jim Angleton said he could skip it, an exemption that apparently made
him unique in CIA history."[39] Since routine screening of employees with
the polygraph was outside the purview of counterintelligence, this story
seems unlikely to be literally true. However, it is part of CIA folklore
highlighting the privilege that came with being "important" enough to
be able to skip the polygraph. Apparently, James Jesus Angleton, the
legendary chief of counterintelligence from 1954 to 1975, contributed
to this lore when he told journalist Joseph Trento: "You know how I
got to be in charge of counterintelligence? I agreed not to polygraph
or require detailed background checks on Allen Dulles and 60 of his
close friends. They were afraid that their own business dealings with
Hitler's pals would come out."[40] Other accounts state a similar number,
but none feature solid archival evidence.[41]

Arbitrary polygraph policies were, however, noted in internal CIA
communications. A 1966 memo, likely from the Interrogation Research
Division, questioned the validity of the agency's Routine Reinvestigation Program (RRIP), which demanded a polygraph exam every five
years from each employee and from overseas returnees of the Office of
Communications (responsible for electronic intelligence in CIA). The
memo noted: "Senior grade personnel frequently had their repolygraph
[sic] waived. Selecting Communications people over all others for more
frequent polygraphing was manifestly unfair." Why were overseas
returnees considered a bigger security threat? The author noted: "Actually, the reverse might be true. The overt person in Washington may
have been studied much more closely than the semi-covert or covert
person overseas."[42]

The problem of "voluntarism" in polygraph tests was also understood within the CIA, in particular whether a signature on the CIA polygraph agreement truly constituted voluntary submission to the test. When the U.S. Civil Service Commission introduced stricter guidelines for polygraph use in the federal government (from which the CIA was largely exempted), the agency noted that it did not fully inform people of their privilege against self-incrimination under the Fifth Amendment in case a polygraph exam led to admissions of criminally relevant information. "We do not dwell on it for fear of having the individual not say anything," the agency noted in an internal memo.[43]

Even after decades of polygraph practice, the CIA could not define what exactly it meant by elusive terms such as "routine" and "voluntary" in its polygraph program. A 1974 list of questions from polygraph examiners to the General Counsel included the following query: "What can a polygraph officer say in response to the question: 'Do I have to take this test to get a job with the Agency?' or 'What happens if I don't take the test?'" Sometimes the polygraph inspired questions that were downright philosophical. One such question went like this: "The standard agreement refers to the polygraph interview as being undertaken of one's own free will. Is this technically or legally correct? How is free will defined in this situation?"[44]

Many CIA officers shared the understanding that the polygraph exam was not really voluntary, particularly if one was the target of a specific investigation. For example, before interrogator and intelligence analyst Frank Snepp published his biting memoir *Decent Interval* in 1977, he was forced to undergo a polygraph exam to establish whether he was working on a book. According to Snepp, "Any CIA officer who refuses a polygraph might as well resign on the spot." Snepp further claimed that an OS interrogator threatened to interpret his admission of having written notes in preparation for a book as admission to having written a complete manuscript.[45] Notwithstanding the fact that *Decent Interval* did not contain classified information, the CIA charged it caused "irreparable harm" to national security by portraying U.S. officials as neglectful and callous when South Vietnam fell in early 1975. In an influential decision, the U.S. Supreme Court in 1980 refused to hear Snepp's appeal to a lower court's verdict that his refusal to submit to the CIA's new Publication Review Board had violated his contract. According to

historian Christopher Moran, "The Snepp precedent effectively heralded an American Official Secrets Act," since government employees
could now be charged for publishing information regardless of whether
they spilled secrets or not. And yet, more prominent CIA employees
such as former DCI William Colby escaped harsh judgment when they
revealed classified information in their memoirs.[46] Therefore, the CIA's
treatment of Frank Snepp starkly highlighted the lack of egalitarianism
when it came to the enforcement of national security through the polygraph or through legal means.

Official polygraph policies also reflected the CIA's participation in
larger social debates about appropriate security measures and gender, sexuality, and personal morals. For example, in 1957 the director
of security ordered that "17 and 18 year old girls" applying for clerical
jobs at the CIA would henceforth not be polygraphed, as "experience
and public relations have dictated."[47] In 1967, the agency further hired a
female officer to debrief female applicants under twenty-five after their
polygraph test "to relieve any anxieties that might develop on the part
of the young woman as the result of her polygraph" and to "supply an
attractive and mature woman to whom the interviewees might confide
if the technical interview ended on an unsatisfactory note from her
standpoint."[48] In the wake of the 1960s, the CIA noted the "changed
morals and ethics of the day," in particular "the acceptance of civil dis-
obedience as a human right if not duty in some circumstances."[49] The
agency recognized that it had to consider adjusting its security procedures. In 1974, it reviewed the "overall propriety of some of the polygraph questions now routinely asked," in particular questions on sexuality. "To recognize the pressures of the times and consider dropping
this question area would not seriously detract from the coverage of the
polygraph interview." The author of the review recognized "that there
may be strong objection to the dropping of this question at this time,"
but advised "a more liberal approach to the whole matter of sex as an
issue of suitability."[50]

Homosexuality, however, proved to be a topic on which the agency
remained rigid. Because the CIA kept its security files, information leading to the uncovering of gay and lesbian Americans grew as
American society slowly became more accepting of homosexuality.
Until increasing public scrutiny led to destruction of the material in

1973, the CIA had kept files of 300,000 persons arrested for "offenses" related to homosexual conduct.[51] Declassified CIA files contain open and oblique references to cases in which polygraph interrogations led to "resignations" of personnel, often without any other evidence of security problems.[52] Here the institutional rationale for the polygraph test again clashed with the need to fit those justifications with social norms outside the CIA's jurisdiction and with the polygraph interview's confrontational methodology. The record only allows glimpses on this topic. For example, a 1957 document stated that in the two-year period between December 1954 and December 1956, the Office of Security terminated 214 applications or current employees: "These 214 cases arose almost totally from disclosures during polygraph examination and the large majority, 195, involved perversion. The rest involved poor credit; blackmail possibilities; crime, such as embezzlement; thievery, and other illegal or unethical activities; disclosure of classified information or association with communist personalities. Of these 214, 1/6 were employees and 5/6 were persons about to enter duty."[53]

Sexual matters appeared to be the default target of security investigations. In 1974 the chief of the Interrogation Branch stated matter-of-factly, "The test of precedence shows the majority of releases [of information obtained during a polygraph] relate to information on an individual's sexual conduct (homosexuality)." Under what conditions could a focus on catching homosexual applicants or employees be justified as part of CIA's national security mission? The 1974 report continued, "Today's interpretation of just what constitutes 'the interest of national security' is vague. We would be hard-pressed to justify release of information on the use of marijuana or homosexuality under some interpretations of 'national security.'"[54] Still, the fact that CIA did not change its policy regarding gay and lesbian employees during the Cold War indicates the power of the "morale" argument (intangible as it was), meaning that officials saw the *esprit de corps* of the agency threatened by openly homosexual employees.

The issue vexed administrators at the very top of the agency. President Gerald Ford's DCI, George H. W. Bush, addressed the more permissive culture of the mid-1970s and probed CIA attitudes. Admissions of drug consumption on the polygraph test rose, for example, from 208 in 1970 to 495 in 1972 among CIA applicants and employees, illustrating

increasing popularity of recreational drug use.[55] Director of Security
Robert Gambino informed Bush in 1976 that the CIA took a "common
sense approach" toward experimentation with illegal drugs among
job applicants, and that "experimentation" was no reason for rejection. "Homosexuals," however, were "immediately disapproved" for
employment, and current agents or analysts were encouraged to resign.
According to Gambino, Bush admitted that

> he had some ambivalent feelings about the CIA's policy toward homo-
> sexuals. He [Bush] noted that this is a question that is always posed to
> him when he addresses a large group of Agency employees. . . . He stated
> that he has no problem with our attitude and policy concerning the so-
> called "closet" homosexual because he recognizes the threat this indi-
> vidual poses to our security and his vulnerability to blackmail. He stat-
> ed, however, that he is undecided as to what his decision may be if we
> were to identify an employee who was an "open" homosexual. He stated
> that he was ambivalent on this point because he did not have any solid
> reasons for denying an "open" homosexual continued employment.[56]

Bush therefore raised the issue of the nexus between the polygraph's
methodology of eliciting personal secrets and the CIA's mission to protect national security secrets. "At this point, Mr. Blake [also of the Security Division] provided the Director with a number of reasons, such
as morale problems, refusal of other employees to be associated with
'open' homosexuals, and the propensity for homosexuals to recruit
their own kind." Bush was not yet convinced, the report noted, but the
CIA did not provide him more specific reasons for targeting homosexuality in its polygraph exams.[57]

We have seen that the CIA began using the polygraph because the
Director of Central Intelligence had been given the responsibility to
protect sources and methods, and because the FBI—at a crucial time
early in the bureaucratic turf wars—had refused to continue screening CIA applicants and employees. This leaves the question why the
CIA continued to use the polygraph. Justification moved from arguments of emergency, present in the first authorization of the polygraph
in 1948, to those of usefulness and experience. Having employed the

polygraph for some time, such claims for usefulness were often made from experience rather than scientific data. For example, a contingency report on the effects of abolishing the polygraph as a screening device declared: "While it has not been conclusively demonstrated that the presence of the polygraph itself contributes something that a straight interrogation by the same interrogator could not produce, experience strongly suggests this to be the case. . . . It seems reasonable to assume that the Agency's polygraph program has some deterrent value in inhibiting hostile penetration attempts." The same document also speculated about morale: "While taking a polygraph test is not regarded by many employees as a particularly enjoyable exercise . . . most seem to regard it at worst as a sort of necessary evil and as a mutual guarantee of bona fides among colleagues. Should the program be dropped, there is a strong possibility that employees would feel less confident in one another."[58]

Practical utility also became the argument the CIA used to defend the polygraph when Congress began to push harder against the institutions of the national security state in the mid-1970s. During the CIA's testimony before the Committee on Government Operations in June 1974, Harold Brownman, Deputy Director for Management and Services, admitted that "validity"—the degree to which polygraph charts measure what they purport to measure—"has been more difficult to evaluate [than consistency in chart interpretation]. . . . We still lack an appropriate scientific base for any conclusions." This did not mean, however, that the polygraph did not do what it was intended to do, Brownman stated. "Validity in the sense of utility" meant that the polygraph delivered reasons to deny clearance to job applicants. A bar graph that can be found in the documents the CIA submitted to Congress indicated that in seven out of the ten years from 1964 to 1973, the majority of security disapprovals had come from the polygraph process, for example 134 out of 152 in 1964.[59] On average, this was about 60 percent.[60]

In short, the polygraph elicited the most reasons for dismissing a person as a security risk or denying him or her employment. As to how precisely the polygraph chart itself had contributed to a negative decision, or whether the mere presence of a polygraph had elicited confessions from intimidated applicants, the CIA did not reveal. Therefore, the agency did not study how exactly the polygraph "worked," but it valued the machine nevertheless for its practical utility. The memoirs of CIA polygraph examiner John Sullivan concur with that conclusion. While the CIA's screening process includes a background investigation, a medical exam, psychological tests, and personal interviews, "a polygraph subject's admission of serious wrongdoing has more impact on a decision to disapprove an applicant than all other parts of the process combined."[61]

The polygraph made decisions "easy to defend," and it produced "in hours" information that background investigations "fail[ed] to uncover in weeks and months." In turn, inconclusive polygraph calls meant that OS had to admit it did not know enough about an applicant, which, in turn, could spark hostility from clearance officials who relied on the polygraph for their final decisions. Consequently, the circumstances of CIA polygraph tests, according to Sullivan, encouraged up-or-down polygraph calls, but did not supply the grounds for a decision.[62]

As impressive as polygraph "successes" might have appeared, they did not keep President Carter's DCI Stansfield Turner (who studied those statistics) from asking his deputy, "Would you give me a simple statement in laymen's language summarizing the generally accepted view of the validity of the polygraph technique?"[63] In his memoirs, Turner also expressed misgivings about the polygraph: "I volunteered for testing twice and each time found it repugnant just to have my honor implicitly questioned. And the sensation of being wired to a machine and not having any idea what it is registering created a sense of tension." Emphasizing that judgments about individuals should not be based solely on their polygraph test, Turner nevertheless insisted that periodic testing "inhibits loose security practices" because of "confessions that were elicited during retesting."[64] For Turner and other leaders, the alleged disciplinary effect of regular polygraph exams therefore was the strongest argument in their favor.

Systematic research into these matters, however, was limited. The priorities of screening applicants for the fast-growing agency favored quick application over careful investigation. Until the mid-1950s, CIA in-house research (from the Security Research Staff, a scientific unit in the Office of Security) on the polygraph was "sporadic," focusing on improving testing technique and question formulation. Here the agency adopted John Reed's "Control Question" method. As a memorandum from 1966 claimed, "These innovations not only improved our product but also improved our 'public image.'"[65] Twenty years after the inception of polygraph screenings, Director of Security Howard Osborn could report that in-house research had established "that polygraph reactions do exist and are used by polygraph examiners in their decision-making process. . . . There has been established a link from polygraph question to polygraph reaction to admission to utility of the admission."[66] What this meant was the rather prosaic fact that the polygraph did measure *something*—physiological responses to questions—and that these responses could be used to elicit admissions from subjects that the agency considered relevant to its security program. But this begged the question of what relevant areas of concern were.

The security relevance of information was outside the realm of technical research. Yet it was crucial in establishing the validity of polygraph screening for security purposes. Again, practice took precedent over research. After the U.S. Civil Service Commission in 1965 had issued instructions that severely limited psychological testing for most categories of federal employment, the CIA stated that "the problem is not one of eliminating invasion of privacy but, rather, of insuring that what is done is warranted." An unknown officer insisted that CIA procedures were "warranted" since they were "reliable and valid." He also admitted, however, that "the next problem is a broader one, that of establishing that there is a relationship between the topic being pursued and the national security. Little of this kind of research has been done."[67]

Another memorandum from the Office of Security (also written in response to congressional inquiries) suggested, "One of the first orders of business would be to explore and come to agreement on what are legitimate topics for a polygraph examination." The document continued,

> Even in CIA there is some problem in this area since we have not clearly defined our area of interest and are periodically accused of delving too far in the sexual area. . . . I do not feel that the question of signing a statement to the effect that the polygraph examination is voluntary enters into the question at this point inasmuch as very few, if any, people would take such

an examination if it were in fact voluntary. [The agency needs] a study of
just what are proper topics to be covered in security interviews in general,
whether or not a polygraph examination is also given.[68]

The central question that defined the task of the Office of Security,
therefore, was the purpose of security procedures in general, not just
the polygraph, and confusion over the benefits of the polygraph was
entangled with confusion over the purpose of security procedures in
general.

This discussion does not suggest that the search for security criteria in employing individuals was in vain, unnecessary, or doomed to
fail. Rather, it highlights that the utility of the polygraph procedure as
part of bureaucratic procedure did not solve the basic problem: that the
Office of Security needed to identify suitable employees and weed out
security risks using the same procedure. The agency asserted, "Little
distinction can be made between suitability and security acceptability.
There are applicants that are rejected solely on security grounds. More
often, however, the weaknesses or vulnerabilities that might make an
individual an unsuitable employee also disqualify him as an acceptable
security risk."[69] This, however, was an unproven assumption. Admissions of past behavior coming to light under during a polygraph exam
raised the question of whether standards of "security" from an intelligence standpoint and cultural standards of "suitability" from a broader
standpoint of sociocultural norms coincided or needed careful bureaucratic distinction.

The discussion above shows that controversies over polygraph
screening in the CIA illustrated "security" as a factor that could never
be disentangled from wider social norms. In fact, the CIA's trouble in
defining suitably loyal, reliable, and trustworthy employees was part of
the larger political legacy of the postwar era. Apart from its legal authorization to conduct security investigations of applicants and employees,
the CIA also had to fulfill the general security and loyalty requirements
assigned by the president. The agency encountered a problem here that
was not of its own making, namely to translate vague definitions of loyalty into specific bureaucratic procedures. President Truman's Executive Order 9835 of March 1947 established the federal government's prerogative to determine the loyalty of every federal employee. President

Eisenhower dismantled Truman's Loyalty Boards, but his Executive Order 10450 called for permanent security protocols. The order stated that "the interests of the National security require that all persons privileged to be employed in the departments and agencies of the Government, shall be reliable, trustworthy, of good conduct and character, and of complete and unswerving loyalty to the United States." To ensure this requirement, the order demanded that "the head of each department and agency of the Government shall be responsible for establishing and maintaining within his department or agency an effective program to ensure that the employment and retention in employment of any civilian officer or employee within the department or agency is clearly consistent with the interests of national security."[70]

The order connected personal character, reliability, loyalty, and national security into a seamless web of requirements. How to spin an equally seamless web of procedures was a different problem. Which specific "behavior, activities, or association" contradicted national security, and what specifically constituted "infamous, dishonest, immoral, or notoriously disgraceful conduct" or "sexual perversion"? It was equally difficult to define the meaning of "sympathetic association" with a "subversive" group.[71] While the Civil Service Commission was responsible for most federal employees, the CIA created its own rules to enforce the requirements of Executive Order 10450, which it included verbatim in its information material for applicants.[72]

We should also acknowledge that CIA officials sometimes showed acute awareness of the problems. An internal 1973 history on personnel security procedures illustrates this awareness. The document stated that while the agency expected that "those employed are of excellent character, and of unquestioned loyalty, integrity, discretion, and trustworthiness," it acknowledged the impossibility of fulfilling this ideal since "few—indeed, if any—individuals consistently evidence outstanding behavioral characteristics." The author opined that "personnel security standards employed during World War II were largely society's consensus of what constituted conventional morality," and continued that since then "a considerable experience factor was developed." In other words, actual cases of defection and information about the "modus operandi" of other foreign intelligence services became known. In addition, constant postwar reshuffling of personnel within the intelligence community made security particularly urgent. Yet despite considerable experience with security procedures by the early 1970s, the author concluded: "The precise yardstick for the measuring of security reliability of an individual continued to be elusive."[73]

We need to return to the fact that the CIA had to appear both threatening to potential opponents and appealing to the best and brightest, most loyal Americans. The synthesis of this double task was to emphasize "professionalism." Resistance to the polygraph highlighted the CIA's struggle to define precisely what it meant when the agency aspired to be a "truly professional intelligence organization," as an Inspector General's survey of 1959 ruminated. For example, professionalism could indicate an elite or egalitarian ethos, bureaucratic procedures or adventure. Especially when the first generation of Ivy League spies left the rapidly growing agency, this question became pertinent. The author of a 1959 survey captured the CIA's struggle to find its professional identity:

> The glamour of espionage is a powerful inducement to some as is the psychological attraction of "being on the inside" in matters of great importance in world affairs. The deeper and more sustaining motivation of serving in the interest of national security is the most durable inducement the Agency has to offer. . . . Some jobs in this Agency are most interesting and challenging but a very large part of our work is deadly monotonous, drudging routine.

Less travel than many hoped for and lack of status and advancement outside the CIA further reduced the attractiveness of intelligence work. The survey concluded, "Compared to the relative freedom of other vocations, intelligence work must be regarded as an abnormal way of life."[74]

In short, the CIA had to balance security with attractiveness to high caliber applicants. John Sullivan also states that "the time that it takes to complete a security processing" continues to be a major deterrent to CIA employment, and if the CIA needs a uniquely qualified person right away, a polygraph test can serve as a preliminary security screening.[75] We can see that the polygraph had to participate in this balancing act by making something "abnormal" part of normal agency life. For example, by 1957, the Security Office suggested that polygraph interrogations of senior employees returning from overseas assignments could be waived "if the last polygraph was of recent date and favorable and no question exists in the security file of the Subject."[76] Due to social pressures, CIA security procedures had to be flexible.

When the Office of Security could not keep up with the regular five-year repolygraph schedule in the mid-1960s, this lapse could have led to increased infiltration. Yet in a 1974 analysis, the Interrogation Research Branch concluded, "Analysis fails to justify use of the polygraph in terms of uncovering penetration attempts or developing serious security information. Not one of the [redacted] repolygraph cases surfaced as a counterintelligence case or case with CI overtones." Instead, the report fell back on "intangible advantages" of the polygraph as deterrence of wrongdoing or infiltration, or "peace of mind available to employees who recognize that their peers have also gone through and face again the possibility of polygraph."[77] What exactly the polygraph was good for thus remained immeasurable.

Espionage and covert operations were at the center of the action in the CIA from the beginning, as we have seen. Thus, it is not surprising that the polygraph took part in secret missions abroad as well.[78] While documentation of the role of the polygraph in foreign covert operations remains thin, the evidence suggests U.S. officials inside and outside the agency were intrigued by the allure of a "modern" interrogation instrument. At the same time, many U.S. field agents distrusted the polygraph and the importance CIA headquarters attached to it. Therefore, the lie detector did not become an uncontested arbiter of truthfulness. Instead, it ended up entangled in the web of CIA bureaucratic infighting and professional competition.

As discussed earlier, in the 1920s, August Vollmer in Berkeley endowed polygraphs with the ethos of modern, scientific policing. It is therefore not surprising to find that two Chinese police administrators of Chiang Kai-shek's nationalist government, Feng Yukun and Frank Lee, became familiar with the polygraph while training in Berkeley in the 1930s. Both men later became part of the Chinese internal secret police under the legendary and controversial General Tai Li.[79] Beginning in 1942, Li acquired American men and equipment as part of the Sino-American Cooperative Organization (SACO), a joint venture made up on the American side of officers from the U.S. Naval Group, China, and OSS officers. As part of this cooperation, the American volunteers in 1945 began a short-lived pilot training program under former FBI agent Charlie Johnston in "modern" policing techniques such as fingerprint identification, ballistic training, and lie detection. According to the memoirs of Rear Admiral Milton Miles, the training took place upon General Li's request, against the objections of both the OSS leadership in Washington and State Department China hands such as John Patton Davies.[80]

U.S. police training, which goes back to the U.S. occupation of the Philippines and America's informal empire in Latin America, became part of Cold War foreign policy as well. This practice was based on the idea that an effective police force could be the basis for anticommunist nation building. According to historian Jeremy Kuzmarov, U.S. policymakers embraced police training as more cost-effective than long-term occupations and less confrontational than outright military intervention. In order to fulfill this mission, U.S. training aimed at enabling indigenous forces to suppress internal dissent through effective access to intelligence. As Kuzmarov puts it, police training therefore "embod[ies] a U.S. imperial style grounded in short-term duty and quest for serviceable information."[81] The fact that lie detectors only made the occasional appearance in police training suggests that, absent constitutional or political restraints, U.S. allies preferred harsher methods and more explicit tools of violence to suppress internal dissent. Lacking checks and balances, even the most "modern" U.S. police technology ended up as blunt instruments of oppression. Nonlethal policing technologies such as rubber bullets and tear gas might have lowered the number of casualties in confrontations between police forces and citizens, but as with the polygraph, they did not in fact bring a democratic ethos. More often than not, U.S.-backed dictators used their American-trained police forces as blunt instruments of political oppression rather than as seed forces to build noncommunist democratic states.

While the CIA at times participated in nation-building efforts, its goals were usually more modest—namely the evaluation of defectors or the recruitment of agents and indigenous rebel forces. Here the polygraph played a larger role. As early as January 1950, DCI Hillenkoetter approved "the principle of testing individuals of all covert offices and of certain individuals in other offices."[82] In July 1950, the OPC (what later became the Directorate of Plans and then the Clandestine Service) "request[ed] all staff personnel to take a polygraph test before departing for a permanent overseas assignment" and demanded "new personnel who are hired for overseas assignments should be tested as soon as possible after their entry on duty."[83] The CIA recruited Ted Shackley—who later participated in some of the CIA's most controversial operations, such as the training of Cuban rebels and the Phoenix program in South Vietnam—from the Army in 1951. Shackley claims that he successfully used the polygraph at a safe house in Frankfurt, West Germany, to test the bona fides of Polish refugees who were suspected of working for the KGB after communist intelligence agencies had effectively operated a sham Polish resistance group, the Freedom and Independence Army, from 1947 to 1950. Shackley avers that he did not allow the polygraph to substitute for his own professional judgment: "I have been willing to use [polygraphs] but never to rely on them as infallible oracles."[84]

An article from the CIA in-house journal *Studies in Intelligence* from 1960 confirms that the Agency began to polygraph potential agents in Europe in 1949 and in the Far East in 1951, and "by 1952 the CIA polygraph program was operating on a world-wide basis. . . . The value of the technique to clandestine operations becomes a thing beyond debate." The article heralded the machine's ability to elicit "not otherwise obtainable admissions of deception," mostly about biographic information. Since the article did not specify what precisely was gained by uncovering this information, the author's praise for the machine as an enforcer of discipline and professionalism is yet again striking:

> A more general dividend realized from the polygraph is its disciplinary effect on the agent. He is usually a better clandestine operator after being polygraphed. He realizes that he is working for a highly professional service, concerned about security for itself and for him. He sees that he will be expected to account for his activities. Loyal agents almost always appreciate this attitude and look with greater respect on the American service after their "ordeal."[85]

This claim sparked a reply from polygraph operator Clark Diangson, who warned against relying on the polygraph instead of the expertise of the case officer: "All too often, the lazy and careless use [of the polygraph] is an excuse to neglect their own most elementary and basic duty—to know everything possible about their agents." Diangson argued that a well-prepared case officer could obtain most necessary information by himself through "an expert's knowledge of the sensitive practices and procedures of foreign services." The author also questioned the disciplinary benefits of the machine: "Agents are human: they do not necessarily 'appreciate our attitude' . . . and the agent who refuses to undergo the ordeal may still be needed and in fact may prove very effective in clandestine operations."[86]

This competition for expertise and authority in the CIA—and in particular in covert operations—is conveyed in many other accounts of CIA foreign operations. According to Duane Clarridge (a CIA officer since 1955 who was later indicted for his involvement in the Iran-Contra affair), overuse of the polygraph reflected a culture of inflexibility in the CIA:

> Clandestine Services afforded polygraphs too much centrality in authentications—and paid the price. Some cultures polygraph more effectively than others. Americans, because of our Puritanical tradition of right and wrong, are good subjects. Arabs and Iranians, for example, are notoriously difficult, because lying under certain circumstances is culturally acceptable. . . . That said, I admit to being a supporter of the polygraph, for I believe that it acts as a deterrent to traitorous and other aberrant behavior.[87]

Apart from the objection that in western culture, too, lying can be considered acceptable under certain conditions, one also has to point out that Clarridge, in this narrative of the polygraph, jumps from issues of individuals to speculative claims about cultures.[88] It is much more likely that language barriers and incomplete background information led to polygraph exams of foreign nationals that defied standard interrogation techniques. But the larger point here is that field agents called upon local knowledge, their instincts, and their experience to assess intelligence assets or agents, while the polygraph represented set procedures. Further, statements about the polygraph show how intelligence officers assert different personal expertise for themselves. For example, while Clarridge, in

the passage quoted above, claims that training countermeasures is possible, James Olsen categorically asserts that such methods "don't work."[89]

John Sullivan's two memoirs give us a further look into this competition between local and standardized knowledge. According to Sullivan, the agency's covert unit and the Interrogation and Research branch
fought a turf war over polygraph operations in the early 1950s, since in
the beginning covert operations made up the majority of the CIA. Sullivan remarks: "Antipathy . . . still exists between the Office of Security and
the clandestine service. . . . Many of the case officers with whom I worked
over the years saw me as a 'cop' who was out to bust their agents and not
as a safeguard against double agents and fabricators."[90] Given the polygraph's prominence in law enforcement, it is not surprising that it made
even CIA polygraph examiners feel they were taking on the role of "cop."

Hired in 1965, Sullivan claims his training "was cursory and, frankly,
not much more challenging than the training I underwent to become an
altar boy. . . . The lack of structure, written tests, lectures on the theoretical aspects of polygraph, etc., raised a question in my mind: 'If this is how
seriously they take training, how serious can they be about testing'?" In
fact, Sullivan concludes, "There was no greater proof of the CIA's distrust
of the polygraph than the fact that, unless admissions were obtained,
subjects passed their tests." Not until 1979, according to Sullivan, did the
CIA begin to refuse to grant clearance to applicants when they had not
confessed to a security-relevant infraction.[91] Throughout his memoir,
Sullivan complains of such lack of respect for the Interrogation Research
Division (only in 1980 was it renamed Polygraph Division), which he
calls "the bastard child of [the Office of] Security" and "the Siberia of
Security"—a grave for incompetent examiners. Polygraphers were called
"operators" to emphasize their status of technicians, rather than interrogators, and every time a new DCI was appointed, Sullivan wondered
"what his attitude regarding polygraph was."[92]

There is only scattered evidence of the use of the polygraph in covert
operations. For example, during Operation Ajax—the effort to overthrow Iranian prime minister Mohammad Mosaddeq in the summer of
1953—the CIA gave the Iranian military attaché in Washington, Colonel
Abbas Farzanegan, a polygraph test before sending him to Tehran to
join the coup.[93] Similarly, in preparing the ouster of Guatemalan President Jacobo Arbenz in 1954, numerous CIA sources were polygraphed

between March 26 and March 30, 1954, by a CIA examiner in a farm-
house, apparently in Panama, while the CIA was training a guerilla force
under Colonel Castillo.[94] Memoirs provide more detail but are hard to
verify. John Sullivan states in his Vietnam memoirs that his heart was in
operational testing, since "these cases were about the CIA's business—
clandestine operations. Being part of that world was important to me."
He saw an extended tour in Vietnam from 1969 to 1975 as an opportunity to "escape from IRD [Interrogation Research Division]'s depress-
ing atmosphere."[95] In Vietnam, Sullivan was confronted head-on with
the many policy conundrums that came with CIA efforts to build an
effective national police in South Vietnam and snuff out communists.
Intelligence sources had to be evaluated on the basis of little background
information and through almost insurmountable language barriers.
Field agents often fell in love with sources (sometimes not just figura-
tively) and expected confirmation rather than doubts about them. Station chiefs only supported the polygraph examiners when they boosted
the right numbers for reports back to Washington. Most exasperating,
according to Sullivan, was the need to cooperate with a deeply corrupt
Special Branch of the South Vietnamese National Police. In these circumstances, "voluntary" cooperation of subjects was a farcical idea.
Many Vietnamese only offered their services under pressure or in hope
of monetary rewards. The polygraph failed to contribute to any of the
successes U.S. policymakers were desperate for: "Being perceived as an
adversary goes with the territory [of being a CIA polygraph examiner],
but the problem was exacerbated in Vietnam. The pressure to recruit
was extraordinary, and the rewards for successful recruitment equally
so." The competition with field agents also meant that confessions were
priced even more highly than usual: "Although it is a bit of an oversim-
plification, it can be said that our successes—getting agents to admit that
they are not who they say they are—are case officers' failures. When an
agent or asset fails a polygraph test, the case officer's roster of agents is
diminished; he might have to retract previously reported information,
and he might be criticized for poor agent handling."[96]

All this meant that polygraph grunts had a thankless job. As was
revealed in the mid-1970s, CIA policies embraced psychological torture
and outright assassinations as means to "pacify" South Vietnam through
local Provincial Reconnaissance Units that were trained, equipped, and

supervised by CIA agents or military officers. While the record, again, shows the occasional use of polygraphs in these units, pressure to demonstrate successes led to much more brutal methods of interrogation.[97]

The competition between polygraph interrogators and case officers consequently was not between man and machine. It was between different types of job description and professional ethos. "Russian spies are trained to beat the polygraph" was a comment Sullivan heard throughout his career, intended to undermine his claim to usefulness.[98] With particular glee, Sullivan then tells the story of his polygraph test with a Cuban source whose chart showed significant reactions that allowed Sullivan to clarify a case. "The test worked on [Cubans] as it does on most people."[99] Accordingly, Sullivan also underscores this competition when he describes his professional humiliation on occasions when he had to tell a suspected double agent that he had passed the polygraph, so that a field agent could signal CIA trust as part of a double bluff.[100] Polygraph conflicts therefore magnified other institutional conflicts. If polygraph tests delivered other parts of the agency what they needed, their standing was high, and vice-versa.

CIA policies also created pressure on the Interrogation Branch/Polygraph Division that defied the assumption that a polygraph examination could be the seamless extension of whatever an examiner wanted out of the test. In one infamous case, Russian defector Yuri Nosenko was held in solitary confinement for almost three years (from 1965 to 1967) under suspicion of being a double agent. Part of the CIA's interest in Nosenko stemmed from the fact that he claimed to have reviewed Lee Harvey Oswald's KGB case file and that there had been no Soviet involvement in President John F. Kennedy's assassination. However, since chief of Counterintelligence Angleton assumed that the KGB had sent Nosenko in order to discredit Anatoly Golitsyn (another KGB officer who had defected six months earlier), Nosenko's interrogators aimed at confirming their suspicion of his guilt rather than examining his story objectively.

Frustrated CIA interrogators confronted Nosenko on several occasions with a barrage of relevant questions, risking "test-tiredness" in their emotionally exhausted subject. According to standard polygraph practice, such testing overkill made the results unreliable.[101] Further, as part of a relentless program of hostile interrogation, Nosenko was given "truth drugs" for at least three sessions with the polygraph. Before the first test in April 1964, Nosenko was told that the polygraph recorded brain waves in order to increase the pressure on him. It had already been decided that he would be told he had flunked the test. The second interrogation in October 1966 lasted eleven days. Nosenko was not allowed to move for hours, making the procedure resemble torture even more closely. According to journalist David Wise, after dissenting CIA officers voiced criticism of the cruelty inflicted upon the prisoner, Nosenko conveniently passed a third round of testing over two non-consecutive days in August 1968.[102] These polygraph interrogations—accompanied by a pitiless program of torture techniques, especially sensory deprivation, humiliation, and disorientation—did not settle the disputes about his bona fides; they also showed that over a decade of research into "brainwashing" techniques had proved useless in a high-profile interrogation.[103]

In other cases the test could also not be bent to the will of the examiner without resorting to outright manipulation. Sullivan states that in the mid-1980s, the Polygraph Division reached a low point when it was discovered that over the years a number of examiners had falsified polygraph charts in order to pass subjects they considered honest but whose charts were nonconclusive. Some examiners had switched relevant with irrelevant questions on the chart (therefore falsifying the evidence of when during a test the subject had shown nervousness); others would redo a test until they had obtained a chart supporting their opinion, which was the only chart they would hand in to their supervisors. With one exception, according to Sullivan, "each examiner who fabricated a test seemed to have done so with the intention of either getting a subject through a test or avoiding an interrogation." In short, if a confrontational interrogation appeared too cumbersome, a number of CIA polygraph examiners chose their hunch over the polygraph chart. Only the veil of secrecy prevented a scandal.[104]

As long as the public perceived the CIA to be competent, polygraph tests appeared to work, while, in turn, every revelation of failure or wrongdoing put the polygraph under pressure. No example illustrates this phenomenon better than the Aldrich Ames case, a scandal that was bad for the CIA and worse for the polygraph. Whatever reputation the lie detector had amassed by sensational press coverage earlier in the twentieth century, it lost in January 1994, when the FBI arrested Ames on charges of selling information to the Soviet Union and Russia that had led to the exposure of at least one hundred CIA sources and the deaths of at least ten agents.

Ames was the son of a CIA officer and joined the agency in 1962. He rose up the ranks in counterintelligence and was eventually responsible for recruiting agents in Eastern Europe and the Soviet Union. By all accounts, Ames was not a communist sympathizer but likely started giving up information in 1985 to finance his and his second wife's expensive lifestyle. This means that questions about communist sympathies upon his polygraph employment test would have been meaningless to him. If anything, Ames was apathetic about the Cold War and cynical about the CIA's purposes.[105] The fact that an employee with an annual salary of $60,000 was able to buy a $500,000 home with cash should have raised red flags, but Ames's claim that his Columbian in-laws were wealthy was apparently never seriously investigated. In addition, press coverage soon focused on the fact that Ames had passed two repolygraphing procedures in 1986 and 1991.

John Sullivan recalls, "A case like this was what many of CIA's anti-polygraph factions had been waiting for." In defense of CIA polygraph operators, Sullivan points out that by the time of his first polygraph test, Ames had already delivered the most destructive documents; even if he had been caught, the damage would have been done. Also, according to Sullivan, the fact that Ames had a bad reputation yet rose to a position where he could do serious damage sheds light on the low status of counterintelligence officers in the CIA. Lastly, polygraph examiners in 1991 had no knowledge of the fact that Ames's prior background investigation had raised the issue of his mysterious wealth. As a result, one change in polygraph policy after the Ames case was the introduction of random testing of current employees.[106] This was meant to provide another layer of quality control and an additional bureaucratic hurdle.[107]

However, this adjustment did not address the question of the test's validity, nor did it solve the practical issue that polygraph exams were never administered on a completely egalitarian basis to all employees, nor according to the exact same standard. Former operations officer David Doyle echoes Sullivan's complaints: "Reliance on the polygraph—many of whose overloaded operators were inadequately trained and improperly briefed—was too great [in the 1980s], and yet paradoxically its results were often ignored. Ames was actively protected when troubling lie detector test results were excused as being of no consequence."[108]

The Ames case led to the reopening of thousands of security files and confronted CIA officers and agents with the dynamics of security overkill. In this context, resentment toward the polygraph further deepened the cultural divide between field officers (and their claims to expertise) and the bureaucratic prerogatives of headquarters. For example, in case officer Robert Baer's memoir *See No Evil,* the trope of local experience vs. top-down policies is illustrated through polygraph anecdotes. Having passed the "dreaded polygraph," Baer became a field officer in 1976, with tours of duty in Europe and the Middle East in the 1980s and 1990s. After the Ames case blew open, Baer had to report to a polygraph test as part of what he saw as a purge within the agency. "I was assigned the meanest, grizzliest polygrapher security had. He'd been around and knew how the game worked. He could tell the difference between a mole and someone who was in the business of meeting foreigners. I was in and out in an hour. My colleagues weren't so fortunate. Too many of them ended up with twenty-three-year-old polygraphers plucked out of the hills of West Virginia—people who thought all foreigners were communists."[109] Embedded in a narrative of clashes between daring field officers and risk-averse superiors, Baer's polygraph experience is meant to represent the superiority of lived experience over bureaucratic inflexibility and American myopia.

Aldrich Ames confessed in jail that he *had* been nervous about his 1986 polygraph. While the KGB was interested in preparing subjects for polygraph exams, there is no evidence suggesting any systematic efforts to research polygraph procedures on the Soviet side, even though polygraphs might have been used on occasion. According to the files of former KGB operative Vasili Mitrokhin, in 1978 the KGB administered a polygraph test on Romeo spy Wilhelm Kahle, an East German illegal working in the West under an assumed identity. When headquarters came to suspect that Kahle merely enjoyed the good life in Paris without sufficient efforts at espionage, he was recalled to Moscow and polygraphed *on the pretext* that he needed to be prepared for his next assignment.[110] In the Ames case, the advice the spy received from his Soviet handlers was this: "Get a good night's sleep, and rest, and go into the test rested and relaxed. Be nice to the polygraph examiner, develop a rapport, and be cooperative and try to maintain your calm."[111] In short, Ames simply had to follow conventional standards of showing sincerity. His chart did show elevated responses on the issue of having been "pitched"—approached by a foreign intelligence service—but this reaction could be explained easily by the nature of Ames's work. After all, intelligence officers were often in touch with foreigners with ambiguous intentions. Ames subsequently called the polygraph "junk science," the usefulness of which lay "somewhere on the scale between the rubber truncheon and the diploma on the wall behind the interrogator's desk."[112] If Ames was cynical about the CIA, his polygraph experience did nothing to alleviate that cynicism.

Whether the polygraph test could ever claim to have caught a spy remains contested. In the case of Edward Lee Howard, a case officer in Moscow who defected in 1985, an argument can be made that it was his dismissal due to admissions of alcoholism, drug use, theft, and cheating during a pre-deployment polygraph exam that pushed him to *start* cooperating with the Soviet Union.[113]

Yet there is also the case of Sharon Scranage, who joined the CIA in 1976. She was transferred to Ghana in 1983, and eventually worked there as an operations support assistant. In Ghana, Scranage—a divorced African American woman who may have felt slighted by the culture of the CIA dominated by white men—began an affair. Her lover was a Ghanaian man named Michael Soussoudis, with whom she shared the identity of American sources and agents in Ghana. Scranage first came under suspicion in 1984, when an inspection team noticed Soussoudis's picture in her apartment. However, according to John Sullivan, the polygraph examiner who interrogated Scranage during a routine test the following year had not been told about any suspicions. When Scranage showed physiological responses to the question of whether she had shared secret information with an unauthorized person, the interrogator managed to get a confession out of her. Scranage pleaded guilty to one count of revealing classified information and two counts of disclosing names of CIA agents and cooperated with an FBI investigation that led to Soussoudis's arrest. Yet, again according to Sullivan, CIA superiors subsequently downplayed the role of the polygraph exam in this affair of a Ghanaian Romeo spy and a lonely American officer.[114] While the exact chronology of events—and the role of different investigative methods—remains unclear, the case of Sharon Scranage does highlight the success of an effective interrogation with the help of a polygraph.

Sullivan's defense of the test as an "art" highlights how the polygraph cannot be separated from the overall culture and procedures of the CIA. In stark contrast, the fact that Congress and the public singled out Ames's polygraph exams emphasizes that the very justification for a practice as confrontational and controversial as the polygraph was that it could in fact detect lies. The Ames case was one of the few occasions when the polygraph's claims for scientific precision had to publicly confront a clear demonstration of failure.

We can conclude that the polygraph adapted to and shaped CIA culture. Given that the CIA was created as America's *central* intelligence agency, an ethos of being the elite unit pervaded the CIA and probably fueled its faithfulness to the polygraph. Furthermore, the polygraph's ability to elicit information from individuals became its strongest argument. In this role, however, it was dependent upon the interrogator who used it and the mission the agency had given them in each particular case.

The quantity of confessions became the substitute for the quality of information. Determining what terms like "security reliability" meant became a secondary problem. As long as no other procedure could produce those results, the polygraph remained in Uncle Sam's service. In John Sullivan's words: "Until a better, less intrusive means of obtaining [information] comes along, [the] polygraph is and should be here to stay. . . . [A]s many problems with and valid criticisms of [the] polygraph as there are, it is the best security-screening device available."[115] Though Sullivan may be correct about the function of the polygraph in the CIA, the public still does not see the polygraph as a "security-screening device"; rather, the public views the polygraph simply as the "lie detector."

The CIA started to experiment with the polygraph because Harry Truman feared an American Gestapo and because of J. Edgar Hoover's jealousy. While it was not inevitable that the CIA would become the strongest supporter of the lie detector among national security agencies, the CIA and the polygraph were a good fit. This chapter's main conclusion is that the polygraph represents the uncertainties and vulnerabilities of the CIA's mission. The fact that the "dreaded" lie detector found a place within the security culture is to a large degree owed to the fact that it helped create what has been called the "clandestine mentality" or "front-line mentality" within agencies that saw themselves as elite.[116] In other words, the polygraph became an initiation ritual—and therefore part of the socialization process within the CIA as a secret society.[117] CIA documents were consequently closer to the truth than their authors might have realized when they stated the polygraph was an "inestimable" and "immeasurable" aid to security. This conclusion starkly contrasts the way polygraph exams often exude to their subject an air of power and mastery of the subject's thoughts and emotions. This may not surprise us, since the performance of power—especially arbitrary power—often reflects weakness and requires a posture of mastery. As political scientist James Q. Wilson reminds us, when policy goals are vague, administration becomes policy, and available technology defines bureaucratic tasks. The availability of polygraphs likely played a role in creating the security policies of the CIA without resolving basic questions of purpose.[118] The polygraph therefore ultimately participated in the construction of the American Cold War by positioning the United States in a security-obsessed posture that deflected from contradictory institutional policies and open-ended goals.

CHAPTER 7

The Polygraph and the Problems of Deterrence

n 1961, Ralph Gerard had an idea. The University of Michigan neurophysiologist had been thinking about ways to break the deadlock in arms control negotiations using the insights of the behavioral science. Maybe the vicious cycle of mutual distrust and rapidly evolving nuclear capabilities could be broken if world leaders could trust each other again.

Gerard thus made the following proposal:

> The argument is simple: given matched power ... opposing nations will resort to actual warfare overwhelmingly as a result of mistrust of the other or of misunderstanding resulting from false information—either suspected or actual. My solution is to ensure that public or other official statements made by key figures are indeed true. This can be done with available lie detection techniques if national leaders will submit to them. . . . The proposal is simply this: all key men, speaking officially for their country in private negotiations or public addresses, subject

182

themselves to lie, or better, truth detection procedures administered by technicians from an opposing country or from the UN. More positively, when a statesman wished to convince the world that he was making a true statement he would subject himself to truth detection.[1]

The polygraph, as envisioned by Gerard, would be used to detect evasions of disarmament agreements and—"more positively"—it would help the truth be heard. Verification would lead to trust.

Gerard's proposal was an intervention in a debate between the supporters of official U.S. nuclear strategy, which depended on maintaining deterrence by constantly updating the nuclear arsenal on the basis of different threat scenarios, and supporters of a universal regime of open government that had inspired the founding of the United Nations and continued to drive the peace movements of the 1950s and 1960s. Particularly the physicists of the Manhattan Project, organizing first at the sites of their work but since 1945 spawning large-scale organizations like the Federation of American Scientists (FAS), were at the forefront of an open government for peace movement.[2] Scientists, scholars, and celebrities, including Norman Cousins, Erich Fromm, and Marlon Brando, joined together in 1957 to form the Committee for Sane Nuclear Policy (SANE), which campaigned for an end to nuclear testing and worked alongside other groups, such as the Committee for non-Violent Action (CNVA), which held a more radical pacifist stance and preferred direct, confrontational action against nuclear installations. While the Vietnam War divided SANE in the 1960s, CNVA built a bridge to the New Left. Various outside groups continued protesting the arms race, especially nuclear rearmament in the early 1980s, until the end of the Cold War and beyond.[3]

This chapter discusses the way a group of scientists—including Ralph Gerard, David Inglis, Jay Orear, and Lewis Bohn—collaboratively imagined the lie detector's role in breaking the vicious cycle between distrust and nuclear armaments. The discussion will show how the lie detector could be envisioned to solve strategic Cold War dilemmas of how to establish cooperation without trust. Yet we will also see that the ideas of supporters of the lie detector went *counter* to prevailing U.S. strategic policy and that the lie detector proved incapable of leading the way toward an alternate political approach to the arms race.

Gerard's scheme to use scientific methods to "read" foreign leaders was not outlandish. In fact, similar ideas had been circulating among scientists, politicians, and nuclear strategists for some time. For example, psychological profiling of opponents and partners alike—with special attention to their sincerity—was standard procedure in U.S. intelligence since Walter Langer's study of Adolf Hitler for the OSS in World War II.[4] Since the 1950s, the CIA used polygraphs to verify the trustworthiness of its agents in covert operations. Gerard was more misguided when he believed the claims of polygraph boosters that testing in private industry had achieved 95% success rates, and that "probably at present, certainly in the immediate future with an appropriate effort, adequate lie detecting techniques are or will be available." Statements such as this illustrate that the *promise* of lie detection was always its greatest strength. This promise made lie detection at home in the technocratic optimism pervasive among scientists. "I cannot but believe," Gerard asserted, "that a mastery of man comparable to mastery of nature will allow men to live together rather than die together."[5] Such hyperbole, reminiscent of early-twentieth-century psychologists such as Hugo Münsterberg, reveled in the pathos of crisis that was the flip side of the euphoria that modern technological and scientific advancement often evoked in its practitioners.

Other measures to control human irrationality did not lack supporters either. In his essay, Gerard rather casually considered methods of "biological manipulation or social reconditioning of the aggressor," such as "manipulat[ing] the brains of whole populations, by pills and the like," as legitimate possibilities to rein in human self-destructive urges. He only dismissed such methods because they lay "far in the future" and were "probably unenforceable." Here the neurophysiologist was voicing interest in methods of mental manipulation and behavior modification that American intelligence agencies had been researching since World War II as well. A little more than a decade passed after Gerard's article before first indications of this research became widely known.[6] Among scientists and intelligence agencies, we can find here alternately a utopian and dystopian literary imagination at work. This imagination guided scientific and national security thinking toward research into ways that the rational and emotional mind could be harmonized.[7]

Eventually, however, scientists focused their efforts more narrowly on the question of how to contain the arms race. Many of their proposals centered on the question of how to verify that each side was abiding by an agreement. Through public discussions and protests, publications, conferences and working groups, and informal meetings with policymakers worldwide, they pushed for a halt in the spiral of escalation. At the University of Michigan, a number of natural and social scientists joined this movement, searching to apply progress in their respective fields of research to issues of arms control and eventual disarmament. Their 1960 proposal for a peace agency in the federal government echoed the language August Vollmer had used in the 1930s in his calls to counter transnational crime with new instruments of scientific policing: "The sudden contraction of the world requires a new, objective look at the sources of conflict and the possible alternatives of action. We have thousands of men studying the most effective ways of applying force; we have very few studying the most effective way of building a new world order. We need to get a new prospective, to see the present as a time for pioneering."[8]

As part of this collective effort, a number of scientists and analysts imagined the lie detector as a method of inspection. As early as 1952, David R. Inglis, a nuclear physicist at the University of Massachusetts and member of the Federation of American Scientists, pondered steps to introduce a control regime of nuclear material and suggested that the lie detector could serve in such an inspections regime. Inglis argued that the longer both superpowers produced weapons-grade material secretly, the harder it would become to agree on sovereign ownership of such material by a neutral agency, or to implement continuous, large-scale inspection of nuclear material in the United States and the Soviet Union by such an agency. Because of uncertain amounts of undeclared stocks of weapons,

> [U]ncertainty exists, [and] each nation may be considered by the other to retain clandestinely within its possession an amount of fissionable material approximately equal to that which it retains legally [under the proposed disarmament plan], and this secreted material will perforce by available for surprise attack. . . . Hence it is imperative that the uncertainty be reduced to the lowest possible figure if a useful amount of disarmament is to be achieved.[9]

In order to check upon past production, Inglis proposed a regime to survey personnel records of scientists, records of relevant production and mining operations, electric power allocation, water consumption, budget surveillance, delivery services, and "the interviewing of personnel including the application of 'lie detector' techniques."[10] In contrast to Gerard's later proposal, Inglis therefore incorporated the polygraph into a larger calculation of risk reduction that targeted nuclear *capabilities* rather than the intentions of political leaders. It was meant to define rational grounds for accepting a low risk of being cheated by the opponent in a control arrangement. Elsewhere, Inglis called this goal "restraint [in the arms race] with sufficient symmetry between the contending nations as not to invite dangerous adventure." By the early 1960s Inglis shared the hope that "a low-level transitional deterrent stage" of arms reduction could buy time to create institutions for "essentially complete national disarmament as the ultimate goal, with greatly reduced danger of accidental war in the meantime."[11] In short, Inglis became more optimistic and was looking for mutual, institutionalized stabilizing measures as the first step toward comprehensive disarmament. He supported a nuclear test ban as the first measure of moderation that could be followed by control of production of nuclear material, control of delivery systems, and eventual elimination of existing weapons.[12]

He was not alone. By the early 1960s, ideas for arms control came in many varieties, with proposals ranging from unilateral disarmament (put forth by SANE luminaries such as Erich Fromm) and calls to categorically reject first use of nuclear weapons, to elaborate schemes of verification that would reduce, if not eliminate, the chance for cheating and gradually introduce a measure of trust. For Inglis, the lie detector mainly worked at a point in inspection where physical measures stopped working: "Unfortunately, it is not possible to verify by technical means whether a nation has gotten rid of all its fissionable material." However, "it might . . . be possible to establish control of stockpiles by questioning the people who should know about them."[13]

Others molded the ideas of Inglis and Gerard into an even more comprehensive arms control system that sought to rekindle democratic voluntarism as a driving force of inspection. Cornell University physicist Jay Orear made an especially bold proposal in the *Bulletin of the*

Atomic Scientists, the publication of the FAS that was a platform to voice ideas about nuclear and many other issues related to the Cold War. In an article titled "A New Approach to Inspection" in the March 1961 issue, Orear discussed "nonphysical techniques that might be incorporated into a disarmament treaty." The basis for such nonphysical inspection would be treaty stipulations that allowed "the international inspectorate the right to ask any citizen questions concerning possible treaty violations." Part of such a regime could be a legal duty to report such violations, a system of punishment and reward ("One prize could be a paid vacation trip around the world for the citizen and his family"), sanctuary for informers, a safe communications system to transmit relevant information, such as specially sealed postal envelopes, and "enthusiastic support on a regular basis through the mass media." Further, "If a reliable lie detector could be developed and proven in field tests, the treaty could give the inspectorate the right to use the instrument."[14]

Utilizing another recent method to get to citizens' thoughts, the article cited a scientific poll that showed strong support for such a theme among the U.S. population. The author was especially enthusiastic about the fact that 80 percent of respondents indicated that they would report persons who secretly made forbidden weapons. The accuracy or significance of this poll is hard to gauge.[15] However, Orear not only sought to encourage supranational loyalty, but to "make use of national loyalty itself to prevent treaty violations." After all, would patriotic citizens not want to uphold the law of the land? The question was whether such a scheme could be realistic, so Orear further suggested polling "key personnel" on scenarios under which they would inform an international inspectorate.[16]

Orear was not alone in assuming that willingness to undergo a lie detector test was a sign of loyalty. Many in the U.S. government held that position. But similar to Ralph Gerard, his proposal assumed that the lie detection regime would have to be administered by a neutral, objective authority. While domestically, U.S. government agencies dealing with national security claimed to have such authority, internationally they would have been asked to surrender it. As Orear failed to notice, it was one thing to ask your own citizens to "volunteer" for such a test, and quite another to cede that privilege to an international inspections regime.

It appears that the promise of lie detection as objective and effective always reached further than what laboratory research bore out. Orear hoped that this missing link could be closed by international cooperation:

> The idea of using a lie detector for inspection of disarmament is an intriguing one. With a foolproof system, disarmament could proceed at its fastest rate. Unfortunately, the field experiments with lie detectors used on criminals shows that lie detection as practiced by police in the U.S. is not as foolproof as would be desired. For this reason, the public acceptance of the lie detector is not high enough for it to be of use in inspection of arms control at present. . . . It would be best if [further] research were conducted jointly by scientists of the East and West.[17]

Yet again, reliable lie detection seemed to depend on the very trust, cooperation, and voluntarism it sought to establish, as well as on a notion of scientific research as completely value-free and objective. Still, inspection by "the people" apparently evoked some optimism at a time when the superpowers were deadlocked over questions of physical monitoring systems of a nuclear test ban. With its appeal to the good sense and higher loyalty of individuals, Orear's proposal was also a perfect example of the hopes of the transnational anti-nuclear movement in the early 1960s. Orear had presented his proposal at the 1960 Pugwash Conference on Science and World Affairs in Moscow. The Pugwash movement had emerged out of the 1955 Russell-Einstein Manifesto, in which preeminent public intellectuals Bertrand Russell and Albert Einstein had called for an international conference of scientists to assess the world situation with regards to atomic weapons. From the first meeting in 1957 in Pugwash, Nova Scotia, to the last conference in 1971, the gatherings would attract nuclear scientists and other scholars from around the world, including the Soviet Union. Orear reported that five Soviet scientists had voiced approval of his scheme, and that Premier Nikita Khrushchev had supported it as well.[18]

While State Department officials in the late 1950s responded coldly to Orear's ideas, he and Gerard were enthusiastic about making common cause. "I am delighted to find somebody thinking along the same lines; the idea of using lie detection seems to me a genuine possibility toward avoiding another war (if it can be done soon enought [sic]!). I have brought my views to the attention of a number of people in government; maybe we can reinforce one another," Gerard wrote Orear in April 1961. Orear responded, "I strongly endorse everything in your paper" and proposed cooperation. Orear also suggested Gerard familiarize himself with the work of Lewis C. Bohn.[19]

Bohn conceptualized the ideas discussed above into an approach called "psychological inspection." As an analyst in the RAND Corporation and member of the Lockheed Electric Company's Systems Research Center, Bohn was at one of the most prominent places to examine psychological issues of nuclear strategy. Created by the Air Force in 1944, this research and development unit of physical and social scientists, based in Santa Monica, California, began with "operational analysis" of the effectiveness of strategic bombing in World War II. Thanks to generous funding from the Ford Foundation, RAND soon expanded to other aspects of military strategy and eventually applied systems analysis to all types of social problems. Some RAND studies became famous for their cool calculations of the unthinkable consequences of nuclear war, and a number of RAND concepts entered everyday language. Bernard Brodie theorized the idea of "deterrence" as mutual fear of retaliation; Albert Wohlstetter created "fail-safe," a system to recall bombers carrying nuclear weapons in cases of false alarm; and Herman Kahn argued for "civil defense"—a massive build-up of nuclear fallout shelters—to calculate what Kahn with breathtaking audacity defined as acceptable human losses in a nuclear war. RAND analysts, the celebrities of Cold War policymaking, created the theoretical basis for the Internet and influenced U.S. military policy in many other ways throughout the Cold War and beyond.[20]

In a paper entitled "Psychological Inspection," Bohn (then at the RAND Social Science Division) explored an approach to arms control, "pursued not in places but in people: in the minds and actions of policymakers, and in the minds and actions of those below the policy level who may have some knowledge of activities, weapons, or installations forbidden by [an arms] agreement."[21] As Bohn stressed, psychological inspection was only complementary to physical inspection regimes, but it carried the distinct advantage that it could pinpoint where to look for violations: the minds of policymakers and engineers. What was needed was just a way to expose guilty knowledge:

Instruments can be arranged to measure and record chemical and electrical responses of the individual being questioned, as has of course been done for some years in psychological research, as well as with the "lie detectors" in domestic crime detection. To propose precise measurements of the physical and mental responses of national decision-makers appears novel, drastic, and (at first) incredible; but the nuclear dangers with which such techniques would be designed to cope are also novel, drastic, and (at first) incredible.[22]

We can see here how the polygraph sparked ideas of technological control, because similar to David Inglis, Bohn saw the abundance of physical material—proliferation of nuclear know-how, the accumulation of fissionable material, ever-growing stockpiles of weapons—as reaching a "point of no return," making exhaustive physical control of such material impossible. As a result, "the military power of nuclear materials that could be kept from international detection is now already intolerably great, and is rising year by year."[23] Among strategic theorists, therefore, mapping the supposedly closed world of the individual mind rather than the limitless physical world became an object of interest, just as the free movement of individuals in mass society had sparked the interest of police administrators in lie detection in the 1920s.

Bohn stressed that the precise regime of psychological inspection would have to be subject to prior agreement. "Political leaders, especially if they have attained top power in totalitarian countries, may be highly experienced in the art of public deception," but "if modern scientific techniques can be employed to uncover this evidence, then possibilities for doing this must be studied seriously."[24] The polygraph, therefore, attracted the interest of scientists who pondered the dilemmas of the nuclear arms race because it fit the bill of a "modern scientific technique" that could provide an escape from such dilemmas.

But what if the polygraph did not work with scientific precision? Here, Bohn went further than his fellow lie detector proponents. RAND analysts prized themselves for calculating even that which could not be calculated. In case of the polygraph, Bohn went on to argue, the very uncertainty of what emotional responses would be revealed in a lie detector test could be made part of the risk calculation of psychological inspection and ultimately lead to deterrence of lies:

The potential evader may well be unable to . . . know with confidence exactly what his chances are of succeeding unless he can know with confidence his own physiological reactions under questioning—and know with confidence the actions that will be taken by any of his rivals, scientists, officers . . . who do learn of his evasion attempts. And if in his over-all choice of action . . . he is faced with these large uncertainties, he may be more effectively deterred from evasion (other things being equal) than in the relatively calculable physical inspection situation.[25]

In other words, Bohn hoped that rational choice would motivate policymakers not to dare the polygraph. Overall, this was a highly technocratic approach that blended out the fact that arms negotiations were as much political as strategic in nature. Therefore, psychological inspection was only one aspect of building an arms control regime, and the polygraph addressed only a small aspect of the problems that verification posed. For example, none of the proposals put forth by Inglis, Orear, Bohn, and Gerard took account of the question what to do after a breach was detected. What if, for political reasons, it was better to ignore minor breaches by the opponent in order not to threaten progress on other fronts? Technology did not provide answers to such political questions.

Still, the lie detector was appealing to these scientists because it allowed them to think creatively about urgent issues of arms control. First, if the lie detector really could uncover deception, it could find a place in inspection regimes when physical evidence of nuclear activity was out of reach. This problem was of particular urgency because the arms race constantly expanded the sphere of physical nuclear activity. In the early 1960s it was indeed about to leave the earth and enter space, defying all physical limits. The lie detector could therefore, at least potentially, contain a globalized strategic conflict. Second, effective lie detection could deter, if not detect, cheating in disarmament regimes, targeting the *intentions,* and not just the capabilities, of the opponent. Social scientists such as David Singer of the University of Michigan, who incorporated ideas of psychological deterrence into their thinking, insisted that progress in nuclear technology, such as the ability to create "cleaner" nuclear explosions due to an improved fission-to-fusion ratio, often could indicate improved defensive *and* offensive capabilities. Therefore, Singer insisted, "we cannot afford to infer intentions and actions from capabilities." He criticized Herman Kahn's demand for credible U.S. first-strike capability, arguing that Kahn "wants us to engage in the sort of behavior which is supposed to deter the U.S.S.R., but which, if employed by them, would almost certainly compel us to opt for a pre-emptive strike." Ultimately, "supra-national political institutions" would have to take control of all weapons unnecessary for domestic policing.[26] Picking up these ideas, Gerard emphasized that if a policymaker wanted to convince the world that he was speaking the truth, passing a polygraph test could amplify the truth and create a kind of "positive evidence" in the court of public opinion.

Finding positive evidence of sincerity posed an ideological problem, as will be discussed below. But for other scientists it was the key to addressing the problem of rapidly escalating crises that could lead to nuclear war. One of RAND's most prominent analysts, Thomas Schelling, theorized ways to anticipate emergencies and enact countermeasures in order to avoid an accidental nuclear war. Schelling based his thinking on the premise that in case of a sudden crisis, "both sides would be emphatically eager, desperately eager, to convey the truth if in fact the truth were reassuring, and to behave in ways that facilitate observation of the truth."[27] Schelling thought about flexible, versatile emergency inspection-observation-communication forces that could stand ready to verify the truth (say, that the Soviet Union was not in fact evacuating its cities in preparation for a nuclear war), but also suggested an instant line of communication between Moscow and Washington. After the Cuban Missile Crisis, that recommendation of a "hotline"—a standing direct communication avenue between Washington and Moscow—became reality. Even though Schelling did not mention the lie detector as part of a flexible crisis truth-verification force, his observations highlight how the prospect of nuclear war inspired thinking about ways to quickly verify the truthfulness of statements if necessary.

Gerard and his allies were enthusiastic about the their ideas and began to lobby for them.[28] In June 1961, Gerard chaired a "planning conference on truth demonstration techniques" that included 23 scientists, among them Bohn and Orear, psychologists David T. Lykken and Joseph Kubis, and Jesse Orlansky of the Institute for Defense Analyses (IDA) in Washington, DC, a nonprofit think tank created in 1956 to assist the federal government with scientific research. Under Orlansky's direction the group issued a report in 1962. Participants recognized the many methodological pitfalls of the polygraph exam and concluded that it would likely be a complementary rather than exclusive means of nonphysical inspection.[29] At another meeting held from July 19 to July 21, 1961, that included members of the State Department's Disarmament Agency and two additional members of the IDA, participants proceeded on the assumption that an arms control agreement was possible and that the USSR would be open to using lie detection as part of the inspections regime. Further, the conference repeated the optimistic assumption that "lie detection by objective measurement of physiological responses has a reliability of 75 to 95 percent" and emphasized the technocratic argument that "the US is interested in determining the cost-effectiveness of lie detection for possible use as one means of inspecting an arms control agreement." Participants also agreed on a wide-ranging research agenda on various aspects of measuring physiological responses to questions.[30]

On September 13, 1961, the IDA finally hosted a conference "Application of Truth Demonstration Techniques to International Politics and Negotiations." The rather modest goal of this meeting was to convince the Department of Defense of the feasibility of exploring the possibilities in lie detection in arms control and "truth demonstration" in political settings when a leader wanted to convince the world of their sincerity. The scientists at this meeting finally also focused on the cultural and political implications of their ideas and held a wide-ranging discussion that included issues such as the influence of cultural orientations toward lying, problems of ambiguous denotative statements, the kind of publicity that polygraph results would receive, and potential disruption of diplomacy if one side were to unilaterally make public statements under a lie detection protocol. However, at the end of the meeting it was agreed that all such questions were "researchable" and that "the contributions of behavioral science are critical in this area of human interactions, world war and peace. Whatever success the particular devices or procedures may have, it is felt that further research is desirable."[31]

The years 1961 and 1962 proved to be the highpoint for enthusiasm about the possibilities of truth detection in the service of arms control and scientific peace research. While Gerard's group of scientists hoped that successful lie detection would over time increase trust between leaders, yet another proposal went the exact opposite route. Walter Morgan, an aircraft production engineer from Missouri, shared with Gerard his scheme of "a dramatic new approach" of instantaneous electronic lie detection/disarmament. Morgan argued that conventional arms control schemes failed because of difficulties in coming to an agreement on inspection regimes and because of potential imbalances of power during any phased disarming process. He therefore insisted that radical measures were in order, namely the use of "tools and techniques" with "such a degree of accuracy as to be reasonably foolproof!" In short, Morgan argued that polygraph interrogation of military leaders could be used to oversee the installation of a global push-button electronic destruct system which would be triggered by a secret electronic signal and disable all atomic weapons (and conventional weapons if so wished) in one stroke. He asserted, "If there is a sincere will for disarmament and the validity of this tool is accepted by heads of state, the problem of trust need no longer exist."[32] This idea of using technology to short-circuit political difficulties attracted endorsements by journalist and peace activist Norman Cousins and Nobel Peace Prize winner Albert Schweitzer.[33]

And yet, it appears that after some promising signals from decision makers, all of these proposals ran into a brick wall in 1962 and quickly dissipated. Senator and Democratic Majority Whip Hubert Humphrey sent Gerard an encouraging letter in August 1962, thanking him for his "fine message" about his "intriguing" research. Air Force Colonel Kent Parrot, a member of the U.S. Arms Control and Disarmament Agency, also expressed appreciation for Gerard's "very interesting paper." However, Parrot also raised the potent question of how often decision makers should be tested, given that politicians often change their minds, and wondered if remote testing might be more acceptable to politicians than being strapped to a polygraph.[34] This was a question Gerard had already inquired about with Howard Baldwin of the Laboratory for the Study of Sensory Systems in Tucson, a manufacturer of telemetric instruments to measure miniscule temperature changes in cows.[35] Other responses from "various 'power elite,'" as Morgan put it to Gerard in February 1962, ranged from generally supportive to outright dismissive. Renowned Johns Hopkins University psychiatrist Jerome Frank, a co-founder of the peace organization Physicians for Social Responsibility, warned Morgan that the greatest difficulty for implementing his idea was that "the United States is not convinced it could survive and protect its way of life in a disarmed world" and that Morgan would first have to convince the public that communism could be fought more effectively without nuclear weapons. Similarly, nuclear physicist William Higinbotham of the Brookhaven National Laboratory, who had worked at Los Alamos for the Manhattan Project, cautioned that "negotiating for instant disarmament involves all the issues that arise in the normal approach. I am afraid it would be impossible for East and West to agree on the nature of the proposed world government in many years of talks." Higinbotham also pointed out "the total dependence on truth verifiers. If they were really that good they would solve many of the major difficulties in the conventional approach to disarmament. . . . I am afraid I don't find anything useful here. I doubt there are any easy or clever solutions and urge the patience and dedication to keep on working for disarmament in spite of the complexities."[36]

These responses concisely identified a number of scientific and political limitations of psychological inspection with the polygraph. In addition, as long as lie detection struggled with fundamental methodological problems, introducing such methods into high-stakes diplomacy was risky. As Chester Darrow of the Institute for Juvenile Research at the University of Illinois in Chicago warned Gerard in 1960, it would be dangerous to give the polygraph "enormous prestige" by "elevating the technic to diplomatic status," since it was possible to beat the test.[37]

Notwithstanding Morgan's exasperation ("Talk about apathy! Talk about defeatism! And these guys are among the best of the 'good guys'!"), lie detector proponents had little to offer in response except pleas for more research and the hope for "a convincing demonstration of the practicality of peace research" with "polygraphic interrogation."[38] In a paper presented at the International Arms Control Symposium Ann Arbor in December 1962, Lewis Bohn repeated his view that deterrence was "at root a psychological matter of influencing human behavior by the widest variety of available means rather than simply a matter of invulnerable nuclear deterrence weapons" and averred that "there is reason to believe that a major research effort could make the simultaneous measurement of a number of [physiological] variables, the so-called 'polygraph', give a highly valid and reliable indication of truthfulness."[39] Ultimately, the Institute for Defense Analyses issued a report to Congress in 1962 (a declassified version was released in 1964 for the hearing of the House Committee on Government Operations on the polygraph in the federal government). This report stated that "although the method of lie detection has been used extensively and is regarded favorably by its practitioners, the degree of its validity is still not known" due to lack of valid research data. Therefore, the team under Jesse Orlansky recommended "a program for research and development in the technology of lie detection" and a "program to develop professional standards for polygraph interrogation throughout the Department of Defense." The report recommended funding of about $500,000 a year for a period of three to five years.[40]

Disappearing in the bowels of the federal government, this report went the way of much scientific work during the Cold War. Moreover, it served as another reminder of the exceptionally wide gap between the claims of polygraph practitioners and the extent of the practice in law enforcement and national security and systematic scientific research on its validity. The enthusiasm of scientists such as Gerard failed to close this gap. By 1968 Gerard responded to a request by Nobel Prize–winning Stanford University biologist Joshua Lederberg for an update on his peace-research activities and reported that after the IDA report his interest in the issue had gradually fizzled out.[41]

As it happened, the development of satellite technology in the mid-1960s opened new doors to physical inspection of nuclear technology.[42] Most importantly, as mentioned above, the need for a mutual agreement on the rules of psychological inspection ran into the dilemma that in order to begin a trust-building inspections regime, sufficient trust and willingness to surrender sovereignty had to exist already. As a result, UN officials armed with lie detectors never entered the scene. Still, the idea of using the knowledge and testimony of individual citizens was attractive enough that it reappeared in discussions of arms control after the end of the Cold War.[43]

We might also wonder if Gerard's proposal would have impressed policymakers even under more promising circumstances. The history of U.S. Cold War policy shows that questions of military preparedness were strictly guarded in Washington. In the words of one of the foremost scholars of American peace movements, "As interest in military-based security increased, citizen peace seekers who emphasized nonmilitary cooperation toward a more just world order appeared as threats to the American way of peace."[44] With a new emphasis on "national security," truth itself became too precious a commodity to be handed over to a neutral body such as the United Nations.

Only once, in 1946, had the United States put forth a comprehensive proposal for UN control over nuclear scientific knowledge, technological know-how, fissionable material, and eventually U.S. bombs. The Acheson-Lilienthal Report had been heavily influenced by J. Robert Oppenheimer's ideas of open science as the model for democratic government. Oppenheimer had envisioned an international Atomic Development Authority with full ownership of uranium mines, nuclear facilities, and laboratories. It included a mutual pledge not to build nuclear weapons, but instead to share all fruits of peaceful nuclear research. For a short moment, such an arrangement (potentially a stepping stone toward "world government") did not seem far-fetched even to hard-headed officials such as Assistant Secretary of War John McCloy and other establishment scientist-policymakers such as Henry Conant.[45]

However, this proposal soon hardened in the hands of U.S. negotiator Bernard Baruch. Soviet leaders turned down the "Baruch Plan" because they mistrusted the neutrality of the UN (the plan disabled the veto powers of the permanent members of the Security Council, including the USSR, on nuclear questions) and because they rejected a physical inspections regime of scientific facilities. Most importantly, Stalin wanted his own bomb. He had spies such as Klaus Fuchs inside the Anglo-American Manhattan Project and an army of Soviet scientists working under the stern leadership of Lavrentyi Beria. It is therefore doubtful that Stalin could have been persuaded to give up his claims for co-equal power status with the United States for any project of joint nuclear control.[46] However, mistrust of collective nuclear security was shared by many U.S. military officials, who were not willing to give up U.S. nuclear weapons before full implementation of control procedures. In fact, Bernard Baruch, a tough, seasoned Wall Street banker with ties to mining corporations, saw the bomb as a "winning weapon"— political bludgeon and insurance policy in one.[47] To some U.S. foreign

policymakers, nuclear weapons in fact seemed to make trust and cooperation with the Soviet Union unnecessary.

Further, sharing nuclear know-how went counter to plans by U.S.
military leaders that already were taking shape during World War II. By
the time American war production was running at full speed in 1943,
its investments in armament production surpassed those of Germany,
Russia, and Britain combined.[48] Even before the Pearl Harbor attack,
U.S. defense officials embarked on plans to cement America's global
strategic supremacy by establishing a global ring of military bases. Notwithstanding estimates that it would take the Soviet Union fifteen to
twenty years to overcome wartime losses, Joint Chief of Staff planners
forged ahead with comprehensive proposals to establish preponderant
global military power. These plans militarized American understandings of geography and continued as part of the formation of the Cold
War.[49] Thus, even before the first nuclear explosion initiated the postwar
era, a strong segment among American foreign policymakers moved
toward a global strategy of deterrence that intended to take advantage
of superior American military capabilities.

In addition to developing other military technologies, by mid-1947
the U.S. military also embarked on a unilateral enlargement of nuclear
capabilities through increased plutonium production, aircraft manufac-
ture, and airbase procurement. Ownership and control of technology
remained a higher priority than disarmament in the uncertain, fluid
political postwar situation. "Our monopoly of the bomb, even though
it is transitory, may well prove to be a critical factor in our efforts to
achieve first a stabilized condition and eventually a lasting peace," Air
Force chief of staff Carl Spaatz asserted in 1946.[50] After the loss of the
U.S. atomic monopoly, policymakers assigned even higher priority to
maintaining a technological lead and an overall position of strength.
"To seek less than preponderant power would be to opt for defeat. Preponderant power must be the objective of U.S. policy," chief of the State
Department Policy Planning Staff Paul Nitze advised in 1952.[51] Nitze
expressed here a U.S. attitude of risk avoidance, which by default came
to favor continued development of nuclear weapons. "We should not
under any circumstances throw away our gun until we are sure the
rest of the world [the Soviet Union] cannot arm against us," President
Truman declared. American ambitions to shape the postwar world in

concert with the Soviet Union, but on American terms, thus almost certainly evaporated with the nuclear blasts over Hiroshima and Nagasaki.
The sheer existence of nuclear weapons amplified existing mistrust and
encouraged confrontation and mutual obstinacy over trust building.[52]

When Gerard wrote his article in the early 1960s, the United States
and the Soviet Union had several thousand nuclear warheads respec-
tively, with the United States still being in the lead. Both possessed thermonuclear bombs with the destructive capabilities of up to twenty-five
megatons (the bomb dropped on Hiroshima had produced an explosion of only fourteen kilotons) and were rapidly developing arsenals of
long-range bombers, submarine-based weapons, and Intercontinental
Ballistic Missiles (ICBMs). Such quick and invulnerable delivery systems opened up the possibility of surprise attacks across the ocean with
as little as fifteen minutes forewarning. Nuclear proliferation took place
at such rapid speed in the 1950s and 1960s that even government insid-
ers such as John Kennedy's and Lyndon Johnson's secretary of defense,
Robert McNamara, later concluded on U.S. policies, "Each individual
decision along the way seemed rational at the time. But the result was
insane."[53] This was another way of saying that U.S. nuclear policy was
all means, no ends. Staying ahead in the competition took the place
of cooperation in nuclear matters. Instead of making the prevention
of nuclear war a top priority, nuclear strategist such as Albert Wohlstetter at the RAND Corporation emphasized the necessity to keep all
options short of total nuclear war open by maintaining U.S. strategic
dominance.[54]

In general, momentum for disarmament during the Cold War often
had a strikingly political character. It ebbed and flowed with the winds
of opportunity and domestic politics in both countries. In the United
States just as in the Soviet Union, critics of official policy could get
into trouble. None other than J. Robert Oppenheimer became the target of intense criticism when he expressed some of his views for the
general public in the essay "Atomic Weapons and American Foreign
Policy," published in 1953 for *Foreign Affairs*. After the inauguration of
the Eisenhower administration and the death of Joseph Stalin earlier
that year, Oppenheimer asserted the necessity for "candor," frank public discussion of the nature of the arms race, even though he conceded
that it was "true that there are secrets that . . . it is important to keep

secret." Yet because "the political vitality of our country largely derives from . . . the interplay, the conflict and debate, . . . which contribute to the making of policy" and "public opinion which is based on confidence that it knows the truth," Oppenheimer demanded "the courage and the wisdom to make public at least what, in all reason, the enemy must now know: to describe in rough but authoritative and quantitative terms what the atomic armaments race is."[55] Oppenheimer did not launch outright criticism of U.S. foreign policy. He even refused to categorically rule out the use of nuclear weapons. But he was not willing to completely give up the ideal of vigorous public debate even on the most sensitive aspects of national security policy, and to break through the culture of euphemisms that started to develop in places like RAND.

A year later, at the first Cold War summit between the United States and the Soviet Union in Geneva in 1955, President Eisenhower surprised the Soviet Union by offering the "Open Skies" initiative, a system of mutual inspections including exchange of blue prints of military installations and aerial photography. Whether Eisenhower's proposal was sincere, and whether the Soviet Union under any circumstances would have accepted it, is still subject for debate. Advisor and MIT professor Walt Rostow might have caught the essence of the problem when he stated in 1982 that Open Skies (which he had helped develop) was "a political and psychological act" but "Eisenhower . . . was deadly serious about the . . . proposal."[56] Could diplomacy be both sincere and aim at scoring points in the competition for world public opinion?

President Eisenhower may not have been interested in taking risks for the sake of arms control. Instead, bold proposals such as "Open Skies" were put forth for propaganda purposes as much as in the expectation that they could be molded into workable compromises. As Kenneth Osgood summarized his study of U.S. propaganda efforts in the 1950s, "Eisenhower attached far greater value to waging and to winning the Cold War than to ending it through negotiations. . . . The objective [of negotiations] became out-maneuvering the opponent in the battle for public opinion; positions were put forward more to win public acclaim than pave the way for compromise at the bargaining table."[57] While there was strong support for a test ban and other agreements in his administration (from the State Department, the president's own Science Advisory Committee, and the CIA, among others), Eisenhower did not use his authority to push an agreement and instead sided with the military and the Atomic Energy Commission, who were vigorously opposed to any agreement with the Soviets. The Soviet Union, on the other hand, in 1957 accepted international seismic control stations on its territory and proposed a universal test ban.

The point to consider here is this: because the United States had no overall strategy as to the goals of arms control, it failed to connect its demands for onsite inspections with a larger vision for comprehensive disarmament. Even after the U.S. Senate gave its approval for a comprehensive test ban in 1958, Eisenhower did not propose such a treaty to the Soviet Union, partly because there was no agreement in his administration that arms control was a moral/political question. "The United States will have to make a purely political decision" with regards to arms control, Eisenhower's own Science Advisory Committee told him in July 1960.[58] In short, insisting on physical inspection to lift the veil of deception and secrecy surrounding the Soviet Union had reached a political limit by 1960, making the United States, not the Soviet Union, appear as the roadblock to real progress. This situation was the context for the search for more creative ways to create a foundation of truth for arms control.

Real disarmament gained momentum by the early 1960s thanks in no small part to the Cuban Missile Crisis of October 1962, which certainly encouraged President Kennedy and Premier Khrushchev to take bolder trust-building measures. Next to shared concerns over proliferation of nuclear technology, especially to China, transnational lobbying by SANE and other grassroots organizations had a significant impact on both sides of the Iron Curtain.[59] Signed in Moscow in August 1963 by the United States, England, and the Soviet Union, the limited test ban treaty outlawed atmospheric tests as well as tests in space and beneath the sea, largely because such tests could be easily detected with existing seismological technology. The issue of physical inspections in the Soviet Union, long a roadblock, was also solved as part of a political give-and-take when Khrushchev at long last agreed to three (instead of two) such inspections a year. The treaty encouraged negotiations of a nonaggression agreement, a freeze in military spending, and other trust building measures. An enthusiastic Khrushchev talked of the agreement as "a real turning point, and the end of the cold war."

And yet, the enthusiasm did not last. A lack of vision, the unresolved issue of Germany, and the political competition over Vietnam and other third-world countries marked the limits that the international system placed on the limited test ban as a first step toward more trust. Further, the sharp protest the test ban engendered in the United States from prominent military leaders, scientists such as Edward Teller, and conservative activists such as Phyllis Schlafly, highlighted the lack of political consensus at home.[60]

Therefore, the affinity of the polygraph with general problems of nuclear strategy and disarmament was more than the shared pathos of mortal danger. Since the days of Hugo Münsterberg, proponents of lie detection had tried to establish trust in an increasingly fractured, diverse, and interconnected society. The nuclear arms race had taken these problems to a global level. Yet lie detection, apart from its methodological flaws, was at heart a nonpolitical solution to political problems. Ralph Gerard was convinced that the way to avoid nuclear war was "not by countervailing force or guile or other move in the strategy of overcoming the opponent." For him, "the hope, rather, [was] in decreasing and eliminating the gamesmanship."[61] It meant to produce a shared commitment to truth when such commitment was lacking in the first place. That was the lie detector's dilemma. In reality, the polygraph never lived up to such hopes. But that did not mean it could not be useful *within* a framework of national security that insisted on American core values of truthfulness, open government, and sincerity, but simultaneously included much gamesmanship to control the role these values should play in U.S. foreign policy. The polygraph's ambivalence—should it be a tool of strategy or cut through the fog of strategic assumptions?—mirrored general ambivalence of U.S. Cold War strategy.

CHAPTER 8

Congress, the Right to Privacy, and the Retrenchment of the Polygraph

In the mid-1960s the polygraph came under sustained attacks by Congress, civil libertarians, and labor unions. The language of "right to privacy" gave coherence to earlier fears about the polygraph and helped create a powerful counter-coalition that started to gain traction by the mid-1970s. Due to persistent lobbying by that coalition, the federal government banned use of polygraphs in private businesses in 1988 through the Polygraph Protection Act. However, this chapter argues that containing the polygraph to the area of "national security" allowed a discourse of emergency to persist: with exceptional powers, the state could claim to defend itself from enemies abroad and at home. The task of keeping watch at the gates of freedom therefore endowed technologies such as the polygraph with special credentials. Voluntarism—on which the polygraph depended methodologically and legally, and from which the national security state had drawn appeal since World War I—was exposed as forced compliance; still, polygraphing persisted under the new special rules of national security.

The 1960s witnessed a considerable reinforcement of defendants' rights in criminal investigations. Anti-polygraph advocates discussed Supreme Court cases such as *Jackson v. Deno* (1964), in which the court decided that a conviction was unconstitutional if based wholly or in part on an involuntary confession, and *Escobedo v. Illinois,* which banned confessions made in absence of legal representation as admissible evidence. (In both cases, the question of the truthfulness of the confession was ruled immaterial.) Furthermore, in its *Schmerber v. California* (1966) decision, the Supreme Court asserted that polygraph exams raised Fifth Amendment issues (protection from self-incrimination) even though it refused to rule one way or the other. On the whole these decisions widened the legal space for polygraph contestation.[1]

In this context, debates over the polygraph flared up with increasing intensity. The House Committee on Government Operations had been at the forefront of legislative investigations of executive secrecy since 1955. It was part of a larger effort by congressional leaders to compensate for having lost power in making foreign policy since World War II. To keep up, between 1946 and 1966 the number of foreign policy subcommittees grew from seven to thirty-one.[2] In April 1964 the House Subcommittee on Foreign Operations and Government Information, which since its inception in 1955 had been chaired by California congressman John E. Moss, held hearings on the "Use of Polygraphs as 'Lie Detectors' by the Federal Government."[3] Moss, who at the time of the hearings was fighting the Johnson administration over what would become the Freedom of Information Act, was a prominent spokesperson for the public's right to know about government operations.[4] In a 1959 speech he had decried secrecy and what he called the "'papa-knows-best' attitude in the executive agencies" that had become "a matter of executive habit in the current cold war." Moss also criticized information control as a weapon of publicity, "the application of slick Madison Avenue advertising techniques to the problems affecting the nation's very survival."[5]

Moss particularly had in mind "Operation Candor," a 1953 propaganda campaign on the dangers of the H-bomb that the Eisenhower administration used to introduce the New Look strategy of heavy reliance on nuclear deterrence. The president sought to tone down widespread hopes for a thaw after Stalin's death in March 1953, which contrasted with his own pessimism about the prospects of ending the Cold War peacefully. Eisenhower chose instead to engage in emotion management, reminding Americans candidly about the direness of the world situation while assuring them of the endurance of American values.[6] In public addresses Eisenhower employed religious language to construe the pursuit of truth as a quintessential element in the achievement of American freedom. He proclaimed, for instance: "We can ignite in mankind the will to win intellectual freedom from the false propaganda and enforced ignorance of Communist tyranny. Through knowledge and understanding, we will drive from the temple of freedom all who seek to establish over us thought control—whether they be agents of a foreign state or demagogues thirsty for personal power and public notice. Truth can make men free!"[7] Like Harry Truman, Dwight Eisenhower saw truth as a Cold War weapon.

Such efforts proved largely futile. For Eisenhower, hysterical witch hunters like McCarthy and public complacency required careful information policy, but official attempts to create a patriotic pageantry of anticommunism enjoyed, at best, mixed success. Occasions such as Loyalty Day parades lost their sway by the early 1960s; expressions of patriotism became as routine as reciting the Pledge of Allegiance; the spirit of democracy became as mundane as paying with coins stamped with the motto "In God We Trust."[8] The national security state, in short, quickly exhausted its willingness to tap into the tradition of American voluntarism. While voluntarism had spun out of control during World War I, amid the prolonged Cold War it seemed to run out of steam.

Nor did attempts to raise morale at home translate into voluntary government transparency. Instead, embarrassing publicity involving a number of polygraph cases in 1962 and 1963 forced congressional investigations that finally lifted the iron curtain that had surrounded the polygraph in U.S. government service. These cases included the defection of two NSA officials, Bernon F. Mitchell and William H. Martin, who had been given partial security clearances based on polygraph exams; a double homicide trial at an Air Force base during which an airman gave a false confession during a polygraph exam; and a highly publicized episode in March 1963, when the Air Force, faced with a Senate investigation on alleged favoritism in the awarding of a defense contract (the TFX airplane), attempted to find the source of a leak to the *Washington Evening Star* by threatening numerous high-ranking military officials with polygraph tests.[9] In particular the last episode, which forced President Kennedy to pledge that nobody would be subjected to a polygraph to find the source of the leak, illustrated a breakdown of the kind of trust-building information control President Eisenhower had in mind. Secretary of Defense Robert McNamara privately admitted that he had been unaware that polygraph exams were a routine part of Pentagon internal investigations.[10] McNamara charged that the investigation "needlessly undermined public confidence" in the Pentagon. Missouri senator Stuart Symington reportedly agreed, arguing that "criticism of defense officials in public was undermining morale."[11]

In its report on a technology it sometimes called "the truth machine," Congress acknowledged that polygraph use meant implicit endorsement:

> There is no "lie detector," neither machine nor human. People have been deceived by a myth that a metal box in the hands of an investigator can detect truth or falsehood. The Federal Government has fostered this myth by spending millions of dollars on polygraph machines. . . . Yet research completed so far has failed to prove that polygraph interrogation actually detects lies or determines guilt or innocence.[12]

This statement was the opening salvo of a report brimming with vigorous condemnation and followed by several specific criticisms: most investigators lacked qualification and training; agencies exercised little oversight; and refusal to submit to a test was noted in employee files. Yet while Congress demanded reform, it also shied away from more fundamental criticism.

Moss and his colleagues took extensive stock of the situation. The committee had sent a detailed questionnaire to fifty-eight federal agencies. Nineteen agencies reported polygraph use. The federal government employed 639 workers authorized to give polygraph exams and owned 512 machines with annual operating costs of four million dollars. In 1963 federal agencies had given approximately 23,000 tests. This number excluded the CIA and the NSA, whose operations "are classified as sensitive security information." The committee found inconsistency in examiner training. While the Office of Naval Intelligence gave a course of only two weeks, other agencies sent operators to courses of four to six weeks at private schools. The Army Polygraph School at Fort Gordon, Georgia, offered "the only formal polygraph course in the Federal Government" with a seven-week course including legal, psychological, and practical instruction. The committee judged it as "completely inadequate since the operator is by far the most important factor in the polygraph technique."[13]

As one example of the kind of improvement the committee hoped to see, its final report cited a new Department of Defense memorandum by Deputy Secretary Cyrus Vance. All polygraph subjects, the memorandum stated, had to be informed of their Fifth Amendment rights against self-incrimination, to give written consent, be informed as to whether the interrogation room contained a two-way mirror, and be notified of any monitoring or recording.[14]

The committee also offered a damning summary of the state of polygraph research. It concluded,

> Federal investigators have given thousands upon thousands of polygraph tests, yet there has been no attempt to determine the validity of the procedure and no attempt to find out whether the polygraph operator really can detect falsehoods. No statistical proof has been compiled despite thousands of cases; no scientific proof has been produced despite thousands of opportunities.

A 1962 Air Force–commissioned study by Dr. Joseph Kubis of Fordham University argued that the polygraph could be beaten through countermeasures such as modified yoga—"the separation of the self from outside stimuli and the maintenance of an abstract frame of mind"—muscle tension, exciting mental imagery, and bodily movement.[15] In criticizing experimental detection technologies, the report highlighted an aborted Federal Aviation Agency (FAA) project to utilize the galvanometer for mass screening of civilian passengers: A passenger would have to "place his hands on electrodes while answering a query as to whether he was carrying explosives aboard the aircraft in his luggage or on his person." However, the committee's main objection to this aborted scheme was that experts considered the galvanometer to be the least reliable of polygraph components.[16]

The investigation's vigorous criticism of the "myth" of the lie detector was not enough to kill federal use. Most of the committee's objections focused on procedures and lack of uniformity in the application of the polygraph. It appears, moreover, that the committee shied away from following up on two much more fundamental dilemmas in polygraph practice. These dilemmas appeared in the committee's proceedings and report but were not reflected in its recommendations and conclusions.

The committee found that "people have come to fear the so-called lie detection examination" because they believed the machine was unbeatable. If the public knew it was not, this would lower the validity of the procedure (even if used only as an interrogation tool). However, informing people of the polygraph's flaws would be "the only justifiable, democratic ethic," as John Lacey, a professor of psychophysiology at Antioch College, put it. In this view, the polygraph was *inherently* undemocratic, since it relied on deception to work. This was a claim American writers and politicians frequently made against communism. Indeed, polygraph supporters themselves admitted the crucial role of deception in the very makeup of a polygraph exam. Fred Inbau, a professor of criminology who had worked with Leonarde Keeler in Chicago, admitted during the hearings that the subject "has got to have some fear of having his lies detected by this technique. . . . If the individual doesn't have this respect for the technique, respect for the examiner, he will not be responsive."[17] In short, bluff was part-and-parcel of the lie detector test as it had been designed by Leonarde Keeler and other lie detector advocates. Yet as with so many aspects of the lie detector test, this assertion was never sufficiently studied. Some research found that believing in the infallibility of the machine did not improve correct calls of deception or truthfulness; other findings suggest that subjects could pass the test more easily with the attitude that the test was fallible.[18]

Balancing protections against self-incrimination against the methodology of polygraph interrogation posed a second dilemma. So-called control questions demanded confessions of some past deeds or experiences causing emotional disturbance. The technique had been developed by Keeler's former collaborator in the Northwestern University Crime Lab, John Reid, in 1947 and was the only fundamental innovation in test procedure since the 1930s. Control questions were based on the theory that proper evaluation of emotional responses to relevant questions during an investigation depended upon the examiner first eliciting a conscious lie to an emotionally arousing yet irrelevant question. As Inbau, Reid's colleague and former co-worker at Keeler's laboratory, explained in the 1948 edition of his textbook:

> If the examiner is fortunate enough to have in his possession certain information about the subject concerning a less serious offense than the one under investigation, and the examiner knows or feels reasonably sure the subject will lie about it, a question based upon such information, coupled with a false reply, will serve very well to indicate the nature of subject's [*sic*] deception responses, if any. . . . If the subject is a suspected first offender, any one of several types of questions may be asked. . . . For instance, "Have you ever stolen over $10?"; "Have you ever cheated on an income tax return?"[19]

Therefore, not only was eliciting a lie an integral part of the polygraph technique as it had been developed after Keeler, but the lie also had to be emotionally relevant to the subject so as to provide the baseline for deceptive responses. It had to be incriminating; it had to be embarrassing.

The committee found, too, that both the Defense Department and the CIA retained information they had acquired during the exam and passed it on their top security official. The report concluded, "The polygraph technique forces an individual to incriminate himself and confess to past actions which are not pertinent to the current investigation. He must dredge up the past so he can approach the polygraph machine with an untroubled soul. The polygraph operators and his superiors then decide whether to defer derogatory information to other agencies or officials." Congressman Cornelius Gallagher amplified upon this view of the lie detector's inherent intrusiveness in his demand that "the use of polygraphs by the Federal Government should be discontinued in all cases immediately until they are proved to be infallible—a day which I doubt will ever come. . . . In my opinion, lie detector tests constitute an insidious search of the human mind and are a breach of the most fundamental human rights."[20]

Witnesses in support of the polygraph interjected the notion of voluntarism. Inbau admitted: "Obviously, when anyone is subjected to this test there is some invasion of privacy. Of course, one basic safeguard against that is that it is not forced upon an individual." However, the committee also heard testimony from all three branches of the armed services confirming that the individual files of employees contained notes of refused polygraph exams and concluded that "the file notation which follows an individual throughout his career often casts a dark shadow on his future."[21]

Given these findings, why did the committee shy away from a principled condemnation of polygraph exams in the federal government? The answer is national security. Of the nineteen federal agencies allowing polygraph use, fourteen reported "security matters," ranging from investigation of security leaks to operational uses in intelligence and counterintelligence activities. The committee noted, "The role the instrument plays in the many-sided efforts to safeguard the Nation's security." Even generally hostile witnesses such as Joseph Kubis insisted that the polygraph was wasted on "trivial situations," but that argument implied that serious matters *were* appropriate for the polygraph. As a result, the committee's recommendation that "lax administrative control over investigators" was to blame for indiscriminate polygraph use left open the possibility for responsible use through correct procedure.[22] The committee forcefully underlined these caveats in their final recommendations:

> The committee recommends that the Federal Government—
> Initiate comprehensive research to determine the validity and reliability of polygraph examinations. Prohibit the use of polygraphs in all but the most serious national security and criminal cases. Improve the training and qualifications of Federal polygraph operators. Restrict the use of two-way mirrors and recording devices during polygraph examinations. Guarantee that polygraph examinations be, in fact, voluntary. Insure that refusal to take a polygraph examination will not constitute prejudice or be made a part of an individual's records except in the most serious national security matters.[23]

The liberal highbrow press underscored the committee's findings. Reporters for the *New Republic* and the *Nation* highlighted the lack of supervision and examiner training and concluded with bristling hostility that the polygraph was "a pernicious instrument that has been seized upon by a society obsessed with gadgetry." The committee had confirmed the "doubts and fears that many responsible people have about the widespread use of polygraphs."[24]

Their recommendations made a case for containment of the polygraph through procedures that would protect individual rights while maintaining national security. Congress therefore confirmed an observation made by historian of technology Theodore Porter, who argues that in the United States, government agencies tend to favor "mechanical objectivity" and neutrality over disciplinary objectivity. Put differently, they prefer rules and procedures that protect the public from arbitrary decisions to the reliable judgment of experts. This preference for standardization expresses, perhaps, the deep distrust of experts in American culture and the relationship of mutual checks between Congress and executive agencies. Most importantly, applying quantifiable rules and procedures allows policymakers and their overseers to transform political questions—questions of values—into administrative questions—questions of numbers: "Quantification is a way of making decisions without seeming to decide."[25]

As a result, congressional orders for more regulation, particularly concerning the qualifications of polygraph examiners, did not threaten the polygraph industry. On the contrary, as a *Business Week* article observed, "Law-enforced standards, the major [polygraph] agencies feel, would help to lift the stigma associated with lie detectors because of the sometimes lurid publicity they have received in police cases." Similarly, *Popular Science* asserted that the polygraph had never been uncritically accepted in Cold War America: "The lie detector has never been popular. This is scarcely surprising. For often its use may imply suspicion and distrust, without direct occasion for either."[26] It was therefore precisely the remedy suggested by Congress—stricter regulations of government procedures—that would provide the polygraph with welcome credentials.

A 1965 article in the trade publication *Supervision* noted these trends. Chicago labor lawyer Lee Burkey commented on the attitude of U.S. labor unions toward the practice of pre-employment polygraph testing: "It seems proper to conclude that an employer can no longer soundly contend that as a management prerogative he is entitled to subject any or all of his employees to polygraphic tests. To do so is to violate the employee's right to privacy and his right against self-incrimination. The emphasis will probably shift from science to civil rights in future cases."[27] The evidence for Burkey's claim was that beginning in the late 1950s, a number of states had initiated restrictions on polygraph use in private business. Beginning with Massachusetts in 1959, twelve states had passed laws of varying stringency by 1973. Some prohibited employers to "require" polygraph tests from current or prospective employees, others added "demand," "subject or cause," or "influence" to the wording in order to rule out forced voluntarism. Penalties ranged from unspecified to $1,000 and/or one year in jail (Alaska). Except for New Jersey and Oregon, most states allowed specific exemptions for law enforcement agencies and federal, state, and local government agencies.[28] The trend toward gradually increased state regulation continued until the arrival of federal legislation. However, contrary to Lee Burkey's juxtaposition of science and civil rights, experts in the psychological (as well as legal and medical) establishment would join the cause of civil rights and provide crucial support for the political efforts that produced the Employee Polygraph Protection Act (EPPA) in 1988.

Public arguments about the polygraph in the 1970s and 1980s—whether in favor or in opposition—were driven by a general sense that the practice was out of control. However, reliable numbers were hard to come by and polygraph discourse remained to a large degree anecdotal, even though a congressional study in 1983 finally provided a comprehensive review of polygraph science. As one of the few academic studies of polygraph use in private business, published in 1978, observed, "Conflicting reports, statistics, and conclusions" surrounded the test, necessitating a survey of the extent, manner, and purpose, as well as rationale for polygraph use in major American businesses.[29] Authors John Holden and Peter Belt estimated the number of annual polygraph exams in the United States to be between 300,000 and 500,000. This vague number underlined the mystique of the practice and its extent. Their survey of 143 returned questionnaires found that approximately 20 percent of respondents used the polygraph. Roughly half of banks and retail businesses replied in the affirmative, followed by transportation (approximately 25 percent). Given that 63 percent of polygraph users indicated that they had been employing the device for ten years or more, the study questioned the perception of rapid rise in polygraph use.

Regarding the rationale for using the test on future and current employees, the survey found that almost all polygraph users employed the test during specific investigations, such as theft of company property. Only about one in three used it to verify data given during the application process or in periodic tests of employee loyalty and honesty. Lastly, nearly half the companies invested in the polygraph rated "speed of obtaining results" as their most important rationale, while "moral or ethical considerations" ranked last. While 62 percent of nonpolygraph users indicated that they would not consider using it under any circumstances, considerable numbers within subcategories of industry (especially transportation) replied they would reconsider their decision not to use the polygraph under certain circumstances. This led the researchers to suggest that "a rather extensive pool of potential polygraph users exists in some areas of business which have not been thought likely to use such services."[30]

In law enforcement, as in the 1920s and 1930s, efforts to reform urban policing propelled the polygraph debate in the 1970s. Police chiefs such as George Tielsch of Seattle shared the belief of his colleagues in New Orleans, Dallas, Miami, and other cities where applicants to the force were subjected to polygraph tests, "to maintain the integrity" of the departments. *Newsweek* reported that in these cities, one in three applicants in the early 1970s was rejected after a polygraph test had revealed "criminal records, unsavory associations, drug use and homosexuality." The response of embattled police departments was expressed by Seattle King County councilman Edward Heavey, who asked: "Why should it be just cops? You can't use it on judges, attorneys, building inspectors and city councilmen. The police feel that everybody's picking on them. You know what kind of a state of mind that encourages."[31] Such statements made an implicit assertion about the polygraph: whoever was in charge of administering it was imbued with social power, while many on the receiving end felt undue power exerted on them. As with polygraph tests in federal agencies, professional and class concerns influenced perceptions of the fairness of the test.

The changing legal landscape and increasing pressure on urban police indicated the tumults of the 1960s. Opposition to the polygraph began to be expressed in civil rights contexts and especially in the discourse of a "right to privacy"; the latter profited from the currency the term acquired in the Supreme Court's 1965 *Griswold v. Connecticut* decision, in which the majority found that the term "right to privacy" was implied in the due process clause of the Constitution. Prominent attorneys such as Alan Westin included anti-polygraph arguments in comprehensive treatments of civil liberties protected under the Constitution and provided wide-ranging arguments that could be used in individual cases of polygraph controversy.[32]

Among civil rights groups, the American Civil Liberties Union (ACLU) expressed these terms of opposition most forcefully. A comprehensive document titled *The Lie Detector as a Surveillance Device,* which the ACLU published in 1973, collected scientific and legal evidence against the polygraph, using (among other sources) the expert testimony compiled by the Moss committee in 1964. Having made an extensive case against polygraph accuracy and reliability, the document turned to "ethical arguments," upon which "few of the labor boards, regulatory agencies and courts which have criticized and rejected the use of polygraph machines" had so far based their criticism.[33] Having collected a host of constitutional arguments, many drawn from Alan Westin's work and based on recent Supreme Court decisions, the document concluded:

> Even if the machine were one hundred percent accurate, however, there are important constitutional principles militating against its utilization. The entire polygraph process can be seen as degrading to human dignity. It can be seen as an invasion of privacy and infringement of fundamental human rights. The technique is contrary to the presumption that one is innocent until proven guilty. It seems to force one into a position of self-incrimination, since the subtle penalties against those who do not take the test are great. . . . Accuracy aside, the polygraph should not be used because it infringes on essential individual liberties.[34]

Trudy Hayden, an ACLU leader on privacy issues, compiled another handbook in 1980 that included information about the legal status of polygraph exams together with information on issues such as credit ratings, medical records, and electronic surveillance.[35]

Polygraph examiners themselves admitted occasionally that the control-question technique was inherently invasive and fueled increasing backlash. The *New York Times* quoted polygraph examiner Rudolph Caputo, who explained that the procedure required relevant, irrelevant, and "control questions," such as "Have you ever stolen?" Caputo explained, "If you can't establish your control questions, you can't get results. You've got to find something that the suspect will lie about." Caputo continued that sexual questions had become problematic as control questions. "Today, I like to stay away from [sexual questions], especially with women. It makes them hostile to you. . . . Furthermore, the woman may suspect your intent, or simply react strongly to sexual matters. When you have emotion, you will get a reading on it, and it may be misleading."[36] This was another problem of the polygraph: It depended on control questions that were embarrassing enough to elicit a likely lie, but also had to be socially acceptable to ask. It became increasingly difficult for interrogators to tread this fine line as advocates of privacy rights chipped away at the polygraph's social acceptance.

The self-perpetuating power of the mysterious "black box" lost its traction the more it was denounced publicly. North Carolina senator Sam Ervin used the floor of the Senate in 1974 to dispel the machine's magic when he asserted that the "self-fulfilling and self-perpetuating myth of infallibility" was the only reason people trusted the lie detector.[37] Law professor Richard Underwood joined this criticism in 1978 when he observed, "It is common to confront the suspect with a recording and then accuse him of lying without going into the interpretation process at all. Apparently, this is a fairly successful method of eliciting confessions."[38] Journalist Jonathan Kwitny echoed this sentiment in an extensive 1978 anti-polygraph exposé in *Esquire* magazine when he reported what people in the business had allegedly told him: "If the average citizen stops believing that lie detectors are infallible, lie detectors will become even less reliable than they are. Blind faith from all concerned is crucial."[39]

Next to the ACLU, labor union leaders were some of the most articulate debunkers of the polygraph. The *New York Times* quoted Lee Burkey, the Chicago lawyer who had overturned countless dismissals on grounds of "failed" polygraph tests, in 1971, insisting that the polygraph was "a deeply ideological thing used by people who desperately long for law and order." Burkey stated that "truly amoral people" easily passed the test, while the straight arrow, "who probably is guilty of some wrongdoing, but perhaps not the theft under investigation, shows all the 'wrong' tracings, believes the machine knows all, and makes damaging confessions."[40] Implied in this statement was the accusation that the polygraph was an attack on honest, sincere American citizens. The fact that a representative of organized labor expressed sentiments similar to the ones traditional, libertarian conservatives had voiced all along illustrates the increasingly closed front against the polygraph.

The ACLU continued its anti-lie detector advocacy into the 1980s. Trudy Hayden authored a number of public statements, arguing that polygraph use comprised a means to defer economic risk from companies to individual workers. This goal led to a bias toward assuming deception and an impetus to drill for personal information and therefore violate workers' privacy:

> It is pointless to discuss polygraph testing in terms of voluntary, willing subjects. The irony of the supposedly "voluntary" test is only emphasized by the insistence of many examiners that their subjects sign a waiver asserting their "voluntary" agreement to be tested. . . . [Employers] are looking for information about their employees' or applicants' past and present lives, thoughts, attitudes, and character, in hopes that such information can help them decide whether a potential employee is a good risk, or whether a current employee has been cheating or stealing. . . . In both content and technique, polygraph tests violate personal privacy as most people understand that elusive, but deeply valued concept.[41]

For the ACLU and labor unions, the ample supply of potential workers allowed employers to exert undue power through the polygraph by demanding a "voluntary" test, given that enough qualified job candidates typically existed who would feel compelled to take it. Risk and responsibility for losses due to employee dishonesty (through theft, etc.) could therefore be unjustly deferred to the working population. No wonder that starting in the early 1960s, unions under the leadership of the AFL-CIO (especially the Retail Clerks International Association) fought for anti-polygraph clauses in arbitration and employment contracts.[42]

For the police and employers, the burden of catching criminals across the country justified their use of polygraph technology. Polygraph examiner Robert Ferguson asserted concisely the machine's value in mass society:

Before World War II, a field investigator could interview many neighbors who really knew the candidate, not only as a boy but also as a youth and young man. Today, with the high rate of population shift and population density, in-depth knowledge of one's neighbors is unknown in many parts of our country. This is the main reason why—with the advent of a very fluid mobile, and unstable society—more and more law enforcement agencies, as well as business firms, are utilizing the skill of polygraphists.[43]

This argument held sway as long as social consensus existed over the means to assess risk. A statement of polygraph examiners collected by the ACLU asserted that all participants in labor relations would profit from widespread testing: "Both the employer and society in general have a legitimate interest in combating dishonesty in American business and industry. The culprit's co-workers also have reason to demand the apprehension of the larcenous or fraudulent employee. Hence the invasion of the thief's privacy is a price that must be paid."[44] Yet insistence on a "right to privacy" marked the beginning of the end of the social consensus that polygraphing represented a happy confluence of the needs of employers and employees.

Overall, as with the issue of anticommunism in the 1950s, we can conclude that the polygraph highlighted social and political controversies rather than alleviate them. Polygraph tests reflected the pertinent risk concerns of American business. They reflected, too, how questions of economic risks connected to political as well as personal data. To discuss the polygraph's significance for U.S. economic, political, or civil rights history independently therefore makes little sense. Due to the way it was used by examiners such as Ferguson, it touched upon all these. Of course the polygraph was only one part of the process of social negotiation, but the controversy surrounding the test illustrates how all sides of the debate perceived their clients to be disadvantaged in anonymous, technology-driven mass society. Civil rights discourse helped polygraph opponents gain the upper hand by allowing them to integrate their specific objections into a larger argumentative framework. The changed social environment of post–Civil Rights America therefore added new potency to the objection that a polygraph might target or deter the wrong person.

The limits imposed in the 1980s on the machine's use further served to legitimize the test. The argument that tighter restrictions would lead to proper testing procedures appeared repeatedly in public discussions on the question of licensing of polygraph examiners. Lie detector examiners themselves favored licensing and continued to insist that unqualified examiners, rather than the methodology of the test itself, were the main cause for popular resistance to the technology.

Indiana senator Birch Bayh echoed that sentiment the same year when he introduced his bill to limit polygraph use to national security–related employment and stated that federal licensing of operators would lead to increased use, "because people would feel that licensing meant the tests are credible."[45] Similarly, Trudy Hayden of the ACLU asserted, "It is sometimes suggested that polygraph abuses could be curbed by regulating practice through licensing statutes. But these would only legitimize a practice that is by its very nature coercive, intrusive, and conductive to harassment and discrimination. Polygraph tests do not need to be regulated; they need to be banned."[46]

Congressional action played an important but also ambiguous role. On the one hand, a string of bills that restricted polygraph use and congressional hearings gave impetus to the anti-polygraph coalition and allowed for public dissemination of arguments against the polygraph. In 1976 the House Government Operations Committee went as far as recommending a universal ban on polygraphs in the federal government. On the other hand, Congress continued to yield to the arguments from the national security establishment that agencies such as the CIA depended on the polygraph and that, given proper supervision and regulation, the technology had its uses. As a result, congressional anti-polygraph activity illustrated the limits of political consensus on national security issues generally. It resulted in strengthening the exceptional status of "national security" as a discourse, justifying received special privileges for agencies entrusted with national security.

Senator Ervin, who from 1961 until his resignation in 1974 chaired the Senate Judiciary Committee's Subcommittee on Constitutional Rights, introduced three anti-polygraph bills—in 1967, 1971, and 1973—as part of a comprehensive Federal Employee Bill of Rights. Each time, his bill passed the Senate but failed in the House of Representatives. When Ervin introduced the bill for the third time, he made an ethical/

constitutional case against the polygraph: "Probably no instrument in modern time so lends itself to threats to constitutional guarantees of individual freedom as the polygraph or so-called lie detector."[47] Ervin, who also chaired the Senate Select Committee to Investigate Campaign Practices (better known as the Watergate committee), was a champion of individual rights. His inquiries into the U.S. Army figured significantly in the passing of the Foreign Intelligence Surveillance Act (FISA) of 1978, which provided judicial and congressional oversight of the government's covert surveillance activities of foreign entities and individuals in the United States. However, on the same grounds, the North Carolinian also opposed federal anti-discrimination and most other civil rights legislation. Like many other opponents of the polygraph, Ervin was pro-civil liberties, but unlike organizations such as the ACLU, he opposed federally enforced civil rights legislation.[48] In short, Richard Nixon's heavy-handed domestic policies succeeded in forging a new political coalition that rallied around the issue of privacy.[49]

As it turned out, it took over a decade of congressional debate until Washington finished negotiating the terms of "right to privacy" regarding the polygraph. A 1974 congressional investigation highlighted both the limited scientific credibility of the device and its ethical/constitutional problems; yet it also illustrated a lack of consensus how to address these problems. The House Committee on Government Operations' initial investigation in 1964–1965 led President Johnson to convene an Interagency Polygraph Committee in November 1965. Despite receiving a research budget of $200,000 from the Pentagon, the committee failed to implement validation studies (i.e., whether a polygraph test could really establish an individual's truthfulness) of the kind Congress had strongly recommended. Other federally funded studies were promised but never materialized, leading the House Committee on Government Operations to conclude in 1976 that the state of research had done "little to persuade the committee that polygraphs, psychological stress evaluators, or voice stress analyzers have demonstrated either their validity or reliability in differentiating between truth and deception, other than possibly in a laboratory situation."[50]

Congress now also gave voice to the arguments against the polygraph on civil liberties grounds. It relied on the 1973 ACLU report and heard testimony from the American Federation of Government Employees

(AFGE); the latter demanded strict regulation of polygraph use because national security investigations created overpowering pressures on individuals to prove their innocence. In his testimony, Henry Dogin, the deputy assistant attorney general in the Criminal Division of the Justice Department, affirmed that the right to remain silent was protected in the Constitution and should serve as a valid reason to refuse polygraph tests in criminal investigations. The Department of Justice opposed the admission of polygraph evidence in trials on the basis of its unproven validity, unresolved constitutional issues, and "undue reliance juries are likely to place on the apparent mechanistic accuracy of polygraph results."[51] Therefore, sentiments from the early Cold War that viewed the polygraph as fundamentally alien to "Anglo-Saxon" liberalism had been combined by the mid-1970s into a coherent, principled case. On the basis of nonvalidity, unreliability, and individual rights violations, the majority of the House Committee on Government Operations recommended "that the use of polygraphs and similar devices be discontinued by all Government agencies for all purposes. . . . The committee finds that the inherent chilling affect [sic] upon individuals subjected to such examinations clearly outweighs any purported benefit to the investigative function of the agency."[52] At no point in the history of polygraph regulations would a federal government body issue a stronger statement against lie detection devices. Subcommittee chairwoman Bella Abzug, a Democrat from New York, was one of Congress's fiercest advocates of civil rights. Abzug's passionate campaigning for women's rights and calls for immediate withdrawal from Vietnam made her anathema to both the liberal and the conservative establishment.[53]

However, the fact that Abzug did not get a majority to join her call for abandoning the polygraph illustrated the limits of consensus in the committee. Her recommendation apparently resulted from heavy infighting among members.[54] The 1976 report included dissenting views from all members of the Republican minority, which supported a different set of recommendations. The Subcommittee on Government Information and Individual Rights, which had held the hearings in 1974, had passed these original recommendations in March 1975 during the Ninety-third Congress. But Abzug had not submitted them for a committee vote and later unilaterally submitted the new recommendation without discussion.[55]

The original set of recommendations, endorsed only by the Republican committee members, also voiced strong reservations about the polygraph. But rather than demanding a complete ban, they called for more government-funded research and clearer information in the Federal Personnel Manual. The latter would emphasize "individual's rights and alternatives when [an employee] is requested to submit to a polygraph test," "uniformity and economy" in training polygraph examiners—ideally at the Army's Military Police School in Fort Gordon, Georgia—and reestablishment of an interagency committee "to make more uniform a number of the agency practices" with regards to polygraph use.[56]

Therefore, partisanship almost certainly played a role in dividing the members of the committee. In the wake of the release of the Pentagon Papers, the Watergate scandal, and subsequent revelations of egregious crimes committed by intelligence agencies, liberal Democrats tended to take a more principled stance against overreach of national security agencies.[57] The report further recommended a drastic reduction in CIA covert action, to be replaced by more open, academic, and scientific collection of intelligence. "Secrecy, elitism, and the mystique of expertise, all must be drastically reduced," it stated.[58] This challenge to executive authority certainly expressed itself in the finding of the committee's Democratic majority to ban the polygraph, a finding that was not shared by its Republican minority.

As a result of this disagreement, Congress did not pass a complete ban on the polygraph, and the federal government instead regulated its limited use. The U.S. Civil Service Commission (CSC, the agency in charge of regulating qualifications for federal employment) by 1968 prohibited the use of polygraphs in screening applicants and appointees for competitive service positions. It estimated in 1973 that this regulation covered 85 to 90 percent of federal civilian employees. Excluded were federal employees not under CSC supervision, such as U.S. attorneys, categories of menial workers, and noncareer executive assignments (often referred to as "political assignments"). Most relevant, however, was the exceptional status CSC regulations created for national security: "An executive agency which has a highly sensitive intelligence or counterintelligence mission directly affecting the national security may use the polygraph for employment screening and personnel investigations of applicants for and appointees to competitive service positions only after receiving written approval from the Chairman of the Civil Service Commission." Executive agencies had to submit a statement on the nature of their mission and a copy of their polygraph regulations; CSC approval had to be renewed annually.[59]

Although these policies apparently reduced the volume of polygraph use in federal agencies, Congress recommended annual reports in agencies with employees not covered by CSC regulations, such as the Federal Reserve System and the U.S. Postal Service. In 1973, federal agencies conducted 6,889 polygraph examinations, half of them (3,081) performed by the NSA. This was a drastic reduction from 1965, when Congress had found almost 20,000 investigations, excluding the NSA (as well as the CIA, which was exempt from reporting any budgetary information to Congress).[60] The committee further found that the U.S. government, in 1973, owned 458 polygraphs, but it complained that the Department of Defense had furnished contradictory numbers on two occasions. Given that federal agencies had to submit their polygraph regulations to the CSC, Congress could further ascertain that departments using the polygraph had all implemented various forms of supervision, mostly by requiring written prior approval of tests from a superior office. Most agencies had no explicit guidelines for medical exams prior to polygraph tests; all agencies assured Congress that refusal to take a polygraph would not be noted in an employee's personnel file and that in the great majority of cases, agencies would not share investigative files with other agencies. Adverse consequences suffered by individuals during investigations that included polygraph tests were open to the regular appeals process.[61]

In short, the 1974 investigation showed considerable but limited reach of administrative control and congressional pressure. Even though Congress realized that exact control over all aspects of government use proved impossible, it undoubtedly had reined in the polygraph by initiating specific bureaucratic guidelines, which the CSC enacted and enforced. But Congress by and large did not challenge the prerogative of the NSA and the CIA; they remained the only two federal agencies allowed to demand polygraph tests from all job applicants and therefore did not have to confront the problem of "voluntary" submission and individual rights. The 1974 investigation generally reflected the far reach of Congress's investigatory efforts in the wake of Watergate, but also the limits these investigations had in terms of changing the deep bureaucratic structures of secret and secretive government. They reflected, too, scant political will to challenge those structures.[62] These limits became apparent when new administrations forcefully asserted executive control over national security policies.

By the 1980s, political winds changed direction. The polygraph received renewed support when the Reagan administration expressed its faith in the test through a number of executive actions and orders. These led to another congressional investigation in 1983 and more political tension. As before, increased use of the polygraph sparked conflict rather than acceptance, and again the polygraph formed a prism for larger political controversies. By highlighting the polygraph's credentials to the discourse of "national security," the federal government also fully acknowledged the role of coercion in its use. In national security–related investigations, the deterrent effect of the polygraph became the government's main argument, since involuntary submission reduced the test's validity. This stance still allowed for restrictions on large-scale lie detector investigations, such as applicant screenings in private business. However, use for reasons of state gained new legitimacy.

After the election of Ronald Reagan in 1980, the executive branch enacted aggressive policies. These included considerable upgrading and expansion of conventional and nuclear armaments (a development begun under Reagan's predecessor Jimmy Carter), covert support for friendly regimes and guerilla organizations in Latin America and elsewhere by the CIA, and an assertive ideological stance toward communism. All these moves were highly controversial and not always well coordinated, which created friction not only between the administration and its critics in Congress and the press, but also internally.[63] Against this backdrop, the Reagan administration proposed National Security Decision Directive 84 (NSDD 84) in March 1983 as well as a new Department of Defense Directive on Polygraph Use.

President Reagan issued NSDD 84 explicitly to protect classified information relating to national security. It included new nondisclosure agreements for all government officials and contract employees holding authorized access to specifically defined categories of classified information obtained from intelligence sources. Such agreements pertained to use of such information in the ever-popular memoir literature by former government executives, but more importantly it targeted the "leaking" of such information to the press. About 128,000 government employees fell into the new category. However, in a much more sweeping move, the Reagan administration also proposed the polygraph as a means to investigate any kind of leak investigation in cases involving classified information. Since almost half of federal employees had some form of security clearance, the General Accounting Office (GAO) estimated that as many as 2.5 million government employees and 1.5 million contractors could potentially be required to take polygraph tests during NSDD 84 investigations. They could expect a variety of adverse actions if they refused. Furthermore, under a proposed Department of Defense polygraph directive, Pentagon employees with access to certain categories of classified information could also be periodically polygraphed to determine their continued eligibility; they would incur repercussions if they refused. In the summer and fall of 1983, the House Committee on Government Operations investigated the potential impact of these regulations, which reversed executive policies implemented in the wake of the 1965 investigation, should they be enacted.[64]

A leak had ignited the first investigation by the House Government Operations Committee in 1964, and leaks continued to drive attempts to widen the net of polygraph tests in the federal government, as committee chairman Jack Brooks, a Texas Democrat, remarked at the time. One such information breach concerned a 1982 headline story in the *Washington Post,* which quoted from a Joint Chiefs of Staff report anticipating considerably larger costs for the Reagan arms buildup than had been announced.[65] This led Brooks to the following conclusion in 1985: "Again, as with the TFX incident almost 20 years earlier, a leak that was embarrassing but not a serious national security problem prompted an investigation to find the source."[66] Polygraph use, therefore, highlighted the political nature of national security discourse and the political uses of information control.

Witnesses before the committee echoed Brooks's sentiment and decried the combined effect of nondisclosure of classified information and threat of polygraph exams. Former Deputy Undersecretary of State George Ball echoed C. Wright Mills's warning that modern technology allowed the power elite to run roughshod over the individual conscience: "So, we must be sure that, in the name of security, we do not adopt measures that discourage the revelation or discussion of actions and policies that violate the standards we purport to follow as a nation."[67] For Ball, NSDD 84 exemplified how the U.S. obsession with the USSR got the best of it and led Americans to use methods that imitated Soviet control of its citizens and clients. Similarly, for CBS Washington correspondent Bob Schieffer, NSDD 84 amounted to "peacetime censorship."[68] A number of other witnesses from the journalist profession also voiced these sentiments, while Congressman Mel Levine, Democrat of California, charged that NSDD 84 was aimed at "inhibiting public scrutiny of Government."[69]

Deputy Assistant Attorney General Richard Willard, who had chaired the interdepartmental committee that had prepared NSDD 84, made the case for the Reagan administration and reiterated the main justifications for government use of the lie detector. As for preemployment screening, Willard conceded, "The polygraph may unfairly screen out some applicants," but "we think that with respect to certain high security jobs, it may be necessary to err on the side of caution." Willard pointed to CIA and NSA screening practices to support that assertion. In addition to criminal investigations and specific administrative investigations, Willard also argued for "the protection of the polygraph" regarding "categories of highly sensitive information that is of great interest to hostile intelligence services," independent of the agency that held such information.[70] Willard therefore justified the polygraph as a protector of information that was of particularly high value to the government: "Use of the technique should be limited to situations where it clearly serves an overriding national interest. Assuring that employees in our intelligence agencies and similarly sensitive positions meet appropriate security standards is such an overriding interest."[71]

Critics asserted that such an argument privileged national security over fairness: "Apparently, the Administration regards the deeply intrusive and humiliating nature of polygraph testing as a virtue when 'national security' is at stake," *Nation* magazine charged.[72] Moreover, such arguments relied on the deterrent effect of the polygraph more than on the actual test results. As Willard pointed out in his written statement, "Indeed, use of the polygraph probably deters many candidates who do not meet security standards from applying in the first place."[73] But how could one prove such an assertion? For the administration, what mattered was their prerogative to use its power over information.

The Reagan administration momentarily went on the defensive but eventually won out. Congress, under Jack Brooks's leadership, suspended implementation of Reagan's initiative until June 1984, the end of the budget year. At the start of an election year that also bore the name of George Orwell's influential novel (a point that was not lost in contemporary press coverage of the issue), Reagan cancelled NSDD 84.[74] Nevertheless, in January 1985 the Pentagon announced that it would implement a one-year test approved by Congress, during which it would periodically polygraph employees with access to classified information. General Richard Stilwell, undersecretary for policy, called the tests "prophylactic flutters" to gauge "the trustworthiness, patriotism and integrity" of Pentagon employees.[75] In November 1985, President Reagan signed an order that authorized "aperiodic, non-life style, counterintelligence-type polygraph examinations" for federal employees with access to classified information, which Congress had approved in June.[76]

However, this victory for national security was quickly followed by a ban on domestic use. Indeed, the most direct effect that the 1983 investigation into NSDD 84 had on public polygraph discussions was its commissioning and funding, through the congressional Office of Technology Assessment (OTA), of the most comprehensive review of polygraph research available at the time.[77] Under the direction of Edward Katkin, professor of psychology at the State University of New York at Buffalo, the study assembled twelve experts from the fields of psychology, psychiatry, political science, law, and medicine. It limited itself to reviewing only scientific evidence for the validity of polygraph tests—in other words, whether or not the tests measured what they claimed to measure: evidence of deception. The study therefore untangled, to an unprecedented degree, different research about the polygraph with regards to utility, civil liberties, and social discipline.

The report presented the incoherent state of polygraph research. The OTA panel, which heard outspoken supporters and opponents of the polygraph, reached conclusions worth quoting at length:

OTA concluded, therefore, that no overall measure or single statistic of polygraph validity can be established based on available scientific evidence. The amount and quality of the evidence depends on the design and conduct of specific studies and the particular application researched. . . . Further, regardless of whether polygraph testing is used in specific-incident investigations or personnel screening, OTA concluded that polygraph accuracy may also be affected by a number of factors: examiner training, orientation, and experience; examinee characteristics such as emotional stability and intelligence; and, in particular, the use of countermeasures and the willingness of the examinee to be tested. In addition, the basic theory (or theories) of how the polygraph test actually works has been only minimally developed and researched. In sum, OTA concluded that there is at present only limited scientific evidence for establishing the validity of polygraph testing.[78]

The OTA study had considerable influence in swaying congressional opinion toward such a ban. Few newspaper stories and politicians' statements from 1983 onward failed to point out its conclusions. In this case, scientific discourse shaped public discourse: since, as the OTA study suggested, polygraph tests tended to exaggerate the number of deceptive subjects (false positives), the polygraph tended to accuse too many people of lying.[79] This undermined it in the public domestic realm where the polygraph was vulnerable to attack on grounds of right to privacy and, in particular, the presumption of innocence. But alternatively, that very same bias bolstered the argument for the polygraph on the basis of national security. As the Reagan administration had asserted in the 1983 hearings on NSDD 84, it was acceptable to err on the side of caution when it came to protecting the nation's secrets, even though that same bias exposed the polygraph to fundamental constitutional and ethical criticism outside the realm of "national security."

The debate also revealed that high-ranking members of the Reagan administration shared the ethos of individual conscience and honor that often led to criticism of the polygraph. When asked by a journalist whether he would ever submit to a polygraph test, Secretary of State George Shultz responded as follows: "The minute, in this government, I am told that I'm not trusted is the day that I leave."[80] He was quickly assured that high-ranking officials would, of course, never be asked to submit to the test. Lowly applicants for federal employment, on the other hand, often did not have the luxury of declining.

Other supporters of the president also fired relentless shots at the polygraph. Nobody represented the conservative-libertarian arguments of the anti-polygraph coalition more forcefully than *New York Times* columnist William Safire. Safire devoted five columns between 1983 and 1988 to his ire against the "inaccurate and always antilibertarian" practice of "Big Brotherism." Safire criticized President Reagan for using the threat of the polygraph "to crack down on internal dissent by using the concern about espionage," and he charged that because of reliance on a faulty technology that was beatable, "both personal liberty and national security suffer."[81] The columnist, a former speechwriter to Richard Nixon and proponent of Reagan's arms build-up, was especially incensed by a 1982 article that illustrated how quickly concerns about espionage could bleed into U.S. domestic institutions. That year, the *Times* printed a story about a Soviet spy in British intelligence, the existence of whom was known to the U.S. government through NSA intercepts of British communications. News of the spy caused a feverish hunt for the source of the leak in the Reagan administration. Suspicion centered on Robert (Bud) McFarlane, then deputy to National Security Advisor William Clark, especially after it became known that McFarlane had failed two polygraph tests. In desperation, McFarlane appealed to *Times* editor Arthur Sulzberger, who personally informed Reagan—after much soul-searching about protection of sources—that McFarlane had not been the source of the story. "Consider what this episode reveals," Safire wrote in 1987. "Bud McFarlane was in fact not the leaker; he was falsely condemned by a Kafkaesque machine whose printout would be decisive with the President of the U.S.; his innocence had to be affirmed by a newspaper that had to decide to break its own rules guarding its ability to get the news."[82]

Safire not only feared for domestic freedom of the press, but he reiterated the charge that the polygraph attacked trust in the individual and their sincerity. His criticism, therefore, went beyond concerns about polygraph inaccuracy: "The best operators will often fail because honest people do get nervous and liars can be trained to beat the system." Safire interpreted Massachusetts senator Edward Kennedy's characterization of the polygraph as an "inaccurate instrument of intimidation" as a nod to his own support for a polygraph ban and thus again illustrated the broad political reach of anti-polygraph sentiment by the 1980s.[83]

By 1987, congressional pressure finally reached critical mass and overcame the still extensive opposition from some, but not all, national security hawks, trade associations, and of course the polygraphists themselves. Long-standing opponents such as Sam Ervin or Birch Bayh had left the Senate by the early 1980s, but after the 1983 hearings on Reagan's NSDD 84, Senate and House Democrats (with support of some Republicans) continued to introduce bills in 1985, 1986, and 1987. On April 23, 1986, the Senate Labor and Human Resources Committee held the last day of congressional hearings on the polygraph, during which the battle lines on the debate presented themselves once again. The United Food and Commercial Workers International Union (a union with 1.3 million members at the time) testified strongly against the polygraph to screen applicants or employees. The American Psychological Association (APA) and the American Pharmaceutical Association (APhA) voiced their reservations about the polygraph test's validity and reliability and strongly supported federal legislation. On the other hand, the American Polygraph Association defended its professional credentials, and trade associations such as the American Bankers Association, the National Grocers Association, the National Wholesale Drug Association, and even the Bowling Proprietors' Association of America either voiced principled opposition to a ban or lobbied for exemptions for their particular trade.[84]

The claims that carried the day were first the argument that the unreliable nature of the test—underscored by the OTA study, which was frequently cited during the hearing—invited abuse, and second that polygraph use apparently had risen dramatically during the preceding decade and needed to be reined in. Democrats still invoked civil liberties, as when Senator John Kerry of Massachusetts asserted in his opening statement that confessions under pressure of an impending lie detector test went against American values: "American courts cannot compel defendants to take these tests and I believe that our basic American values are corrupted when we mandate these tests as a condition for employment."[85] Yet the Senate Committee on Labor and Human Relations also heard testimony from psychologists, most prominently David C. Raskin of the University of Utah, who shared concern over superficial polygraph exams that utilized broad questions but voiced support for the polygraph in specific investigations. Apparently, it was especially the observation by experts such as Raskin that polygraph screening tests falsely identified innocent persons that reassured committee chairman Senator Orrin Hatch of Utah in his support for the bill. For Hatch, the fairness of the "tradeoff" between the legitimate concerns of employers and the invasive means of the polygraph was the issue.[86] In short, Congress concluded that quantity of polygraph exams interfered with quality. The more polygraph exams, the higher the number of innocent victims. This logic demanded curtailment of quantity but also made room for exceptions, especially for the federal government, where Congress could demand higher quality standards for examiners.

The EPPA prohibited business in the broadest possible language to use any kind of lie detection technology for any kind of purpose or to discriminate in any way against prospective or current employees on the basis of an action related to the EPPA.[87] The act further created clear penalties (fines up to $10,000) and defined authority for the secretary of labor to enforce the act. It further prohibited any form of waiver as part of employment agreements. The act therefore eliminated forced voluntarism and created clearly delineated implementation mechanisms, the crux of much civil rights legislation in the past. The act did exempt polygraph tests for specific investigative purposes in cases of theft and defined a number of explicit conditions employers needed to fulfill before they could request, but not order, a test.

But the EPPA also affirmed exemptions for government and justified these exemptions with notions of national security: government employees on any level were untouched by the act; nothing in the act could be interpreted as prohibiting the federal government from performing "its intelligence or counterintelligence function" through lie detector tests, whether that effected applicants, employees, or "experts or consultants" under contract with the Pentagon, the Department of Energy, the CIA, or the FBI in connection with counterintelligence activities.[88]

The act also defined the limits of test questions, specifically outlawing those pertaining to religious or political beliefs and sexual matters, and outlined advance notice of the purpose, limits to the test procedure, and rights against disclosure or other adverse consequences of the test. In short, the history of the polygraph and the American Cold War ended with the federal government's assertion of regulatory power domestically, while it also showcased the power of national security as a discourse that allowed—and indeed demanded—exemptions from regular procedure.

After the House of Representatives passed its version in November 1987 by a vote of 254 to 158, the Senate approved a bill in March 1988 by a vote of 69 to 27. A House-Senate conference in May agreed on a compromise bill, which was passed again by both houses by similar margins. President Reagan signed the bill in June. It went into effect in December 1988. The fact that the Senate version of the EPPA was co-sponsored by Democrat Edward Kennedy, chairman of the Senate Labor Committee and perhaps the Senate's most prominent liberal, and Republican Orrin G. Hatch, demonstrated again how broad the anti-polygraph coalition had become. At the time, Kennedy and Hatch had been at odds with each other over the nomination of Robert Bork to the Supreme Court and issues relating to abortion. Kennedy declared on the floor of the Senate that "if you are an altar boy, you probably will fail it. You would have a sense of conscience and potential guilt. But who passes it? The psychopaths, the deceptive ones."[89] The marriage of libertarians' respect for sincerity and liberals' concerns over civil rights had won the day.

The EPPA created minimum restrictions in twenty-nine states that had not passed their own law at the time. Those states lay mainly in the South and parts of the Midwest. Unsurprisingly, congressional opposition mostly came from those states. For example, Texas congressman Tom Delay called the law "the criminal protection act."[90]

Opponents of the EPPA identified two major issues of contention, which illustrate the polygraph's role in extending federal power and, in turn, the role of national security discourse in this extension. For one, the Department of Justice objected to the EPPA on grounds of free-market ideology and federalism. In 1986 Assistant Attorney General John R. Bolton asserted, "The terms and conditions of private employment, to the maximum extent possible, should be decided in the private marketplace. . . . Polygraph misuse may be more appropriately deterred by restricting the conditions under which polygraphs are administered rather than prohibiting their use altogether. The states are better equipped to make those determinations."[91] Two years later, Assistant Attorney General Stephen J. Markman testified: "To preempt the states in this context, where there is no evidence for an overriding need for national policy uniformity, would do violence to an important underlying principle of our union—the belief in the ability and responsibility of the states generally to govern the affairs of its citizens."[92]

Congressional supporters of the EPPA countered that there was a need for national conformity, since often employers located in states with polygraph restrictions would send employees across state borders for the procedure. Yet Congress failed to realize that the metaphorical border between national security–related and other uses might not hold either. During the debate about the EPPA, this inconsistency was not lost on opponents of the bill. Republican senator Malcolm Wallop of Wyoming fulminated, "On the one hand, we allow the national security agency, the CIA, the Defense Department, and other agencies to use the polygraph to conduct their investigations. Standards are set to ensure that the tests are fair and accurate. Yet we turn around and tell American companies that they cannot use the same test to protect their security."[93]

In its testimony before Congress, the National Retail Merchants' Association (NRMA) also pointed to past exemptions that Congress had granted to the Department of Defense, CIA, and other national security–related uses of the polygraph. By allowing such exemptions, the NRMA stated, Congress "apparently overwhelmingly acknowledged the usefulness of the polygraph in protecting our national security. Yet, the same interests which make the polygraph a useful tool for protection against theft of information make it a useful tool for protecting against theft of cash and merchandise."[94]

Even supporters of the EPPA joined in the charge that the law made a nonsensical distinction between private and government employment. Labor lawyer Sheldon Engelhard asserted, "The exemptions were purely political, having nothing to do at all with the recognized view that polygraphs aren't reliable."[95] Either the polygraph as a screening tool was helpful or not.

As for the questionable distinction between domestic and foreign realm, columnist William Safire eloquently expressed this problem in 1983 when he criticized Reagan's order to extend polygraph use to any government official dealing with sensitive material, which had found expression in the EPPA as well: "Talk about slippery slopes—first the spies; now on the 'consistency' excuse, everyone in Government; next, Congressmen and journalists, and finally everyone will be required to prove himself innocent on the machine, lest a refusal lead to the presumption of guilt."[96] If one goal of polygraphing was to protect sensitive information, how many other exceptional powers could the government claim to protect its secrets? How far could it reach into the domestic realm to protect its secrets from foreign powers, or indeed from any kind of public disclosure? When did a specific investigation turn into a potentially abusive fishing expedition?

Commentators also noticed how failure to distinguish between protection against information leaking on the one hand and counterespionage on the other could cast suspicion on the patriotism of individual Americans. In a televised 1984 panel discussion on "The Media and Government Leaks," PBS host Ford Rowan pointed out that traitors would likely "give secrets to the other side, not journalists." But what about the motives of people who leaked to the press? Rowan listed vanity, ambition (with Henry Kissinger as a prime example), but also patriotism: "People want to right a perceived wrong, or correct a mistake in strategy—the whistle-blower idea." On the same panel, historian Allen Weinstein agreed: "One administration's 'leaker' is an opposition's 'loyal American underground.'" Weinstein further underlined the political character of information control when he stated that agreement on counterespionage measures usually appeared in times "in which the purposes and definitions of the national interest were generally agreed upon by the society's leadership."[97] That meant that by the same token, those same measures could become controversial if society could not reach a consensus on their purpose.

While outsourcing means the export of governmental functions from the public to the private sector, polygraph discussions in connection with national security issues also illustrated moves in the opposite direction. When criticizing Reagan's NSDD 84 and its provisions to enforce information control, critics particularly pointed to the danger of giving the government the right to virtually license information and therefore treat public ownership of knowledge according to the rules of private knowledge. Even "voluntary" nondisclosure agreements were against the spirit of the First Amendment, as University of Michigan law professor Lee Bollinger argued before Congress, since the public's right to free information would have to trump any agreements between individuals and the government: "We all have an interest," Bollinger testified, "in stopping the Government from trying to shape public discussion, whether the government seeks to do that through punishment or through offering inducements to them. . . . It would not be sufficient for the Government to point to the fact that the voluntarily contracted with the Government to refrain from criticizing the Government."[98] Just as private business had tried for decades to protect its knowledge with the polygraph, the government appeared to do the same in the name of national security.

The EPPA sidestepped all these issues. In the end, an unusually broad coalition of civil rights groups such as the ACLU, labor lawyers and unions, high-powered Wall Street bankers, scientific experts from the AMA and APA, and libertarian conservatives, as well as persistent political pressure from Congress, managed to contain the polygraph. Significantly, what had changed from the 1950s was not the breadth but the depth of both polygraph use and opposition to it.[99]

However, the EPPA was a victory of regulation that shifted social risk from employees back to employers in domestic labor relations. By defining strict rules for polygraph use, it created a deterrent effect *for employers,* which moved risk toward the side of the prospective user of the test. As the *Journal of Small Business Management* concluded at the time, "Small businesses should refrain from utilizing such examinations [polygraph tests]. The law and regulations are extremely complex. To correctly interpret and apply the law, small businesses will have to hire legal counsel, the cost of whose advice is likely to outweigh the benefits gained from the polygraph results."[100]

In fact, beginning at the latest in the early 1960s, a number of lawsuits had resulted in substantial settlements for individuals who sued their employer after they had refused or allegedly failed polygraph tests.[101] In 1965 the federal Equal Employment Opportunity Commission, which President Johnson had turned into a major vehicle to press businesses working under contract with the federal government to implement civil rights laws, stated that it considered the polygraph a discriminatory labor practice.[102] A 1988 *Business Week* article cited the case of a Maryland appeals court that awarded $1.3 million to a former

Rite-Aid employee, who in the course of an internal investigation of stock shortages was fired after she had refused to take a polygraph test. The article, titled "Privacy," discussed the polygraph in connection with a host of other issues of privacy in the workplace such as random drug testing, confidentiality for people infected with HIV/AIDS, computer and phone surveillance, and employer access to FBI databases. The article's conclusion reflected the general tenor of rights discourse in the late 1980s: "Most workplace privacy issues pose . . . difficult questions. They pit the needs of the company against the worker's feelings of dignity and worth. To sacrifice much of the latter would make work life untenable. So the U.S. must decide which rights of a citizen in society should extend to an employee in the corporation—and in what form."[103]

This context of resistance to polygraph exams as an issue of privacy and individual rights in the workplace was echoed by legal scholars, who concluded by the end of the decade that "these [polygraph] suits have been based on a variety of legal theories, including public policy tort, defamation, invasion of privacy, intentional infliction of emotional distress, racial discrimination, and negligence, to name a few."[104] A quip among lawyers called the EPPA the "Lawyer Full Employment Act" in anticipation of lawsuits arising from it.[105]

It must also be emphasized that limiting the lie detector did not mean an untarnished victory for privacy in domestic labor relations. Rather, it meant a renegotiation of social power in relation to workplace testing. While factors such as the increasing use of litigation to enforce rights allowed for more effective resistance to the polygraph, new drug tests or methods of surveillance such as computer or phone surveillance simply shifted the ground in personnel testing. The same year that the polygraph was largely banned from the private workplace, the American Management Association published a survey of 1,005 human resource managers. It showed that 48 percent of companies now used drug tests in some form on their employees (up from 21 percent in 1986). Of those companies using drug tests, 96 percent stated they would not hire a positive applicant and 25 percent that they would fire current positive employees (the real number might have been higher). On the other hand, polygraph testing fell from 10.7 percent in 1987 to 8.7 percent in 1988 (probably in anticipation of the EPPA). About 30 percent of companies operating in states without polygraph legislation still used it, with retailers in those states the most common practitioners (71 percent) followed by the banking and security industries.[106] In short, drug tests by the late 1980s had not only become a replacement for the polygraph but had already become far more widespread.[107]

Polygraph controversies thus resulted in an ambiguous draw by the end of the Cold War. On the one hand, the notion of privacy—which had gained importance in other constitutional discussions as well, most prominently with the Supreme Court's abortion decision *Roe v. Wade* in 1973—scored a victory when Congress declared widespread pre-employment screenings in private business as an invasion of workers' privacy. Even though the question of constitutionality was left open, the 1988 Employee Polygraph Protection Act eventually expressed a polit-ical consensus that this practice was unacceptable. On the other hand, national security asserted its claim as an exceptional area where unruly practices such as polygraphing were necessary. Therefore, the Cold War ended with an act of Congress stipulating that a practice incompatible with American freedom at home was nevertheless necessary to protect that same freedom from external danger. Moreover, the very efforts to limit polygraph use through regulation normalized the practice and boosted the test's credentials. This conclusion highlights how the ethos of security gave rise to a separate sphere of governmental power to pro-tect a self-proclaimed free society.

Epilogue

In April 2008 the cable news channel MSNBC reported that the Pentagon had issued a new hand-held lie detection device to U.S. soldiers:

> The new device, known by the acronym PCASS, for Preliminary Credibility Assessment Screening System, uses a commercial TDS Ranger hand-held personal digital assistant with three wires connected to sensors attached to the hand. An interpreter will ask a series of 20 or so questions in Persian, Arabic, or Pashto: "Do you intend to answer my questions truthfully?" "Are the lights on in this room?" "Are you a member of the Taliban?" The operator will punch in each answer and, after a delay of a minute or so for processing, the screen will display the results: "Green," if it thinks the person has told the truth, "Red" for deception, and "Yellow" if it can't decide.

According to MSNBC, the U.S. Army had purchased 94 PCASSs for $7,500 each from a company called Lafayette Instruments in Lafayette, Indiana. The device was not to be used on U.S. personnel. While the Pentagon claimed 82 to 90 percent accuracy from three studies conducted with volunteers (223 persons in all), MSNBC reported that this statistic disregarded inconclusive findings, the inclusion of which dropped the instrument's success rate to 62 to 70 percent. "It's virtually impossible to do a validity study in a war zone," project manager Donald Krapohl, special assistant to the director at the Defense Academy for Credibility Assessment, was quoted as saying. "That's the best that we can do right now. But if you come back next year or in five years, I might have a different answer for you." Army counterintelligence official David Thompson added, "Once this capability is introduced and word spreads of its use, militia or insurgent related individuals will be less likely to attempt to gain admittance [as correctional officers]."[1]

In its efforts to police occupied Iraq and Afghanistan, the Army was updating the polygraph. For me, the above statements have a far-cical ring. After all, the polygraph had promised to deliver its scientific credentials for decades, yet validation always remained just beyond the horizon. At the same time, this new lie detector story illustrates that perceived emergency and the powerful discourse of "national security" continue to imbue lie detection technology, and other technologies of identification, with exceptional authority. Similarly, during a conference that the National Research Council organized in 2009 to explore the possibilities of utilizing the behavioral sciences to support military intelligence, speakers found that none of the "various technologies with potential application in the intelligence field" had been "subjected to a careful field evaluation."[2] While Department of Defense Intelligence Operations Specialist Anthony Veney insisted that PCASS "has been a godsend on the battlefield" in Iraq, Afghanistan, and in counter-narcotic operations in Colombia, Harvard University psychiatrist Robert Fein cautioned, "I think we can do better than put something out there that has such limitations."[3] In his 2011 testimony to Congress, cognitive scientist Philip Rubin found "a lack of appreciation among many of those in the intelligence community for the value of objective field evaluations and how inaccurate informal 'lessons learned' approaches to field evaluation can be." This cultural difference between application and research in the field was exacerbated, according to Rubin, by the sense of urgency felt by soldiers and intelligence operators thrown into dangerous situations: "This sense of urgency can lead to pressure to use available tools before they are evaluated—and even to ignoring the results of evaluations if they disagree with the users' conviction that the tools are useful."[4]

Paradoxically, the very logic of emergency that justified the use of lie detection technology in the first place continues to be the principle obstacle to viable evaluations of its effectiveness.

The attacks of September 11, 2001, have often been used to justify the use of torture—the term itself being contested by the CIA—in order to gain crucial intelligence quickly. In the case of waterboarding and other techniques, informed consent of the subjects is, of course, not a consideration.[5] But in the twenty-first century, the search for new lie detection technologies continued as well. As literary scholar Melissa Littlefield puts it, "The anxiety created by 9/11 has enabled a particular kind of presentation that privileges technoscientific advancement while returning to many of the assumptions foundational to traditional polygraphy and fingerprinting."[6] Like the Cold War, the War on Terror has spiraled into a larger project of policing various frontiers of U.S. influence and predicting and controlling the human mind. For example, physicist John Marburger III, who directed the Office of Science and Technology Policy under President George W. Bush, prefaced a report on the possibilities of combating terrorism with the support of social, behavioral, and economic sciences thus:

> The events of September 11, 2001 profoundly affected the lives of all Americans and were a call to action to which American and our government have responded in many ways. . . . Our ability to maintain our American way of life also depends on our understanding of human behavior, which is the domain of the social, behavioral, and economic sciences. We must investigate the psychological and neurobiological mechanisms of stress, fear and courage; the powerful networks of human social exchange that sustain individuals and families; the special needs and strengths of groups as a function of their history and culture; the principles of economic growth and decline; and the attitudes and beliefs that lead people to vote and sustain a democracy.[7]

Therefore, as during the second half of the twentieth century, in the early twenty-first century lie detection continued to be part of a larger, comprehensive policy to assert U.S. national security on a variety of fronts.

As with the Soviet enemy, some Americans associated their new opponent also with a quasi-natural tendency to lie. For example,

Republican congressman Duncan Hunter Jr. asserted on the C-Span program *Washington Journal* in 2013:

> In the Middle Eastern culture, it is looked upon with high regard to get the best deal possible no matter what it takes, that includes lying. . . . People barter back and forth and try to get the best deal for each other. Iran is the epitome of that, they have lied over and over. They are liars. The Iranian government lie [*sic*] all the time. So, why trust them now?

Upon questioning by the moderator of the show, Hunter admitted that this was "a big generalization" but refused to qualify his statements.[8] Similarly, the contention that Russian politics is exceptionally prone to propaganda and a disbelief in objective truth has remained a discernable trope in American public discussions.[9]

National security policy after 9/11 also included the polygraph. Anecdotal evidence suggests that the CIA continued the operational use of polygraph exams in the hunt for terrorists or to protect its secret operations in conflict zones. For example, according to anonymous sources interviewed by journalist Seymour Hersh, when an officer of Pakistan's powerful military intelligence organization, the Inter-Services Intelligence (ISI), walked into the U.S. embassy in Islamabad in 2010 and claimed to have intelligence about the whereabouts of Osama bin Laden, he was given a polygraph exam (which he passed) to confirm his bona fides.[10] According to CNN reporting in 2013, "Some CIA operatives involved in the agency's missions in Libya, have been subjected to frequent, even monthly polygraph examinations, according to a source with deep inside knowledge of the agency's workings. The goal of the questioning, according to sources, is to find out if anyone is talking to the media or Congress."[11] Scientist Stephen Fienberg, who had directed a National Research Council study on the topic, noted that after the attacks of September 11, only the Department of Energy was willing to critically question and minimize its use of the polygraph.[12] In 2002, the FBI, which hitherto had used the polygraph mainly in cases where its employees worked with other intelligence agencies relying on the technology, expanded its use of polygraph exams. Those subject to screenings now included "all FBI employees assigned to counterintelligence, counterterrorism, and security programs." More broadly, the bureau emphasized, "All FBI employees will be subject to random selection at any time."[13] Since the implementation of this policy, stories about FBI analysts who had their security clearance revoked after "failed" polygraph examinations have surfaced.[14] As in earlier times, public criticism of the unreliability of the test followed immediately. The subhead to a 2002 article in *Mother Jones* titled "Lie Detector Roulette" read: "Everyone admits that polygraphs are unreliable. So why are government employees subjected to tests that can ruin their careers?"[15]

And so polygraph controversies continued. In 2013, the Drug Enforcement Agency agreed to settle a lawsuit filed by fourteen contractors who had been denied employment due to failed or refused polygraph tests. After the agency discovered that one of its contract translators was related to a suspect, it required around a hundred translators to be polygraphed and informed twenty-seven of them afterward that they had failed the test. Questions included "very personal and even alarming questions about their lives, including about their sexual practices and crimes such as bestiality, court documents said."[16] In 2014, the National Reconnaissance Office, responsible for espionage in space, announced an overhaul of its polygraph program after examiners had told the *McClatchy* news agency in 2012 that they had been encouraged to probe into the private lives of employees against Pentagon directions to limit questions to security-relevant areas, and that the agency rewarded examiners for the number of admissions they achieved. On the other hand, admission of serious crimes such as child molestation remained unreported in some cases. An Inspector General report denied that such practices were official policy and blamed "inefficient testing practices," a claim that employees and contractors for the NRO disputed.[17]

Further, despite polygraph examiners' claims that countermeasures were inefficient, in 2013 federal authorities opened an investigation against Douglas Williams, a former Oklahoma police polygrapher, for teaching polygraph countermeasures to unsuitable people planning to infiltrate security agencies. In interviews with journalists Marisa Taylor and Cleve Wootson, officials referred to the Obama administration's Insider Threat Program, launched in 2011 in the wake of the discovery that Private Chelsea (then known as Bradley) Manning had downloaded large numbers of classified documents and distributed them to the organization Wikileaks. The program encourages federal employees to report a range of "risky" behaviors of their co-workers. McClatchy reported that federal agencies gave about 70,000 polygraph tests a year. An unnamed security official charged, "Prosecutors are trying to make an example of [Doug Williams]. . . . It serves to elevate polygraph to something it hasn't been before, that teaching countermeasures is akin to teaching bomb making, and that there's something inherently dis- loyal about disseminating this type of information." Further, former Army Reserve intelligence officer and anti-polygraph activist George Maschke claimed that a federal agent targeted him online by posing as an Islamic terrorist seeking to help pass a polygraph test.[18] In Septem- ber 2015, a Federal Court in Oklahoma City sentenced Williams to two years in prison.[19]

In other words, polygraph controversies continued to be enmeshed in larger debates over the appropriateness of security policies. Notwith- standing efforts by federal agencies to ease anxieties, for example by producing informational videos showing content, relaxed employees, polygraph tests still cause apprehension about invasion of privacy on all fronts.[20]

In an area where privacy concerns appear less urgent, the test has also been expanded in the United States and in Great Britain to a differ- ent group of people feared and ostracized by the general population: sex offenders.[21] Its use can, again, be explained by assumptions about the inherent dishonesty of a population (in this case individuals suppos- edly in denial about their sexual urges) and a governmental program of producing confessions and managing risk by constant monitoring of the "abnormal" individual.[22] Even in Germany, where the polygraph had been found unconstitutional in 1956, the Supreme Court in 1998 reversed itself somewhat and based any bans on the technology only on its unreliability, therefore opening up possibilities for limited appli- cations in Germany and other countries where the polygraph has been in limited use.[23]

In the early twenty-first century, however, the polygraph might very well be in the process of being replaced by new technologies of truth that promise visual access to the human brain, most prominently in the form of brain "imaging" or "scanning." Yet, as Melissa Littlefield has shown, these new "mind reading" machines continue to make assump- tions about the nature of mind and body that are directly inherited from the polygraph. Just as the polygraph did in the mid-twentieth century, "Brain Fingerprinting" and its latest competitor, functional magnetic resonance imaging (fMRI), promises that *finally* a scientifically sound way to identify liars has been discovered. Both methodologies utilize a questioning technique directly drawn from the Guilty Knowledge Test developed by David Lykken for the polygraph. The fMRI and Brain Fingerprinting also assume that lies can be localized in the body, only now through sequences of three-dimensional images of the brain, which means that the measurement takes place directly at the central, not the peripheral, nervous system.

In this endeavor, the new techniques continue to encounter the same methodological problems as the polygraph. First, the intention to lie cannot be localized in the body, because of the logical problem that one cannot unambiguously infer a cause from its consequence, and because deception is not a physical phenomenon but a discursive construct, the content of which depends on the experimental design one chooses. Second, all bodily activity takes place within an organism, in an interdependent system that requires evaluation as a whole. Additionally, truth technology makes a fundamental assumption about lying as an increase of cranial activity. This assumption itself has not been proven and could easily be challenged on evolutionary grounds. Lastly, image-based lie detection is open to the same potential countermeasures as the polygraph.[24] Yet many scientists, politicians, security experts, and others are enthralled. It might very well be its aesthetic fit with the authority of photographic realism that makes lie detection through brain imaging so attractive.[25] In the end, lie detection technologies are still based on highly problematic methodological assumptions that are disguised by representational compression into a dynamic curve or a colorful image.

Governmental power appears to become less centralized in comparison to the twentieth century, with Big Business an equal partner to Big Government. To some observers, a new kind of totalitarian government began to creep up on citizens through the guise of benevolent empire. Echoing C. Wright Mills, political theorist Sheldon Wolin insisted that democracy requires truth-telling and that the "inverted totalitarianism" of the United States in the early twenty-first century is based on a fundamental deception of the people about the political

system they live in.[26] Here the contrast of new surveillance technology
to the polygraph is most startling. Rather than confronting individuals
in a heightened state of alert during a test that requires definite "yes"
or "no" answers, technologies such as data mining of online activity or
tracking of cell phone use follow individuals in their private and professional consumption of technology. In fact, "life logging" encourages
individuals to self-monitor using web-based, linked technology, thus
creating a seamless record of everyday activity that is open for analysis.
Whether individuals' mental health or their ability to escape manipulation might not require them to keep some of their experiences hidden,
even to themselves, is a question usually not considered by supporters
of self-surveillance.[27] By intimately connecting technology with our
own sense of self, we assume that smart phones and other devices simply become extensions of ourselves rather than tools that can be used
for different purposes. As writer Charles Howarth puts it,

> We now view technology not just as empowering but as self-actualizing
> as well. Because it's positioned as key to our authentic selves, we are
> newly intimate with it. This sounds utopian. It seems as if technolo-
> gy is finally reaching its potential: It is no longer the threat to human
> freedom, but its driving force. . . . The result is that we become blind
> to technology's dark side—its potential to be misused in ways that en-
> croach on our privacy. How can we see the privacy implications of our
> smartphones when we see them first as the key to the authentic self, or
> the Google Car when it looks so cute, or Google Glass when we believe
> that it will allow us to transcend our bodies to allow a new mastery of
> the world.[28]

Yet surveillance technologies do have governmental agendas and
ideological precepts. The dominant ideology of western liberalism
since the 1970s has been the ideology of the free individual in pursuit of
their authentic self in direct competition with other selves.[29] Neoliberal
individuals see themselves as human capital, their pursuits of freedom
governed through risk management, audits, budgeting, and other indirect governmental techniques that urge individuals to hone their marketable skills. To some critics, neoliberal society is turning college students (but by implication all of society) into "excellent sheep," capable
of performing but lacking introspection.[30] In this sense, government

in the early twenty-first century is centered on a particular notion of the core value of freedom, namely "a type of regulated freedom that encourage[s] or requires[s] individuals to compare what they did, what they achieved, and what they were, with what they could or should be."[31] In this sense, surveillance technology animates individuals to "freely" develop their talents and does not inflict direct violence on individuals, as long as they remain within the limits of acceptable behavior in the marketplace. The neoliberal self can be refashioned indefinitely and therefore does not require probing into its depth.

Linked technologies such as databases of biometric data can give the experience of freedom through effortless travel or enjoyment of social benefits. Yet it is wise to consider that identification based on surveillance does not *require* freedom. After all, slaves were the first individuals in the United States whom the government attempted to authenticate through ID. Therefore, *inclusion* and *exclusion*, rather than freedom, should be seen as among the goals pursued by ID projects and other surveillance technologies.

Further, identification through methods such as iris scans, electronic fingerprints, voice pattern analysis, and so on separates information from the body and is based on parameters that are chosen, just as with the polygraph, with an eye toward sensitivity and specificity, that is, the ability to correctly identify culprits and innocents. As with the lie detector, choice of parameters can lead to misidentification. Government by identification through disembodied aggregates of data is therefore based on constant surveillance, assessment, and classification of bodies, all of which include possibilities for error and open avenues of punishment if the citizen refuses cooperation.[32]

Facial expression analysis can also be seen as part of a larger trend of defining parameters of normal versus abnormal bodies in their expression of affect. Psychologist Paul Ekman's "Automated Facial Expression Analysis" model is being employed to develop face-reading software for uses not only in human-computer interaction and psychological therapy, but also in forensic investigations.[33] Ekman became famous for his research in the nonverbal communication of emotions. He argued that expression of emotions was determined by evolution and therefore universal among humans. His book *Telling Lies* and his cooperation with the television series *Lie to Me* made Ekman the most prominent proponent of using facial expressions (especially so-called micro-expressions, such as pursing of the lips) to identify emotions, but also to deceive.[34] Ekman's ongoing project is to create a comprehensive map of emotions as expressed by the human face through his "Facial Action Coding System." Ekman's work in combining analysis of facial expression with other nonverbal clues has been incorporated by the Transportation Security Administration (TSA) into their Screening Passengers by Observation Technique (SPOT), which began in 2006 and has been criticized—by, among others, proponents of the polygraph such as David Raskin, a retired professor of psychology at the University of Utah—for being unconfirmed by peer-reviewed research and implemented inconsistently.[35] One former TSA Behavior Detection Officer called the SPOT program "complete bullshit."[36]

As various forms of lie detection have gone mainstream, lie detection techniques based on nonverbal clues and other behavioral science techniques are increasingly marketed as how-to guides for the average citizen or business owner. Former CIA or FBI officers often write such guides.[37] The value of imbuing everyday life with intelligence techniques remains questionable and may be seen as part of the larger culture of security that developed in the wake of the 9/11 attacks. We are increasingly asked not to look away when our fellow citizens involuntarily reveal private information about themselves. Such inquisitiveness violates what sociologist Erving Goffman defined as the essence of civilized behavior.[38] What kind of society we create when we hover like drones over our fellow citizens as if they were enemies remains to be seen.[39]

I conclude by highlighting four particularly significant legacies of the history of the polygraph for the early twenty-first century. First, the polygraph carved out a separate sphere for itself: a legal space where a different calculus of state power applies. Defenders of this separate sphere maintain that war is governed by different rules than peace, and that the executive branch of government must respond to emergencies with the full powers of the laws of war.[40] The history of the polygraph suggests that only by maintaining continued existence of a warlike state of international affairs has the executive managed to maintain wider powers. Therefore, administrations will be encouraged to secure for themselves wider powers by claiming interests of "national security" and thus prolonged states of emergency. The history of the polygraph is part of a larger political history of the United States in which an ideology of permanent emergency has been developing since the 1940s. The more normalized this ideology of emergency is becoming—in other words, the more phrases like "national security," "terrorist," and other discursive constructs lose their initial strangeness—the harder it becomes to recognize them as ideological and to challenge the assumptions they rest upon. Technologies like the polygraph and newer truth technologies play a crucial role in this process of normalization since their ideological claims come cloaked in scientific objectivity.

Second, the polygraph, especially as conceived by Leonarde Keeler, moved from the margin to the center of American society (participating in the definition of both terms in the process). Its targets were, first, the mentally ill, then criminals, gays, and foreigners, and then finally everybody. It shares this history with other technologies of surveillance and identification such as fingerprinting. British authorities began to experiment with fingerprint identification techniques to administer Indians, whom they considered pervasively dishonest, after the Indigo Disturbances of the 1860s; American fingerprint experts at first worked in Manila to put down indigenous rebellions against U.S. rule in the Philippines.[41] In contrast to colonial practices, the polygraph was a domestic technology: it was from the beginning used in the United States. Its history shows that the broad category of "national security" has the power to marginalize an ever-expanding list of categories of citizens. Once established as a separate sphere, "national security" can expand at a moment's notice and reach deeply into domestic society. As August Vollmer claimed in the 1920s, modernity crosses borders. Traditional understandings of the separation of domestic and foreign sphere, as expressed for example in the National Security Act of 1947, therefore increasingly lose meaning. The idea that freedom at home and freedom abroad cannot be separated was at the heart of U.S. national security policies throughout the twentieth century. As a result, after the terrorist attacks of September 11, 2001, the polygraph was one technology that immediately expanded its reach.

Third, the history of the polygraph shows that the promise of technology often reaches further than its ability to deliver. Yet this shortcoming might not keep federal agencies from using technologies for purposes other than the ones originally advertised. Despite lack of scientific credentials and persistent calls for more research, the polygraph maintained its authority to a large part because it became imbued with the aura of national security. Again, we can find a similar development in other surveillance technologies, such as the TSA's SPOT program or the biometric ID card the United States and other Western countries have been aggressively pursuing. Further, DNA testing, or "genetic fingerprinting," also appears to take on the role of utopian "truth machine," of unassailable forensic technology free of human error. Alas, human error—whether in sample collection or record keeping—has a way of creeping back into the system. Yet when national security is concerned, even experimental technologies can appear ready to go.[42]

Lastly, the history of the lie detector suggests that technology fails in its promise to alleviate political controversies. If anything, the lie detector test exacerbated controversies over the appropriateness of security procedures. Its use was renegotiated over decades. Technologies, I conclude, will remain controversial as long as the purpose of their use is controversial. As central as "national security" has become in American political discourse, its meaning remains foggy and its implementation is often classified. The lie detector shares in this pervasive legacy of the Cold War.

NOTES

Introduction

1. Charles M. Blow, *Fire Shut Up in My Bones: A Memoir* (Boston: Houghton Mifflin Harcourt, 2014), 203–4.
2. George Shultz, quoted in Don Oberdorfer, "Shultz Backs 'Voluntary' Polygraph Tests at State," *Washington Post*, April 29, 1988, A4.
3. On this theme see Andrea Friedman, *Citizenship in Cold War America: The National Security State and the Possibilities of Dissent* (Amherst: University of Massachusetts Press, 2014).
4. Walter A. McDougall, ... *The Heavens and the Earth: A Political History of the Space Age* (Baltimore: Johns Hopkins University Press, 1997), 7. For a powerful illustration of the influence of Cold War considerations on science pedagogy, see Christopher J. Phillips, *The New Math: A Political History* (Chicago: University of Chicago Press, 2015).
5. Daniel Yergin, *Shattered Peace: The Origins of the Cold War and the National Security State* (Boston: Houghton Mifflin, 1977), 193.
6. Lionel Trilling, *Sincerity and Authenticity* (Cambridge, MA: Harvard University Press, 1972); Jack Lynch, *Detection and Deception in Eighteenth-Century Britain* (Burlington: Ashgate, 2008); Karen Haltunen, *Confidence Men and Painted Women: A Study of Middle-Class Culture in America, 1830–1870* (New Haven, CT: Yale University Press, 1982).
7. Walter A. McDougall, *Freedom Just Around the Corner: A New American History, 1585–1828* (New York: HarperCollins, 2004); Gary Lindberg, *The Confidence Man in American Literature* (New York: Oxford University Press, 1982); Stephen Mihm, *A Nation of Counterfeiters: Capitalists, Con Men, and the Making of the United States* (Cambridge, MA: Harvard University Press, 2007).
8. John Kucich, *The Power of Lies: Transgression in Victorian Fiction* (Ithaca, NY: Cornell University Press, 1994). See Oscar Wilde, "The Decay of Lying: An Observation" (1889), http://virgil.org/dswo/courses/novel/wilde-lying.pdf.
9. See David Runciman, *Political Hypocrisy: The Mask of Power from Hobbes to Orwell and Beyond* (Princeton, NJ: Princeton University Press, 2008), 74–115.

10. See John Bew, *Realpolitik: A History* (New York: Oxford University Press, 2016). Meinecke's book *Machiavellianism: The Doctrine of Raison d'Etat and Its Place in Modern History from 1924* is quoted on 159.

11. See Mary L. Dudziak, *Cold War Civil Rights: Race and the Image of American Democracy* (Princeton, NJ: Princeton University Press, 2000).

12. J. Edgar Hoover, *Masters of Deceit: The Story of Communism in America and How to Fight It* (New York: Holt, 1958), 194–95; Laura A. Belmonte, *Selling the American Way: U.S. Propaganda and the Cold War* (Philadelphia: University of Pennsylvania Press, 2008).

13. See Gordon H. Barland, "Foreign Use of the Polygraph—Summary, v. 5.1," May 25, 1995. Document in author's possession. Countries with "major" polygraph capabilities, either private or public, were Bosnia, Canada, Croatia, El Salvador, India, Israel, Japan, Korea, Mexico, Poland, Romania, Russia, Serbia, Slovenia, South Africa, Taiwan, and Turkey.

14. See Ken Alder, *The Lie Detectors: The History of an American Obsession* (New York: Free Press, 2007), 271.

15. See Ellen Herman, *The Romance of American Psychology: Political Culture in the Age of Experts* (Berkeley: University of California Press, 1995).

16. Alan Trachtenberg, "Lincoln's Smile: Ambiguities of the Face in Photography," *Social Research* 67, no. 1 (Spring 2000): 9, 12; Gregory Fried, "True Pictures," *Common-Place* 2, no. 2 (January 2002), http://www.common-place.org/; Christian Parenti, *The Soft Cage: Surveillance in America From Slavery to the War on Terror* (New York: Basic Books, 2004), 37; James West Davidson, *"They Say": Ida B. Wells and the Reconstruction of Race* (New York: Oxford University Press, 2009), 1–5.

17. See Geoffrey C. Bunn, "The Hazards of the Will to Truth: A History of the Lie Detector" (Ph.D. diss., York University, 1998), 41–43.

18. Geoffrey C. Bunn, *The Truth Machine: A Social History of the Lie Detector* (Baltimore: Johns Hopkins University Press, 2011), 51–93, quotes on 53, 65. On Marston's test of women, see 156. Bunn's account ends at the time of World War II and neglects to explain why the polygraph prevailed after criminology, psychology, and the popular press turned against it after the 1930s.

19. R. Thomas, *Detective Fiction and the Rise of Forensic Science* (Cambridge: Cambridge University Press, 1998), 22.

20. Melissa M. Littlefield, *The Lying Brain: Lie Detection in Science and Science Fiction* (Ann Arbor: University of Michigan Press, 2011).

21. Robert Michael Brain, *The Pulse of Modernism: Physiological Aesthetics in Fin-de-Siècle Europe* (Seattle: University of Washington Press, 2015). Brain notes that the new physiological aesthetics were part of the larger transformation of western understandings of human nature in the nineteenth century. This theme is explored more broadly in Barry Sanders, *Unsuspecting Souls: The Disappearance of the Human Being* (Berkeley: Counterpoint Press, 2009).

22. Stephen Kern, *The Culture of Time and Space, 1880–1918* (Cambridge, MA: Harvard University Press, 1983). Mackinder presented his argument about the crucial importance of the Eurasian heartland before World War I. See Halford J. Mackinder, "The Geographical Pivot of History," *Geographical Journal* 23, no. 4 (April 1904); he developed it in more detail in his book *Democratic Ideals and Reality* (1919; New York: Holt, 1942); the reference to closed geography is on 29.

23. See Frank Ninkovich: *Modernity and Power: A History of the Domino Theory in the 20th Century* (Chicago: University of Chicago Press, 1994); Frank Ninkovich, *The*

Wilsonian Century: U.S. Foreign Policy since 1900 (Chicago: University of Chicago Press, 1999).

24. See Anders Stephanson, "Cold War Degree Zero," in *Uncertain Empire: American History and the Idea of the Cold War,* ed. Joel Isaac and Duncan Bell (New York: Oxford University Press, 2012), 19–50, quotes on 21.

25. See Perry Anderson, *American Foreign Policy and Its Thinkers* (New York: Verso, 2015), 55; Thomas J. McCormick, *America's Half-Century: United States Foreign Policy in the Cold War and after* (1989; reprint, Baltimore: Johns Hopkins University Press, 1995).

26. See John A. Thompson, *A Sense of Power: The Roots of America's Global Role* (Ithaca, NY: Cornell University Press, 2015).

27. For a useful discussion of the idea of a "High Cold War" that ended in 1963, see Andrew J. Bacevich, *The New American Militarism: How Americans Are Seduced by War* (2005; New York: Oxford University Press, 2013), 177–79. Alternatively, see the anthology of essays in Lorenz Lüthi, ed., *Regional Cold Wars in Europe, East Asia, and the Middle East: Crucial Periods* (Stanford: Stanford University Press, 2015). These essays collectively argue for four moments in which the international Cold War system was transformed, namely 1953–1956, 1965–1969, 1978–1983, and 1986–1989. While highlighting the regional peculiarities of different Cold War subsystems and the importance of a variety of actors, this volume still shows the usefulness of the systemic concept of "Cold War" to describe the international system after World War II.

28. Alan Nadel, *Containment Culture: American Narratives, Postmodernism, and the Atomic Age* (Durham, NC: Duke University Press, 1995), 2.

29. Melvyn P. Leffler, *A Preponderance of Power: National Security, the Truman Administration, and the Cold War* (Stanford: Stanford University Press, 1992), 446.

30. Gyan Prakash, *Another Reason: Technology and the Imagination of Modern India* (Princeton, NJ: Princeton University Press, 1999), 159. For a similar approach see James C. Scott, *Seeing Like a State: How Certain Schemes to Improve the Human Condition Have Failed* (New Haven, CT: Yale University Press, 1998).

31. Parenti, *Soft Cage,* 13–32.

32. Alfred W. McCoy, *Policing America's Empire: The United States, The Philippines, and the Rise of the Surveillance State* (Madison: University of Wisconsin Press, 2009); on the general theme of the interpenetration of domestic and colonial U.S. state building after 1898, see Alfred W. McCoy and Francisco A. Scarano, eds., *Colonial Crucible: Empire in the Making of the Modern American State* (Madison: University of Wisconsin Press, 2009).

33. See Michael Adas, *Dominance by Design: Technological Imperatives and America's Civilizing Mission* (Cambridge, MA: Belknap Press of Harvard University Press, 2006); Michael Adas, *Machines as the Measure of Men: Science, Technology, and Ideologies of Western Dominance* (Ithaca, NY: Cornell University Press, 1989).

34. See Prakash, *Another Reason,* 178–200.

35. James T. Sparrow, *Warfare State: World War II Americans and the Age of Big Government* (New York: Oxford University Press, 2011), 12. For the term "corporatism" to analyze the role of so-called functional groups and their role in shaping U.S. foreign policy since the 1920s, see Michael J. Hogan, "Corporatism," in *Explaining the History of American Foreign Relations,* ed. Michael J. Hogan and Thomas G. Paterson, 2nd ed. (New York: Cambridge University Press, 2004), 137–48.

36. Michael J. Hogan, *A Cross of Iron: Harry S. Truman and the Origins of the National Security State, 1945–1954* (New York: Cambridge University Press, 1998).

37. Aaron Friedberg, *In the Shadow of the Garrison State: America's Anti-Statism and Its Cold War Grand Strategy* (Princeton, NJ: Princeton University Press, 2000). While Friedberg emphasizes the limits to American national security statism, Sparrow underscores its radical expansion during World War II.

38. Recent works that emphasize the crucial role of partisan politics in Cold War policy debates and decisions include Robert David Johnson, *Congress and the Cold War* (New York: Cambridge University Press, 2006); Julian E. Zelizer, *Arsenal of Democracy: The Politics of National Security—From World War II to the War on Terrorism* (New York: Basic Books, 2009); Campbell Craig and Fredrik Logevall, *America's Cold War: The Politics of Insecurity* (Cambridge, MA: Belknap Press of Harvard University Press, 2009).

39. The term "global nationalism" is borrowed from John Fousek, *To Lead the Free World: American Nationalism and the Cultural Roots of the Cold War* (Chapel Hill: University of North Carolina Press, 2000).

40. See Michael S. Sherry, *In the Shadow of War: The United States since the 1930s* (New Haven, CT: Yale University Press, 1995); Tom Engelhardt, *The End of Victory Culture: Cold War America and the Disillusioning of a Generation* (New York: Basic Books, 1995).

41. Recent studies of Congress that do not mention polygraph investigations include David M. Barrett, *The CIA and Congress: The Untold Story from Truman to Kennedy* (Lawrence: University Press of Kansas, 2005); Johnson, *Congress and the Cold War*; Kathryn S. Olmsted, *Challenging the Secret Government: The Post-Watergate Investigations of the CIA and FBI* (Chapel Hill: University of North Carolina Press, 1996).

42. Sam C. Sarkesian, John Allen Williams, and Stephen J. Cimbala, *U.S. National Security: Policymakers, Processes, and Politics* (Boulder: Lynne Rienner, 2008), 4.

43. Melvyn P. Leffler, "National Security," in *Explaining the History of American Foreign Relations*, ed. Hogan and Paterson, 126. See this essay for further literature on the topic.

44. Melvyn P. Leffler, *Safeguarding Democratic Capitalism: U.S. Foreign Policy and National Security, 1920–2015* (Princeton, NJ: Princeton University Press, 2017), 24.

45. David Campbell, *Writing Security: United States Foreign Policy and the Politics of Identity* (Minneapolis: University of Minnesota Press, 1992), 30, 31.

46. John Lewis Gaddis, *Strategies of Containment: A Critical Appraisal of American National Security Policy during the Cold War*, rev. ed. (New York: Oxford University Press, 2005), esp. 82.

47. See Raymond L. Garthoff, *Soviet Leaders and Intelligence: Assessing the American Adversary during the Cold War* (Washington, DC: Georgetown University Press, 2015), 97.

48. Paul N. Edwards, *The Closed World: Computers and the Politics of Discourse in Cold War America* (Cambridge, MA: MIT Press, 1996), 7.

49. On the concept of path dependency and its usefulness for history, see John Lewis Gaddis, *The Landscape of History: How Historians Map the Past* (New York: Oxford University Press, 2002), 80–81.

50. Theodore M. Porter, *Trust in Numbers: The Pursuit of Objectivity in Science and Public Life* (Princeton, NJ: Princeton University Press, 1995), 8.

51. Neil Postman, *Technopoly: The Surrender of Culture to Technology* (New York: Vintage Books, 1992), 71, 93, 127.

Chapter 1: How the Polygraph Does and Does Not Work

1. David T. Lykken, *A Tremor in the Blood: Uses and Abuses of the Lie Detector,* rev. ed. (New York: Plenum Trade, 1998); see esp. 7–19.
2. Mark L. Knapp, *Lying and Deception in Human Interaction* (Boston: Pearson, 2007), 4–10.
3. For an overview of current research on behavioral clues and deception, see Bella DePaulo, *The Hows and Whys of Lies* (CreateSpace Independent Publishing Platform, 2010).
4. See Dan Ariely, *The (Honest Truth) about Dishonesty: How We Lie to Everyone— Especially Ourselves* (New York: HarperCollins, 2012), 27.
5. National Research Council: Committee to Review the Scientific Evidence on the Polygraph, Division of Behavioral and Social Sciences and Education, *The Polygraph and Lie Detection* (Washington, DC: National Academies Press, 2003).
6. Ibid., 94–97.
7. Ibid., 4, 5, 6.
8. See ibid., 65–76.
9. Ibid., 83.
10. Ibid., 96.
11. Ibid., 35.
12. Ibid., 37.
13. Ibid., 5–6.
14. Ibid., 37–43.
15. John F. Sullivan, *Gatekeeper: Memoirs of a CIA Polygraph Examiner* (Dulles, VA: Potomac Books, 2007), 238.
16. See Gordon H. Barland, "The Polygraph Test in the USA and Elsewhere," in *The Polygraph Test: Lies, Truth, and Science,* ed. Anthony Gale (Beverly Hills, CA: Sage, 1988), 75–95.
17. Geoffrey C. Bunn, *The Truth Machine: A Social History of the Lie Detector* (Baltimore: Johns Hopkins University Press, 2011), 95.

Chapter 2: Truth to Remake Society

1. See J. Anthony Lukas, *Big Trouble: A Murder in a Small Western Town Sets Off a Struggle for the Soul of America* (New York: Simon and Schuster, 1997).
2. See Daniel T. Rodgers, *Atlantic Crossings: Social Politics in a Progressive Age* (Cambridge, MA: Belknap Press of Harvard University Press, 1998).
3. See John M. O'Donnell, *The Origins of Behaviorism: American Psychology, 1870– 1920* (New York: New York University Press, 1985).
4. See Matthew Hale Jr., *Human Science and Social Order: Hugo Munsterberg and the Origins of Applied Psychology* (Philadelphia: Temple University Press, 1980); Jutta Spillmann and Lothar Spillmann, "The Rise and Fall of Hugo Münsterberg," *Journal of the History of the Behavioral Sciences* 29, no. 4 (October 1993): 322–38; Frank J. Landy, "Hugo Münsterberg: Victim or Visionary?," *Journal of Applied Psychology* 77, no. 6 (December 1992): 787–802; Phyllis Keller, *States of Belonging: German-American Intellectuals and the First World War* (Cambridge, MA: Harvard University Press, 1979), 7–118; Tal Golan, *Laws of Men and Laws of Nature: The History of Scientific Expert Testimony in England and America* (Cam-

bridge, MA: Harvard University Press, 2004), 218–26. Quote from Keller, *States of Belonging*, 6.

5. Quoted in Matthew Frye Jacobson, *Barbarian Virtues: The United States Encounters Foreign Peoples at Home and Abroad, 1876–1917* (New York: Hill and Wang, 2000), 62.

6. See Eric Rauchway, *Murdering McKinley: The Making of Theodore Roosevelt's America* (New York: Hill and Wang, 2003).

7. "Who Planned the Steunenberg Murder?," *New York Times*, April 29, 1906, X1; on anarchism in the United States at the time, see Paul Avrich, *Sacco and Vanzetti: The Anarchist Background* (Princeton, NJ: Princeton University Press, 1991), 45–57.

8. Hugo Münsterberg, "Experiments with Harry Orchard," manuscript, Hugo Münsterberg Papers, Boston Public Library, Boston, p. 3; Borah quoted in Melvyn Dubofsky, *"Big Bill" Haywood* (New York: St. Martin's Press, 1987), 49; on the transatlantic discourse of an international anarchist conspiracy at the turn of the twentieth century, see Matthew Carr, *The Infernal Machine: A History of Terrorism* (New York: New Press, 2006), 37–57.

9. Oscar King Davis, "Orchard Tells about Murders," *New York Times*, June 6, 1907, 1.

10. George Kibbe Turner, "Introductory Note to the Confession and Autobiography of Harry Orchard," *McClure's Magazine*, July 1907, 295.

11. Davis, "Orchard Tells about Murders," 1.

12. Oscar King Davis, "Defense Badgers Orchard in Vain," *New York Times*, June 9, 1907, 1.

13. *Denver Post*, May 17, 1907, found in folder 1: Harry Orchard, box 6, J. Anthony Lukas Papers, Part 4 (Additions 1984–1997), Wisconsin Historical Society, Madison.

14. "The Confession and Autobiography of Harry Orchard," *McClure's Magazine*, November 1907, 126–27.

15. See Clay Motley, "Making Over Body and Soul: *In His Steps* and the Roots of Evangelical Popular Culture," in *The Great American Makeover: Television, History, Nation*, ed. Dana Heller (New York: Palgrave Macmillan, 2006), 85–103.

16. Hugo Münsterberg, *On the Witness Stand: Essays on Psychology and Crime*, 2nd ed. (New York: Clark Boardman, 1933), 74.

17. Münsterberg, "Experiments with Harry Orchard," 1.

18. Ibid., 6, 5.

19. Ibid., 8.

20. Münsterberg, *On the Witness Stand*, 95.

21. Ibid., 98.

22. Münsterberg, "Experiments with Harry Orchard," 7.

23. Ibid., 21.

24. For this quote and similar press reactions, see Lukas, *Big Trouble*, 599–600.

25. One strong theme emerging from Lukas's book is the weight that both unions and state authorities/mine owners assigned to influencing public opinion during the trial. See ibid., 634.

26. "Dr. Münsterberg's Theory," *New York Times*, October 3, 1907, 8.

27. See Peter Carlson, *Roughneck: The Life and Times of Big Bill Haywood* (New York: W.W. Norton, 1983), 97–142.

28. James quoted in Spillmann and Spillmann, "Rise and Fall of Hugo Munsterberg," 328.

29. Cattell quoted in Hale, *Human Science and Social Order*, 107. Hale's otherwise exemplary study blames what the author considers overly conservative positions on

Münsterberg's German background. Similarly, Ken Alder emphasizes that "Münsterberg preferred the autocratic institutions of his homeland" to explain differences with James. See Alder, *The Lie Detectors: The History of an American Obsession* (New York: Free Press, 2007), 46.

30. Herbert Nichols, "The Psychological Laboratory at Harvard," *McClure's Magazine*, November 1893, 409.

31. This point is also made in Melissa M. Littlefield, *The Lying Brain: Lie Detection in Science and Science Fiction* (Ann Arbor: University of Michigan Press, 2011), 23.

32. Moritz Benedikt quoted in Stephen Kern, *A Cultural History of Causality: Science, Murder Novels, and Systems of Thought* (Princeton, NJ: Princeton University Press, 2004), 232. On Lombroso, see also Daniel Pick, *Faces of Degeneration: A European Disorder, c. 1848–c. 1918* (New York: Cambridge University Press, 1989), 109–52.

33. Kern, *Cultural History of Causality*, 6.

34. See Bunn, *Truth Machine*, 116–33; Alder, *Lie Detectors*, 47.

35. Hugo Münsterberg, "The Prevention of Crime," *McClure's Magazine*, November 1908, 751, 754, 755.

36. Münsterberg, "Nothing but the Truth," *McClure's Magazine*, October 1907, 536, 535.

37. Münsterberg, *Psychology and Industrial Efficiency* (Boston and New York: Houghton Mifflin, 1913), 169, 181.

38. See Robert Michael Brain, "The Ontology of the Questionnaire: Max Weber on Measurement and Mass Investigation," *Studies in the History and Philosophy of Science* 32, no. 4 (2001): 647–84.

39. Ibid., 16.

40. See Winifred Gallagher, *Rapt: Attention and the Focused Life* (New York: Penguin Press, 2009).

41. See for example Gail Bederman, *Manliness and Civilization: A Cultural History of Gender and Race in the United States, 1880–1917* (Chicago: University of Chicago Press, 1995); Ann Douglas, *The Feminization of American Culture*, 2nd ed. (New York: Farrar, Straus and Giroux, 1998); Michael Kimmel, *Manhood in America: A Cultural History* (New York: Knopf, 1996).

42. Münsterberg, *American Problems*, 11–12.

43. Münsterberg, "Prevention of Crime," 756; Münsterberg, *American Problems*, 89.

44. See Hale, *Science and Social Order*, 110.

45. Münsterberg, "Prevention of Crime," 77.

46. See Alder, *Lie Detectors*, 49–50.

47. *Lancet*, November 1865, quoted in Robert G. Frank Jr., "The Telltale Heart: Physiological Instruments, Graphic Methods, and Clinical Hopes, 1854–1914," in *The Investigative Enterprise: Experimental Physiology in Nineteenth-Century Medicine*, ed. William Coleman and Frederic L. Holmes (Berkeley: University of California Press, 1988), 212.

48. See Hughes Evans, "Losing Touch: The Controversy over the Introduction of Blood Pressure Instruments into Medicine," *Technology and Culture* 34, no. 4 (October 1993): 784–807.

49. William M. Marston, "Systolic Blood Pressure Symptoms of Deception," *Journal of Experimental Psychology* 2, no. 2 (September 1917): 128, 162 (emphasis in original).

50. See Littlefield, *Lying Brain*, 48–66.

51. Marston, "Systolic Blood Pressure Symptoms of Deception," 156.

52. William M. Marston to Robert Yerkes, April 4, 1918, folder "MEDICINE and

Related Sciences; "Com on Psychology: Projects; Deception Test, 1918," National Academy of Sciences, Washington, DC.

53. Michael H. Hunt, *The American Ascendancy: How the United States Gained and Wielded Global Dominance* (Chapel Hill: University of North Carolina Press, 2007), 140.

54. Münsterberg, *Psychology and Industrial Efficiency*; for Yerkes' admiration for Münsterberg as a mentor, see Hale, *Science and Social Order*, 57.

55. William Marston to Robert Yerkes, September 20, 1917, folder "EX Com: Com on Psychology; Projects: Deception Test, 1917," National Academy of Sciences.

56. Leila Zenderland, "The Debate over Diagnosis: Henry Herbert Goddard and the Medical Acceptance of Intelligence Testing," in *Psychological Testing in American Society*, ed. Michael M. Sokal (New Brunswick, NJ: Rutgers University Press, 1987), 46–73.

57. Leila Zenderland, *Measuring Minds: Henry Herbert Goddard and the Origins of American Intelligence Testing* (New York: Cambridge University Press, 1998), 261–81.

58. Zenderland, *Measuring Minds*, 281–94.

59. See Daniel J. Kevles, "Testing the Army's Intelligence: Psychologists and the Military in World War I," *Journal of American History* 55, no. 3 (December 1968): 565–81.

60. James Reed, "Robert M. Yerkes and the Mental Testing Movement," in Sokal, *Psychological Testing in American Society*, 88–89.

61. See Michael M. Sokal, "Introduction," in Sokal, *Psychological Testing in American Society*, 1–20.

62. Richard W. Hale to Charles Warren, November 27, 1917, folder "EX Com: Com on Psychology; Projects: Deception Test, 1917," National Academy of Sciences (hereafter cited as "Com on Psychology").

63. William Marston to Robert Yerkes, November 27, 1917, "Com on Psychology."

64. E. L. Thorndike to Robert Yerkes, n.d., "Com on Psychology."

65. See William Marston to Robert Yerkes, November 13, 1917, "Com on Psychology."

66. Marston's work during World War I is elsewhere described in Alder, *Lie Detectors*, 50–53.

67. Richard W. Hale to Charles Warren, November 27, 1917, "Com on Psychology."

68. William Marston to Robert Yerkes, December 4, 1917, "Com on Psychology." Marston published his results as William M. Marston, "Psychological Possibilities in the Deception Tests," *Journal of Criminal Law and Criminology* 11, no. 4 (February 1921): 551–70.

69. William M. Marston to Robert Yerkes, December 10, 1917, "Com on Psychology"; William M. Marston to Robert Yerkes, December 19, 1917, "Com on Psychology"; Robert Yerkes to Newton Baker, December 22, 1917, "Com on Psychology."

70. William M. Marston and John E. Anderson, "Report on Deception Tests," December 19, 1918, 3, in folder "MEDICINE and Related Sciences; "Com on Psychology: Projects; Deception Test, 1918," National Academy of Sciences (hereafter cited as MEDICINE, 1918).

71. Ibid., 4. The problem of the reliability of Marston's tests is also addressed in Alder, *Lie Detectors*, 50.

72. William M. Marston and John E. Anderson, "Report on Deception Tests," December 19, 1918, 3, MEDICINE, 1918.

73. John Shepard to Robert Yerkes, December 14, 1917, in folder "MEDICINE and Related Sciences; "Com on Psychology: Projects; Deception Test, 1917," National Academy of Sciences, Washington, DC (hereafter cited as MEDICINE, 1917).

74. See "Report on Deception Tests," by William M. Marston and John E. Anderson, December 19, 1918, 2, MEDICINE, 1918.
75. John Shepard to Robert Yerkes, December 14, 1917, MEDICINE, 1917.
76. William Marston to Robert Yerkes, January 21, 1918, MEDICINE, 1918.
77. William Marston to Robert Yerkes, February 23, 1918, ibid. Marston tried systematic follow-up work, but he could only administer three more tests to African Americans. He concluded that the man he had judged guilty, one Horace Drear, "had a guilty consciousness concerning some act of his, but I certainly don't have enough negro b.p. data to approach scientific or even workable exactitude in tests of colored men." Ibid. "Norm plus excitement" was Marston's term to describe the blood pressure base line at the beginning of the test, measuring regular blood pressure plus the excitement coming from the test situation itself. See William M. Marston, *The Lie Detector Test* (New York: Smith, 1938), 53.
78. Quote from Marston, *Lie Detector Test*, 66; on Marston's logical fallacy, see Alder, *Lie Detectors*, 52.
79. Herbert Langfeld to Robert Yerkes, October 8, 1917, "Com on Psychology."
80. A. H. Sutherland, review of Münsterberg's *Grundzüge der Psychotechnik*, quoted in Landy, "Hugo Münsterberg," 791.
81. C. G. Jung to Charles William Eliot, October 15, 1907, folder 23: Hugo Münsterberg, box 5, J. Anthony Lukas Papers, Wisconsin Historical Society, Madison, WI.
82. See William Marston, "Report on Deception Tests," submitted October 9, 1917, to Robert Yerkes, "Com on Psychology." This document illustrates Marston's ideas for a practicable deception test before his NRC work began.
83. Marston, "Psychological Possibilities in the Deception Tests," 553.
84. Ibid., 5.
85. Ibid., 5–6.
86. Ken Alder masterfully tells Larson's and Keeler's story and its significance for the history of police reform and administration of justice. See Alder, *Lie Detectors,* passim.
87. August Vollmer, *The Police and Modern Society* (Berkeley: University of California Press, 1936), 81.
88. Background on Vollmer comes from Gene E. Carte and Elaine H. Carte, *Police Reform in the United States: The Era of August Vollmer, 1905–1932* (Berkeley: University of California Press, 1975); Alfred E. Parker, *The Berkeley Police Story* (Springfield, IL: Thomas, 1972); Thomas J. Deakin, *Police Professionalism: The Renaissance of American Law Enforcement* (Springfield, IL: Thomas, 1988), 89–103.
89. August Vollmer, "Predeliquency," in *IACP Proceedings, 1919* (New York, 1971), 77.
90. Speech quoted in Care and Carte, *Police Reform in the United States,* 57.
91. Münsterberg, *On the Witness Stand,* 76.
92. Vollmer, *Police and Modern Society,* 4.
93. See Robert C. Wadman and William Thomas Allison, *To Protect and to Serve: A History of Police in America* (Upper Saddle River, NJ: Prentice Hall, 2004), 82–106; Samuel Walker, *Popular Justice: A History of American Criminal Justice* (New York: Oxford University Press, 1980), 127–93.
94. Vollmer, *Police and Modern Society,* 237.
95. Vollmer, *Police and Modern Society,* 6.
96. See Eric H. Monkkonen, *Crime, Justice, History* (Columbus: Ohio State University Press, 2002), 154–70.

97. Vollmer quoted in Carte and Carte, *Police Administration in the United States*, 76; see also Walker, *Popular Justice*, 187–89. In 1910 an African American was the first person to be convicted of murder only on the basis of a fingerprint. In 1919 the first businesses started fingerprinting of employees. Stories of amnesiacs who required identification by fingerprinting circulated widely and were often used to justify introduction of fingerprint databases; see Christian Parenti, *The Soft Cage: Surveillance in America From Slavery to the War on Terror* (New York: Basic Books, 2004), 49–59.

98. See Alder, *Lie Detectors*, 17–27.

99. John Larson, *Lying and Its Detection: A Study of Deception and Deception Tests* (Chicago: University of Chicago Press, 1932).

100. See Alder's discussion of the two models in "To Tell the Truth: The Polygraph Exam and the Marketing of American Expertise," *Historical Reflections* 24, no. 3 (1998): 505–20; Alder, *Lie Detectors*, 76–78; Alder, "A Social History of Untruth: Lie Detection and Trust in Twentieth-Century America," *Representations* 80, no. 1 (Fall 2002): 12–14.

101. See Alder, *Lie Detectors*, 63–73.

102. See for example John A. Larson and G. W. Haney, "Cardio-Respiratory Variations in Personality Studies, "*American Journal of Psychiatry* 11 (1932): 1035–81.

103. Vollmer quoted in Alder, "Social History of Untruth," 16. On the survey see Alder, *Lie Detectors*, 126–27.

104. See the detailed discussion in Alder, *Lie Detectors*, 119–53.

105. Leonarde Keeler to August Vollmer, December 17, 1929, folder "Keeler, Leonarde," box 7, in Charles A. Keeler Papers, Bancroft Library, University of California, Berkeley.

106. See Alder, *Lie Detectors*, 163–78.

107. See Jill Lepore, *The Secret History of Wonder Woman* (New York: Alfred A. Knopf, 2014); Geoffrey Bunn, "The Lie Detector, Wonder Woman, and Liberty: The Life and Work of William Moulton Marston," *History of the Human Sciences* 10, no. 1 (1997): 91–119; Alder, *Lie Detectors*, 181–95.

108. Eloise Keeler, *The Lie Detector Man: The Career and Cases of Leonarde Keeler* (West Palm Beach: Telshare Publishing, 1983), 149.

109. See Eloise Keeler, "The Lie Detector," manuscript, folder "The Lie Detector," box 694, National Theater Project Papers, Library of Congress, Washington, DC.

110. Marston, *Lie Detector Test*, 15, 112.

111. For the trial, see J. E. Starrs, "'A Still-Life Watercolor': Frye v. United States," *Journal of Forensic Sciences* 27, no. 3 (July 1982): 684–94; quote from trial transcript, 691, 692.

112. Quoted ibid., 685.

113. See Alder, *Lie Detectors*, 53; Golan, *Laws of Men and Laws of Nature*, 253. While Golan's general argument is plausible, his assertion that Judge McCoy had no other reason to reject Marston's expertise than fear for the integrity of the Common Law system relies on an uncritical reading of the success rates Marston reported in his early experiments.

114. C. T. McCormick, "Deception-Tests and the Law of Evidence," *California Law Review* 15, no. 6 (September 1927): 498–99.

115. See Alder, *Lie Detectors*, 146–47, 253.

116. On the history of letting juries hear testimony, see George Fisher, "The Jury's Rise as Lie Detector," *Yale Law Journal* 107, no. 3 (December 1997): 575–713.

117. See Alder, *Lie Detectors*, 256–57.
118. Littlefield, *Lying Brain*, 25–35.
119. Alder, *Lie Detectors*, 29; However, as Littlefield shows, crime fiction preceded press coverage in developing fantasies of an almighty machine to detect lies. See Littlefield, *Lying Brain*, 11.
120. See Bunn, *Hazards of the Will to Truth*, 121–22. The term "invention" still proves powerful when talking about the origins of the lie detector. In advertising historian Jill Lepore's 2014 book about William Marston, her publisher chose to describe Marston as the "inventor" of the lie detector, notwithstanding Bunn's persuasive argument against applying this term.
121. See Alison Winter, "The Making of 'Truth Serum,' 1920–1940," *Bulletin of the History of Medicine* 79, no. 3 (Fall 2005): 500–533.
122. See Rhodri Jeffreys-Jones, *The FBI: A History* (New Haven, CT: Yale University Press, 2007), 81–99; Walker, *Popular Justice*, 182–84.
123. Hoover article in *The National Police Officer* (July 1931), quoted in Claire Bond Potter, *War on Crime: Bandits, G-Men, and the Politics of Mass Culture* (New Brunswick, NJ: Rutgers University Press, 1998), 57; second quote, 2.
124. See Matthew Cecil, *Hoover's FBI and the Fourth Estate: The Campaign to Control the Press and the Bureau's Image* (Lawrence: University Press of Kansas, 2014).
125. See Richard Gid Powers, *G-Men: Hoover's FBI in American Popular Culture* (Carbondale: Southern Illinois University Press, 1983); Potter, *War on Crime*.
126. For Hoover's interest in Marston's World War I work on lie detection, see William Marston to Albert L. Burrows, July 29, 1935, folder "MEDICINE and Related Sciences; "Com on Psychology: Projects; Deception Test, 1918," National Academy of Science. Burrows had forwarded a request for reports from Marston from J. Edgar Hoover to the NRC.
127. E. P. Coffey, "Memorandum for Mr. Nathan, re: Review of Book Entitled The Lie Detector Test by Dr. William M. Marston," May 11, 1938, FBI Freedom of Information Act file of William M. Marston, http://www.antipolygraph.org; John S. Bugas to J. Edgar Hoover, July 13, 1939, FBI Freedom of Information Act file of William M. Marston, http://www.antipolygraph.org.

Chapter 3: World War II, National Security, and the Search for Loyal Citizens

1. Responding to the request by one Capt. Stanford Moses, who had seen a demonstration by August Vollmer, the Bureau stated, "The results to be obtained by the use of the polygraph . . . would not justify the expenditure entailed." Letter, February 17, 1923, folder 15183–167, box 688, RG 80: General Correspondence of the Secretary of the Navy, National Archives and Records Administration (NARA), Washington, DC.
2. Five days after the Pearl Harbor attacks, Marston contacted President Franklin Roosevelt, ending his letter with a "personal pledge of loyalty and devotion to the greatest cause on earth." Yet Marston's offer remained unanswered. William Marston to Franklin Roosevelt, December 12, 1941. FBI Freedom of Information Act file of William M. Marston. http://www.antipolygraph.org.
3. Dael Wolfle, "The Lie Detector: Methods for the Detection of Deception," October 4, 1941, folder "A&P: Emergency Com in Psychology: Methods for Detection of Deception: Wolfle D, 1941," National Academy of Science, Washington, DC. In

1935 Hoover sent agent E. P. Coffey to Chicago to observe Keeler. While Coffey returned a convert and the FBI did purchase a Keeler Polygraph, which it secretly tested, Hoover remained on the public record as a polygraph skeptic. See Ken Alder, *The Lie Detectors: The History of an American Obsession* (New York: Free Press, 2007), 227.

4. See James H. Capshew, *Psychologists on the March: Science, Practice, and Professional Identity in America, 1929–1969* (New York: Cambridge University Press, 1999), 39–48.

5. Wolfle, "Lie Detector"; For Keeler's card trick, see Alder, *Lie Detectors,* 9.

6. Wolfle, "Lie Detector."

7. See Alder, *Lie Detectors,* 200, on Keeler's failed induction test in 1942.

8. Only 0.5 percent of drafted Americans failed to report or deserted soon after arrival in the military, in contrast to 12 percent in World War I and 20 percent during the Vietnam War. See Gary Gerstle, *American Crucible: Race and Nation in the Twentieth Century* (Princeton, NJ: Princeton University Press, 2001), 189. In addition to over 300,000 Japanese and Japanese Americans, about 11,000 Germans and German Americans were also interned. See Stephen Fox, *American Gulag: A Biography of German American Internment and Exclusion in World War II* (New York: Peter Lang, 2000).

9. Richard Whittingham, *Martial Justice: The Last Mass Execution in the United States,* 2nd ed. (Annapolis: Naval Institute Press, 1997). On Keeler's role see 107–13.

10. Ralph W. Pierce, "Memorandum for Colonel Alton C. Miller," August 14, 1944, folder "Miscellaneous Papers Pertaining to Polygraph Matters," POW Special Projects Division, Administrative Branch, Decimal File 1943–1946, box 1627, RG 389: Records of the Office of the Provost Marshal General, 1941-, National Archives and Records Administration (NARA), College Park, MD (hereafter cited as Misc Polygraph Matters); Alton C. Miller, "Memorandum for Lt. Col. Ralph W. Pierce," August 21, 1944, Misc Polygraph Matters.

11. See Ralph W. Pierce, "Report of Temporary Duty," January 24, 1945, Misc Polygraph Matters.

12. Erikson quoted in Ellen Herman, *The Romance of American Psychology: Political Culture in the Age of Experts* (Berkeley: University of California Press, 1995), 49.

13. Leonarde Keeler, "Report," September 12, 1945, folder "POW Screening Project," POW Special Projects Division, Administrative Branch, Decimal File 1943–1946, box 1627, RG 389, NARA.

14. List of questions, folder, "POW—Polygraph—Screening of POWs," Provost Division, Criminal Investigation Branch, General Correspondence, 1947–1951, box 1705, RG 389, NARA (hereafter cited as POW—Polygraph).

15. "Memorandum for Col. Alton C. Miller," June 8, 1945, POW—Polygraph.

16. Ralph W. Pierce, "Memorandum to Col. Franklin W. Reese," August 30, 1945, folder: "Screening of POWs by Use of Polygraph, 1945," POW/Civilian Internee Information Center, box 10, RG 389, NARA.

17. Leonarde Keeler, "Report," September 12, 1945, folder "POW Screening Project," POW Special Projects Division, Administrative Branch, Decimal File 1943–1946, box 1627, RG 389, NARA.

18. Ron Robin, *Barbed-Wire College: Educating German POWs in the United States during World War II* (Princeton, NJ: Princeton University Press, 1995), 29.

19. See ibid., 137–42.

20. Ralph W. Pierce, "Memorandum to Col. Franklin W. Reese," August 30, 1945, folder: "Screening of POWs by Use of Polygraph, 1945," POW/Civilian Internee Information Center, box 10, RG 389, NARA.

21. Robin, *Barbed-Wire College*, 142–43.

22. This assessment is based on Robert D. Billinger Jr., *Hitler's Soldiers in the Sunshine State: German POWs in Florida* (Gainesville: University Press of Florida, 2000).

23. Leonarde Keeler to Betsy Bunnell, October 16, 1940, folder "Letters from Leonarde Keeler to Various Relatives, 1932–1948," carton 2, Leonarde Keeler Papers, Bancroft Library, University of California, Berkeley.

24. On accusations of totalitarianism against FDR, see Benjamin L. Alpers, *Dictators, Democracy and American Public Culture: Envisioning the Totalitarian Enemy* (Chapel Hill: University of North Carolina Press, 2003), 34–35, 105–7.

25. See Tim Weiner, *Legacy of Ashes: The History of the CIA* (New York: Doubleday, 2007), 46–48. On the use of Nazi scientists after World War II, see Annie Jacobsen, *Operation Paperclip: The Secret Intelligence Program That Brought Nazi Scientists to America* (Boston: Little, Brown, 2014); Eric Lichtblau, *The Nazis Next Door: How America Became a Haven for Hitler's Men* (New York: Houghton Mifflin Harcourt, 2014), which also discusses the use of war criminals by U.S. intelligence agencies.

26. See Udi Greenberg, *The Weimar Century: German Emigres and the Ideological Foundations of the Cold War* (Princeton, NJ: Princeton University Press, 2015).

27. See Norbert Frei, *Adenauer's Germany and the Nazi Past: The Politics of Amnesty and Integration* (New York: Columbia University Press, 2002).

28. Gerard J. Forney [Col., Corps of Engineers] to Scientific Investigation Section, Office of the Provost Marshal General, November 1945, Folder "Miscellaneous Papers Pertaining to Polygraph Matters," Provost Division, Criminal Investigation Branch, General Correspondence, 1947–1951, box 1705, RG 389, NARA; Forney to Office of the [Army] Provost Marshal General, Jan. 23, 1946, Folder "Miscellaneous Papers Pertaining to Polygraph Matters," Provost Division, Criminal Investigation Branch, General Correspondence, 1947–1951, box 1705, RG 389, NARA.

29. See John G. Linehan, "The Oak Ridge Polygraph Program, 1946–1953," *Polygraph* 19, no. 2 (1990): 131–37; Alder, *Lie Detectors*, 204–12.

30. Quoted in Lineham, "Oak Ridge Polygraph Program," 133. This article is not footnoted, but the author had access to unpublished material by Chatham and Trovillo.

31. See Jessica Wang, *American Scientists in an Age of Anxiety: Scientists, Anticommunism, and the Cold War* (Chapel Hill: University of North Carolina Press, 1999), 148–82. The quote from Thomas's article is on 150.

32. See Lineham, "Oak Ridge Polygraph Program," 135.

33. "Lie Detector Tests Given at Plant," *Washington Post*, December 21, 1951, 18.

34. Hugh Gusterson, *Nuclear Rites: A Weapons Laboratory at the End of the Cold War* (Berkeley: University of California Press, 1996), 68; See also Joseph P. Masco, "Lie Detectors: On Secrets and Hypersecurity in Los Alamos," *Public Culture* 14, no. 3 (2002): 441–67; Masco, *The Nuclear Borderlands: The Manhattan Project in Post-Cold War New Mexico* (Princeton, NJ: Princeton University Press, 2006).

35. See Alder, *Lie Detectors*, 210–11.

36. Anthony Leviero, "US Tests Staff by Lie Detectors," *New York Times*, December 20, 1951, 1, 20.

37. "Lie Detector Expert Accuses A.E.C. Aides," *New York Times*, April 29, 1953, 13. See

also Dick Smyther, "Controversy Looms over Conflicting Reasons for Lie Detector Discontinuance," *Oak Ridger*, April 14, 1953, 1.

38. See Priscilla J. McMillan, *The Ruin of J. Robert Oppenheimer and the Birth of the Modern Arms Race* (New York: Viking, 2005).

39. U.S. Atomic Energy Commission, *Findings and Recommendations of the Personnel Security Board in the Matter of J. Robert Oppenheimer: Texts of Principal Documents and Letters of Personnel Security Board* (Washington, DC: U.S. Government Publishing Office, 1954), 13.

40. Charles Thorpe, *Oppenheimer: The Tragic Intellect* (Chicago: University of Chicago Press, 2006), 4.

41. See Kai Bird and Martin J. Sherwin, *American Prometheus: The Triumph and Tragedy of J. Robert Oppenheimer* (New York: Alfred A. Knopf, 2005), 391–430; David K. Hecht, *Storytelling and Science: Rewriting Oppenheimer in the Nuclear Age* (Amherst: University of Massachusetts Press, 2015), 57.

42. U.S. Atomic Energy Commission, *Findings and Recommendations of the Personnel Security Board in the Matter of J. Robert Oppenheimer*, 2.

43. See Ellen Schrecker, *Many Are the Crimes: McCarthyism in America* (Princeton, NJ: Princeton University Press, 1998), 266–70, 286–93.

44. U.S. Atomic Energy Commission, *Findings and Recommendations of the Personnel Security Board in the Matter of J. Robert Oppenheimer*, 14.

45. Ibid., 15.

46. As the AEC report acknowledged, "We are acutely aware that in a very real sense this case puts the security system of the United States on trial, both as to procedures and as to substance." U.S. Atomic Energy Commission, *Findings and Recommendations of the Personnel Security Board in the Matter of J. Robert Oppenheimer*, 1.

47. Thorpe, *Oppenheimer*, 18.

48. This account is based on Howard L. Rosenberg, *Atomic Soldiers: American Victims of Nuclear Experiments* (Boston: Beacon Press, 1980), 40–55. Quotes on 47, 53.

49. See Scott Kirsch, *Proving Grounds: Project Plowshare and the Unrealized Dream of Nuclear Earthmoving* (New Brunswick, NJ: Rutgers University Press, 2005).

50. See ibid., esp. 120–22.

51. Quote from Joseph P. Masco, "Engineering Ruins and Affect," in *Cultures of Fear: A Critical Reader*, ed. Uli Linke and Danielle Taana Smith (New York: Pluto Press, 2009), 40. The deeply ambiguous response to the public display of nuclear weapons and their threat from 1945 to 1963, when the United States conducted atmospheric testing, is tracked through a variety of sources by Robert A. Jacobs, *The Dragon's Tail: Americans Face the Atomic Age* (Amherst: University of Massachusetts Press, 2010); Michael A. Amundson and Scott C. Zeman, ed., *Atomic Culture: How We Learned to Stop Worrying and Love the Bomb* (Boulder: University Press of Colorado, 2004). For a treatment that focuses on movies, see Jerome F. Shapiro, *Atomic Bomb Cinema: The Apocalyptic Imagination on Film* (New York: Routledge, 2002).

52. See Geoffrey C. Bunn, "Spectacular Science: The Lie Detector's Ambivalent Powers," *History of Psychology* 10, no. 2 (2007): 156–78; Ken Alder, "America's Two Gadgets: Of Bombs and Polygraphs," *Isis* 98, no. 1 (2007): 124–37.

53. Leonarde Keeler, "A Method for Detecting Deception," *American Journal of Police Science* 1, no. 1 (1930): 48.

54. Fred E. Inbau, *Lie Detection and Criminal Interrogation* (Baltimore: Williams &

Wilkins, 1942), 9. Clarence Lee, who worked with Keeler in Berkeley and later opened a competing lie detection business, used the same technique. See Clarence D. Lee, *The Instrumental Detection of Deception: The Lie Test* (Springfield, IL: Thomas, 1953), 102; See also the recommendation by law professor Lawrence Taylor, *Scientific Interrogation: Hypnosis, Polygraphy, Narcoanalysis, Voice Stress and Pupillometrics* (Charlottesville, VA: Michie Company, 1984), 198.

55. See Thomas Klein, Wilfriede Otto, and Peter Grieder, eds., *Visionen, Repression, und Opposition in der SED, 1949–1989* (Frankfurt/Oder: Frankfurter Oder Editionen, 1996); Konrad H. Jarausch, ed., *Dictatorship as Experience: Toward a Socio-Cultural History of the GDR* (New York: Berghahn Books, 1999).

56. William Graebner, *The Age of Doubt: American Thought and Culture in the 1940s* (Prospect Heights, IL: Waveland Press, 1991); Margot A. Henriksen, *Dr. Strangelove's America: Society and Culture in the Atomic Age* (Berkeley: University of California Press, 1997); Andrew Jamison and Ron Eyerman, *Seeds of the Sixties* (Berkeley: University of California Press, 1994).

Chapter 4: The Polygraph and the Specter of Totalitarianism Within

1. See Alan Brinkley, *The End of Reform* (New York: Vintage Books, 1995); Gary Gerstle, *American Crucible: Race and Nation in the Twentieth Century* (Princeton, NJ: Princeton University Press, 2001), 128–236; Elizabeth Borgwardt, *A New Deal for the World: America's Vision for Human Rights* (Cambridge, MA: Harvard University Press, 2005); James T. Sparrow, *Warfare State: World War II Americans and the Age of Big Government* (New York: Oxford University Press, 2011).

2. See Kevin M. Kruse and Stephen Tuck, ed., *Fog of War: The Second World War and the Civil Rights Movement* (New York: Oxford University Press, 2012); Michael C.C. Adams, *The Best War Ever: Americans and World War II*, rev. ed. (Baltimore: Johns Hopkins University Press, 2015); John Bodnar, *The "Good War" in American Memory* (Baltimore: Johns Hopkins University Press, 2010).

3. See Richard H. Pells, *The Liberal Mind in a Conservative Age: American Intellectuals in the 1940s and 1950s* (Hanover, NH: Wesleyan University Press, 1985).

4. Reinhold Niebuhr, *The Children of Light and the Children of Darkness: A Vindication of Democracy and a Critique of Its Traditional Defense* (New York: Charles Scribner's Sons, 1944), X.

5. See George Cotkin, *Existential America* (Baltimore: Johns Hopkins University Press, 2003).

6. Arthur M. Schlesinger Jr., *The Vital Center: The Politics of Freedom* (Boston: Houghton Mifflin, 1949), 52.

7. See Richard Fox, *Reinhold Niebuhr: A Biography* (San Francisco: Harper and Row, 1987), 224–25.

8. See Paul S. Boyer, *By the Bomb's Early Light: American Thought and Culture at the Dawn of the Atomic Age* (New York: Pantheon, 1985), 1–26.

9. Erich Fromm, *Escape from Freedom* (1941; New York: Holt, 1994), xiii–xiv, 251. On Fromm's remarkable popular success, background, psychology, political activism, and transnational network of support, see Lawrence J. Friedman, assisted by Anke M. Schreiber, *Love's Prophet: The Lives of Erich Fromm* (New York: Columbia University Press, 2013).

10. See Vance Packard, *The Hidden Persuaders* (New York: Penguin Books, 1957).

11. Rahv quoted in Pells, *Liberal Mind in Conservative Age*, 82–83.

12. "A Report to the President Pursuant to the President's Directive of January 31, 1950 [NSC-68]," *FRUS, 1950: National Security Affairs; Foreign Economic Policy*, Vol. 1, 245, http://images.library.wisc.edu/FRUS/EFacs/1950v01/reference/frus.frus1950v01.i0008.pdf.

13. See Pells, *Liberal Mind in Conservative Age*, 83–96. For popular images of communism as a concentration camp and the constructed nature of "escape" stories circulating in Western media in the 1940s and 1950s, see Susan L. Carruthers, *Cold War Captives: Imprisonment, Escape, and Brainwashing* (Berkeley: University of California Press, 2009).

14. See Matthew W. Dunne, *A Cold War State of Mind: Brainwashing and Postwar American Society* (Amherst: University of Massachusetts Press, 2013).

15. See Friedrich A. Hayek, *The Road to Serfdom: Text and Documents; the Definitive Edition* (Chicago: University of Chicago Press, 2007); Ludwig von Mises, *Omnipotent Government: The Rise of the Total State and Total War* (1944; Indianapolis: Liberty Fund, 2007).

16. Benjamin L. Alpers, *Dictators, Democracy, and American Public Culture: Envisioning the Totalitarian Enemy, 1920s–1950s* (Chapel Hill: University of North Carolina Press, 2003), 253.

17. See Alfred W. McCoy, *A Question of Torture: CIA Interrogation from the Cold War to the War on Terror* (New York: Holt, 2006); McCoy, *Torture and Impunity: The U.S. Doctrine of Coercive Interrogation* (Madison: University of Wisconsin Press, 2012); McCoy, *The CIA's Secret Research on Torture: How Psychologists Helped Washington Crack the Code of Human Consciousness* (Venice, CA: Now & Then Reader, 2014), e-book.

18. Background on Morse comes from Mason Drukman, *Wayne Morse: A Political Biography* (Portland: Oregon Historical Society Press, 1997); A. Robert Smith, *The Tiger in the Senate: The Biography of Wayne Morse* (New York: Doubleday, 1962).

19. Wayne Morse, "Constitutional Safeguards Required in Loyalty Procedures," speech, January 17, 1952 (Washington, DC: Government Printing Press, 1952), 4, 2.

20. Ibid., 1, 2.

21. The *New York Times* only reported Morse's speech as "denouncing as un-American the use of the Lie Detector in testing federal job applicants" but not the caveats Morse had expressed. See Anthony Leviero, "Morse Denounces Lie Detector Use," *New York Times*, January 18, 1952, 9.

22. See Pells, *Liberal Mind in Conservative Age*, 280–81.

23. The order was leaked to columnist Drew Pearson, who published it. See Drew Pearson, "Double Talk Ascribed to Lovett," *Washington Post*, March 1, 1952, B13.

24. *Reporter* staff received information from Morse's office and subsequently contacted citizens who had written Morse after his 1952 speech. See for example the form letter, William Berg to Mrs. Paul Preas, February 15, 1954, folder "Lie Detector," box A 77, Wayne Morse Papers, University of Oregon, Eugene (hereafter cited as Wayne Morse Papers). Upon publication, *Reporter* editor Max Ascoli sent Morse a thank-you note for the "great help" the senator and his staff had been; see Max Ascoli to Wayne Morse, May 14, 1954, Wayne Morse Papers.

25. Dwight Macdonald, "The Lie-Detector Era: Part I," *Reporter*, June 8, 1954, 11.

26. Quoted in Stephen J. Whitfield, *A Critical American: The Politics of Dwight Macdonald* (Guilford, CT: Archon Books, 1984), 89.

27. Macdonald, "Lie Detector Era: Part I," 10, 11.

28. The informant's real name was Arthur Banks. Banks had written Wayne Morse, who very likely forwarded his letter to Macdonald later. Some of Banks's complaints to Morse appeared verbatim in Macdonald's piece. See Arthur S. Banks to Wayne Morse, February 2, 1952, Wayne Morse Papers.

29. Dwight Macdonald, "The Lie-Detector Era: Part II," *Reporter,* June 22, 1954, 24.

30. Ibid., 24, 25.

31. Ibid., 27. The magazine's cover on the June 8, 1954, lie detector issue underlined this focus. It featured a drawing of a bespectacled, suited, middle-aged man strapped to a polygraph. In the background a man in a white doctor's coat administered the test.

32. C. Wright Mills, *The Power Elite* (New York: Oxford University Press, 1956), 300, 308, 304.

33. Macdonald, "Lie Detector Era: Part II," 23.

34. On *Reporter* editor Max Ascoli, see Hugh Wilford, *The Mighty Wurlitzer: How the CIA Played America* (Cambridge, MA: Harvard University Press, 2008), 230–31; Stanley Lichtenstein, letter to the editor, *Reporter,* July 20, 1954, 3.

35. Dwight Macdonald, "The Root Is Man, Part I," *politics* 3 (April 1946): 99.

36. C. Wright Mills, "The Powerless People: The Role of Intellectuals in Society," reprinted in John H. Summers, ed., *The Politics of Truth: Selected Writings of C. Wright Mills* (New York: Oxford University Press, 2008), 18.

37. Pauline S. Preas to Wayne Morse, January 27, 1952, Wayne Morse Papers; Gene B. Rutledge to Wayne Morse, January 21, 1952, Wayne Morse Papers.

38. Elsa Kruuse to Wayne Morse, June 7, 1954, Wayne Morse Papers.

39. Pauline S. Preas to Wayne Morse, January 27, 1952, Wayne Morse Papers.

40. William H. Whyte Jr., *The Organization Man* (New York: Simon and Schuster, 1956), 195–96.

41. See Steven Watts, *Self-Help Messiah: Dale Carnegie and Success in Modern America* (New York: Other Press, 2013).

42. "Lie Detector Tests on Workers," *Business Week,* April 18, 1951, 24.

43. Robert N. Tuthill to Wayne Morse, May 5, 1952, Wayne Morse Papers.

44. Joseph and Stewart Alsop, "Lie-Detector Piling up Records," *Washington Post,* February 21, 1954, B5.

45. See Eric Alterman, *Sound and Fury: The Washington Punditocracy and the Collapse of American Politics* (New York: HarperCollins, 1992), 48–50.

46. See Daniel Wickberg, "What Is the History of Sensibilities? On Cultural Histories, Old and New," *American Historical Review* 112, no. 3 (June 2007): 661–84.

47. M. W. de Laubenfels to Wayne Morse, January 21, 1952, Wayne Morse Papers; Jerry J. Bell to Wayne Morse, February 6, 1952, Wayne Morse Papers; Vernon White to Wayne Morse, March 3, 1952, Wayne Morse Papers; Howard Wriggens to Wayne Morse, February 6, 1952, Wayne Morse Papers.

48. John R. Porter to Wayne Morse, January 19, 1952, Wayne Morse Papers; Allen McConnell to Wayne Morse, February 6, 1952, Wayne Morse Papers.

49. Andrea Friedman, *Citizenship in Cold War America: The National Security State and the Possibilities of Dissent* (Amherst: University of Massachusetts Press, 2014), 5.

50. Macdonald, "Lie Detector Era: Part II," 29.

51. See Michael Wreszin, *A Rebel in Defense of Tradition: The Life and Politics of Dwight Macdonald* (New York: Basic Books, 1994), 178.
52. Lionel Trilling, *The Liberal Imagination: Essays on Literature and Society* (New York: Viking, 1950), xi.
53. See Martin Jay, *The Dialectical Imagination: A History of the Frankfurt School and the Institute of Social Research, 1923–1950* (London: Heinemann, 1973); T. W. Adorno, Else Frenkel-Brunswik, Daniel J. Levinson, R. Nevitt Sanford, *The Authoritarian Personality* (New York: Norton, 1950); David Riesman, with Nathan Glazer and Reuel Denney, *The Lonely Crowd: A Study of the Changing American Character* (New York: Doubleday, 1950).
54. Trilling, *Liberal Imagination*, 219, 220.
55. See Jonathan Gathorne-Hardy, *Sex: The Measure of All Things: A Life of Alfred C. Kinsey* (Bloomington: Indiana University Press, 2000).
56. A *Washington Post* article from 1952 noted, "The Lie Detector operators in government know more about the sex lives of more persons, with the possible exception of Dr. Kinsey, than anybody." Quoted in Macdonald, "Lie Detector Era: Part II," 29.
57. Life Magazine quoted in Whitfield, *Culture of the Cold War*, 185.
58. Trilling, *Liberal Imagination*, 227.
59. David K. Johnson, *The Lavender Scare: The Cold War Persecution of Gays and Lesbians in the Federal Government* (Chicago: University of Chicago Press, 2004), 41–64.
60. See ibid., 73.
61. See ibid., 166.
62. See Robert D. Dean, *Imperial Brotherhood: Gender and the Making of Cold War Foreign Policy* (Amherst: University of Massachusetts Press, 2001), 111.
63. See Alder's discussion in *Lie Detectors*, 225.
64. Douglas M. Charles, *Hoover's War on Gays: Exposing the FBI's "Sex Deviates" Program* (Lawrence: University Press of Kansas, 2015), 257.
65. Matt Apuzzo, "Uncovered Papers Show Past Government Efforts to Drive Gays from Jobs," *New York Times*, May 21, 2014, A13.
66. See Andrea Friedman, "The Smearing of Joe McCarthy: The Lavender Scare, Gossip, and Cold War Politics," *American Quarterly* 57, no. 4 (December 2005): 1105–29.
67. See Claire Bond Potter, "Queer Hoover: Sex, Lies, and Political History," *Journal of the History of Sexuality* 15, no. 3 (Fall 2006): 355–81.
68. See Daniel Patrick Moynihan, *Secrecy: The American Experience* (New Haven, CT: Yale University Press, 1997).
69. Gary Kinsman and Patrizia Gentile, *The Canadian War on Queers: National Security as Sexual Regulation* (Vancouver: University of British Columbia Press, 2010), 3, 4, 7.
70. Ibid., 171.
71. See ibid., 168–90.
72. See Jennifer V. Evans, "Decriminalization, Seduction, and 'Unnatural Desire' in East Germany," *Feminist Studies* 36, no. 3 (Fall 2010): 552–77.
73. Edwin M. Yoder Jr., *Joe Alsop's Cold War: A Study of Journalistic Influence and Intrigue* (Chapel Hill: University of North Carolina Press, 1995).
74. See Jonathan Haslam, *Near and Distant Neighbors: A New History of Soviet Intelligence* (New York: Farrar, Straus and Giroux, 2015), 97, 204–5. One successful recruitment through a honey trap for a homosexual man was the case of John Vassal, a British naval clerk who provided intelligence to the GRU, Soviet military intel-

ligence, before being exposed by defector Anatoly Golitsyn in 1961. See Haslam, *Near and Distant Neighbors*, 180, 197.

75. Oleg Kalugin, *Spymaster: My Thirty-two Years in Intelligence and Espionage against the West* (New York: Basic Books, 2009), 254–55.

76. "Justice by Gadget," *Reporter*, June 9, 1953, 1.

77. Macdonald, "Lie Detector Era: Part I," 16.

78. Quoted in W. H. Lawrence, "McCarthy Proposes Lie Detector Test Him and Army Witnesses," *New York Times*, March 22, 1954, 19.

79. Quoted in W. H. Lawrence, "Welch Questions the Authenticity of McCarthy's Data," *New York Times*, June 2, 1954, 1.

80. Alger Hiss, *In the Court of Public Opinion* (New York: Alfred A. Knopf, 1957), 16, 32, 33.

81. "Lie Detector Test Offered Chambers, Alger Hiss," *Washington Post*, August 17, 1948, 1.

82. See Sam Tanenhaus, *Whittaker Chambers* (New York: Random House, 1997), 255–56, for Hiss's complaint about the leak.

83. See Victor S. Navasky, *Naming Names*, rev. ed. (New York: Hill and Wang, 2003). On the cultural construction of denunciation as a patriotic act despite many cultural caveats against informing on fellow citizens, see Olaf Stieglitz, *Undercover: Die Kultur der Denunziation in den USA* (Frankfurt: Campus Verlag, 2013).

84. Alder, *Lie Detectors*, 221.

85. Whittaker Chambers, *Witness* (Chicago: Regnery Gateway, 1952), 574.

86. See ibid., 85, 507, 509, 769.

87. Chambers later withdrew active support for McCarthy's loyalty investigations and advised McCarthy against demanding a polygraph test for Charles Bohlen upon Bohlen's nomination for ambassador to the Soviet Union to avoid a stigma for the new ambassador. See Tanenhaus, *Whittaker Chambers*, 477.

88. Hiss testimony quoted in Tanenhaus, *Whittaker Chambers*, 252–53. Sydney Hook wrote in the *New York Times Book Review*, "One misses the passionate protest and burning sense of outrage usually found in the writings of those who consider themselves victimized." Quoted ibid., 496.

89. See Tanenhaus, *Whittaker Chambers*, 416.

90. Positive polygraph stories in the 1940s include "Fangs and Polygraphs," *New Yorker*, September 4, 1948, 18; Dean Jennings, "Father of the Modern Cop," *Reader's Digest* 23 (May 1947); David Redstone, "The Case of the Dormitory Thefts," *Reader's Digest* 23 (December 1947).

91. See Highway Patrol, "Lie Detector," folder 6, box 66, United Artists Corporation Records, Series 7.2: ZIV-TV Script Files, 1950–1964, Wisconsin Historical Society, Madison.

92. See Margot A. Henriksen, *Dr. Strangelove's America: Society and Culture in the Atomic Age* (Berkeley: University of California Press, 1997), 70–75; Whitfield, *Culture of the Cold War*, 133–41. On the sexualized depiction of communism, see Cynthia Hendershot, *Anti-Communism and Popular Culture in Mid-Century America* (Jefferson, NC: McFarland, 2003), 9–17.

93. Whitfield, *The Culture of the Cold War*, 28.

94. See K. A. Cuordileone, *Manhood and American Political Culture in the Cold War* (New York: Routledge, 2005).

95. Thayer quoted in Dean, *Imperial Brotherhood*, 141–42.

96. See Athan Theoharis, *Chasing Spies: How the FBI Failed in Counterintelligence but Promoted the Politics of McCarthyism in the Cold War Years* (Chicago: Ivan R. Dee, 2002).
97. Dulles quoted in Dean, *Imperial Brotherhood*, 127.
98. Edward A. Shils, *The Torment of Secrecy: The Background and Consequences of American Security Policies* (Glencoe, IL: Free Press, 1956), 16–17.
99. Ibid., 43.
100. See Richard Hofstadter, "The Paranoid Style in American Politics," in *The Paranoid Style in American Politics and Other Essays* (New York: Vintage Books, 1967), 24.
101. Rhodri Jeffreys-Jones, "Why Was the CIA Established in 1947?," in *Eternal Vigilance? 50 Years of the CIA,* ed. Rhodri Jeffreys-Jones and Christopher Andrew (Portland: Frank Cass, 1997), 31. For the involvement of Allen and John Foster Dulles in the transatlantic economic elite, see Stephen Kinzer, *The Brothers: John Foster Dulles, Allen Dulles, and Their Secret World War* (New York: St. Martin's Griffin, 2014).
102. "The use of the lie detector has spread throughout the Government and spilled over into private life." Joseph and Stewart Alsop, "Lie-Detector Piling up Records."
103. Marilyn French, "Oh, My Employees Are All Honest," *American Business* 21 (August 1951): 49.
104. William E. Mayer, "Why Did So Many GI Captives Cave In?," *U.S. News and World Report,* February 24, 1956, quoted in Ron Robin, *The Making of the Cold War Enemy: Culture and Politics in the Military-Intellectual Complex* (Princeton, NJ: Princeton University Press, 2001), 164.
105. See Robin, *Making of Cold War Enemy,* 170–81; Dominic Streatfeild, *Brainwash: The Secret History of Mind Control* (New York: Thomas Dunne Books, 2007), 12; Dunne, *Cold War State of Mind,* 31.
106. See Rhodri Jeffreys-Jones, *We Know All About You: The Story of Surveillance in Britain and America* (New York: Oxford University Press, 2017), 96.
107. Summers, ed., *Politics of Truth,* 9.
108. See Robert H. Zieger, "The Evolving Cold War: The Changing Character of the Enemy Within, 1949–63," *American Communist History* 3, no. 1 (June 2004): 3–23.
109. Michael S. Sherry, *In the Shadow of War: The United States since the 1930s* (New Haven, CT: Yale University Press, 1995), 216.
110. Francis E. Rourke, *Secrecy and Publicity: Dilemmas of Democracy* (Baltimore: Johns Hopkins University Press, 1961), vii, 33.

Chapter 5: Truth and National Security in the American Cold War

1. Quoted in Anders Stephanson, *George Kennan and the Art of Foreign Policy* (Cambridge, MA: Harvard University Press, 1989), 192.
2. See Giorgi Agamben, *State of Exception* (Chicago: University of Chicago Press, 2005); Andrea Friedman, *Citizenship in Cold War America: The National Security State and the Possibilities of Dissent* (Amherst: University of Massachusetts Press, 2014), makes a similar point, see p. 7.
3. Anders Stephanson, "Commentary: Ideology and Neorealist Mirrors," *Diplomatic History* 17 (April 1993): 285.
4. See Melvyn P. Leffler, "National Security," in *Explaining the History of American Foreign Relations,* ed. Michael J. Hogan and Thomas G. Paterson, 2nd ed. (New York: Cambridge University Press, 2004), 126.

5. George Orwell, "Politics and the English Language," in *Selected Writings*, ed. George Bott (London: Heinemann, 1958), 85, 86.

6. Cable, March 18, 1942, in Warren F. Kimball, ed., *Churchill and Roosevelt: Their Complete Correspondence*, vol. 3 (Princeton, NJ: Princeton University Press, 1984), 421; Franklin D. Roosevelt, "Informal Extemporaneous Remarks on Receiving the Delegates to the Dumbarton Oaks Conference," August 23, 1944, in Samuel Rosenman, ed., *The Public Papers and Addresses of Franklin D. Roosevelt*, vol. 12 (New York: Russell and Russell, 1938–1950), 233; W. Averell Harriman and Elie Abel, *Special Envoy to Churchill and Stalin, 1941–1946* (New York: Random House, 1975), 279.

7. See Frank Costigliola, *Roosevelt's Lost Alliances: How Personal Politics Helped Start the Cold War* (Princeton, NJ: Princeton University Press, 2012).

8. See Anders Stephanson, "Cold War Origins," in *Encyclopedia of American Foreign Relations*, ed. Alexander deConde, Richard Dean Burns, Fredrik Logevall, vol. 1 (New York: Scribner, 2002), 223–39.

9. See Nikolas Rose, *Governing the Soul: The Shaping of the Private Self* (New York: Routledge, 1989), 31–35.

10. Edward W. Barrett, *Truth Is Our Weapon* (New York: Funk and Wagnalls, 1953), 131.

11. See Brett Gary, *The Nervous Liberals: Propaganda Anxieties from World War I to the Cold War* (New York: Columbia University Press, 1999).

12. I will use the definition of "propaganda" as "attempting to influence a society . . . by disseminating opinions, information, or misinformation through the available media." Abram N. Shulsky and Gary J. Schmitt, *Silent Warfare: Understanding the World of Intelligence* (1991; Washington, DC: Potomac Books, 2002), 84.

13. See Wendy L. Wall, "America's 'Best Propagandists': Italian Americans and the 1948 'Letters to Italy' Campaign," in *Cold War Constructions: The Political Culture of U.S. Imperialism, 1945–1966*, ed. Christian G. Apply (Amherst: University of Massachusetts Press, 2000), 91–108; Gary D. Rawnsley, "The Campaign of Truth: A Populist Propaganda," in *Cold War Propaganda in the 1950s*, ed. Gary D. Rawnsley (New York: St. Martin's Press, 1999), 31–46; Ahmed Khalid al-Rawi, "The Campaign of Truth Program: US Propaganda in Iraq during the Early 1950s," in *Religion and the Cold War: A Global Perspective*, ed. Philip Muehlenbeck (Nashville: Vanderbilt University Press, 2012), 113–38.

14. See Hugh Wilford, *The Mighty Wurlitzer: How the CIA Played America* (Cambridge, MA: Harvard University Press, 2008).

15. See Walter L. Hixson, *Parting the Curtain: Propaganda, Culture, and the Cold War, 1945–1961* (New York: St. Martin's Press, 1997); Scott Lucas, *Freedom's War: The American Crusade against the Soviet Union* (New York: New York University Press, 1999); Giles Scott-Smith and Hans Krabbendam, eds., *The Cultural Cold War in Western Europe, 1945–1960* (New York: Routledge, 2004); Johanna Granville, "'Caught with Jam on Our Fingers': Radio Free Europe and the Hungarian Revolution of 1956," *Diplomatic History* 29, no. 5 (November 2005): 811–39.

16. Memorandum "U.S. Views on Capturing Initiative in Psychological Field," April 14, 1950, in U.S. Department of State, *Foreign Relations of the United States (FRUS), 1950: Central and Eastern Europe; the Soviet Union*, vol. 4, 297, http://digicoll.library.wisc.edu/cgi-bin/FRUS/FRUS-idx?type=browse&scope=FRUS.FRUS1.

17. "Telegraphic Message of Feb. 22, 1946," in George F. Kennan, *Memoirs: 1925–1950* (Boston: Little, Brown, 1967), 555; Harry S. Truman, "Going Forward with a

Campaign of Truth" (address, April 20, 1950), in *Department of State Bulletin (DSB)* 22 (May 1, 1950): 669; William Webb, "Memorandum by Under Secretary of State (William Webb) to the President," June 23, 1950, in *FRUS*, vol. 4 (1950): 313.

18. William Benton, "Freedom of Information Throughout World Insures Peace" (address, April 7, 1948), in *DSB* 18 (April 18, 1948): 519; George V. Allen, "The Voice of America," *DSB* 19 (November 7, 1948): 568; "Campaign of Truth Intensifies Activity in Field of Religion" (press release, February 4, 1952), in *DSB* 26 (February 18, 1952): 252.

19. Douglas Schneider, "America's Answer to Communist Propaganda Abroad" (address, December 6, 1948), in *DSB* (December 19, 1948): 774; "A Report to the President Pursuant to the President's Directive of January 31, 1950 [NSC-68]," *FRUS, 1950: National Security Affairs; Foreign Economic Policy,* vol. 1, 243, http:// images.library.wisc.edu/FRUS/EFacs/1950v01/reference/frus.frus1950v01.i0008. pdf (emphasis added).

20. "A Report to the President Pursuant to the President's Directive of January 31, 1950 [NSC-68]," 252.

21. Kennan, "Telegraphic Message," 551.

22. [George Kennan], "The Sources of Soviet Conduct," *Foreign Affairs* 25 (July 1947): 568, 574, 676.

23. George Kennan, "Totalitarianism in the Modern World," in *Totalitarianism,* ed. Carl J. Friedrich (1954; New York: Universal Library, 1964), 24, 28, 34.

24. See David C. Engerman, *Modernization from the Other Shore: American Intellectuals and the Romance of Russian Development* (Cambridge, MA: Harvard University Press, 2003), 253.

25. See Chandak Sengoopta, *Imprint of the Raj* (London: Macmillan, 2003); Christian Parenti, *The Soft Cage: Surveillance in America From Slavery to the War on Terror* (New York: Basic Books, 2004), 48–49; Melissa M. Littlefield, *The Lying Brain: Lie Detection in Science and Science Fiction* (Ann Arbor: University of Michigan Press, 2011), 104.

26. Leon Trotsky, "Their Morals and Ours," in Leon Trotsky, John Dewey, and George Novack, *Their Morals and Ours: Marxist vs. Liberal Views on Morality* (New York: Pathfinder Press, 1973), 36, 37.

27. See the discussion in Steven Lukes, *Marxism and Morality* (Oxford: Oxford University Press, 1985), 118–38. On philosopher John Dewey's perceptive observation that Marxists such as Trotsky bound their goals of bettering the world to a specific means, violent revolution, and therefore reversed the proper relation between ends and means, see 121.

28. See Piers Brendon, *The Dark Valley: A Panorama of the 1930s* (New York: Alfred Knopf, 2000), 252–53.

29. Quoted in John Lamberton Harper, *The Cold War* (New York: Oxford University Press, 2011), 9.

30. The most thoughtful analysis of Kennan's emotional rhetoric in the "Long Telegram" and elsewhere is Frank Costigliola, "'Unceasing Pressure for Penetration': Gender, Pathology, and Emotion in George Kennan's Formulation of the Cold War," *Journal of American History* 83 (March 1997): 1309–39.

31. See Engerman, *Modernization from the Other Shore,* 273–85.

32. Kennan, "Telegraphic Message," 559. See George V. Allen, "Thought Control in the Soviet Union I–III," *DSB* 25 (November 5, November 26, December 3, 1951); George V.

Allen, "Our World Information Program" (address, March 5, 1949), in *DSB* 20 (March 13, 1949): 324.

33. Dean Acheson, *Present at the Creation: My Years in the State Department* (New York: Norton, 1969), 375.

34. See John J. Mearsheimer, *Why Leaders Lie: The Truth about Lying in International Politics* (New York: Oxford University Press, 2011).

35. Hull quoted in Paul Kennedy, *The Rise and Fall of the Great Powers: Economic Change and Military Conflict from 1500 to 2000* (New York: Random House, 1987), 361; "A Report to the President Pursuant to the President's Directive of January 31, 1950 [NSC-68]," 257.

36. NSC-68, 314.

37. See Alex Roland, "The Military-Industrial Complex: Lobby and Trope," in *The Long War: A History of U.S. National Security Policy since World War II,* ed. Andrew J. Bacevich (New York: Columbia University Press, 2007), 335–70.

38. James Q. Wilson, *Bureaucracy: What Government Agencies Do and Why They Do It* (New York: Basic Books, 1989), 189.

39. Dulles, quoted in Immerman, "Brief History of the CIA," 24. For early budget numbers for covert operations (estimated, since CIA budgets remain classified), see Immerman, "Brief History," 21. Personnel in clandestine operations went from 302 in 1949 to 1,531 in 1951.

40. See Tim Weiner, *Legacy of Ashes: The History of the CIA* (New York: Doubleday, 2007).

41. Richard Bissell, Thomas I. Emerson, James E. Newman, and Harold Stein to [Secretary of the Treasury] Snyder, May 24, 1946, in Michael J. Hogan, *A Cross of Iron: Harry S. Truman and the Origins of the National Security State, 1945–1954* (New York: Cambridge University Press, 1998), 50.

42. On the joint British-FBI intelligence cooperation inside the United States, and the visit of FBI agents to London to study British intelligence practices before Donovan's famed report of June 1941, see Douglas M. Charles, "'Before the Colonel Arrived': Hoover, Donovan, Roosevelt, and the Origins of American Central Intelligence, 1940–41," *Intelligence and National Security* 20, no. 2 (June 2005): 225–37.

43. See David F. Rudgers, *Creating the Secret State: The Origins of the Central Intelligence Agency, 1943–1947* (Lawrence: University Press of Kansas, 2000).

44. The National Security Act of 1947, Section 102, July 26, 1947, in Michael Warner, ed., *Central Intelligence: Origin and Evolution* (Washington, DC: Center for the Study of Intelligence, Central Intelligence Agency, 2001), 29–30.

45. "National Security Council Directive No. 3," in U.S. Department of State, *Foreign Relations of the United States (FRUS), 1945–1950: Emergence of the Intelligence Establishment,* http://www.state.gov/www/about_state/history/intel/index.html.

46. This sketch is based on Immerman, "Brief History of the CIA," 1–22.

47. "National Security Act of 1947," Section 102, July 26, 1947, in Warner, *Central Intelligence,* 29–30.

48. Rhodri Jeffreys-Jones, *The CIA and American Democracy,* 3rd ed. (New Haven, CT: Yale University Press, 2003), 47.

49. See Carolyn Eisenberg, "The Myth of the Berlin Blockade and the Early Cold War," in *Cold War Triumphalism: The Misuse of History after the Fall of Communism,* ed. Ellen Schrecker (New York: New Press, 2004), 174–200; see esp. note 7 for evidence of U.S. expectation of a Soviet move against Berlin.

50. SSU was considerably larger than CIG at the time. Stacked with old OSSers, "it was SSU that kept alive the spirit of the old OSS and eventually bequeathed it to the CIA," according to CIA historian Michael Warner. See "Preface," in Michael Warner, ed., *The CIA under Harry Truman* (Washington, DC: Center for the Study of Intelligence, Central Intelligence Agency, 1994), xvi.

51. The bureaucratic give-and-take can be followed through the documents published in *FRUS, 1945–1950: Emergence of the Intelligence Establishment*. See esp. NSC 4, December 17, 1947, and NSC 4-A, December 9, 1947, docs. 252 and 253, which established the organizational separation of overt and covert activities. Quotes from "Memorandum from the Deputy Director of Central Intelligence (Wright) to the Chief of the Interagency Coordinating and Planning Staff, Central Intelligence Agency (Childs)," December 2, 1947, doc. 251; quote from draft directive to the Central Intelligence Agency, which is enclosed in doc. 253.

52. "Director of Policy Planning Staff (Kennan) to Under Secretary of State (Lovett) and Secretary of State Marshall," memo, May 19, 1948, in *FRUS, 1945–1950: Emergence of the Intelligence Establishment*, doc. 276; Undersecretary of State Robert Lovett quoted in "Memorandum for the President of the Discussion at 12th Meeting of the National Security Council," June 3, 1948, doc. 282. See also Immerman, "Brief History of the CIA," 15–18, 20–21.

53. See Lawrence R. Houston, "Memorandum for the Director: 'Responsibility and Control for OPC,'" October 19, 1948, in Warner, *CIA under Harry Truman*, 235–39.

54. Truman quoted in David F. Rudgers, "The Origins of Covert Action," *Journal of Contemporary History* 35, no. 2 (2000): 260.

55. "Memorandum from the General Counsel of the Central Intelligence Agency (Houston) to Director of Central Intelligence Hillenkoetter," September 25, 1947, in *FRUS, 1945–1950: Emergence of the Intelligence Establishment*, doc. 241.

56. "National Security Council Directive to Director of Central Intelligence Hillenkoetter," December 17, 1947, *FRUS, 1945–1950*, doc. 257.

57. "Memorandum from the Deputy Director of Central Intelligence (Wright) to the Chief of the Interagency Coordinating and Planning Staff, Central Intelligence Agency (Childs)," December 2, 1947, *FRUS, 1945–1950*, doc. 251.

58. "National Security Council Directive on Office of Special Projects" (NSC 10/2), June 18, 1948, *FRUS, 1945–1950*, doc. 292.

59. John Prados, *Safe for Democracy: The Secret Wars of the CIA* (Chicago: Ivan R. Dee, 2006), 148.

60. On Allen Dulles's public style, see Peter Grose, *Gentleman Spy: The Life of Allen Dulles* (New York: Houghton Mifflin, 1994), esp. 414–16.

61. Amy Zegart, *Flawed by Design: The Evolution of the CIA, JCS, and NSC* (Stanford, CA: Stanford University Press, 1999), 208.

62. Memorandum by Kennan, paraphrased in "Department of State Briefing Memorandum," December 17, 1947, *FRUS, 1945–1950: Emergence of the Intelligence Establishment*, doc. 256.

63. Kennan to [Sec. of State George] Marshall, March 15, 1948, quoted in Wilson D. Miscamble, *George F. Kennan and the Making of American Foreign Policy, 1947–1950* (Princeton, NJ: Princeton University Press, 1992), 105; see 106–11 for discussion of Kennan's role in the creation of the OPC.

64. The strategic and ideological importance—the "real" and symbolic role—is noted in Jeffries-Jones, *CIA and American Democracy*, 51.

65. On the Italian elections, see James Edward Miller, *The United States and Italy, 1940–1950: The Politics of Stabilization* (Chapel Hill: University of North Carolina Press, 1986), 213–71; quote in "Memorandum from the Director of the Policy Planning Staff (Kennan) to the Under Secretary of State (Lovett) and Secretary of State Marshall," June 16, 1948, *FRUS, 1945–1950: Emergence of the Intelligence Establishment*, doc. 289.

66. See Athan Theoharis, "A New Agency: The Origins and Expansion of CIA Covert Operations," in Theoharis et al., *Central Intelligence Agency*, 155–88.

67. "Draft Proposal NSC Directive," May 5, 1948, *FRUS, 1945–1950: Emergence of the Intelligence Establishment*, doc. 270; "Policy Planning Staff Memorandum," May 4, 1948, *FRUS, 1945–1950*, doc. 269.

68. "Policy Planning Staff Memorandum," May 4, 1948, *FRUS, 1945–1950*, doc. 269.

69. Ibid.

70. Frank G. Wisner, "Memorandum for the Director of Central Intelligence: 'OPC Projects,'" October 29, 1948, in Warner, *CIA under Harry Truman*, 242.

71. Kennan, *Memoirs, 1925–1950*, 403–4; Kennan's statement of regret was made to historian Wilson Miscamble in 1989. See Miscamble, *George F. Kennan and the Making of American Foreign Policy*, 109.

72. Kennan address, January 23, 1947, quoted in Stephanson, *George Kennan and the Art of Foreign Policy*, 97.

73. See Scott Lucas and Kaeten Mistry, "Illusions of Coherence: George F. Kennan, U.S. Strategy, and Political Warfare in the Early Cold War, 1946–1950," *Diplomatic History* 33, no. 1 (January 2009): 39–66.

74. See Jeffreys-Jones, *CIA and American Democracy*, 30–32.

75. See excerpts from the report (of which apparently until today no copy has been located) in Grose, *Gentleman Spy*, 445–48, quote on 447–48.

76. NSC 20/4, "Report by the National Security Council on U.S. Objectives with Respect to the USSR to Counter Soviet Threats to U.S. Security," November 23, 1948, U.S. Department of State, *FRUS, 1948: General; the United Nations*, vol. 1, 668. http://digicoll.library.wisc.edu/cgi-bin/FRUS/FRUS-idx?type=browse&scope=FRUS.FRUS1.

77. U.S. Office of Management and Budget, *The Budget for the Fiscal Year 2005, Historical Series* (Washington, DC: Government Printing Press, 2004), 45–50.

78. See Kennedy, *Rise and Fall of the Great Powers*, 384, 436.

79. See Hogan, *Cross of Iron*. Contrast with Aaron L. Friedberg, *In the Shadow of the Garrison State: America's Anti-statism and Its Cold War Grand Strategy* (Princeton, NJ: Princeton University Press, 2000).

80. Walter L. Pfortzheimer [Chief, CIA Legislative Liaison Division], "Memorandum for the Record," January 28, 1947, in Warner, *CIA under Harry Truman*, 107.

81. Hogan, *Cross of Iron*, 66.

82. See Robert David Johnson, *Congress and the Cold War* (New York: Cambridge University Press, 2006), 130–33.

83. Michael Warner, "Historical Perspective," in Warner, ed., *Central Intelligence*, 6.

84. Harold D. Lasswell, "The Garrison State," *American Journal of Sociology* 46 (January 1941): 455–68. Lasswell saw his construct not as a strict prediction, but as an ideal type of state, certain features of which could come about at different times in different form.

85. Friedrich A. Hayek, *The Road to Serfdom: Text and Documents; the Definitive Edition* (Chicago: University of Chicago Press, 2007), 69. This book assumed a much

stricter developmental logic inherent in types of societies than did Lasswell. See also Friedberg, *In the Shadow of the Garrison State,* 34–61, on public debates at the time.

86. The term "crisis internationalism" to define Wilson's influence in twentieth-century U.S. foreign policy comes from Frank Ninkovich, *The Wilsonian Century* (Chicago: University of Chicago Press, 1999).

87. "Report on the Covert Activities of the Central Intelligence Agency," September 30, 1954, 5, 12, 13, CREST.

88. Lilienthal diary, June 24, 1946, quoted in Kai Bird and Martin J. Sherwin, *American Prometheus: The Triumph and Tragedy of J. Robert Oppenheimer* (New York: Alfred A. Knopf, 2005), 346.

Chapter 6: Immeasurable Security

1. Francis Gary Powers with Curt Gentry, *Operation Overflight: The U-2 Spy Pilot Tells His Story for the First Time* (New York: Tower Publications, 1970), 23.

2. See the declassified, but heavily redacted, internal CIA history by Gregory W. Pedlow and Donald E. Welzenbach, *The CIA and the U-2 Program, 1954–1974* (Washington, DC: Central Intelligence Agency, [1992] 1998), 1–93; Curtis Peebles, *Shadow Flights: America's Secret Air War against the Soviet Union* (Novato, CA: Presido, 2000).

3. See Michael R. Beschloss, *Mayday: The U-2 Affair; The Untold Story of the Greatest U.S.-U.S.S.R. Spy Scancal* (New York: Harper and Row, 1986).

4. Ibid., 352.

5. "Statement Concerning Francis Gary Powers," in *Hearing before the Committee on Armed Services,* U.S. Senate, 87th Congress, second session, on Francis Gary Powers, March 6, 1962 (Washington, DC: Government Printing Office, 1962), 25.

6. Powers, *Operation Overflight,* 312.

7. See Matthew M. Aid, *The Secret Sentry: The Untold Story of the National Security Agency* (New York: Bloomsbury Press, 2009), 52–55.

8. "Office of Security: Statement of Mission and Functions," September 2, 1957, p. 1, CIA Records Search Tool (CREST), National Archives and Records Administrations (NARA), College Park, MD.

9. "1947" [no date, but in likelihood a document written by the CIA history staff as part of an internal history of security procedures], quote on p. 13, CREST. See also Rhodri Jeffreys-Jones, *The FBI: A History* (New Haven, CT: Yale University Press, 2007), 141–45.

10. R. H. Hillenkoetter [DCI], Memorandum on "Study Project on Technical Investigative Method in Time of Emergency," August 23, 1948, CREST.

11. [Redacted], [Chief of Inspection and Security], Memorandum to the Director of Central Intelligence, March 18, 1949, CREST.

12. See Sheffield Edwards, [Director of Security] to Director of CIA, Office Memorandum, May 20, 1949, CREST; [redacted], message to Sheffield Edwards, May 24, 1949 (containing approval of request for unvouchered funds), ibid.

13. [Redacted], [Chief, Inspection and Security Staff], Memorandum to Director of Central Intelligence, January 3, 1950, CREST.

14. Sheffield Edwards [Director of Security], "Memorandum for Director of Central Intelligence," April 13, 1953, CREST.

15. Allen Dulles [Director of Central Intelligence], "Memorandum for Director of Security," May 21, 1953, CREST.
16. [Redacted], [Acting Director of Security], "Memorandum to Mr. Jerome D. Fenton, Chairman, USCIB Special Committee," September 19, 1955, p. 2, CREST.
17. See "Memorandum from the National Security Council Representative on Internal Security (Coyne) to the President's Special Assistant for National Security Affairs (Cutler) and the Executive Secretary of the National Security Council (Lay)," February 8, 1955, *Foreign Relations of the United States, 1950–1955, The Intelligence Community, 1950–1955*, doc. 205, https://history.state.gov/historicaldocuments/frus1950–55Intel/d205.
18. Sheffield Edwards, [Chief, Inspection and Staff Security], "Memo to the Executive," January 17, 1950, CREST.
19. Stansfield Turner, [Director of Central Intelligence], "Subject: Reinvestigation/Repolygraph Program," September 19, 1978, CREST.
20. "Personnel Security in CIA: Report of Investigation by The Inspector General," October 10, 1963, 4, 5, CREST.
21. Sheffield Edwards, [Director of Security], Memorandum for the General Counsel [of the CIA], April 24, 1957, CREST.
22. "Polygraph Agreement," CREST.
23. Richard Helms, [Director of Central Intelligence], "Memorandum for Director of Security, Subject: Polygraph Program," February 21, 1970, CREST.
24. See L. K. White [CIA Deputy Director/Administration], Memorandum for the Record: "The General Mark Clark Task Force," November 27, 1954, CREST.
25. [Redacted], "Memorandum for the Record of the Clark Committee," February 1, 1955, CREST.
26. [Redacted], "Diary Notes," October 23, 1964, CREST.
27. George H. W. Bush, [Director of Central Intelligence] to Bella Abzug, February 25, 1976, CREST.
28. [Redacted], [Executive Secretary, Security Committee], "Response to Certain Recommendations Made in a House Subcommittee Staff Report Entitled 'Security Clearance Procedures in the Intelligence Agencies,'" January 16, 1980, p. 4, CREST.
29. Tom Gilligan, *CIA LIFE: 10,000 Days with the Agency,* 2nd ed. (Boston: Intelligence e-Publishing Company, 2003), 239, 240.
30. James M. Olson, *Fair Play: The Moral Dilemmas of Spying* (Dulles, VA: Potomac Books, 2006), 258.
31. Scott D. Breckinridge, *CIA and the Cold War: A Memoir* (Westport: Praeger, 1993), 12, 13.
32. Philip Agee, *Inside the Company: CIA Diary* (New York: Stonehill, 1975), 22.
33. Ibid., 22, 25.
34. Ibid., 26, 27.
35. Lindsay Moran, *Blowing My Cover: My Life as a CIA Spy* (New York: G. P. Putnam's Sons, 2005), 17, 27.
36. "Interim Assignment Branch: 1953 Progress Report," p. 5, CREST.
37. Director of Security, "Accomplishments of the Security Division during Fiscal Year 1954 and Objectives for Fiscal Year 1955," August 31, 1954, p. 6, CREST.
38. [Redacted], [Acting Chief, Personnel Security Division], Memorandum to Director of Security, May 7, 1956, CREST.
39. John H. Richardson, *My Father the Spy: An Investigative Memoir* (New York: HarperCollins, 2005), 85. As was shown, in the late 1940s CIA polygraph policies were not yet fully developed.

40. Original citation in Joseph Trento, *The Secret History of the CIA* (Rosevile, CA: Prima Publishing, 2001), 478. Quoted in David Talbot, *The Devil's Chessboard: Allen Dulles, the CIA, and the Rise of America's Secret Government* (New York: HarperCollins, 2015), 333–34.

41. See William R. Corson, *The Armies of Ignorance: The Rise of the American Intelligence Empire* (New York: Dial Press, 1977), 378–79.

42. [Redacted], Memorandum to Deputy Director of Security and Chief, Interrogation Research Division, February 21, 1966, CREST.

43. "Comparison of Agency Documentation and Procedures with the Requirements of the CSC FPM [Federal Personnel Manual] Letter No. 736–4," June 2, 1969, CREST.

44. [Redacted], [Chief, Interrogation Branch], "Memorandum for Deputy Director of Security, Subject: Legal Issues, Interrogation Branch," May 10, 1974, CREST.

45. Frank Snepp, *Irreparable Harm: A Firsthand Account of How One Agent Took On the CIA in an Epic Battle over Secrecy and Free Speech* (Lawrence: University Press of Kansas, 2001), 59; Snepp, *Decent Interval: An Insider's Account of Saigon's Indecent End, Told by the CIA's Chief Strategy Analyst in Vietnam* (Lawrence: University Press of Kansas, [1977] 2002).

46. Christopher Moran, *Company Confessions: Secrets, Memoirs, and the CIA* (New York: Thomas Dunne Books/St. Martin's Press, 2016), 201. Introduced in 1889, the British Official Secrets Act prohibits government employees from obtaining and disclosing any information potentially useful to the enemy without prior authorization. After a 1911 revision, and in contrast to U.S. law, the burden of proof as to whether an individual had been engaged in espionage or not rested with the accused. See Christopher Andrew, *Defend the Realm: The Authorized History of MI5* (New York: Vintage Books, 2010), 39.

47. Sheffield Edwards, [Director of Security], "Memorandum for Acting Director of Central Intelligence," August 7, 1957, CREST.

48. [Redacted], [Chief/Interrogation Research Division, Chief, Personnel Security Division], "Memorandum for Acting Deputy Director of Security for Personnel Security, Subject: Post-Polygraph Interview Program," December 8, 1967, CREST; [redacted], Chief, Personnel Security Division, Memorandum for Chief, Executive and Planning Division, September 3, 1969, CREST.

49. [Redacted], [Chief, Interrogation Branch], "Memorandum for Director of Security, Subject: Role of Polygraph in the Reinvestigation Program," April 12, 1974, CREST.

50. [Redacted], [Chief, Interrogation Branch], "Memorandum for Deputy Director of Security, Subject: Polygraph Policy Review," April 25, 1974, CREST.

51. President's Commission on CIA Activities within the United States [popularly known as Rockefeller Commission], *Report to the President by the Commission on CIA Activities within the United States* (Washington, DC: Government Printing Office, 1975), 249.

52. See, for example, an Inspector General report from 1962, which mentions "the son of an influential man" who admitted he was gay during a CIA polygraph test. In this case, the CIA referred the case to the congressional representative. "The difficult decision of whether to tell the father his boy was a homosexual was thus up to the Congressman—not CIA." Inspector General study, August 17, 1962, p. 17, CREST.

53. Lyman B. Kirkpatrick, [Inspector General of the CIA], "Memorandum for Director of Central Intelligence, Subject: An Analysis of Agency Methods for Handling Personnel Security Cases," April 19, 1957, 8–9, CREST.

54. [Redacted], [Chief, Interrogation Branch], "Memorandum for Deputy Director of Security, Subject: Polygraph Policy Review," April 25, 1974, CREST.

55. "Office of Security Weekly Staff Meeting," July 12, 1973, p. 3, CREST.

56. Robert W. Gambino, "Memorandum for the Record, Subject: Briefing of DCI," September 1, 1976, p. 3, 4, CREST.

57. Ibid., 5.

58. "Summary of Contingency Planning for the Abolition of Non-Operational Polygraphy (Objective B57103)," n.d., p. 2, 3, CREST.

59. U.S. Congress, House, *The Use of Polygraphs and Similar Devices by Federal Agencies: Hearings before a Subcommittee of the Committee on Government Operations, House of Representatives, June 4 and 5, 1974*, 93rd Cong., 2nd sess. (Washington, DC: Government Printing Office, 1974), 647, 644; bar chart on 645, without numbers.

60. E. H. Kneche, [Deputy Director of Central Intelligence], "Memorandum for Director of Central Intelligence, Subject: Polygraph Testing," March 3, 1977, CREST.

61. John F. Sullivan, *Gatekeeper: Memoirs of a CIA Polygraph Examiner* (Dulles, VA: Potomac Press, 2007), 5.

62. Ibid., 5, 31.

63. Stansfield Turner, [Director of Central Intelligence], "Memorandum for Deputy Director of Central Intelligence, Subject: Polygraph Testing," March 3, 1977, CREST.

64. Stansfield Turner, *Secrecy and Democracy: The CIA in Transition* (Boston: Houghton Mifflin, 1985), 69.

65. [Redacted], "Memorandum for the Record, Subject: Polygraph Research and Development, 1948–1956," [handwritten date: 1966], CREST.

66. Howard Osborn, [Director of Security], "Memorandum for Deputy Director for Support, Subject: Significant Accomplishments, Office of Security—FY 1968, p. 3, CREST.

67. [Redacted], Memorandum for the Record, no date, CREST.

68. [Redacted], Memorandum for Deputy Director of Security and Chief, Interrogation Research Division, January 16, 1966, CREST.

69. "Personnel Security in CIA: Report of Investigation by The Inspector General," TAB A, p. 4, October 10, 1963, CREST.

70. Executive Order 10450, as amended October 13, 1953, May 27, 1954, August 2, 1954, and August 5, 1954, p. 1, 2, CREST.

71. Ibid., 6, 7–8.

72. See Applicant Information Sheet No. 2, CREST.

73. [Redacted], *Security Program of the Central Intelligence Agency 1941–1968: Vol. II, Personnel Security*, May 1973, 5, 8–10, 15, 31–32, CREST.

74. [Redacted], "Inspector General's Survey of the CIA Career Service, December 1959," pp. 18, 19, 20, CREST.

75. Sullivan, *Gatekeeper*, 7.

76. [Redacted], [Chief, Personnel Security Division], Memorandum for the File, November 29, 1957, CREST.

77. [Redacted], [Chief, Interrogation Branch], "Memorandum for Director of Security, Subject: Role of Polygraph in the Reinvestigation Program," April 12, 1974, CREST.

78. See Alan B. Trabue, *A Life of Lies and Spies: Tales of a CIA Covert Ops Polygraph Interrogator* (New York: Thomas Dunne Books, 2015).

79. Frederic Wakeman Jr., "American Police Advisors and the Nationalist Chinese Secret Service, 1930–1937," *Modern China* 18, no. 2 (April 1992): 107–37.

80. See Milton Miles, *A Different Kind of War* (Garden City, NY: Doubleday, 1967), 200.

See also Roy Olin Stratton, *SACO: The Rice Paddy Navy* (Pleasantville, NY: C. S. Palmer, 1950), 338–39.

81. Jeremy Kuzmarov, *Modernizing Repression: Police Training and Nation-Building in the American Century* (Amherst: University of Massachusetts Press, 2012), 6.

82. R. H. Hillenkoetter, [Director of Central Intelligence], memorandum to Chief, I&SS, January 10, 1950, CREST.

83. "OPC Regulation No. 20–20," July 13, 1950, CREST.

84. Ted Shackley, with Richard Finney, *Spymaster: My Life in the CIA* (Dulles, VA: Potomac Books, 2005), 21, 80.

85. Chester C. Crawford, "The Polygraph in Agent Interrogation," *Studies in Intelligence* 4 (Summer 1960): 32, 35, 32, 35–36.

86. Clark R. Diangson, "Communication to the Editors: Reservations on the Polygraph," *Studies in Intelligence* 5 (Fall 1961): 58, 59, 60.

87. Duane R. Clarridge with Digby Diehl, *A Spy for All Seasons: My Life in the CIA* (New York: Scribner, 2002), 146, 407.

88. See Sissela Bok, *Lying: Moral Choice in Public and Private Life* (New York: Vintage Books, 1979).

89. Olsen, *Moral Dilemmas of Spying*, 258.

90. Sullivan, *Gatekeeper*, 21.

91. Ibid., 29, 30.

92. Ibid., 40, 47, 60.

93. Mark J. Gasiorowski, "The 1953 Coup d'Etat against Mosaddeq," in *Mohammad Mosaddeq and the 1953 Coup in Iran*, ed. Mark J. Gasiorowski and Malcolm Byrne (Syracuse: Syracuse University Press, 2004), 241. Farzanegan was the main Iranian collaborator with the CIA in the military network that participated in the coup and later became minister of post and telegraph. See Gasiorowski, "The 1953 Coup d'Etat against Mosaddeq," 258, 264.

94. George E. Filbing, "The LC Flutter Excursion into [redacted]", April 2, 1954, rough draft of report. Filbing, "SPARKLE AND SPARKLE #1," April 2, 1954, rough draft of report. Documents available at www.antipolygraph.org.

95. Sullivan, *Gatekeeper*, 42, 48.

96. John F. Sullivan, *Of Spies and Lies: A CIA Lie Detector Remembers Vietnam* (Lawrence: University Press of Kansas, 2002), 174.

97. See Alfred W. McCoy, *A Question of Torture: CIA Interrogation, from the Cold War to the War on Terror* (New York: Holt, 2006), 60–71.

98. Sullivan, *Gatekeeper*, 29.

99. Ibid., 71.

100. Ibid., 68.

101. See the testimony of polygraph interrogator Richard O. Arther to the House Select Committee on Assassinations in 1979. U.S. Congress, House of Representatives, 95th Cong., 2nd sess., "The Analysis of Yuri Nosenko's Polygraph Examination," submitted by Richard O. Arther (Washington, DC: Government Printing Office, 1979), 193–94.

102. See David Wise, *Molehunt: The Secret Search for Traitors That Shattered the CIA* (New York: Random House, 1992), 131–48, esp. 146–47; Richard J. Heuer Jr., "Nosenko: Five Paths to Judgment," *Studies in Intelligence* 31, no. 3 (Fall 1987): 71–101, reprinted in H. Bradford Westerfield, *Inside the CIA's Private World: Declassified Articles from the Agency's Internal Journal, 1955–1992* (New Haven, CT: Yale University Press, 1995), 379–414.

103. See Dominic Streatfeild, *Brainwash: The Secret History of Mind Control* (New York: Thomas Dunne Books, 2007), 323–31.

104. Sullivan, *Gatekeeper,* 163–71, quote on 166.

105. See David Wise, *Nightmover: How Aldrich Ames Sold the CIA to the KGB for $4.6 Million* (New York: HarperCollins, 1995); Tim Weiner, David Johnston, and Neil A. Lewis, *Betrayal: The Story of Aldrich Ames, an American Spy* (New York: Random House, 1995).

106. Sullivan, *Gatekeeper,* 186. See the findings and recommendations of the Senate Select Committee on Intelligence after investigating the Ames case, reprinted in Loch K. Johnson and James J. Wirtz, eds., *Intelligence: The Secret World of Spies; An Anthology,* 4th ed. (New York: Oxford University Press, 2014), 328–40.

107. Sullivan, *Gatekeeper,* 186. In fact, counterintelligence officer Dan Payne had flagged Ames's finances as an area of concern, but questions during the 1991 polygraph test had been deliberately kept vague in order to suggest a routine procedure and thus to avoid tipping off Ames. See John Diamond, *The CIA and the Culture of Failure: U.S. Intelligence from the End of the Cold War to the Invasion of Iraq* (Stanford, CA: Stanford University Press, 2008), 218.

108. David W. Doyle, *True Men and Traitors: From the OSS to the CIA, My Life in the Shadows* (New York: Wiley, 2001), 250.

109. Robert Baer, *See No Evil: The True Story of a Ground Soldier in the CIA's War on Terrorism* (New York: Three Rivers Press, 2002), 20–21, 232.

110. See Christopher Andrew and Vasili Mitrokhin, *The Sword and the Shield: The Mitrokhin Archive and the Secret History of the KGB* (New York: Basic Books, 1999), 449–50.

111. Quoted in Weiner, Johnston, and Lewis, *Betrayal,* 90. Victor Cherkashin, who handled Ames for the KGB, also claims that the Soviets provided Ames with a list of anticipated questions for a conspicuous public meeting with Soviet officers in May 1986 in order to create an alibi in case Ames responded positively to the polygraph question about meeting foreign nationals; However, other parts of Cherkashin's account show ignorance about the polygraph, as when he claims that "voice level" is one of the measurements. See Victor Cherkashin and Gregory Feifer, *Spy Handler: Memoir of a KGB Officer: The True Story of the Man Who Recruited Robert Hanssen and Aldrich Ames* (New York: Basic Books, 2005), 188, 202.

112. Aldrich Ames to Steven Aftergood [American Federation of Scientists], November 28, 2000. http://www.fas.org/sgp/othergov/polygraph/ames.html.

113. See Robert Wallace and H. Keith Melton, *Spycraft: The Secret History of the CIA's Spytechs, from Communism to Al-Qaeda* (New York: Plume, 2009), 153–55.

114. See Sullivan, *Gatekeeper,* 127–29; Philip Hager and Ronald J. Ostrow, "U.S. Swaps Spy for 8 Ghanaians Who Aided CIA," *Los Angeles Times,* November 26, 1985, http://articles.latimes.com/1985-11-26/news/mn-1944_1_cia-training. Biographical details about Scranage come from [author redacted], "CIA, Ghana, and the [redacted]," *Studies in Intelligence* 34 (Fall 1990): 27. The vast majority of this article remains classified.

115. Sullivan, *Gatekeeper,* 7, 9.

116. This includes the National Security Agency (NSA), which began polygraphing applicants and employees in 1951. See James Bamford, *The Puzzle Palace: Inside the National Security Agency, America's Most Secret Intelligence Organization* (New York: Viking Penguin, 1982), 144, 163–64.

117. See Fred M. Kaiser, "Secrecy, Intelligence, and Community: The U.S. Intelligence Community," in *Secrecy: A Cross-Cultural Perspective*, ed. Stanton K. Tefft (New York: Human Sciences Press, 1980), 273, 280.

118. James Q. Wilson, *Bureaucracy: What Government Agencies Do and Why They Do It* (New York: Basic Books, 1989), 43.

Chapter 7: The Polygraph and the Problems of Deterrence

1. Ralph W. Gerard, "To Prevent Another World War: Truth Detection," *Journal of Conflict Resolution* 5, no. 2 (June 1961): 212, 216.

2. See Jessica Wang: *American Science in an Age of Anxiety: Scientists, Anticommunism, and the Cold War* (Chapel Hill: University of North Carolina Press, 1999).

3. See Charles DeBenedetti, *The Peace Reform in American History* (Bloomington: Indiana University Press, 1980); Lawrence Wittner, *One World or None: A History of the Nuclear Disarmament Movement through 1953* (Stanford, CA: Stanford University Press, 1993); Wittner, *Resisting the Bomb: A History of the World Nuclear Disarmament Movement, 1965–1970* (Stanford, CA: Stanford University Press, 1997).

4. See Thomas Omestad, "Psychology and the CIA: Leaders on the Couch," *Foreign Policy* 95 (Summer 1994): 105–22.

5. Gerard, "To Prevent Another World War," 215–16, 217.

6. Ibid., 214. See John Marks, *The Search for the "Manchurian Candidate:" The CIA and Mind Control*, rev. ed. (New York: Norton, 1991).

7. For example, Hungarian-born British writer Arthur Koestler argued in his 1967 book *The Ghost in the Machine* for a universal drug regiment to counteract the evolutionary mismatch between rationalizing and emoting brain. See David Cesarani, *Arthur Koestler: The Homeless Mind* (London: Heinemann, 1998), 493.

8. The Center for Research on Conflict Resolution, "Proposal for a Peace Agency in the National Government," August 1960, box 16, Ralph W. Gerard Papers, University of California, Irvine, Rare Books and Manuscripts collection.

9. D. R. Inglis, D. A. Flanders, M. S. Freedman, and A. H. Jaffer, *A Specific Proposal for Balanced Disarmament and Atomic Control* [dated December 1, 1952], 31, in CIA Records Search Tool (CREST), National Archives and Records Administration (NARA), College Park, MD.

10. Ibid., 32, 34.

11. David R. Inglis, "Transition to Disarmament," in *America Armed: Essays on United States Military Policy*, ed. Robert A. Goldwin (Chicago: Rand McNally, 1962), 92, 93–94.

12. See David R. Inglis, *Testing and Taming of Nuclear Weapons* (New York: Public Affairs Committee, 1960).

13. Ibid., 25.

14. Jay Orear, "A New Approach to Inspection," *Bulletin of the Atomic Scientists* 17, no. 3 (March 1961): 107, 108.

15. In October 1961, another poll showed that 81 percent of Americans preferred a nuclear war to rule by communists. See Wittner, *Resisting the Bomb*, 449.

16. See Orear, "New Approach to Inspection," 109.

17. Ibid., 110.

18. Ibid., 109. See also Wittner, *Resisting the Bomb*, 32–37.

19. Gerard to Orear, April 19, 1961; Orear to Gerard, April 24, 1961, box 16, Ralph Gerard Papers.

20. See Alex Abella, *Soldiers of Reason: The RAND Corporation and the Rise of the American Empire* (Orlando: Harcourt, 2008).

21. Lewis C. Bohn, *Psychological Inspection*, [dated February 19, 1960, unpublished], 3, 4, in CREST.

22. Ibid., 8–9.

23. Ibid., 21.

24. Ibid., 9–10.

25. Ibid., 27.

26. J. David Singer, "Testing: A Strategic Appraisal," *The Nation*, January 13, 1962, 26; J. David Singer, "The Strategic Dilemma: Probability versus Disutility: A Review of Herman Kahn, *On Thermonuclear War*," *Journal of Conflict Resolution* 5, no. 2 (June 1961): 201; J. David Singer, "Weapons Technology and International Stability," *Centennial Review* 5, no. 4 (Fall 1961): 434.

27. T. C. Schelling, "A Special Surveillance Force," in *Preventing World War III: Some Proposals*, ed. Quincy Wright, William M. Evan, and Morton Deutsch (New York: Simon and Schuster, 1962), 93.

28. When the article was reprinted in an anthology of disarmament proposals in 1962, Gerard added in his postscript: "The manuscript was also circulated earlier and, by one avenue or another (including some personal effort in Washington), the government became interested in further exploration of the ideas here presented." Ralph Gerard, "Truth Detection," in Wright, Evan, and Deutsch, *Preventing World War III*, 59.

29. "Planning Conference on Truth Demonstration Techniques: Minutes of Meeting," June 9, 1961, box 16, Ralph Gerard Papers.

30. "Lie Detection for Arms Control Inspection," July 19, 1961, box 16, Ralph Gerard Papers; "Research to Improve the Objective Measurement of Autonomic Responses for Use in Lie Detection," July 20–21, 1961, box 16, Ralph Gerard Papers..

31. The September meeting did not include members of the State Department anymore, which suggests a less than enthusiastic response to the earlier conferences. "Memorandum to the File on Lie Detection, Minutes of a Meeting," September 20, 1961, box 16, Ralph Gerard Papers.

32. Walter C. Morgan, "New Tools for Disarmament," April 15, 1962, box 16, Ralph Gerard Papers, 1.

33. Morgan sent Schweitzer a manuscript in March 1961. Schweitzer called Morgan's idea "discovery" and thanked him for his "valuable shipment." Albert Schweitzer to Walter Morgan, April 14, 1961, box 16, Ralph Gerard Papers. Cousins called Morgan's idea "a most valuable approach" and a "most exciting proposal." Norman Cousins to Walter Morgan, September 7, 1961, box 16, Ralph Gerard Papers.

34. Hubert Humphrey to Ralph Gerard, August 2, 1962, and Kent Parrot to Ralph Gerard, September 4, 1962, both box 16, Ralph Gerard Papers.

35. See Howard Baldwin to Ralph Gerard, January 17, 1962, box 16, Ralph Gerard Papers; Gerard also requested information about "ultraminiature radio-telemetering equipment" from Electro-Med, Inc., a company from Minneapolis. See "Bulletin," Electro-Med., Inc., January 26, 1962, box 16, Ralph Gerard Papers.

36. Walter Morgan to Ralph Gerard, February 3, 1962, box 16, Ralph Gerard Papers; Jerome Frank to Walter Morgan, February 8, 1962, box 16, Ralph Gerard Papers; W. A. Higinbotham to John Fowler, January 29, 1962, box 16, Ralph Gerard Papers.

37. Chester R. Darrow to Ralph W. Gerard, July 6, 1960, box 16, Ralph Gerard Papers.

38. Walter Morgan to Ralph Gerard, February 3, 1962, box 16, Ralph Gerard Papers.

39. Lewis C. Bohn, "Whose Nuclear Test? Non-Physical Inspection and the Nuclear Test Ban," December 1962, box 16, Ralph Gerard Papers.

40. Jesse Orlansky, "An Assessment of Lie Detection Capability," declassified version, July 1964, Institute for Defense Analyses, Research and Engineering Support Division, IX, XI, 32, http://fas.org/sgp/othergov/polygraph/ida1964.pdf (accessed November 30, 2014).

41. Joshua Lederberg to Ralph Gerard, n.d.; Ralph Gerard to Joshua Lederberg, August 5, 1968. Joshua Lederberg Papers, http://profiles.nlm.nih.gov/ps/browse/Resource-Browse/TYPE/Correspondence/CID/BB/YEAR/1968/p-sort/chron-corr/MONTH (accessed November 30, 2014).

42. See Amrom H. Katz, *Verification and Salt: The State of the Art and the Art of the State* (Washington, DC: Heritage Foundation, 1980).

43. See Joseph Rotblat, "Toward a Nuclear Weapon-Free World: Societal Verification," *Security Dialogue*, 23, no. 51 (1992): 51–61.

44. DeBenedetti, *Peace Reform in American History*, 138.

45. See Kai Bird and Martin J. Sherwin, *American Prometheus: The Triumph and Tragedy of J. Robert Oppenheimer* (New York: Alfred A. Knopf, 2005), 339–49.

46. See David Holloway, *Stalin and the Bomb: The Soviet Union and Nuclear Technology, 1938–1956* (New Haven, CT: Yale University Press, 1994); Vladislav M. Zubok, *A Failed Empire: The Soviet Union in the Cold War from Stalin to Gorbachev* (Chapel Hill: University of North Carolina Press, 2007), 1–93.

47. See Lloyd C. Gardner, *Architects of Illusion: Men and Ideas in American Foreign Policy, 1941–1949* (Chicago: Quadrangle Books, 1970), 171–201.

48. See table in Paul Kennedy, *The Rise and Fall of the Great Powers: Economic Change and Military Conflict from 1500 to 2000* (New York: Random House, 1987), 355.

49. See Melvyn P. Leffler, "The American Concept of National Security and the Beginnings of the Cold War, 1945–48," *American Historical Review* 89, no. 2 (April 1984): 379. On the militarization of the discipline of geography, see Matthew Farish, *The Contours of America's Cold War* (Minneapolis: University of Minnesota Press, 2010).

50. Quoted in Melvyn P. Leffler, *A Preponderance of Power* (Stanford, CA: Stanford University Press, 1992), 116.

51. Nitze is quoted ibid., 446.

52. See Campbell Craig and Sergey Radchenko, *The Atomic Bomb and the Origins of the Cold War* (New Haven, CT: Yale University Press, 2008); Wilson D. Miscamble, *From Roosevelt to Truman: Potsdam, Hiroshima, and the Cold War* (Cambridge, MA: Cambridge University Press, 2007); Leffler, *Preponderance of Power*, 114–16 (Truman quoted on 115).

53. See Richard Rhodes, *Arsenals of Folly: The Making of the Nuclear Arms Race* (New York: Alfred A. Knopf, 2007) (McNamara quoted on 99).

54. See Andrew J. Bacevich, *The New American Militarism: How Americans are Seduced by War* (New York: Oxford University Press, 2005), 147–73.

55. J. Robert Oppenheimer, "Atomic Weapons and American Foreign Policy," *Foreign Affairs* 30 (July 1953): 530, 532.

56. Rostow quoted in Victor Rosenberg, *Soviet-American Relations, 1953–1960* (Jefferson, NC: McFarland, 2005), 79.

57. Kenneth Osgood, *Total Cold War: Eisenhower's Secret Propaganda Battle at Home and Abroad* (Lawrence: University Press of Kansas, 2006), 7, 213.

58. See Jeremy Suri, "America's Search for a Technological Solution to the Arms Race: The Surprise Attack Conference of 1958 and a Challenge for 'Eisenhower Revisionists,'" *Diplomatic History* 21, no. 3 (Summer 1997): 417–51; Martha Smith-Norris, "The Eisenhower Administration and the Nuclear Test Ban Talks, 1958–1960: Another Challenge to 'Revisionism,'" *Diplomatic History* 27, no. 4 (September 2003): 503–41; Zuoyue Wang, *In Sputnik's Shadow: The President's Science Advisory Committee and Cold War America* (New Brunswick, NJ: Rutgers University Press, 2008), quote on 141.

59. See Matthew Evangelista, *Unarmed Forces: The Transnational Movement to End the Cold War* (Ithaca, NY: Cornell University Press, 1999); see also Wittner, *Resisting the Bomb*, 415–32.

60. Melvyn P. Leffler, *For the Soul of Mankind: The United States, the Soviet Union, and the Cold War* (New York: Hill and Wang, 2007), 186–92 (Khrushchev quote on p.188). On resistance, see Wittner, *Resisting the Bomb*, 428.

61. Gerard, "To Prevent Another World War," 215.

Chapter 8: Congress, the Right to Privacy, and the Retrenchment of the Polygraph

1. See Lee Burkey, "Privacy, Property, and the Polygraph," *Labor Law Journal* 18, no. 2 (February 1967): 88–89.

2. Robert David Johnson, *Congress and the Cold War* (New York: Cambridge University Press, 2006), xvii.

3. Francis E. Rourke, *Secrecy and Publicity: Dilemmas of Democracy* (Baltimore: Johns Hopkins University Press, 1961), 43; U.S. Congress, House, *Use of Polygraphs as "Lie Detectors" by the Federal Government, Hearings before a Subcommittee of the Committee on Government Operations, House of Representatives*, 88th Cong., 2nd Sess. (Washington, DC: Government Printing Office, 1964) [henceforth "Congress, *1964 Hearings*"]; U.S. Congress, House, *Use of Polygraphs as "Lie Detectors" by the Federal Government, Tenth Report by the Committee on Government Operations* (Washington, DC: Government Printing Office, 1965) [henceforth "Congress, *1965 Report*"].

4. See Michael R. Lemov, *People's Warrior: John Moss and the Fight for Freedom of Information and Consumer Rights* (Lanham, MD: Rowman and Littlefield, 2011).

5. John E. Moss, "What You Don't Know *Will* Hurt You," address upon accepting the John Peter Zenger Award for Freedom of the Press, January 10, 1959, http://www.johnmossfoundation.org/foi/zengersp.htm.

6. See Ira Chernus, "Operation Candor: Fear, Faith, and Flexibility," *Diplomatic History* 29, no. 5 (November 2005): 779–809; for the term "emotion management" to refer to early Cold War government policies that treated emotions as public, sustainable and subject to political manipulation, see Guy Oakes, *The Imaginary War* (New York: Oxford University Press, 1994), esp. 47–50.

7. Dwight Eisenhower, "Address at the Columbia University National Bicentennial Dinner," May 31, 1954, *New York Times*, June 1, 1954, 6.

8. Richard M. Fried, *The Russians Are Coming! The Russians Are Coming!: Pageantry and Patriotism in Cold War America* (New York: Oxford University Press, 1998).

9. See Congress, *1965 Report*, 3–5. On the NSA defectors Mitchell and Martin, who defected due to disillusionment with NSA's aggressive spy flights into Soviet territory,

see James Bamford, *The Puzzle Palace: Inside the National Security Agency, America's Most Secret Intelligence Organization* (New York: Penguin Books, 1983), 177–96.

10. "Telephone Recordings: Dictation Belt 17B.2. Using Polygraphs in Tracing Defense Department Leaks," April 3, 1963, Presidential Recordings, Telephone Recordings, President's Office Files, Papers of John F. Kennedy, Kennedy Presidential Library, Boston, MA, at https://www.jfklibrary.org/Asset-Viewer/Archives/JFKPOF-TPH -17B-2.aspx.

11. McNamara quoted in Jack Raymond, "McNamara Scores Inquiry on Plane," *New York Times,* March 13, 1963, 1; Symington paraphrased in Jack Raymond, "'Abuse' Is Laid to Senate Aides in Plane Inquiry," *New York Times,* March 22, 1963, 5.

12. Congress, *1965 Report,* 1.

13. Ibid., 7, 14, 15.

14. Ibid., 19.

15. Ibid., 25, 12, 13.

16. Congress, *1964 Hearings,* 186.

17. Congress, *1965 Report,* 12, 13; Congress, *1964 Hearings,* 18.

18. Indiana University psychologist R. C. Davis found that Keeler's card trick did not make test subjects more responsive: R. C. Davis, "Physiological Responses as a Means of Evaluating Information," in *The Manipulation of Human Behavior,* ed. Albert D. Biderman and Herbert Zimmer (New York: John Wiley and Sons, 1961), 153; on the other hand, see Leonard Saxe, "Science and the CQT Polygraph: A Theoretical Critique," *Integrative Physiological and Behavioral Science* 26, no. 3 (1991): 223–31.

19. Inbau, *Lie Detection and Criminal Interrogation,* 15.

20. Congress, *1965 Report,* 19–20.

21. Congress, *1964 Hearings,* 8; Congress, *1965 Report,* 20.

22. Congress, *1965 Report,* 29; Congress, *1964 Hearings,* 349; Congress, *1965 Report,* 17.

23. Congress, *1965 Report,* 2. Committee member Robert P. Griffin objected to "the general tenor of the report which tends to discredit the polygraph and its use." However, he agreed with what turned out to be the consensus view, that "there is need for more research to document the validity and reliability of polygraph exams." *1965 Report,* 45.

24. Stanley Meister, "Lie Detectors: Trial by Gadget," *Nation,* September 28, 1964, 176; Robert Burkhardt, "How to Successfully Lie to the Lie Detector," *New Republic,* May 16, 1964, 7.

25. Theodore M. Porter, *Trust in Numbers: The Pursuit of Objectivity in Science and Public Life* (Princeton, NJ: Princeton University Press, 1995), 8.

26. "Business Uses the Lie Detector," *Business Week,* June 18, 1960, 106; Robert Christie, "Do Lie Detectors Lie?," *Popular Science,* September 1963, 203.

27. William E. Lissy, "Labor Law," *Supervision* 27 (October 1965): 15.

28. See John Shattuck, Patricia Brown, and Stephen Carlson, *The Lie Detector as a Surveillance Device* (New York: American Civil Liberties Union, 1973), 49–51. In addition, several cities such as Madison, Wisconsin, as well as Cincinnati and Akron, Ohio, adopted similar provisions starting in 1965. For the laws that had been enacted by 1965 (Alaska, California, Illinois, Kentucky, Massachusetts, New Mexico, Oregon, Rhode Island, Washington), see Congress, *1965 Hearings,* 549–61.

29. The following data come from John A. Belt and Peter B. Holden, "Polygraph Usage among Major U.S. Corporations," *Personnel Journal* 57 (February 1978): 80–86.

30. Ibid., 85.

31. "Cops vs. Lie Detectors," *Newsweek,* February 26, 1973, 52.

32. See Alan F. Westin, *Privacy and Freedom* (New York: Atheneum, 1967).

33. Shattuck et al., *Lie Detector as Surveillance Device*, 30.

34. Ibid., 44–45.

35. Trudy Hayden and Jack Novik, *Your Right to Privacy: The Basic ACLU Guide for Your Rights to Privacy* (New York: Avon Books, 1980).

36. Quoted in James Lincoln Collier, "Again, the Truth Machine," *New York Times Magazine*, November 25, 1973, 108, 110.

37. Quoted in Frye Gaillard, "Polygraphs and Privacy," *The Progressive* 38 (September 1974): 44.

38. Quoted in Richard H. Underwood, "Truth Verifyers: From the Hot Iron to the Lie Detector," *Kentucky Law Journal* 84 (Spring 1995/1996): 628.

39. Jonathan Kwitny, "The Dirty Little Secret of Lie Detectors," *Esquire* 89 (January 1978): 73.

40. Ben A. Franklin, "Lie Detector's Use by Industry Rises; Rights Peril Feared," *New York Times,* November 22, 1971, 45.

41. Trudy Hayden, "Employers Who Use Lie Detector Tests," *Business and Society Review* 41 (Spring 1982): 16.

42. For examples, see Shattuck et al., *Lie Detector as Surveillance Device,* 54–55.

43. Robert J. Ferguson Jr., *The Scientific Informer* (Springfield, IL: Charles C. Thomas Publisher, 1971), 145.

44. Council of Polygraph Examiners, Newsletter (undated), quoted in Shattuck et al, *Lie Detector as Surveillance Device,* 33.

45. Birch Bayh, quoted in "Outlaw Lie-Detector Tests?," *U.S. News and World Report,* January 30, 1978, 46.

46. Trudy Hayden, "Employers Who Use Lie Detector Tests," *Business and Society Review* 41 (Spring 1982): 21.

47. "Congressional Record, Senate, Dec. 20, 1973," quoted in U.S. Congress, House, *The Use of Polygraphs and Similar Devices by Federal Agencies: Hearings before a Subcommittee of the Committee on Government Operations, House of Representatives, June 4 and 5, 1974*, 93rd Cong., 2nd sess. (Washington, DC: Government Printing Office, 1974) [henceforth "Congress, *1974 Hearings*"], 85.

48. Background on Ervin comes from Karl E. Campbell, *Senator Sam Ervin, Last of the Founding Fathers* (Chapel Hill: University of North Carolina Press, 2007).

49. See ibid., 185–245.

50. U.S. Congress, House, *Report No. 94-795: The Use of Polygraphs and Similar Devices by Federal Agencies: Thirteenth Report by the Committee on Government Operations together with Separate and Dissenting Views*, 94th Cong., 2nd sess. (Washington, DC: Government Printing Office, 1976) [henceforth "Congress, *1976 Report*"], 12.

51. See Congress, *1974 Hearings*, 191, quote on 415.

52. Congress, *1976 Report*, 46.

53. See Judith Nies, *Nine Women: Portraits from the American Radical Tradition* (Berkeley: University of California Press, 2002), 237–67.

54. "Bill Jones, counsel to the full Government Operations Committee, thinks that you may have trouble obtaining approval of the polygraph report by the full committee. This is perhaps borne out by [Jack] Brooks's giving you a proxy for the Women's Conference Bill, but not for the polygraph report." Memo, September 30, 1975, box

155: Folder "Civil Rights and Human Rights, Polygraph Tests," Bella Abzug Papers, Special Collections, Columbia University, New York.

55. See Congress, *1976 Report,* 55–57.

56. Ibid., 51, 52, 53.

57. See Richard H. Blum, ed., *Surveillance and Espionage in a Free Society: A Report by the Planning Gorup on Intelligence and Security to the Policy Council of the Democratic National Committee* (New York: Praeger, 1972).

58. Richard H. Blum, "Intelligence and Security: Issues and Directions for America," ibid., 314.

59. Congress, *1976 Report,* 20.

60. Ibid., 25.

61. For a summary of departmental polygraph regulations, see ibid., 39–45.

62. See Kathryn S. Olmsted, *Challenging the Secret Government: The Post-Watergate Investigations of the CIA and FBI* (Chapel Hill: University of North Carolina Press, 1996).

63. See John Lewis Gaddis, *Strategies of Containment: A Critical Appraisal of American National Security Policy during the Cold War,* rev. ed.(New York: Oxford University Press, 2005), 353–79; Frances Fitzgerald, *Way Out There in the Blue: Reagan, Star Wars, and the End of the Cold War* (New York: Simon and Schuster, 2000).

64. For the GAO report, see U.S. Congress, House, *Review of the President's National Security Decision Directive 84 and the Proposed Department of Defense Directive on Polygraph Use: Hearing before a Subcommittee of the Committee on Government Operations, House of Representatives,* 98th Cong., 1st sess. (Washington, DC: Government Printing Office, 1983), 8–17 [henceforth "Congress, *NSDD 84 Hearing*"].

65. See George C. Wilson, "Arms Costs Could Exceed Plans by $750 Billion, Leaders Told," *Washington Post,* January 8, 1982, A1.

66. Jack Brooks, "Polygraph Testing: Thoughts of a Skeptical Legislator," *American Psychologist* 40, no. 3 (March 1985): 351.

67. Congress, *NSDD 84 Hearing,* 92.

68. See ibid., 99; see also the numerous newspaper editorials against *NSDD 84* that were submitted for the record by the American Society of Newspaper Editors, 430–47.

69. Ibid., 109.

70. Ibid., 167–68.

71. Ibid., 168.

72. Dorothy J. Samuels, "What if the Lie Detector Lies?," *Nation,* December 3, 1983, 567.

73. "Statement of Richard K. Willard, Deputy Assistant Attorney General, U.S. Department of Justice, before the Legislation and National Security Subcommittee of the Committee on Government Operations, U.S. House of Representatives," Congress, *NSDD 84 Hearing,* 207.

74. "Canceled Order," *Time,* February 27, 1984, 86.

75. "Fluttering the Pentagon," *Newsweek,* January 14, 1985.

76. "Reagan Disputed by Rep. Brooks on Polygraph Directive's Meaning," *New York Times,* January 9, 1986, A14.

77. U.S. Congress, Office of Technology Assessment (OTA), *Scientific Validity of Polygraph Testing: A Research Review and Evaluation* (Washington, DC: Congress of the U.S., Office of Technology Assessment, 1983).

78. Ibid., 96.

79. See ibid., 97.

80. "Schultz, a Flutter," *Newsweek,* December 30, 1985, 20.

81. William Safire, "Reagan, Fluttered," *New York Times,* May 2, 1983, A19; Safire, "Reagan's Dark Side," *New York Times,* December 26, 1985, A27.

82. Safire, "The Polygraph Lied," *New York Times,* March 5, 1987, A27.

83. Safire, "The Sweat Merchants," *New York Times,* February 29, 1988, A19; Safire, "One Blow for Liberty," *New York Times,* May 26, 1988, A35.

84. Over fifty professional associations submitted statements to the Senate. See U.S. Congress, Senate *Hearing before the Committee on Labor and Human Resources, U.S. Senate on S. 1815, To Prevent the Denial of Employment Opportunities by Prohibiting the Use of Lie Detectors by Employers Involved in or Affecting Interstate Commerce,* 99th Cong., 2nd sess. (Washington, DC: Government Printing Office, 1986) [henceforth "Congress, *1986 Hearing*"], 283–522.

85. Congress, *1986 Hearing,* 5.

86. See Hatch's opening statement, as well as Raskin's written and oral testimony, ibid., 1–3; 59–87.

87. See the full text of the law in http://www.fas.org/sgp/othergov/polygraph/eppa. html.

88. Ibid.

89. Quoted in Adam Clymer, *Edward M. Kennedy: A Biography* (New York: Harper-Collins, 1999), 435; on the congressional fights over civil rights in the late 1980s, see 406–74.

90. The *New York Times* called Hatch "an unusual ally" of Kennedy. Delay quoted in "Conferees Back Bill Curbing Device to Detect Lies," *New York Times,* May 18, 1988, A17. States that by 1988 had curbed polygraph tests were Connecticut, New Jersey, Alaska, California, Delaware, Hawaii, Idaho, Iowa, Maine, Maryland, Massachusetts, Michigan, Minnesota, Montana, Oregon, Pennsylvania, Rhode Island, Vermont, Washington, West Virginia, and Wisconsin. See Irvin Molotsky, "Senate Votes for Limits on Polygraph Testing," *New York Times,* March 4, 1988, A21.

91. John R. Bolton to Thomas P. O'Neill, March 11, 1986, reprinted in Congress, *1986 Hearing,* 8, 10.

92. U.S. Congress, Senate, "Statement of the Department of Justice," Committee Serial No. 100–23 (Washington, DC: Government Printing Office, 1988), 106.

93. Statement by Malcolm Wallop, Congress, *1986 Hearing,* 12.

94. U.S. Congress, Senate, "Statement of the National Retail Merchants Association," Committee Serial No. 100–23 (Washington, DC: Government Printing Office, 1988), 246.

95. Engelhard quoted in "Business and the Law," *New York Times,* November 28, 1988, D2.

96. Safire, "Reagan, Fluttered."

97. "Democracy versus Secrecy: Should the United States Have an Official Secrets Act? Suppressing Leaks: Is Polygraph Testing Acceptable in a Democracy?," *Center Magazine,* September/October, 1984, 61, 63.

98. Congress, *NSDD 84 Hearings,* 112. See also the testimony of Lucas A. Powe of the University of Texas, ibid., 134–51.

99. As the *Wall Street Journal* remarked at the time, applicants for and employees in a variety of positions in the financial sector had been required to take polygraph tests. A 1987 survey of 160 large banks had shown that 78 percent of those institutions were using polygraph tests in some fashion on their employees. Albert R. Karr,

"Law Limiting Use of Lie Detectors Is Seen Having Widespread Effect," *Wall Street Journal*, July 1, 1988, 1.

100. Janell M. Kurtz and Wayne R. Wells, "The Employee Polygraph Protection Act: The End of Lie Detector Use in Employment Decisions?," *Journal of Small Business Management* 27, no. 4 (October 1989): 77.

101. Examples of successful lawsuits from 1961 and 1965 are cited in Lee Burkey, "Privacy, Property, and the Polygraph," *Labor Law Journal* 18, no. 2 (February 1967): 88.

102. Equal Employment Opportunity Commission, "Brief against Polygraphs as a Discriminatory Labor Practice," cited in Shattuck et al., *Lie Detector as Surveillance Device*, 49.

103. John Hoerr et al., "Privacy," *Business Week*, March 28, 1988, 63.

104. Robert B. Fitzpatrick, "Polygraph Testing of Employees in Private Industry: A Legal Overview," *Federal Bar News & Journal* (March/April, 1988), 132.

105. Rene Shermar, "Polygraph Suits? That's No Lie," *National Law Journal*, September 5, 1988, 8.

106. See the tables in Eric Rolfe Greenberg, "Workplace Testing: Who's Testing Whom?," *Personnel*, May 1989, 39–43.

107. The Supreme Court's 1966 *Schmerber v. California* decision, which ruled that an involuntary blood test administered to determine guilt in a traffic accident was neither a violation of Fifth Amendment rights against self-incrimination nor Fourth or Fourteenth Amendment rights against unreasonable search and seizure, opened the legal avenue toward widespread use of mandatory drug tests in private industry. See http://law.jrank.org/pages/12953/Schmerber-v-California.html.

Epilogue

1. Bill Dedman, "New Anti-Terror Weapon: Hand-held Lie Detector," *NBC News*, April 9, 2008, http://www.msnbc.msn.com/id/23926278.

2. Robert Pool, rapporteur; Planning Committee on Field Evaluation of Behavioral and Cognitive Sciences-Based Methods and Tools for Intelligence and Counterintelligence; National Research Council, *Field Evaluation in the Intelligence and Counterintelligence Context: Workshop Summary* (Washington, DC: National Academies Press, 2010), 9.

3. National Research Council, *Field Evaluation*, 15, 16.

4. "Behavioral Science and Security: Statement of Philip E. Rubin, Ph.D., before the Subcommittee on Investigations and Oversight Committee on Science, Space, and Technology, U.S. House of Representatives," April 6, 2011, 14. Available at https://science.house.gov/sites/republicans.science.house.gov/files/documents/hearings/2011%2004%2001%20RubinTestimony.pdf.

5. Spencer Ackerman, "CIA Torture Appears to Have Broken Spy Agency Rules on Human Experimentation," *Guardian*, June 15, 2015, https://www.theguardian.com/us-news/2015/jun/15/cia-torture-human-experimentation-doctors.

6. Melissa M. Littlefield, *The Lying Brain: Lie Detection in Science and Science Fiction* (Ann Arbor: University of Michigan Press, 2011), 138.

7. *Combatting Terrorism: Research Priorities in the Social, Behavioral, and Economic Sciences:* Report of the National Science and Technology Council, Subcommittee on Social, Behavioral and Economic Sciences (Washington, DC: Government Printing Office, 2005).

8. Matt Wilstein, "GOP Rep Says Haggling Proves 'Lying' Is Part of 'Middle Eastern Culture,'" *Mediaite,* December 4, 2013, http://www.mediaite.com/tv/gop-rep-says -haggling-proves-lying-is-part-of-middle-eastern-culture/.

9. See James Garden, "Neo-McCarthyism and the US Media: The Crusade to Ban Russia Policy Critics," *Nation,* June 8, 2015, https://www.thenation.com/article/neo -mccarthyism-and-us-media/.

10. See Seymour M. Hersh, *The Killing of Osama bin Laden* (London: Verso, 2016), 16.

11. "Exclusive: Dozens of CIA Operatives on the Ground during Benghazi Attacks," *CNN,* August 1, 2013, http://thelead.blogs.cnn.com/2013/08/01/exclusive-dozens-of-cia-opera tives-on-the-ground-during-benghazi-attack/?hpt=hp_t4 (accessed June 25, 2017).

12. Stephen E. Fienberg and Paul C. Stern, "In Search of the Magic Lasso: The Truth about the Polygraph," *Statistical Science* 20, no. 3 (August 2005): 259.

13. Federal Bureau of Investigation, *The Personnel Security Polygraph Program* (Washington, DC: U.S. Justice Department, Federal Bureau of Investigation, 2002).

14. Jessica Schulberg, "The FBI Insists It Doesn't Fire People over Polygraphs. This Man Says It Happened to Him," *Huffington Post,* October 17, 2016, http://www .huffingtonpost.com/entry/fbi-polygraphs-countermeasures_us_57ffe22ce40162 c043ae621?section=&.

15. Brendan I. Koerner, "Lie Detector Roulette," *Mother Jones,* November/December 2002, http://www.motherjones.com/politics/2002/11/lie-detector-roulette.

16. Marisa Taylor, "DEA Settles Suit Alleging Government Lie Detector Abuses," *McClatchy,* May 7, 2013, http://www.mcclatchydc.com/2014/05/07/226776_dea-settles -suit-alleging-government.html?sp=/99/323/&rh=1#storylink=cpy.

17. Marisa Taylor, "Spy Satellite Agency Says It Fixed Its 'Broken' Polygraph Program," *McClatchy,* May 14, 2014, http://www.mcclatchydc.com/2014/05/15/227598/spy-satellite -agency-says-it-fixed.html?sp=/99/323/.

18. Marisa Taylor and Cleve R. Wootson Jr., "Seeing Threats, Feds Target Instructors of Polygraph-beating Methods," *McClatchy,* August 16, 2013, http://www.mcclatchydc .com/2013/08/16/199590/seeing-threats-feds-target-instructors.html#.Ug9v4FPOmhZ.

19. Andrea Nobel, "Former Oklahoma City Cop Gets Two Years in Prison for Polygraph Coaching," *Washington Times,* September 23, 2015, http://www.washingtontimes. com/news/2015/sep/23/douglas-williams-former-oklahoma-city-cop-gets-two/.

20. See Jeff Stein, "NSA Lie Detectors No Sweat, Video Says," *Washington Post,* June 14, 2010, http://voices.washingtonpost.com/spy-talk/2010/06/facing_nsas_lie_detector_ relax.html.

21. See Daniel T. Wilcox, ed., *The Use of the Polygraph in Assessing, Treating, and Supervising Sex Offenders* (Hoboken, NJ: Wiley, 2009).

22. Andrew S. Balmer and Ralph Sandland, "Making Monsters: The Polygraph, the Plesythmograph, and Other Practices for the Performance of Abnormal Sexuality," *Journal of Law and Society* 39, no. 4 (December 2012): 593–615.

23. See Mark Schüssler, *Polygraphie im deutschen Strafverfahren* (Frankfurt a.M. et al: Lang, 2002).

24. Littlefield, *Lying Brain,* 118–40.

25. See Bettina Paul and Sigmund Egbert, "Lügendetektion per Neuroimaging," *Krim J: Kriminologisches Journal* 46, no. 3 (2014): 153–67.

26. See Sheldon S. Wolin, *Democracy Inc.: Managed Democracy and the Specter of Inverted Totalitarianism* (Princeton, NJ: Princeton University Press, 2008).

27. See Evgeny Morozov, *To Save Everything, Click Here: The Folly of Technological Solu-*

tionism (New York: PublicAffairs, 2013), 273. On the notion of free will and unpredictability, see David Edmonds and Nigel Warburton, *Philosophy Bites Again* (New York: Oxford University Press, 2014), 125–33 (interview with philosopher Daniel Dennett).

28. Charles Howarth, "Technology Is Making Us Blind: The Dangerous Complacency of the iPhone Era," *Salon*, November 29, 2014, http://www.salon.com/2014/11/29/technology_is_making_us_blind_the_dangerous_complacency_of_the_iphone_era/.

29. Pierre Dardot and Christian Laval, *The New Way of the World: On Neoliberal Society* (New York: Verso, 2009).

30. William Deresiewicz, *Excellent Sheep: The Miseducation of the American Elite* (New York: Free Press, 2014).

31. Peter Miller and Nikolas Rose, *Governing the Present: Administering Economic, Social and Personal Life* (Malden, MA: Polity Press, 2008), 9.

32. See David Lyon, *Identifying Citizens: ID Cards as Surveillance* (Malden, MA: Polity Press, 2009).

33. See Kelly A. Gates, *Our Biometric Future: Facial Recognition Technology and the Culture of Surveillance* (New York: New York University Press, 2011), 22.

34. See Paul Ekman, *Telling Lies: Clues to Deceit in the Marketplace, Politics, and Marriage* (New York: Norton, 1985); Ekman, *Why Kids Lie: How Parents Can Encourage Truthfulness* (New York: Penguin Books, 1991).

35. See Sharon Weinberger, "Airport Security: Intent to Deceive?," *Nature* 465 (2010): 412–15.

36. Jana Winter and Cora Currier, "Exclusive: TSA's Secret Behavior Checklist to Spot Terrorists," *The Intercept*, March 27, 2015, https://theintercept.com/2015/03/27/revealed-tsas-closely-held-behavior-checklist-spot-terrorists/.

37. See Pamela Meyer, *Liespotting: Proven Techniques to Detect Deception* (New York: St. Martin's Press, 2012); Philip Houston, Michael Floyd, and Susan Carnicero, with Don Tennant, *Spy the Lie: Former CIA Officers Teach You How to Detect Deception* (New York: St. Martin's Press, 2012). While Meyer uses Ekman's concept of microexpressions, Houston et al. reject the method as unreliable and mainly discuss rhetorical strategies of liars and behavioral clues. See also Joe Navarro with Tony Sciarra Poynter, *Dangerous Personalities: An FBI Profiler Shows You How to Identify and Protect Yourself from Harmful People* (Emmaus, PA: Rodale Press, 2014).

38. See Malcolm Gladwell, "The Naked Face: Can You Read Thoughts Just by Looking at Them?," *New Yorker*, August 5, 2002, 49.

39. See Vicente L. Rafael, "Trayvon Martin and Edward Snowden," *historynewsnetwork*, July 28, 2013, http://historynewsnetwork.org/article/152783.

40. See John Yoo, *War by Other Means: An Insider's Account of the War on Terror* (New York: Atlantic Monthly Press , 2006).

41. See Chandak Sengoopta, *Imprint of the Raj: How Fingerprinting Was Born in Colonial India* (London: Pan Books, 2004); Alfred W. McCoy, *Policing America's Empire: The United States, the Philippines, and the Rise of the Surveillance State* (Madison: University of Wisconsin Press, 2009).

42. See Gates, *Our Biometric Future*; Michael Lynch, Simon A. Cole, Ruth McNally, and Kathleen Jordan, *Truth Machine: The Contentious History of DNA Fingerprinting* (Chicago: University of Chicago Press, 2008).

INDEX

JOHN PHILIPP BAESLER was born in Germany. He received an MA in history and philosophy from Heidelberg University in 2001 and a PhD in history from Indiana University Bloomington in 2009. He is currently associate professor of history at Saginaw Valley State University in Michigan, where he teaches the history of U.S. foreign relations. He lives with his wife, historian Jennifer Stinson, their daughter, Charlotte, and their cat, Signe, in East Lansing, Michigan.